AMERICAN JEWISH IDENTITY POLITICS

American Jewish Identity Politics

EDITOR
Deborah Dash Moore

THE UNIVERSITY OF MICHIGAN PRESS

Ann Arbor

Published in the United States of America by
The University of Michigan Press
Manufactured in the United States of America
♾ Printed on acid-free paper

2011   2010   2009   2008   4   3   2   1

A CIP catalog record for this book is available from the British Library.

Library of Congress Cataloging-in-Publication Data

American Jewish identity politics / edited by Deborah Dash Moore.
        p.   cm.
     ISBN-13: 978-0-472-11648-5 (cloth : alk. paper)
     ISBN-10: 0-472-11648-7 (cloth : alk. paper)
     ISBN-13: 978-0-472-03288-4 (pbk. : alk. paper)
     ISBN-10: 0-472-03288-7 (pbk. : alk. paper)
     1. Jews—United States—History—20th century.   2. Jews—United
States—History—21st century.   3. Jews—United States—Identity.
4. Jews—United States—Cultural assimilation.   5. Judaism—United
States.   I. Moore, Deborah Dash, 1946–
E184.355A45   2008
973'.04924—dc22   2007052488

Grateful acknowledgment is given to Bill Aron for the photographs introducing the essays.

Acknowledgments

These essays owe their existence to the foresight and generosity of David W. Belin, an alumnus of the College of Literature, Science and the Arts, the Business School, and the Law School of the University of Michigan. A distinguished public servant, Belin served as counsel to the Warren Commission, which investigated President John F. Kennedy's assassination, and was executive director to the Rockefeller Commission, which investigated CIA activities within the United States. Belin, of Des Moines and New York, was equally engaged in issues confronting American Jews during these tumultuous decades. A founding Chairman of Reform Judaism's Outreach Commission and founding member of the Jewish Foundation for the Righteous, Belin initiated action on aspects of intermarriage and the Holocaust, two key elements of American Jewish identity politics. His leadership reflected his concern for the future of American Jewry and stimulated him to endow an annual lectureship in 1991 to provide a forum for the discussion of contemporary Jewish life in the United States. Each year since 1991 the Jean and Samuel Frankel Center for Judaic Studies of the University of Michigan has brought a distinguished scholar to campus to address diverse dimensions of American Jewish culture. The essays collected here represent the best of these lectures revised for publication.

The task of assembling the essays was made easier by the assistance of Naamah Paley, Sally Wong, and Matt Weingarden. Joshua Friedman handled the editorial revisions and index with care and skill. I am pleased to acknowledge the incisive comments of two readers for the Press, Allan Arkush and Riv-Ellen Prell, who substantially improved the introduction. Phil Pochoda's enthusiasm for the project and Sarah Remington's help carried us over rough spots. A grant from the University of Michigan's Office of the Vice President for Research made possible the inclusion of photographs by Bill Aron, a participant observer in the identity politics of American Jews for over three decades.

Deborah Dash Moore
Ann Arbor, September 19, 2007

Contents

Introduction

Deborah Dash Moore

Identity politics exploded in the United States in the 1970s. Awakened by student activists in the civil rights movement and the New Left, the politics of identity responded to the rise of black power. Feminism's insight that the personal is political as well as a turn toward a revival of European ethnicity provided language to express new insights regarding authority within the United States and abroad. As women came to identify what Betty Friedan called "the problem that has no name," they stirred others suffering from discrimination to find their voice.[1] "Sisterhood is powerful," like "Black is beautiful," inspired more than those who championed the slogans.[2] They became models for political action for Jews as for other Americans. The scholar Matthew Frye Jacobson dates the birth of identity politics "in the showdown over Zionism" at the Conference on New Politics in Chicago two months after the Israeli victory in the Six Day War "(and, not incidentally, in the slights that women . . . felt *as women* at that same meeting)."[3] Reverberations of that stormy beginning would extend across two decades.

David W. Belin, born in 1928, an accomplished lawyer who had just finished serving on the Warren Commission investigating the death of President John F. Kennedy, seemed to be far removed from the younger generation of activists attending the Conference on New Politics. Yet he, too, would find himself drawn within the orbit of questions raised by identity politics. What did identity politics mean for American Jews? It meant trying to bring Jewishness together with political elements of an identity. Jewish identity acquired a self-conscious valence lacking for an earlier generation that had grown up in dense urban neighborhoods. Politics now extended into all reaches of society and culture, including Jewish life. What did it mean to be an American Jew? Was this a religious question? A question of ethnicity? Perhaps a political question? How did Jews understand themselves as individuals and as members of a group in the United States? Although David Belin had grown up during the Great Depression in Iowa, coming east to attend college and the University of Michigan Law School, as a father of four children, a liberal, a lawyer, and a Jew active in the movement of Reform Judaism, he became increasingly engaged in seeking new ways to understand what it meant to be a contemporary American Jew. In 1991 he endowed a lecture series at the University of Michigan in American Jewish Public Affairs. He sought through these annual lectures to build a bridge between university scholars and American Jews. Eager to explore issues raised by identity politics as they affected American Jews, he turned mostly to members of the baby boom generation for some answers. Those answers, as well as the questions, form the basis of the articles collected in this volume.

I arrived at the University of Michigan in 2005 as director of Judaic Studies. I had been invited, a decade earlier, to give one of the early Belin lectures. Now I looked at a shelf full of published lectures, a rainbow of muted colors in soft covers, and realized that they opened a window on several decades of American Jewish life. Each one separately marked a particular moment in perspective. Taken together, however, they represent a generation of scholars grappling with questions raised by identity politics as they were configured among American Jews. Although most of these lectures were not in conversation with each other, publishing them together initiates a dialogue that enriches their individual insights.

These previously published essays reflect several layers of identity politics. On one level, they interrogate the recent past of American Jews, starting with their experiences of World War II. Without the flourishing of identity politics and the white ethnic revival, many questions about American Jewish history might never have been explored. Those who adopted identity politics often saw Jews as an ethnic group in the United States, one connected both to other Americans and to other Jews throughout the world and in the past. On another level, these essays express ideas nourished in universities during the turbulent 1970s and 1980s. Those years marked the expansion of Jewish studies as a field in the United States and the establishment of American Jewish studies as an area of specialization.[4] There is, however, a third layer, a personal one. Most of the scholars writing about American Jewish affairs also participated in those affairs as activists. They agitated for equal rights for Jewish women, they built Jewish studies programs within universities, they took stands on the conflicts and wars between Israel and its neighbors, they struggled for new understandings of Judaism in the wake of the radical evil of the Holocaust, and they experimented with innovative forms of Jewish religious life. These essays thus embody a type of knowledge drawn from participation as well as research, and they speak to audiences seeking to reconsider narratives of change and continuity.

Given the timeliness of these essays and their responsiveness to political questions of the moment, why, one might ask, should they be republished? The answer lies in their very timeliness, for they teach us not only about their subject but also about how issues were framed and debated during our fin de siècle, the end of the twentieth century and beginning of the twenty-first. The authors of these articles include several—most notably Arthur Green, Alvin Rosenfeld, and the late Egon Mayer—who could be thought of as founding fathers of this new generation of Jewish scholars. Green in theology, Rosenfeld in literature, and Mayer in sociology influenced younger academics like Arnold Eisen. A slightly different relationship exists among the historians. Several come to their subject through the study of American history, including Hasia Diner, Stephen Whitfield, and Jonathan Sarna, while others approach through the portal of Jewish history, such as Paula Hyman and Jeffrey Gurock. Taken together they reveal the varied sources of American Jewish studies. Finally, one must note that in many cases these essays anticipate major books on the subject. Reading them now reveals how ideas took shape within the political pressures of the moment.

Those who embraced the politics of identity initially turned away from the vision of integration that had animated the civil rights movement in the years after World War II. Jacobson sees both conservative and liberal tendencies in this embrace of what he calls "Ellis Island ethnicity." According to Jacobson, an antimodernism that imagined an immigrant past in warm colors of family solidarity and struggle fueled a new aggressiveness directed against affirmative action strategies adopted by African Americans in the late 1960s. Desires to rectify past injustices by creating a society where individuals would be judged not by group attributes yielded to calls for recognition of group differences and assertions of collective pride in seemingly unchangeable identities of ethnicity, race, and gender.[5]

In any case, white descendants of European immigrants pursued an aggressive form of politics symbolically recognized by the federal government in 1972 in the Ethnic Heritage Studies Program Act.[6] This legislation underwrote programs in ethnic and immigration studies within and outside of universities. Such recognition helped to solidify the viability of identity politics in the United States. Gays and lesbians adopted similar strategies of parades and protest, proclaiming the political significance of sexuality.

However, because individual identities are layered, debates over identity politics often forced individuals to decide which single identity mattered most. Did one's gender as a woman trump one's ethnicity as a Jew? Did one's homosexuality take precedence over one's racial identity? What happened when one expression of identity politics came into conflict with another? Should one speak out against anti-Semitism in the woman's movement?[7] Should one defend Zionism from attack by civil rights advocates? Nowhere did these demands to choose a single identity resonate more than among American Jews because so many of them played leading roles as activists in the 1960s and 1970s civil rights, antiwar, and feminist movements, and as supporters of black power and the new white ethnics.[8]

That heritage of activism extended all the way back to the beginning of the twentieth century when immigrant Jews championed diverse radical movements for social change. Socialism, anarchism, trade unionism, and communism competed for their allegiances. During the Great Depression, ideological fissures fractured the radical Left into splinter groups that postwar anticommunist purges failed to heal. Divisions among Jews raised questions of loyalties: to Soviet Communism, to Socialist Zionism, to anti-Stalinist social democracy, even to anti-anti-Communist liberalism.[9] Yet a new postwar synthesis emerged in the 1950s that often went by the name of liberalism. Many Jews supported integration and civil rights, social welfare programs and trade unionism, civil liberties and religious freedom, internationalism in the United Nations, and the new State of Israel. This synthesis shattered on the shoals of 1960s politics: desegregation in northern cities, the war in Vietnam, the arms race, and Israel's new status after the Six Day War.[10]

American Jews fiercely debated every "must" and "should" of their loyalties. Their collective identity seemed hopelessly hyphenated (though written without a hyphen). Were they Jewish Americans, analogous say to Italian Americans? Or were they American Jews, similar to American Catholics and Protestants? Did ethnicity matter more than religion? And what was ethnicity without religion, without language, without memory? What was the meaning of American? Did it suggest only citizenship or membership in a nation? Did it imply participation in a culture grounded in English and connected to a history of settlement? Could they as the children or grandchildren of Yiddish-speaking immigrants from Eastern Europe lay claim to this American language and history? What, in fact, did

"Jew" mean? Perhaps this was merely an expression of family sentiment, a way of identifying parents and grandparents. Or did it have a public dimension, referring to a long history of suffering and persecution? Maybe the term *Jew* suggested ties to biblical ancestors.

These arguments among American Jews reconsidered earlier struggles with issues of identity. In the years around World War I, immigrant and second-generation Jews debated whether and how they should prioritize their multiple identities. Were they Americans first? Jews first? Such philosophers as Horace Kallen, who argued for cultural pluralism, or political figures as Louis Brandeis, who championed Zionism as integral to being a good American Jew, disputed such writers as Israel Zangwill, who proclaimed the virtues of assimilation in the melting pot. In the 1970s additional categories appeared. Perhaps Jews were women first? And what did each of these identities mean? If one affirmed that one was "Jewish" first and foremost, did that mean a religious identity or a national one, an ethnic one or a political one? Soon, the language of identity politics entered these arguments. Jews had their "Uncle Jakes" analogous to "Uncle Toms" among African Americans.[11] "Jake" apparently pandered to gentile expectations of conciliatory Jewish behavior, refusing to defend aggressively Jewish interests. As the scholar Michael Staub has shown, arguments often escalated. They threatened, at times, to drive some Jews out of the Jewish community itself.[12]

American Jews engaged these debates at a moment when they had achieved an unprecedented level of security, affluence, integration, and freedom in the United States. As the only large community of Jews basically unscarred by the catastrophe of the Holocaust, American Jews entered the postwar world ready to accept a position of leadership among world Jewry. They simultaneously tackled twin challenges: to assist hundreds of thousands of Jews displaced by the war and to support the establishment of a struggling Jewish state in the context of a changing social, economic, and political scene in the United States. After the war American Jews left large cities like New York, Chicago, Philadelphia, and Cleveland where they had previously concentrated and settled in newer cities like Los Angeles and Miami. They also moved in large numbers to the suburbs. The generation that had gone to war used the GI Bill to help them attend college or professional school and obtain mortgages. They eagerly contributed funds to build synagogues and Jewish community centers in these new locales of Jewish life to nourish an American Jewish identity in their children, the baby boom generation. They also supported an extensive array of Jewish communal organizations devoted to social welfare, recreation, health, and education. Looking at this American Jewish world in 1963, the philosopher Harold Weisberg observed with a mixture of awe and disdain that "Jewish life in the United States is expressed primarily through a culture of organizations."[13] Belonging to a Jewish community took precedence over belief in Judaism among American Jews. Jewish accommodation to American congregational models of affiliation effectively papered over the fact that faith had not been the bedrock of Judaism.[14] Since Jews did not want their children growing up feeling insecure or inadequate, they tackled enduring anti-Semitic barriers to Jewish advancement, especially discrimination in jobs, housing, and public accommodations like hotels. If the New York Jewish beauty Bess Myerson could be chosen Miss America in 1945, then Jews could be accepted as Americans without denying their Jewish identity.[15] Or so they hoped.

Political arguments had always flourished among Jews, but in the wake of the depression and World War II a broad consensus had emerged. That consensus located Jews among the Democratic Party's urban wing. They supported the New Deal's social welfare provisions and they championed the rights of labor to unionize to negotiate from strength to secure a decent livelihood. They advocated a generous understanding of the public sphere; housing, utilities, transportation, education, libraries, and culture all deserved government support and regulation. Their optimism was tempered, however, by their experience of World War II and the mass murder of European Jews. These events prompted them to defend the idea and reality of a Jewish state, to seek international cooperation through the United Nations and an end to colonialism. The creation of Israel and other new nations in Africa and Asia in the postwar decades represented in their eyes the triumph of liberation movements. Jews similarly understood the struggle for civil rights at home, including fair employment practices and an end to discrimination in housing, resorts, and university education as efforts to achieve justice, to make the United States a more equal society.

After the war Jews also sought recognition as a legitimate American religious group. As the United States adopted the idea of the Judeo-Christian tradition as its distinctive democratic credo, Judaism achieved a measure of equality with Protestantism and Catholicism.[16] Protestant, Catholic, Jew epitomized the American version of the Judeo-Christian tradition.[17] But Jews did not just accept this context of interreligious understanding. In the postwar years Jewish organizations, especially the American Jewish Congress, mounted legal challenges to practices like Bible reading in the public schools and Christmas and Easter celebrations that intertwined church and state.[18] These cases increased the stress on the easy optimism that held the Judeo-Christian tradition together.

As many Jewish goals for civil rights and civil liberties were adequately met by the mid-1960s, Jewish political consensus eroded. Jews attacked during the McCarthy years as "communistic" were effectively frozen out of the community. Suburban and new urban politics raised different issues and required other coalitions from those in older large cities. Increasingly virulent argument dominated Jewish political debates as a new generation emerged.[19] Maturation of Jewish baby boomers coincided with the rise of identity politics. They came to be associated with one another, but in unstable terms.

In the 1970s a Jewish counterculture arose in response to the black power movement and the cultural politics of other minority groups. Young Jews involved in loose-knit religious groups called a *havurah,* "incorporated much of the language of these movements into their own definitions of their ethnicity." They were recasting Judaism as part of a generational rebellion against the synthesis their parents had crafted, "but this was not their only motivation," argues anthropologist Riv-Ellen Prell.[20] They believed that social transformation was possible, and they "claimed that shared Jewish activities were important acts of protest."[21] They were reconfiguring Jewish politics, making the personal political. In the vision of one activist, this generation was transforming itself "from Jewish radicals to radical Jews."[22]

These engagements with issues of identity intersected with the tumultuous story of identity politics among Americans of every description. To simplify drastically, one path of identity politics began in the 1960s with organized activism for racial justice, and continued with opposition to the Vietnam War and agitation for women's rights. In the 1980s this road wound through not altogether symbolic turf wars over race, ethnicity, gender, and sexuality. The trail ended at the mall, with Gen X in hot pursuit of identity-through-lifestyle, with personal investments in culture-as-virtual-politics, commitments that curiously enough have echoed aspects of counterculture conceits popular back in the late 1960s.

Weisberg had noticed as early as 1963 how much had changed in the ideologies of American Jews. He summarized these shifts: "the disappearance of assimilationism as a serious ideological option, the abandonment of secularist ideologies, the replacement of Marxist, humanist, and liberal ideologies with existentialist theologies and ideologies, the effective

So by 60s shift is from assimilationism to fear of dying out (existentialism)

armistice in the warfare between science and theology, the enormous growth of organized Jewish religion coupled with the serious decline of liberal theologies, the success of political Zionism and the subsequent, perhaps consequent, failure of Zionist ideologies and parties."[23] Less than a decade later another series of issues had risen to the forefront of the consciousness of young Jews: the Holocaust and its meanings, Israel and identification with Zionism, feminism as women's liberation, intermarriage and betrayal of Jewish community, the fate of Soviet Jewry and how it should be rescued, and the authority of Judaism and a religious identity. (Yiddish and homosexuality as alternative countercultural Jewish identities developed later in the final decades of the century.)

By the 1970s a specific, Jewishly inflected identity politics that stemmed from Jewish involvement in New Left politics animated American Jews. Voices of this counterculture, as Prell describes them, "emphasized the culpability of three institutions in the assimilation of American Jews."[24] These were the Jewish communal federations that coordinated fund-raising for local, national, and international organizations, large impersonal synagogues, and middle-class, materialistic, suburban Jewish families.

Young Jews disaffected from established Jewish communal organizations and bitterly opposed to their priorities and leadership mounted attacks that drew upon intriguing mixtures of support for Zionism, concern for the Holocaust, belief in feminism, and advocacy of public religious behavior. But rather than weld these issues into a coherent political program, they wielded them as clubs to attack "the establishment." Thus it was not unusual to see college-aged Jews demanding greater religious observance from Jewish organizations at the same time as they proudly asserted the importance of Jewish difference from other Americans and roundly condemned American Jews' failure to rescue coreligionists during the Holocaust. No particular logic connected religious observance with rescuing Jews during the Holocaust and militantly asserting Jewish difference from Christian Americans. Rather, the threads that linked Jewish identity politics stemmed from a confluence of political, social, and cultural trends in American society. It was partly a generational revolt, partly an effort to learn from history, partly the allure of the counterculture, partly a response to traumatic violent events that shook American cities, including political assassinations, student takeovers of universities, antiwar protests that ended in deaths, riots by African Americans, and strikes that pitted Jewish union members against black advocates of community control.

The historian Ezra Mendelsohn outlines a typology of Jewish politics in the modern era before the heyday of identity politics. From the 1880s until after World War II people asked not "Who is a Jew?" but "What is a Jew?" Were Jews a nation, a people, a religious group, or just a group of individuals whose Jewishness was a private matter?[25] With the rise of identity politics, the question "Who is a Jew?" became more prominent. The possibility now arose that a Jew could lose her Jewish identity if she adopted the wrong politics. Can a Jew identify with black liberation? Or does that identification mean the person has betrayed his Jewishness? Can a Jew be a feminist? Can a feminist be a Jew? Are these contradictory identities or complementary ones? Are Jews necessarily feminists in some ideal typical sense? Is a Jew a supporter of Israel's right to exist? Are Jews necessarily supporters of Israel's right to exist? Does a Jew retain her Jewish rights within the community if she intermarries? No longer could one claim an identity as a Jew and then adopt whatever politics one desired. The issue was no longer, "What is to be done?" but rather, "Where do I stand?" Politics and identity were intertwined. The former helped to define the latter as much as the latter shaped the former.

Jews often referenced their identity politics using terms popular in the United States. Jewish Defense League (JDL) slogans referred to their perception that Jews had been tragically and damnably passive during the Holocaust. "Never Again" promised resistance to Nazi extermination. The JDL popularized the slogan along with "Every Jew a 22." The latter referenced a 22-caliber gun for self-defense. The JDL adopted these slogans along with a militant stance modeled on the Black Panthers. Now, the slogans suggested, Jews would be armed and able to defend themselves against murderous anti-Semitism. But JDL used the phrases to mobilize lower-middle-class Jewish youth both to protect their urban neighborhoods from gangs and criminals and to struggle against the Communist Soviet state. They aimed in the latter case to win permission for Soviet Jews to emigrate by standing up to U.S. government authority and by challenging the priorities of Jewish communal organizations.[26]

Jewish identity, ambiguously located among changing American interpretations of ethnicity, religion, people, and race, lent itself to political redefinition. For many Jews what mattered was politics, and politics therefore defined Jewish identity. Those politics centered on hotly contested issues, most notably feminism, Israel, the Holocaust, intermarriage, and religion. Two examples may suffice. "Radicals Invade Federation, Glue 200 Mezuzahs to Doors" announced a headline in a Los Angeles paper.[27] The chosen site for this political action—the Jewish Federation Council building—represented the pinnacle of the organized American Jewish community. The Federation coordinated fund-raising for many different Jewish health, welfare, social service, and recreational organizations. But it deliberately did not fund religious groups to avoid religious partisanship among proponents of Reform, Conservative, and Orthodox Judaism. The Federation imagined itself as the civic space of American Jews, and that space, its leaders concurred, should be free of religious identification.[28] The college students conducting their Sunday-morning raid on the Federation disagreed. Their demand for public religious identification reflected a new aggressiveness among young Jews. It also expressed their conviction that pluralism and consensus politics produced an anemic Jewish community. The absence of mezuzahs on its doorframes symbolized the Federation's ignorance of its rich religious heritage. This outward sign of Jewish identification represented defiance toward a politics of accommodation in the eyes of the youth, though the mezuzah itself with its small parchment scroll quoting from the Shema (the Jewish prayer proclaiming the unity of God) had rarely been enlisted in such political gestures. Now the mezuzah was coming to stand for a generic Jewish identity rather than reflect a specific religious commitment. "Jewish Women Call for Change" declared the 1972 manifesto of Ezrat Nashim, a Jewish feminist consciousness-raising group.[29] Having committed themselves to feminist Jewish identity, these women struggled to make room within the Jewish community for their vision of Judaism. They demanded that women be granted membership in synagogues, be counted in a prayer minyan of ten adult Jews, and be allowed to participate fully in congregational life. Symbolism did not matter to them as it did for the two young women involved in the project to glue mezuzahs to the doorframes of the Federation building. Yet both groups of women were engaged in Jewish identity politics.

The activism of identity politics fractured the Jewish community. Although efforts to fight anti-Semitism continued to unite Jews of all stripes, a wide range of issues propelled American Jews into different camps divided by their understanding of who was a Jew.

Perhaps most divisive was the status of the State of Israel. After the Yom Kippur war of October 1973 a number of American Jewish activists organized Breira (Alternative). They argued for peaceful coexistence of Israelis and Palestinians. Although these ideas would form the basis of the Oslo accords twenty years later, in the mid-1970s they were considered provocative and inappropriate, threatening to undermine American support for Israel. Breira articulated a dissenting position among American Jews: recognize

Palestinians as a nation and urge that Israelis consider a two-state solution. Breira maintained that American Jews could simultaneously support and criticize Israel. Loyalty to and identification as Jews did not require accepting decisions of Israeli political figures. Indeed, the organization's very name challenged a phrase popular in Israel at the time, *eyn breira,* meaning "there is no choice" but to accept the status quo. After the victory of the Likud party in 1977 and Menachem Begin's election as prime minister, conservative American Jews orchestrated a deft attack on Breira that smeared the organization. Writers associated with Americans for a Safe Israel, a group founded in 1971 to "persuade American Jews to reject a 'peace for territory' solution and only accept 'peace for peace,'" tarred Breira's leaders and members as self-hating Jews, anti-Zionists with communist and socialist pasts, traitors to the Jewish community, or unwitting fellow travelers.[30] With Breira's demise, conflict over Israel among American Jews diminished. Neither New Jewish Agenda nor Americans for Peace Now, which emerged in the 1980s, mounted the sort of linked critiques of the American Jewish establishment and Israeli political leaders that had characterized Breira.

While conflict over Israel gradually became less intense due to suppression of dissent and emergence of consensus, conflict over the Holocaust and its meanings intensified in the 1980s and 1990s. In some ways connections drawn between the Holocaust and the subsequent establishment of Israel contributed to arguments about the meaning of the Holocaust. Increasingly Americans of all backgrounds recognized the significance of the genocide of European Jews. Yet the establishment of the United States Holocaust Memorial Museum, which reflected that recognition, provoked debates over the uniqueness of the Holocaust. At stake was how one viewed the war, events leading up to the war, and what happened after it ended. Was this a singularly Jewish catastrophe with its roots in anti-Semitism, the culmination of centuries of persecution of Jews? Or was the extermination of European Jews one example of genocide in a century filled with mass murders? Many Americans tried to answer, "Both."[31] As the Holocaust moved onto prime-time television in the nine-hour miniseries *Holocaust* that premiered in 1978, it also raised anew questions about how the Holocaust should be represented. Were popular culture portrayals inappropriate on the grounds of "taste" or "seriousness"? Discussions that had largely been confined to the Jewish press now took place in front of a large non-Jewish audience.[32]

In the context of identity politics, it was no longer enough to remember the murder of European Jews, to see anti-Semitism as a form of racism, to resolve to dismantle discrimination in the United States, and to support the right of Jews to have their own state. Such attitudes, which characterized the "Jewish greatest generation" that fought in World War II, lacked clarity and commitment in the eyes of their children. The Holocaust increasingly came to occupy a central place in the identity politics of American Jews. What one thought of the Holocaust, what lessons one derived from it, how one commemorated it mattered a great deal.[33] When her daughter came home from first grade and asked, "Where were you in the Holocaust, Mommy?" the feminist scholar Paula Hyman, born after the war, was moved to write an article in the *New York Times Magazine*. Hyman questioned the emphasis on role-playing enactments of Holocaust scenarios at Jewish summer camps and the centrality that the Holocaust had achieved in Jewish school curriculums. She asked whether Holocaust consciousness should stand at the emotional heart of Jewish study.[34] As the Holocaust entered Jewish identity politics, Jews stopped referring to it as a rationale for civil rights activism or opposition to McCarthyism. The Holocaust no longer served as a touchstone for liberal politics. It could not be summoned to justify building synagogues, or integrating bus stations and restaurants, or fighting poverty.[35]

As Alvin Rosenfeld demonstrates in his article, the Holocaust became Americanized. Americans, Jewish Americans included, were disinclined to contemplate unfathomable evil as expressed in the systematic mass extermination of European Jews. The trade-off for greater recognition of the importance of the Holocaust seemed to be a dilution of its significance. Americans universalized the Holocaust. They began to apply the term to other catastrophes. Americans also searched for life-affirming messages in the Holocaust. The most notable example of this desire appeared in the popularity of Anne Frank's diary. Americans preferred to emphasize not her miserable death in Bergen-Belsen at the age of fifteen but her optimistic affirmation of humanity's fundamental goodness.

Rosenfeld points out that the usual division of those involved in the murder of European Jewry into three camps shifts in the United States. Instead of concentrating on the actions of perpetrators, victims, and bystanders, attention is paid to two new categories—rescuers and survivors. The change in focus obscures the primary importance of the former categories. Thus a popular movie like *Schindler's List* portrays only tangentially the perpetrators and victims. Choosing Oskar Schindler and the Jews he rescued to be the subject of the film misrepresents the Holocaust. Through such reframing the event is fundamentally distorted. Most Jews were killed; most Nazis murdered Jews. Schindler and his Jews are the exception. The desire to retrieve some "moral idealism from a history of mass murder" ultimately distorts understanding, making it ever more difficult to retain the sense of outrage and despair inherent in any effort to comprehend such a catastrophe.

One of the mysteries of the transformation and Americanization of the Holocaust into a component of the identity politics of American Jews is how it came to be accepted that American Jews ignored the Holocaust in the years after the end of World War II. Hasia Diner sets out to discover the trajectory of identity politics that connects a youthful attack upon the American Jewish establishment with the popularization of the Holocaust in American life.

In 1967 Arthur D. Morse, the executive television producer of *CBS Reports*, published a best-selling book, *While Six Million Died*, subtitled "a chronicle of American apathy." As its cover proclaimed, Morse told "the breathtaking story of how America ducked chance after chance to save the Jews."[36] The book marked an opening salvo in what would become a mounting attack on the Roosevelt administration for failing to rescue European Jews, one that paralleled efforts by American historians to knock Franklin Delano Roosevelt off the pedestal where American Jews and other liberals had placed him. Morse's book was followed by scholarly studies; perhaps the most influential was David Wyman's *The Abandonment of the Jews*, which appeared fifteen years later.

Diner suggests a parallel path, rooted in the rebellious identity politics of the 1970s. In those years young Jews adopted Morse's critique, aiming it not at the Roosevelt administration but at the leadership of American Jews. Along with blaming American Jews for failing to rescue their European cousins, these young Jews also condemned American Jews for not remembering the Holocaust, not placing it at the forefront of their consciousness. The charges stuck. Indeed, a blue-ribbon commission headed by former Supreme Court justice Arthur Goldberg was impaneled in the 1980s to evaluate and judge American Jews. Held up to standards of identity politics, American Jews of the war years failed miserably. Where were the protests? The rallies? And as a mark of their lack of interest, they did not even care to mourn the deaths, to commemorate the cultural destruction, to ponder the meaning of the Holocaust.[37] Yet Diner shows that this powerful version of history is wrong. American Jews did remember, did mourn, did commemorate. The Holocaust remained burned in their consciousness. But the politics of identity erased it from history. The children didn't realize what their parents had done.

Religious debates increasingly polarized American Jews as they internalized their spiritual identity. Arnold Eisen describes how a private Jewish consciousness comes to guide and shape American Jewish practice. The choices Jews make—what holidays to observe, what rituals to perform, what commandments to follow—derive from their own interior sense of identity. By the 1980s even moderately affiliated Jews had moved so far from their parents Jewish "culture of organizations" that they rarely gave credence to communal norms in their assessment of their own behavior. In part this reflected their conviction that Jewishness was both ascribed and achieved. Thus Jews had choice, and yet they remained connected to other Jews through ancestors and children.

For Eisen, American Jews perform the politics of Jewish religious identities most dramatically within their families, around their private dining room tables at mealtimes. This reduces the risk that observance will enter the public non-Jewish sphere. In addition, by focusing Jewish religious practices on children, adults can minimize the extent of their own Jewish identities. "One is not affirming ethnic distinctiveness or religious truth," Eisen argues, by lighting Sabbath candles or blessing the wine, "but merely passing on a tradition, helping to bring the family together." A movement that may have started with affixing mezuzahs to the doorframes of the Federation building seems to have produced personal religious practices that express identity but are devoid of belief.

Of course, as another generation of children matured, they often disagreed with their parents' practices, either adopting more rigorous religious observance or intermarrying. Both actions challenged their parents' religious identities and politics. Young Jews who "returned" to Orthodox or Hasidic Judaism often refused to eat in their parents' homes because their parents did not keep sufficiently kosher kitchens. These children enacted their religious behaviors in public for all to see, and they emphasized the importance of strict interpretations of religious requirements.[38] At the other end of the spectrum, young Jews who intermarried often denied that they were still Jews, thus disrupting the chain of generations that had been so central to their parents' identities.

Jonathan Sarna sees both tendencies as extending back in American history. Both the drive for religious renewal and revitalization by a young, native-born generation and the desire to assimilate and intermarry with Christian Americans have long histories. Tensions between the two over the course of three centuries have strengthened pluralism in American Jewish life. The freedoms of the United States coupled with disestablishment of religion, especially at the national level, encouraged American Jews to develop competing and even contradictory traditions of behavior.

The competitive dimensions of contemporary religious pluralism can be seen most clearly in the changing fluid relationship of Orthodox and Conservative Jews. Whether in rabbinic leadership, synagogue practices, or membership, few distinctions sharply demarcated orthodox from conservative. But with the rise of identity politics in the 1970s, demands on Orthodoxy and Conservatism escalated. Feminist Jews urged the latter to move beyond mixed seating that had previously been the symbol of equality between men and women in American Judaism. Now feminists called for recognition of women as constituent members of a prayer quorum (minyan), acceptance of women as prayer leaders, training of women as rabbis, scholars, and cantors. Their demands were met. These dramatic changes aligned Conservative Judaism with an egalitarianism identified as American. By contrast, efforts to convince Orthodox rabbis to modify Jewish law *(halakhah)* to allow Jewish women to study traditional texts, or to permit them to form their own prayer groups, provoked as much opposition as support. Women had a place in Judaism, Orthodox leaders affirmed, but it was not identical to that of men.

The politics of religious identity extended into the public sphere beyond the synagogue. In the 1980s clothing styles for men and women came to mark religious identities. Orthodox women adopted modest forms of dress, wearing long skirts and blouses and covering their hair if married. Different types of head coverings for men, from knitted *kipot* to elaborate fur-trimmed hats, signified their allegiance to versions of Orthodoxy. Other public behaviors, including where one ate, entered the language of religious identity politics. Although one needed to know how to "read" the evidence, it was widely available for in-group members. The process of differentiation described by Jeffrey Gurock reached well beyond the rabbis and leaders he discusses. The politics of identity helped to draw rigid lines between two groups of religious Jews who once shared much in common.

New directions in Jewish theology in America accompanied these trends. In response to the rise of identity politics in religion, Arthur Green argues for a Jewish theology that includes all Jews. Indeed, the legacy of Hasidism, the pietist movement of mystical Judaism, is too valuable to remain only with its adherents. It belongs to all Jews because it speaks a rich language of sacred texts, of prayer and nature, and of God's immanence. Green locates an Eastern European tradition of theologizing that connects contemporary Jewish thinkers with Hasidic masters of the nineteenth century. This tradition reaches American Jews through the exemplary career of renowned philosopher and civil rights activist Rabbi Abraham Joshua Heschel, who was born in Poland, educated in Germany, and immigrated to the United States before World War II. Green places himself within this spiritual lineage. He emphasizes that Judaism is a garment "that is completely natural." There is no need to defend Judaism or to define it in terms that are basically foreign to it. Instead, this neo-Hasidic religious reflection rests upon recovery of the "kabbalistic-hasidic tradition" that potentially possesses a power to transform American Jewish spirituality.

Although women have contributed to this new spirituality, the Jewish feminist movement has moved more often toward an egalitarian than a mystical understanding of Judaism. Paula Hyman speaks powerfully of Jewish feminism's centrality to the identity of its adherents. They can no more part with their feminism than with their Judaism; both are integral to their personhood. Jewish feminists distinguished themselves from many of the Jewish women active in the American feminist movement by refusing to privilege one identity over another or to separate their identity as women from their identity as Jews. Since neither took priority, Jewish feminists conducted a dual struggle against sexism and discrimination in the Jewish community and against anti-Semitism in the feminist movement. They were remarkably successful. Within less than two decades from the early organizing years of the 1970s, women had broken down long-standing barriers to their participation as equals in Jewish religious life and won recognition as rabbis, scholars, and leaders. Their successes helped to establish feminism as an enduring fault-line separating Jewish religious groups. Simultaneously, Jewish women summoned the courage to speak out about anti-Semitism in diverse segments of the women's movement. Their attacks on anti-Zionism, anti-Judaism, and stereotypes of Jewish women (e.g., as "Jewish American Princesses") promoted healthy dialogue and gradually changed gentile women's attitudes.[39]

For Jewish women disappointed with radicalism, Jewish feminism also offered an alternative path. Because of its own radical critique of Judaism that reflected a deep commitment to Jewish identification, Jewish feminists spoke to Jews on the left in a common language. If feminists often disparaged the organized Jewish community and dissented from its policies, Jewish feminists provided a model of constructive engagement and critique. Situated between competing constituencies and claiming legitimacy in both, Jewish feminists provided a bridge back to Judaism. Betty Friedan, one of the founders of second-wave feminism, had been estranged from her Jewish identity but rediscovered its significance through the path blazed by Jewish feminists.

Questions of Jewish culture entered the realm of identity politics some-

what later than feminism. While Jews always enjoyed the game of identifying other Jews in popular culture, the issue of whether American Jewish
culture even existed engaged them less often. Steven Whitfield tries to
wrestle a position out of contradictory definitions of culture, of Jewishness,
and of being American. He juggles multiple possibilities, from diffuse understandings of American Jewish culture that include all Jews and set no
boundaries, to maximalist interpretations that limit American Jewish culture to works by Jews that explicitly deal with Jewish themes. The latter
perversely truncates a writer's or artist's identity, reducing it to only some
Jewish fraction, leaving unaccounted the American side. It is a dilemma ex-
acerbated by struggles over identity politics. However, postmodern notions
of hybridity may offer alternatives.

Perhaps the most enduring arena of identity politics can be found in
the bitter debates over intermarriage. Both Egon Mayer and Sylvia Barack
Fishman use measured language and similar social science methodologies
to come to rather different conclusions. Mayer's optimism that "America is
different" leads him to argue that intermarriage in the United States does
not resemble the "radical assimilation" studied by Todd Endelman in Europe. Fishman's darker view of the same trends sees intermarriage destroying necessary boundaries demarcating Jews from other Americans. Without
conversion to Judaism by the gentile spouse, intermarried families tend to
compromise with the dominant Christian culture. Neither Fishman nor
Mayer indulges in the polemics and name-calling that has characterized
discussion of intermarriage. However, Mayer alludes to some of the
provocative advertisements published by Orthodox Jews in response to the
decision by Reform Jews to welcome converts to Judaism. Conversely, Fishman cites the imputation of "racism" leveled at Jews who desire endogamy.

Yet intermarriage has engendered hyperbolic rhetoric. Former prime
minister of Israel Benjamin Netanyahu referred to rising intermarriage rates
among American Jews as "a Silent Holocaust."[40] Fears for the future of Jewish life in America have focused on intermarriage. Statistics from the national Jewish population survey in 1990 fueled frantic efforts to revamp
American Jewish organizational priorities. Fund-raising campaigns focused
on "continuity," raising the specter of a North American continent with
barely any Jews, bereft of political influence, a tiny minority due to intermarriage. Calls were heard to exclude Jews who intermarried from positions of authority, to keep them out of synagogue boardrooms and classrooms. Indeed, intermarriage vied with homosexuality as touchstones of
identity politics at the end of the twentieth century.[41] It is a tribute to their

scholarly commitments that both Mayer and Fishman, though they stand on opposite sides of the intermarriage fence, still speak with respect and civility about one of the hot political topics agitating American Jews.

The course of Jewish identity politics eventually narrowed. By the end of the twentieth century, as Mayer and Fishman suggest, Jewish identity politics had coalesced around either Jewishness as ineluctable or Jewishness as elective. Were Jews a chosen people or a choosy people? The idea of selecting affiliation, practice, or belief undermined the premise of identity politics since it suggested the mutability of identities and hence of any political ideologies codependent with them.

Identity politics have waned in the twenty-first century, but have not disappeared. A concern for social and racial justice, environmentalism, and questions of war and peace increasingly occupy the center of a new generation's political consciousness. Although it is too early to characterize their politics, the question "What is to be done?" has acquired fresh importance. This American Jewish generation seeks to differentiate itself from its parents, the baby boomers. Thus it seeks alternatives to identity politics in coalitions that bring Jews and their Jewishness to the forefront of efforts to make a better and more humane world.

Notes

1. Betty Friedan, *The Feminine Mystique* (New York: Dell, 1963), 11.
2. Sara M. Evans, *Personal Politics: The Roots of Women's Liberation in the Civil Rights Movement and the New Left* (New York: Knopf, 1979).
3. Matthew Frye Jacobson, *Roots Too: White Ethnic Revival in Post–Civil Rights America* (Cambridge: Harvard University Press, 2006), 225.
4. Paul Ritterband and Harold S. Wechsler, *Jewish Learning in American Universities: The First Century* (Bloomington: University of Indiana Press, 1994), 211–15, 233–35.
5. Jacobson, *Roots Too*, 117–246.
6. Arthur A. Goren, "Inventing the 'New Pluralism,'" in *The Politics and Public Culture of American Jews* (Bloomington: Indiana University Press, 1999), 205–23, especially 220–22.
7. Letty Cottin Pogrebin writes in *Deborah, Golda, and Me: Being Female and Jewish in America* (New York: Doubleday, 1991), 203, that only one of her articles "has won and lost friends and influenced people so dramatically that it could be called a cause celebre." That article, "Anti-Semitism in the Women's Movement" appeared in the June 1982 issue of *Ms.* magazine and allowed her to confront the conflict between her identity as a woman and a Jew. It is reprinted in *Deborah, Golda, and Me*, 205–28.
8. Debra L. Schultz, *Going South: Jewish Women in the Civil Rights Movement* (New York: New York University Press, 2001), 100–108, discusses the tensions for Jewish

women in Mississippi in the 1960s. "Acting in accord with one of several identities in a given political situation does not preclude bringing all of oneself to the situation," she writes (105).

9. Arthur Liebman, *Jews and the Left* (New York: Wiley, 1979).

10. On the 1940s and 1950s see Stuart Svonkin, *Jews against Prejudice: American Jews and the Fight for Civil Liberties* (New York: Columbia University Press, 1997); on the 1950s, 1960s, and 1970s see Marc L. Dollinger, *Quest for Inclusion: Jews and Liberalism in Modern America* (Princeton: Princeton University Press, 2000), 129–41.

11. M. Jay Rosenberg, "To Jewish Uncle Toms," reprinted from *Jewish Frontier* (1969) in *The Jewish 1960s: An American Sourcebook,* ed. Michael E. Staub (Waltham, MA: Brandeis University Press, 2004), 232–36. The reference to "Uncle Jake" is on p. 229.

12. Michael E. Staub, *Torn at the Roots: The Crisis of Jewish Liberalism in Postwar America* (New York: Columbia University Press, 2002), especially chaps. 5 and 6.

13. Harold Weisberg, "Ideologies of American Jews," in *The American Jew: A Reappraisal,* ed. Oscar I. Janowsky (Philadelphia: Jewish Publication Society, 1964), 347.

14. Marshall Sklare, *Conservative Judaism: An American Religious Movement* (New York: Schocken, 1972), 19–42.

15. Edward S. Shapiro, *A Time for Healing: American Jewry since World War II* (Baltimore: Johns Hopkins University Press, 1992), 8–10.

16. Deborah Dash Moore, "Jewish GIs and the Creation of the Judeo-Christian Tradition," *Religion and American Culture* 8, no. 1 (1998): 31–54.

17. Will Herberg, *Protestant, Catholic, Jew: An Essay in American Religious Sociology* (Garden City, NY: Doubleday, 1960).

18. Naomi Cohen, *Jews in Christian America: The Pursuit of Religious Equality* (New York: Oxford University Press, 1992).

19. Svonkin, *Jews against Prejudice.*

20. Riv-Ellen Prell, *Prayer and Community: The Havurah in American Judaism* (Detroit: Wayne State University Press, 1989), 70.

21. Prell, *Prayer and Community,* 76.

22. Prell, *Prayer and Community,* 80.

23. Weisberg, "Ideologies of American Jews," 339.

24. Prell, *Prayer and Community,* 81.

25. Ezra Mendelsohn, *On Modern Jewish Politics* (New York: Oxford University Press, 1993), 5–35.

26. Janet L. Dolgin, *Jewish Identity and the JDL* (Princeton: Princeton University Press, 1977), especially chap. 3. "The broader categorization, Jew/non-Jew, was not based on action. These were categories of being," she writes; "it is the significance and meaning of *Jewishness* rather than Judaism with which JDL was concerned" (71–72).

27. *Jewish Post and Opinion,* November 14, 1969, 4, in Staub, *The Jewish 1960s,* 239.

28. Jonathan S. Woocher, *Sacred Survival: The Civil Religion of American Jews* (Bloomington: Indiana University Press, 1986).

29. Jacob Rader Marcus, ed. *The American Jewish Woman: A Documentary History* (New York: Ktav, 1981), 894–96.

30. Jack Wertheimer, "Breaking the Taboo: Critics of Israel and the American Jewish Establishment," in *Envisioning Israel: The Changing Ideals and Images of North American Jews,* ed. Allon Gal (Jerusalem: Magnes Press of the Hebrew University; Detroit: Wayne State University Press, 1996), 401.

31. Edward Linenthal, *Preserving Memory: The Struggle to Create America's Holocaust Museum* (New York: Viking, 1995).

32. Alan Mintz, *Popular Culture and the Shaping of Holocaust Memory in America* (Seattle: University of Washington Press, 2001), 23–26.

33. Peter Novick, *The Holocaust in American Life* (Boston: Houghton Mifflin, 1999), 1–15.

34. Paula Hyman, "New Debate on the Holocaust," *New York Times Magazine,* September 14, 1980.

35. Staub, *Torn at the Roots,* 45–75.

36. Arthur D. Morse, *While Six Million Died: A Chronicle of American Apathy* (New York: Random House, 1967).

37. Seymour Maxwell Finger, *American Jewry during the Holocaust: A Report by the Research Director, His Staff, and Independent Research Scholars Retained by the Director for the American Jewish Commission on the Holocaust* (New York: Holmes and Meier, 1984).

38. Haym Soloveitchik, "Rupture and Reconstruction: The Transformation of Contemporary Orthodoxy," *Tradition* 28, no. 4 (1994): 64–130.

39. Jacobson, *Roots Too,* 292–302.

40. Samuel G. Freedman, *Jew vs. Jew: The Struggle for the Soul of American Jewry* (New York: Simon and Schuster, 2000), 73–79.

41. See the contributors to *A Statement on the Jewish Future: Text and Responses* (New York: American Jewish Committee, 1997).

The Politics of Holocaust Identity

Holocaust Memorial, Los Angeles, 2006. Courtesy of Bill Aron.

When Jews Were GIs: How World War II Changed a Generation and Remade American Jewry

Deborah Dash Moore

It is a commonly accepted, if rarely explored, truism that World War II marked a turning point for American Jews. Everyone knows that after the war American Jews moved to the suburbs, entered the professions, achieved a secure middle-class status, acquired political clout, and became accepted as Americans by their fellow citizens. The formidable prewar barriers of anti-Semitic discrimination and prejudice appeared to melt away: each succeeding year after the war fewer and fewer Americans admitted to pollsters that they disliked Jews or feared that Jews had too much power.[1] Here was the American success story so aptly described by Charles Silberman in his book *A Certain People* or personified in Alan Dershowitz's remarkable autobiography *Chutzpah*.[2] Of course, social scientists recognized that Jews were well prepared to take advantage of the postwar era of economic abundance and social mobility. Both their culture and social position during the Great Depression provided them with tools to transform themselves into middle-class, liberal suburbanites.[3]

I am not interested in revising this postwar portrait so much as exploring its dynamics. I also want to examine how it happened that after a devastating world war in which Jews sustained many times more deaths than Americans, American Jews emerged with the resilience and optimism to press their specifically Jewish claims upon the world. How did a Reform rabbi come to speak before the United Nations gathered at Lake Success to

This essay was originally presented on March 7, 1994, at the Jean and Samuel Frankel Center for Judaic Studies, University of Michigan, Ann Arbor.

urge them eloquently to support the establishment of a Jewish state in Palestine?[4] From where did the courage come to oppose quotas limiting Jewish enrollment in colleges in the face of the opportunities offered by the GI bill? What led Jewish defense agencies—from the patrician American Jewish Committee to the populist American Jewish Congress, from the socialist Jewish Labor Committee to the bourgeois Anti-Defamation League— to overhaul their programs in the early cold war years and embark upon new approaches to combating discrimination and prejudice, methods that differed radically from those of the prewar period?[5] In an era of political quietism and social conformity, American Jews not only rushed to the suburbs to purchase single-family homes and build synagogue centers, but they also aggressively pursued programs of liberal change.[6] The conjunction of these behaviors deserves the historian's attention.

If we accept the truism that World War II was a watershed for American Jews, it behooves us to look more closely at Jewish experience on the home front and in military service during the war years. Even a cursory appraisal should prove illuminating, though it neglects such important topics as Jewish women's work in war industries or the attitudes of immigrant or even second-generation parents toward their children's decision to enlist.

Most American Jews and their fellow citizens did not see active military service; rather they experienced the war on the home front. Thus the home front should serve as our starting point. The vast majority of American Jews made their homes in the nation's largest cities. In fact, New York and Chicago accounted for over half the American Jewish population. Contemporaries often saw this concentration as problematic. As the historian Salo Baron observed in an address on what war had meant to American Jewish community life, for decades "observers of American Jewish life have deplored the . . . agglomeration of nearly two-thirds of American Jewry within a radius of two hundred miles from Times Square."[7] No matter where one put the emphasis, urban America was the Jewish home front.

In the beginning of his history of America's fight at home and abroad during World War II, William O'Neill notes that "America has changed so much that those who grew up in the interwar years remember a nation that, to a significant degree, no longer exists." He then points out that "to modern eyes the most striking feature of American cities in 1941 was the absence of people of color." Rather, "what most impressed foreign visitors was the remarkably varied ethnic backgrounds of white Americans."[8] Irrespective of size, the cities Jews called home shared common characteristics. Ethnicity animated their neighborhoods, influenced occupational distribution, and dominated politics. Here Jews were one ethnic group among many. Jewish religion, culture, politics, and occupations stemmed from immigrant origins. Divisions among Jews—of class, birth, background, ideology, and religion—ultimately paled before the differences separating Jews from other immigrants, mostly Catholics, many from peasant cultures. Their interaction with each other, and with the local, often Protestant, elites, shaped each city's character.[9]

In every city except New York, Jews were simply one struggling minority among others. Jews in New York City enjoyed the luxury of numbers and diversity. Almost two million strong and roughly 30 percent of the population, they were the city's largest single ethnic group. Because of their critical mass, their internal differences did count. New York Jews could separate themselves from their fellow Jews on the grounds of ideology or religion, class or politics, and still find enough other similar Jews to fill an apartment house, an organization, or even a neighborhood. Gerson Cohen, the future chancellor of the Jewish Theological Seminary, grew up speaking Hebrew in an immigrant household, an unusual pattern of Jewish family culture. When he was a teenager he met a Polish boy who had studied "within the Hebrew secular system of Poland. He and I played ball together, talking away in Hebrew, from which I drew the following inference: New York City was a place where people, however isolated they were from the mainstream, did not need to be alone."[10]

The diversity and numbers of New York Jews allowed them to settle large sections of the city and to endow those areas with a Jewish ambiance. Growing up in East Flatbush, Victor Gotbaum remembered that section of Brooklyn as "really insulated, wrapped in a false sense of security, what with Jews to the left of you and to the right of you and across the street from you." Although they shared the streets with other ethnics, New York Jews often were remarkably provincial. "Much later," the labor leader continues, "I was impressed when my Chicago friends told me that right across the street there might be a Polish family and a Polish gang ready to get you. I never had that problem. Neither did most Jews raised in Brooklyn. When you went to school the minority would be two or three non-Jews per class."[11] The writer Grace Paley "grew up being very sorry for Christians. My idea was that there were very few of them in the world."[12] Kate Simon knew that Italian immigrants lived on the east side of LaFontaine Street but she considered them "just Jews who didn't talk Yiddish. They didn't go to synagogues, either, but a lot of Jews didn't."[13] Comfortable in their own world, New York Jews rarely ventured outside of it. "The Jewish immigrant world branded upon its sons and daughters marks of separateness even while encouraging them to dreams of universalism."[14]

The organized Jewish community in northeastern and Midwestern cities presented a picture of institutional completeness. Schools of all types—religious, congregational, communal, Zionist, Yiddishist, socialist, communist—and of all levels—elementary, secondary, vocational, college, teacher training, graduate—flourished or expected to flourish. Jews established hospitals, orphanages, old-age homes, homes for delinquents and unwed mothers, community centers, settlement houses, and young men's and women's Hebrew associations. Gender provided a fulcrum for organization, and women's organizations represented a wide political and religious spectrum. Even occupational groups reflected ethnic background. There were organizations of Jewish public school teachers and policemen, unions of Jewish garment workers and bakers, of Yiddish writers and social workers. Most numerous were the small societies of Jews from the same home towns in the old country, *landsmanshaftn.* These groups directly linked Jews with their European cousins. Religious activities increasingly fractured along denominational lines with growing distinctions among Reform, Conservative, and Orthodox. Finally, national Jewish organizations, from fraternal orders to Zionist groups, participated through their branches in local city life.[15]

Although few Jews growing up in the big cities in the 1930s were aware of the extent and diversity of Jewish organizational activity, most participated in public expressions of Jewishness, and many engaged in activities under Jewish auspices. Urban Jews knew about synagogues, even if they did not attend them, as most did not; indeed, they were as likely to walk by them on the streets as they were to pass a church. Similarly, Jews were conscious of the Yiddish dailies that shared newsstands with English-language papers, and they experienced the rhythm of the Jewish calendar because they refrained from school, or work, or shopping like others in their neighborhood. In the metropolitan milieu, even the secular worlds of work, commerce, and recreation reflected Jewish associations. Special sales in local stores coincided with Jewish holidays like Rosh Hashanah or Passover, promoting patterns of consumption linked to Judaism. Strikes in Jewish industries, especially the garment trades, resonated throughout the streets of Jewish neighborhoods. Young Jews played basketball and attended dances at the local Jewish community center; the lucky ones would spend summer vacations at Jewish country resorts, cottages, or camps; and all had some friends who became bar mitzvah at the age of thirteen.[16]

Just as young Jews were aware of a Jewish world, they were similarly conscious of discrimination and prejudice. "Almost every Chicago boy born into the 1930s Depression and the pre–World War II years had a Siamese twin brother: fear. A cold, knowing terror that a pogrom of science-fiction dimensions might soon be launched from Hitler's Germany." Clancy Sigal's awareness came from radio broadcasts. "It took no brains to figure this out," Sigal recalled, "just a pair of ears to listen to Adolf's harangues from Berlin, rebroadcast on one of the city's radio stations, and enough filial piety to tune in on the tales of Old Country persecution by parents who never forgot the Cossacks." For many of Sigal's friends on the West Side, "the question was, Do we run again, or do we resist?"[17] One did not have to encounter anti-Semitism to know it existed, even to plan one's life and tailor one's aspirations so that one would avoid it. "I knew that I was a good student and that I was going to apply for graduate school," Maxwell Greenberg, a Harvard-educated lawyer recalled. "I knew that there were quotas in various graduate schools. I also knew that if I worked very hard and made good grades, and did everything that was expected of me by my parents and by society, that I would qualify for graduate school."[18] Jewish vocational patterns often reflected this reality. Few Jews tried to obtain engineering degrees, for example, because prospects for employment were slim. Some Jews changed their names to increase their chances at jobs in large firms.[19] But most navigated the prejudice and discrimination as facts of life. Compared to the violent anti-Semitism in Europe, the American brand seemed tame.

Then the war came and uprooted Jews from their established routines, comfortable neighborhoods, and mundane affairs. Initially, however, the war did not seem to change their lives. Jews read the papers, raised funds, and sent packages of food to help Polish Jews, the newest victims of Nazi attack. They protested and urged their political representatives to help rescue Jewish refugees desperately trying to leave Europe. They signed affidavits of support to assist near or distant relatives obtain visas. They helped the Yishuv, the Jewish settlement in Palestine, as it struggled against the encroaching reality of war. But at the same time they held banquets and dinners to raise monies for their local synagogues and hospitals. They continued their intramural political struggles. They celebrated the ordinary rounds of holidays and family occasions, births and weddings, bar mitzvahs and confirmations.

When the United States declared war in December 1941 after the Japanese attack on Pearl Harbor, Jews threw themselves into the war effort together with their fellow citizens. Some young Jews did not wait to be drafted but enlisted in the armed forces. But only a minority chose to leave college as Nathan Perlmutter left Georgetown University to enlist.[20] The majority followed the more common track of continuing to work or remaining in school until called by their draft boards. A few intrepid individuals were forced to battle American anti-Semitism in order to enlist, the experience of one recent Yale graduate. Rebuffed by biased Manhattan recruiters who refused to enroll him in the navy's officer corps, Martin Dash went down to Baltimore to use his relatives' address to sign up.[21] Seymour Graubard faced similar problems with Air Force Intelligence. A Columbia Law School graduate, Graubard had a deferral from the draft but "was insistent on getting into action. All my non-Jewish friends were accepted, but my application was lost three times running. I was finally informed by a sympathetic Air Corps officer that the Air Corps didn't want Jews." Graubard then pulled strings to get a commission in the army.[22] A handful of Jewish pacifists faced a different dilemma. Convinced that World War II "would be an imperialist one," committed Jewish socialists like Paul Jacobs had to decide: "should we or should we not support the Allies against the Nazis and the Italian Fascists?"[23]

Many more American Jews shared Nathan Perlmutter's sentiments; when asked why he wanted to join the marines, Perlmutter told a surprised recruiter, "I want to fight Fascism."[24] Most Americans saw Japan, not the Nazis, as the crucial enemy. "The primary objective of our war is to defeat the Japs—not Hitler, and certainly not Nazism," reported Ari Lashner with dismay. He found among his fellow recruits in the Maritime Service Radio Cadet School "no sympathy for what I presented as the fundamental issue of the war: the defeat of Fascism." While Lashner praised a healthy skepticism of American soldiers toward naive and idealistic slogans of war, he recognized that their sentiments derived from prejudice. "With the Japs it's different. They hate the Japs."[25]

Jews entering the armed forces faced a choice in how to identify themselves; they were asked to indicate their religion on their dog tags. As a confirmed socialist and secularist, Jacobs initially told the army air corps that he had no religion "and then found out that this made me fair game for all the chaplains. After being bombarded for a week by suggestions that I attend Catholic, Protestant, Hebrew, and I even think Christian Science services, I gave up." He had his "dogtags stamped with the initial 'H' for Hebrew, thus at least removing myself from the anxious ministry of the other groups."[26]

Approximately 550,000 Jewish men and women served in the United States armed forces during World War II, the equivalent of thirty-seven divisions. The participation of 11 percent of the Jewish population in the service or 50 percent of the men age eighteen to forty-four ensured that few Jewish families would not have a close relative in uniform.[27] Widespread involvement in the military turned Jews into fighters. They became seasoned soldiers, competent in handling arms and comfortable in taking risks. It was the only generation of American Jews to know military life firsthand. The experience changed their lives, their perceptions of the world, and their self-understanding as Jews. "The experience of the war years," Lucy Dawidowicz observed, "had a transfiguring effect on American Jews and on their ideas of themselves as Jews."[28]

Military service lifted Jews out of their cities and sent them to bases located often in rural areas of the country, especially the South and West. The first encounter produced a kind of culture shock. "I was in a strange land among people who hardly spoke my own language," wrote one GI from Brooklyn. "On this foreign soil one could not find lox or bagels or pumpernickel. Here Southern fried and grits were the popular delicacies."[29] To many Jews' amazement, "this foreign soil" was indeed America. The United States turned out to be a Protestant nation, not a Catholic one. Jews in the armed services discovered a world beyond their provincial neighborhoods. "Most of us were kind of insulated," Abe Shalo remembered; "we had very little knowledge of the rest of the country. Whatever we learned about the United States was for the most part from geography books. . . . we knew very little about the people." And the geography books "didn't tell you how different the average American was."[30] Jews acknowledged their surprise upon realizing how Protestant the United States was. They had mistaken the heavily Catholic cities of their childhoods for the entire country.

Jews also discovered the diversity of the Jewish diaspora and how different Jews were from each other.[31] Stationed in Calcutta, India, David Macarov enjoyed hospitality for soldiers at "a weekly tea at the magnificent home of Lady Ezra, and a kosher chicken dinner" prepared each week by Mrs. Gubbay. Writing to his family in Atlanta, Macarov admitted: "When I mention these people, I am sure that the first question which enters your mind is 'Are they Indians?' . . . Yet I know that what you really mean is 'Are they dark skinned?' And I find that I get very angry at the question, and am tempted to answer, 'What difference does it make?'" "Perhaps," Macarov continued, "you don't realize what a remarkable accomplishment that is for me. Born and bred in the South, it did not matter what I *thought*, I *felt* an instinctive prejudice against dark skins." Though he knew the attitude to be wrong, he did not think he could overcome it. Yet after living among Indian Jews for several months, Macarov discovered that he not only no longer felt revulsion toward dark-skinned people, "but don't see how it could have existed."[32]

The army introduced other Jews to racial discrimination and prejudice. One recruit stationed in Virginia observed a Jim Crow incident on a bus— a Negro soldier who refused to sit in the rear was forced to get off. Writing home to family in Brooklyn, he described the matter and concluded: "It is about time that all JIM CROW laws were abolished in the South. . . . Such a move would prove how truly and genuinely we mean our war aims."[33] This awareness and anger at civil discrimination—and its contradiction of clearly articulated American wartime ideals—stimulated in many Jews a commitment to civil rights.

The armed forces similarly gave Jews new perspectives on anti-Semitism. Greenberg remembered that the first time he was "labelled a Jew or a kike was in the Army."[34] His experience was not uncommon. "You know, Dad, there is anti-Semitism. I have found it in the army," wrote Lillian Kimberg, a WAC. Although most Jewish soldiers encountered anti-Semitism in the service, many thought that daily living together reduced prejudice.[35] Kimberg discovered that "many of the girls have never seen a Jew." But she felt that, as "a representative of my religion," she "showed them that Jews are people like all other in the world."[36] Some were less sanguine about the impact an individual could make. Victor Gotbaum recalled many incidents and "statements about our cowardice and Jewish unwillingness to fight. I was deeply upset by it. Here we were fighting the Nazis, and then this madness in the United States Army!"[37] Lashner wrote: "We are either despised, mocked, or magnanimously tolerated."[38]

Other Jewish soldiers felt empowered to undercut American anti-Semitism. "As a GI, I wasn't going to take shit from anybody," Joseph Bensman recalled. "So when I had a civilian teacher in the army school who was anti-Semitic, anti-Roosevelt, and antiwar, I denounced him for propagandizing in class and had him put on the carpet." As the future sociologist knew, "lots of personal abuse was built into the system. I understood that, but I also realized that anti-Semitism was illegal."[39] Jews in the armed services understood that they had the right as Americans to oppose anti-Semitism. Some contended that as they approached the battlefield, anti-Semitism declined and that it disappeared completely under the pressure of battle. The teenage Leon Uris wrote to his father in 1944 that he "fought beside

Catholics, Protestants and Mormons, Indians, Irish, Italians, Poles. They liked me because I was a good man and a regular fellow." After two years of serving in the marines in the Pacific, the future novelist was convinced that "it's not the religion we look at, but the man himself."[40]

Corresponding to this perception of a declining anti-Semitism came renewed respect for Judaism by Jewish GIs. Jews turned to religion in the armed forces to assert their identity. "It could only happen here," Albert Eisen wrote to his mother. "I went to Jewish Services tonight. I think I can count on the fingers of one hand the times I have gone before." "However," he explained, "as a minority, it becomes necessary for us to declare ourselves to those who, unfortunately, are imbued with anti-Semitic sentiments."[41] A few actually *did* find comfort in religion, despite a militantly secular and radical Jewish upbringing. Harold Paris grew up in Brooklyn within a secular Jewish milieu and "was never religious." "Now I somehow want to be very much. I go to services on Tuesday and Friday," the nineteen-year-old admitted to his immigrant parents, somewhat apologetically. "I feel better when I do. It gives hope for things to come."[42] A soldier in the Third Army recalled a Yom Kippur service in Europe: "Our headgear were the steel helmets, and every soldier carried his rifle, which he placed between his feet when sitting, and slung to his shoulder when certain prayers required him to stand." "At such times," he wrote, "there would be an ominous rustling of government issued hardware throughout the theater."[43] The blend of American weapons and Jewish worship—steel helmets as yarmulkes—kindled powerful imagery and confirmed a dual sense of belonging. Surveying Jewish soldiers' attitudes toward Judaism immediately after the war, Moses Kligsberg argued that they "perceived in it an imposing and powerful force." The war strengthened their identity as Jews.[44]

Chaplains, by contrast, marveled at how little Jews knew about their religion and culture and, correspondingly, how strong was the appeal of kosher salami and gefilte fish.[45] Few perceived any Jewish religious revival in the foxholes, despite popular press accounts of Christian renewal. Some found that Jewish servicemen became aware "that to be Jewish is no crime, rather a natural fact, just as much as being a Catholic, Methodist, Baptist, Lutheran."[46] Morris Adler concluded from his experience as chaplain what subsequent Jewish population surveys would confirm, namely, how the plethora of American Jewish organizations touch just a handful of American Jews. As a rabbi, he never realized "the extent and depth of the widespread, militant, boundless ignorance of matters Jewish which characterize large sections of Jewry." Searching for an analogy, he suggested that "they are Israelites of a pre-Sinaitic era. It is not that they have turned their backs upon Judaism but that they have never faced it." Rabbis and Jewish leaders "do not have to overcome a bitter opposition and rejection. Culturally, we are presented with a *tabula rasa*," Adler exclaimed.[47]

Fighting for their country empowered American Jews. In the armed services they came to identify with America and its ideals. "This feeling of affiliation with a great power and the sense that they are symbolizing the principles for which this power went to battle" made many of the same young Jewish men "begin to consider the Jewish religion as a positive asset."[48] A Jewish chaplain thought that because the military "respects the heritage of the Jew and encourages the active identification of every fighting man with his religious civilization," Jews left the service with both components of their identities as Jewish Americans enhanced.[49] Kligsberg concluded that almost all "came back from the war with a feeling of pride in their Jewishness, with an awakened interest in Jewish life and with a readiness to carry out actively certain Jewish responsibilities."[50]

Jews serving in the army in Europe experienced the liberation of the Buchenwald concentration camp as a turning point. There their Jewish and American identities intersected; as American soldiers, they recognized the horror of anti-Semitism and their need to be Jews. "I came out of World War II with such a feeling of guilt that I felt I had to do something," Marty Peppercorn admitted. Growing up in the Bronx, "I had been a typical Jewish boy raised in a Jewish home, accustomed to Jewish values, and certainly my friends were all Jewish. Then, during World War II, after going into the . . . camps and observing what went on, I became ardently Jewish."[51] "Something happened to me in the Army of Occupation," Gotbaum mused. "The war was over, and soon after we entered a little town in Germany I went to all possible religious services. . . . I had to go to a synagogue and be with other Jews."[52]

Even professional Jewish soldiers recognized how powerfully the revelations of the camps influenced their own behavior. Irving Heymont of the Third Army was placed in charge of the Landsberg displaced persons camp in September 1945. In his first speech before the inmates, the twenty-seven-year-old major articulated his identification with the Jews forced to live there. "As I speak to you tonight, I can also be called a sort of DP," he told his audience. "We know what you suffered in the Nazi concentration camps—and not just through newspaper reports. My Regiment liberated a concentration camp." Many years later Heymont concluded that "the few months I spent at Landsberg had a greater impact on my outlook on life than any other experience in my career, including infantry combat in both World War II and the Korean War." Though he was unaware of it at the time, Heymont subsequently reflected that "Landsberg made me a conscious Jew again—not a religious Jew, seeking the ways of the Lord—but an affirmed member of the Jewish people."[53]

Jewish socialists and communists filtered the discovery of the death camps through their ideology. Jacobs, who was not sent overseas (perhaps, he speculated, because of his known Trotskyist background), remembered that when the German war crimes trials began, he "was not very much interested in them. My feelings of political ambivalence about the war were still fairly strong, although they had been shaken by the ghastly photos of the concentration-camp victims. But I couldn't help reflecting bitterly how neither the United States nor Britain had done very much to help either the Jews or the political victims of the Nazis until after Hitler marched into Poland."[54] Despite his army service, Irving Howe recalled that "at war's end we didn't know much about the Holocaust. . . . It took a couple of years for a horror of such immensity to sink in." Pondering his delayed reaction, he speculated, "it may be that by then I had become less ideological and more responsive morally." Kligsberg thought that "the greater the estrangement, the stronger was the blow and spiritual shock when they came face-to-face with the Jewish tragedy in Europe."[55]

For those who stayed at home, distance muted the horror of the extermination of European Jewry. Accounts appeared in the press, especially Jewish newspapers, surrounded by descriptions of battles and the destruction of war.[56] American Jews responded by contributing generously to the war effort: They purchased millions of dollars of war bonds; the working-class Brooklyn Jewish neighborhood of Brownsville bought fifteen million dollars worth.[57] Civilian defense volunteers wrote letters to servicemen and ran canteens for soldiers home on furlough. Jews participated in blood drives and scrap metal drives; they collected old clothing and books and magazines. In addition, Jews contributed to specifically Jewish organizations to rescue refugees, support the Yishuv, or save Jewish scholars and their students. They also raised substantial monies for Russian War Relief; in Philadelphia, thousands gave through *landsmanshaftn*, B'nai B'rith lodges, women's auxiliaries, and sisterhoods.[58] Even such insular Jewish communities as the six thousand Syrian Jews in Bensonhurst, Brooklyn, enthusiastically supported the home front.[59]

In the spring of 1945, American Jews watched in shock and disbelief as the sweet fruits of allied victory turned bitter under the staggering revelations of the death camps. The Allies won the war against Hitler too late to rescue most European Jews. Not until General Dwight Eisenhower invited the press corps and politicians and moviemakers to tour the concentration camps did the horror strike home. Shepard Broad found it hard to believe the catastrophe until the Allies "actually physically entered the concentration camps and saw the disaster."[60] Like Broad, Peppercorn knew what had happened but it did not really register. "[M]y indignation was there but I never could visualize just how physical and malignant this whole thing had been. . . . And some of the things I'll never forget as long as I live. I guess I can still smell them."[61] Only when they saw the photographs and films of living human skeletons in striped uniforms, the mountains of dead bodies, the bulldozers pushing corpses into mass graves, the piles of human hair, baby clothes, and eyeglasses, did American Jews realize, most for the first time, what had happened.[62] Susan Sontag calls it "a negative epiphany." She came across photographs of Bergen-Belsen and Dachau "by chance in a bookstore in Santa Monica in July 1945. Nothing I have seen—in photographs or in real life—ever cut me as sharply, deeply, instantaneously." "Indeed," she writes, "it seems plausible to me to divide my life into two parts, before I saw those photographs (I was twelve) and after."[63]

American Jews reeled under their losses, trying to make sense of the disaster. The six million murdered during the six long years of war constituted a third of the Jewish people and almost two-thirds of the Jews of Europe. "Our tiny people has sacrificed twenty-five times more lives in this war than Great Britain on all her battlefields, on the sea, under the sea, in the air and throughout the years of bombings. This is in absolute figures," wrote an anguished editorialist.[64] Liberation not only came too late for European Jewry, but it also failed to liberate those who survived, the refugees or displaced persons, DPs for short.[65]

Aghast at the ravages of anti-Semitism, Zionists demanded free Jewish immigration to Palestine and the establishment there of a Jewish commonwealth. Jews were losing patience with the politics of gestures. The Jews alone "are told to wait; to stand outside; to watch the remnants of their people ground to death in Europe . . . while the gates of Palestine, *where they would be welcome as nowhere else in the world,* are forcibly shut upon them," yelled the American Zionist Emergency Council. Frustrated at the continued unwillingness of the victorious United Nations to pay attention to the Jewish plight, American Zionists escalated their campaign to win converts to their cause among Americans of goodwill and among the rank and file of American Jewry. "The ghosts of 5,000,000 dead already haunt the forthcoming Conference in San Francisco" that would establish a permanent international world organization. "We ask the world how great must this ghastly company grow before the voice of those still living will be heard?"[66]

If the Allies were reluctant to listen, especially Great Britain, which controlled immigration to Palestine, American Jews were ready to act. Convinced by the war of the virulence of anti-Semitism and the need to fight it vigorously, convinced too of the impossibility of securing American Jewish life without providing a secure future for world Jewry, they swelled the membership rolls of American Zionist organizations and began to politick in earnest. "I became a Zionist after World War II, thinking that Jews, with their lives in jeopardy, must have a haven somewhere on this planet," the union leader Gus Tyler recalled.[67] Others went further in their conversion to Zionism. Even when in recent years it became fashionable to attack Israel for its shortcomings, many of these Zionists demurred. Talking at a casual gathering of fellow labor leaders with the Israeli consul many years after the establishment of the state, Gotbaum refused to join in the friendly criticism. "I guess I'm an emotional party-liner in this case," he told his colleagues. "Since I helped to liberate Buchenwald, I feel Zionism as a *faith*. I can never be critical of Israel."[68] In the war's aftermath, American Jews transformed faith into politics.[69]

American Jews learned more than the bitter lessons of Jewish political impotence from World War II. They acquired new perspectives on themselves and their country through their participation in the armed services of the United States. American wartime propaganda declared the struggle against the Axis to be between democracy and fascism, between the values of equality and those of racism, between freedom and totalitarianism.[70] Patriotic fervor also enlisted most American religious groups. Shortly after the war in Europe began, the president of the Jewish Theological Seminary established the Conference on Science, Philosophy and Religion and Their Relation to the Democratic Way of Life. The conference included seventy-nine leading American thinkers and religious figures. Seeking "to create a framework for the preservation of democracy and intellectual freedom" in response to the rise of European totalitarianism, the conference proclaimed that American ideals were rooted in biblical tradition and sustained by the biblical religions of Christianity and Judaism.[71] The concept of a Judeo-Christian tradition of democracy gained widespread currency as the American alternative to fascism. American fascist and anti-Semitic groups had preempted the term *Christian* in the 1930s.[72] *Judeo-Christian* suggested an anti-fascist basis for democratic values. The idea "was to invoke a common faith for a united democratic front."[73]

As GIs learned, the American way was not supposed to include prejudice and discrimination. On his way home from California to his wife and family in New York City, Bernard Zaritsky felt his spirits soar, until he got off the train in New Mexico and bought a paper. "In it I found that one hundred thousand Jews were being kicked around in the old football game, politics. The Arabs threatened to revolt if the Jews were let into Palestine . . . [A]nd the war, supposedly over, was just beginning for these people . . . my people." Then Zaritsky headed for a store to buy a glass of milk when he saw the sign: "No Jews, No Soldiers, No Negroes, No Dogs, Allowed in these Premises!" He concluded bitterly: "We didn't win any war. . . . This wasn't the United States of America."[74] Although the war failed to eradicate anti-Semitism in the United States, wartime propaganda discredited it and encouraged Jews to oppose it.

Even Jews remaining at home identified the American victory as a Jewish one, feeling strengthened by it. The legal scholar Robert Burt remembers how as a youngster he celebrated V-E day in Philadelphia with his maternal grandfather, a "relentlessly secular" Russian Jewish immigrant. When the German surrender was announced in May 1945, he writes, "My grandfather immediately went into his basement and returned arms filled with small American flags, party hats, horns, and other noisemakers and bags of paper confetti. We dressed for the celebration and went out into the street, where he outfitted other neighborhood children." Burt's account would not be unusual, except that his grandfather later admitted that "on the day the war began . . . he had bought all of these supplies and stored them for the inevitable day when America would win the war. And the relevant triumph for him," Burt recognized, "was not the final end, not when the Japanese surrendered four months later. The victory was in Europe. It was also, as I think he saw it, a victory over Europe."[75] Over a Europe that had persecuted Jews for centuries.

Perhaps the war's mixed messages to American Jews complemented each other. If Jews could be targeted for destruction and could not rely upon the world's democracies for a timely rescue, then they had to rely upon themselves. The logic of the Jewish need for independent political power—a state of their own—pressed upon American Jews. A United Jewish Appeal activist after he left the service, Peppercorn thought that almost everyone was "motivated toward the creation of a Jewish state." He had no doubt that it was "the solution" to the DP camps.[76] The war also gave

American Jews a new self-confidence. As Americans, Jews could rely upon themselves; they could fight anti-Semitism and win. The American victory in the war was their victory as much as anyone else's. The dawn of the American century marked the start of their own self-confident era, American Jewry's era.

The war had disrupted American Jewish society, fueling new movements, releasing previously untapped energies, exploding the boundaries of a provincial urban world. Participation in the service interrupted the lives of many young Jews. Some found it impossible to return home to pick up the tangled threads of family, work, and education that had been attenuated during their military years. Their war experience had unsettled them; they had seen too much to resume their mundane lives where they had left them. "One quick furlough home" to Chicago convinced writer Clancy Sigal "that my beloved old neighborhood was a slummy shtetl, my hangout pals narrow-minded schlumps. Along with practically the entire West Side younger generation which fled either to Chicago's northern suburbs or to California, I took off without a backward glance."[77] Like Sigal, these footloose young men sought greener pastures, a fresh future filled with promise, a chance to try something new freed from familiar constraints. They remembered the other America they had glimpsed during training, or en route to the Pacific war theater, or perhaps while recovering from a wound. With a brash self-confidence they decided to pioneer thousands of miles away from home. Eager for another adventure, they determined to take a chance, to rely upon themselves.

This self-confidence appeared in many aspects of postwar American Jewish life. It not only fueled vast migrations of American Jews to the suburbs and to such new cities as Miami and Los Angeles, but it also restructured household relationships around the nuclear family unit. The GI bill sent many more Jews to college than would have been able to go had the war not intervened in their lives. For those American Jews of the wartime generation, the acquisition of a college education hastened their social mobility. The self-understanding Jewish GIs took away from their wartime experience encouraged in many a deep commitment to the State of Israel as the "answer" to the Holocaust even as it led most Jews away from ideological politics into the liberal Democratic camp. It strengthened as well a religious consensualism among Jews, most visible in the rapid growth of the Reform and Conservative movements, and tolerance for those Jews who were both more and less religious than the consensual middle. In an essay written in 1946, Abraham Duker argued that the army chaplaincy "furnished a laboratory for the blending of the religious groupings." He found a pattern of worship emerging that discarded both extreme Orthodoxy and extreme Reform but included mixed pews, head covering for men, English prayers, and Hebrew hymns sung in traditional melodies.[78]

Perceived Jewish weakness and failure to rescue their European brethren shaped an intense concern for unity among Jewish communal leaders; it became the watchword of a generation that also developed communal structures to implement its desire for cooperation. A deep dedication to democracy, equality, and individualism, understood as core American values opposed to fascism, permeated much of American Jewish culture: religious school curriculums, summer camp programs, defense agency goals, women's organizations' activities.

How much of this endured the test of time? Among the generation that went to war, a great deal. For example, a 1993 survey by Alan Fisher of the politics of Los Angeles Jews shows that its generally older leadership (in its sixties and seventies) maintained a much more liberal political profile than the majority of Los Angeles Jews. Despite enormous demographic, social, and cultural changes that have occurred in the City of Angels since the late-1960s, this generation has retained its fundamental commitment to values shaped in the crucible of World War II.[79] Much of the Jewish communal agenda continues to reflect these commitments. Israel's centrality for Jewish fund-raising and American Jews' support of the state endure despite significant sociopolitical changes. Even as Jews begin to adjust their communal budgets, leading philanthropists of an older generation emphatically reject the idea that money raised for Israel is charity. "I give seven-figure money every year, and I don't give it to charity," Max Fisher told a reporter. "Charity is what you give a homeless person on the street. I give money because I'm a partner with the state of Israel in a sacred cause."[80] Indeed, probably many American Jews still hold a romantic image of Israel as a land peopled by heroes who made deserts bloom and rescued Jews from the destructive snares of anti-Semitism, an image shaped by Jewish GIs like Leon Uris. (In fact, Jews are not alone in searching out Ari Ben Canaans when they visit Israel. Gentile Americans share similar myths about the Jewish state.)

How much did the generation of Jewish GIs transmit to their children? That is more difficult to assess. Certain prewar choices and constraints disappeared. It became commonplace for American Jewish youth to attend college just as most boys after the war marked the end of several fitful years of Jewish education with bar mitzvah ceremonies.[81] Indeed, the popularity of bar mitzvah encouraged bat mitzvah ceremonies to spread among American Jews who wanted and could afford to give their daughters a Jewish education. Nuclear family households still appear to be the norm among American Jews, and migration continues to be chosen by many Jews when they decide to start a career or family or when they choose to retire. Such mobility heightens distances among relatives, though American Jews appear to have acclimated themselves to maintaining family ties through telephone calls and occasional visits. The dispersion of American Jews today presents a striking contrast with the Jewish urban world in the prewar years when a subway ride from the Bronx to Brooklyn was a major journey—indeed, when it was rare for Jews in the Bronx even to meet Jews from Brooklyn unless they went to a Catskill resort or a college campus. Not that parochial enclaves do not exist; they do. But Jewish horizons have broadened, not only about the United States but also regarding the diversity of the Jewish diaspora. Jews are also much more comfortable among Christians than they were in the prewar period, and many Jews no longer think of themselves as members of an ethnic group, the self-evident reality of the prewar years.[82]

How did American Jews, who had experienced discrimination and prejudice in the years prior to World War II, acquire today's freedom to choose to be Jews? How did a distinctive Jewish pattern emerge linking wealth and education with political liberalism, secularism, and a steadfast commitment to Israel? The possibility of a new Jewish synthesis emerged after World War II from changes it effected in a crucial generation. For Jewishness to become a matter of choice, the subtle and not-so-subtle barriers of discrimination in education, housing, and employment had to be dismantled. Prejudice against Jews had to lose its respectability. Jews had to work at opening society before they could thrive in it and fashion an American Judaism appropriate to such a free milieu. Only then could they discover the "crisis of freedom"; the opportunity offered by an increasingly open society to intermarry and the challenge it presented to maintain Jewish distinctiveness and collective continuity.[83] The generation who went to war, returned ready and able to transform American Jewry. We live with their heritage today.

Notes

1. Charles Herbert Stember, "The Recent History of Public Attitudes," in *Jews in the Mind of America* (New York: Basic Books, 1966), 60–73.

2. Charles E. Silberman, *A Certain People: American Jews and Their Lives Today* (New

York: Summit Books, 1985), part 1; Alan M. Dershowitz, *Chutzpah* (New York: Simon and Schuster, 1991).

3. Nathan Glazer, "Social Characteristics of American Jews," in *The Characteristics of American Jews* (New York: Jewish Education Press, 1965), 37–39.

4. Abba Hillel Silver, *Vision and Victory: A Collection of Addresses, 1942–1948* (New York: Zionist Organization of America, 1949), 124–33; Marc Lindsey Dollinger, "The Politics of Acculturation: American Jewish Liberalism, 1933–1975," Ph.D. diss., University of California, Los Angeles, 1993, 149.

5. On the American Jewish Committee, see Naomi Cohen, *Not Free to Desist: A History of the American Jewish Committee, 1906–1966* (Philadelphia: Jewish Publication Society, 1972), 333–39; on the American Jewish Congress, see Dollinger, "The Politics of Acculturation," 154–55, 167–74; on the Anti-Defamation League, see Deborah Dash Moore, *B'nai B'rith and the Challenge of Ethnic Leadership* (Albany: SUNY Press, 1981), 123–33, 228–30.

6. During the twenty years after the war, one out of three American Jews moved to the suburbs. Arthur Hertzberg, *The Jews in America: Four Centuries of an Uneasy Encounter* (New York: Simon and Schuster, 1989), 321. Jews spent a billion dollars to construct a thousand new synagogues in the postwar era. Dollinger, "The Politics of Acculturation," 153.

7. Salo W. Baron, "What War Has Meant to Community Life," *Contemporary Jewish Record* 5 (1942): 500.

8. William L. O'Neill, *A Democracy at War: America's Fight at Home and Abroad in World War II* (New York: Free Press, 1994), 7.

9. Deborah Dash Moore, "On the Fringes of the City: Jewish Neighborhoods in Three Boroughs," in *The Landscape of Modernity*, ed. David Ward and Olivier Zunz (New York: Russell Sage, 1992), 253–54.

10. Gerson Cohen, "The Scholar as Chancellor," in *Creators and Disturbers,* ed. Bernard Rosenberg and Ernest Goldstein (New York: Columbia University Press, 1982), 217; Ira Rosenwaike, *Population History of New York City* (Syracuse: Syracuse University Press, 1972), 100–112.

11. Victor Gotbaum, "The Spirit of the New York Labor Movement," in Rosenberg and Goldstein, *Creators and Disturbers,* 246.

12. Grace Paley, "The Writer in Greenwich Village," in Rosenberg and Goldstein, *Creators and Disturbers,* 289–90.

13. Kate Simon, *Bronx Primitive* (New York: Viking, 1982), 39.

14. Irving Howe, "The New York Intellectuals," in *Decline of the New* (New York: Harcourt, Brace and World, 1970), 216–17.

15. June Sochen, *Consecrate Every Day: The Public Lives of Jewish American Women, 1880–1980* (Albany: SUNY Press, 1981), 50–74; Hannah Kliger, ed., *Jewish Hometown Associations and Family Circles in New York* (Bloomington: Indiana University Press, 1992), 35; Abraham J. Karp, "Overview: The Synagogue in America," in *The American Synagogue,* ed. Jack Wertheimer (Cambridge: Cambridge University Press, 1987), 13–23.

16. Andrew R. Heinze, *Adapting to Abundance: Jewish Immigrants, Mass Consumption, and the Search for American Identity* (New York: Columbia University Press, 1992), 68–85; Arthur Liebman, *Jews and the Left* (New York: John Wiley, 1979),

261–62; Deborah Dash Moore, *At Home in America: Second Generation New York Jews* (New York: Columbia University Press, 1981), chap. 3; Susan A. Glenn, *Daughters of the Shtetl: Life and Labor in the Immigrant Generation* (Ithaca: Cornell University Press, 1990), 177–82.

17. Clancy Sigal, "Hollywood during the Great Fear," *Present Tense,* spring 1982, 45–46.

18. Maxwell E. Greenberg, "Oral Memoirs," in *"Not the Work of a Day": Anti-Defamation League of B'nai B'rith Oral Memoirs* (New York: Anti-Defamation League of B'nai B'rith, 1987), 2:8–9.

19. Greenberg noted that the first Jewish lawyer accepted at the Los Angeles law firm of O'Melveny and Myers was Richard Sherwood, who had changed his name from Shapiro. Greenberg, "Oral Memoirs," 2:28–29.

20. Nathan Perlmutter, *A Bias of Reflections* (New Rochelle: Arlington House, 1972), 103–4.

21. Conversation with Martin Dash, November 9, 1992.

22. Seymour Graubard, "Oral Memoirs," in *Not Work of a Day,* 2:21–22.

23. Paul Jacobs, *Is Curly Jewish?* (New York: Vintage, 1973), 127–28.

24. Perlmutter, *A Bias of Reflections,* 103–4.

25. Ari Lashner, "An Evening's Discussion," in "Correspondence," *Furrows,* June 1943, 30.

26. Jacobs, *Is Curly Jewish?* 129.

27. S. C. Kohs, "Jewish War Records of World War II," *American Jewish Year Book* 47 (1946): 167; Isidor Kaufman, *American Jews in World War II* (New York: Dial, 1947), 1:349. This represented an average rate of participation.

28. Lucy S. Dawidowicz, *On Equal Terms: Jews in America, 1881–1981* (New York: Holt, Rinehart and Winston, 1982), 129.

29. Quoted in Moses Kligsberg, "American Jewish Soldiers on Jews and Judaism," *YIVO Annual of Jewish Social Science* 5 (1950): 264.

30. Quoted in Marianne Sanua, "From the Pages of the *Victory Bulletin,*" *YIVO Annual of Jewish Social Science* 19 (1990): 308.

31. Jews from small towns discovered how different New York Jews were.

32. "Ben Zion," pseudonym of David Macarov, entry no. 11, YIVO Essay Contest: My Experiences and Observations as a Jew and a Soldier in World War II, 18–19, YIVO Institute for Jewish Research, New York.

33. Quoted in Sanua, "Pages of *Victory Bulletin,*" 318.

34. Greenberg, "Oral Memoirs," 2:10.

35. Kligsberg, "American Jewish Soldiers," 258.

36. Kimberg, quoted in *Jewish Youth at War,* ed. Israel E. Rontch (New York: Marstin Press, 1945), 105.

37. Gotbaum, "New York Labor Movement," 249.

38. Lashner, "An Evening's Discussion," 31.

39. Joseph Bensman, "The Sociologist on the Cutting Edge," in Rosenberg and Goldstein, *Creators and Disturbers,* 374.

40. Uris, quoted in Rontch, *Jewish Youth at War,* 225.

41. Eisen, quoted in Rontch, *Jewish Youth at War,* 43.

42. Paris, quoted in Rontch, *Jewish Youth at War,* 147.

43. Quoted in Kligsberg, "American Jewish Soldiers," 263.

44. Kligsberg, "American Jewish Soldiers," 62.

45. Edward T. Sandrow, "Jews in the Army—a Short Social Study," *The Reconstructionist,* March 17, 1944, 1.

46. Letter from Rabbi Leonard Greenberg, *The Reconstructionist,* May 18, 1945, 24.

47. Morris Adler, "The Chaplain and the Rabbi," *The Reconstructionist,* April 6, 1945, 11.

48. Kligsberg, "American Jewish Soldiers," 263.

49. Sandrow, "Jews in the Army," 17.

50. Kligsberg, "American Jewish Soldiers," 265.

51. Martin Peppercorn, interview, July 20, 1977, 4, Oral History Archives, Institute of Contemporary Jewry, Hebrew University, Jerusalem.

52. Gotbaum, "New York Labor Movement," 250–51.

53. Irving Heymont, *Among the Survivors of the Holocaust* (Cincinnati: American Jewish Archives, 1982), 25, 109.

54. Jacobs, *Is Curly Jewish?* 133.

55. Howe, "The New York Intellectuals," 285; Kligsberg, "American Jewish Soldiers," 260.

56. Deborah E. Lipstadt, *Beyond Belief: The American Press and the Coming of the Holocaust, 1933–1945* (New York: Free Press, 1986), 267–78.

57. Gerald Sorin, *The Nurturing Neighborhood: The Brownsville Boys Club and Jewish Community in Urban America, 1940–1990* (New York: New York University Press, 1990), 96.

58. Philip Rosen, Robert Tabak, and David Gross, "Philadelphia Jewry, the Holocaust, and the Birth of the Jewish State," in *Philadelphia Jewish Life, 1940–1985,* ed. Murray Friedman (Ardmore, PA: Seth Press, 1986), 36.

59. Sanua, "Pages of *Victory Bulletin,*" 287.

60. Shepard Broad, interview, April 10, 1977, 9, Oral History of the United Jewish Appeal, Oral History Archives, Institute of Contemporary Jewry, Hebrew University, Jerusalem.

61. Peppercorn, interview, 5, 8.

62. There is extensive debate among historians over the extent to which American Jews knew about the Holocaust at the time. Certainly the leadership and those who read the Jewish press knew. But as Deborah Lipstadt argues, it was, for the majority of the masses, "beyond belief." See Rosen, Tabak, and Gross, "Philadelphia Jewry," 54–55, for their assessment, with which I agree. "Philadelphia Jewry certainly wanted to do whatever could be done; it lacked the unity necessary to decide what had to be done, the sense of urgency necessary to implement their decisions, and the will to risk its tenuous position in this country in all-out effort."

63. Susan Sontag, *On Photography* (1977; reprint, New York: Anchor, 1990), 19–20.

64. Trude Weiss-Rosmarin, "These Are Our Losses," *Jewish Spectator,* May 1945, 5.

65. Paul R. Mendes-Flohr and Jehuda Reinharz, eds., *The Jew in the Modern World* (New York: Oxford University Press, 1980), 520.

66. American Zionist Emergency Council, quoted in "The Spurned Ally," *Jewish Spectator,* April 1945, 5.

67. Gus Tyler, "The Intellectual and the ILGWU," in Rosenberg and Goldstein, *Creators and Disturbers*, 174–75.

68. Gotbaum, "New York Labor Movement," 250.

69. Baron, "What War Has Meant," 507.

70. Henry L. Feingold, *A Time for Searching: Entering the Mainstream, 1920–1945* (Baltimore: Johns Hopkins University Press, 1992), 251–59; Stember, "Public Attitudes," 78–85.

71. "Historical Statement," Conference on Science, Philosophy and Religion, Joseph and Miriam Ratner Center for the Study of Conservative Judaism, Jewish Theological Seminary, New York. For a Christian statement, see Henry A. Wallace, "Judaism and Americanism," *Menorah Journal*, July–September 1940, 127–37.

72. Leonard Dinnerstein, *Uneasy at Home: Antisemitism and the American Jewish Experience* (New York: Columbia University Press, 1987), 179.

73. Mark Silk, *Spiritual Politics* (New York: Simon and Schuster, 1988), 42.

74. "Liba," pseudonym of Bernard Zaritsky, entry no. 16, YIVO Essay Contest: My Experiences and Observations as a Jew and a Soldier in World War II, 11–12, YIVO Institute for Jewish Research.

75. Robert Burt, "My Crowd: Jews, Lawyers, and America," paper presented at the Conference on Jews and the Law in the United States, University of Wisconsin, November 14–17, 1991, 6–7.

76. Peppercorn, interview, 13.

77. Sigal, "Hollywood," 46.

78. Abraham G. Duker, "On Religious Trends in American Jewish Life," *YIVO Annual of Jewish Social Science* 4 (1949): 62–63.

79. Alan M. Fisher, "Jewish Organizational Leaders, the Jewish Laity, and Non-Jewish Neighbors in Los Angeles: A Demographic and Socio-Political Comparison," Wilstein Institute Research Report, fall 1993, iv–v.

80. Douglas Feiden, "Jewish Charities Turn to Priorities at Home," *The Forward*, March 25, 1994, 4.

81. Abraham G. Duker, "Emerging Culture Patterns in American Jewish Life," in *The Jewish Experience in America*, ed. Abraham J. Karp (New York: Ktav, 1969), 5:402, observed as early as 1950 a trend among Reform and secular Yiddishists to adopt the bar mitzvah ceremony.

82. Barry A. Kosmin et al., *Highlights of the CJF 1990 National Jewish Population Survey* (New York: Council of Jewish Federations, 1991), remark that "being Jewish as defined by cultural group membership is the clear preference of three of the four identity groups" (28).

83. Thomas Morgan, "The Vanishing American Jew," *Look*, May 5, 1964, 42–46.

Curt Lowen, Holocaust survivor, Los Angeles, 2006. Courtesy of Bill Aron.

The Americanization of the Holocaust

Alvin H. Rosenfeld

Sixty years after the end of World War II, how do we look back upon and understand that catastrophic event? In particular, what do we make of the almost total devastation of European Jewry brought on by Hitler and his collaborators?

In an effort to discover answers to questions of this kind, the American Jewish Committee carried out a series of studies to determine what people in several countries—among them, the United States, France, Germany, and Great Britain—know about the Holocaust.[1] The findings are not encouraging, especially with respect to the levels of historical knowledge among Americans. When asked, "What does the term 'the Holocaust' refer to?" 38 percent of American adults and 53 percent of high-school students replied that they did not know or answered incorrectly. Higher percentages of American adults (65 percent) and high-school students (71 percent) seemed not to know that approximately six million Jews were killed by the Nazis and their allies. Presented with the names "Auschwitz, Dachau, and Treblinka," 38 percent of the same adults and 51 percent of the high-school students failed to recognize these as concentration camps. It is little wonder, then, that the scholars who carried out this survey concluded that a "serious knowledge gap exists for both adults and youth in the United States with regard to basic information about the Holocaust."[2]

The Europeans did better, with adults and students in Germany scoring the highest among the national population groups surveyed in these studies. But then we confront a seeming paradox, for while the Americans knew the least about the Holocaust, they seemed to *care* the most, with large per-

This essay was originally presented on March 20, 1995, at the Jean and Samuel Frankel Center for Judaic Studies, University of Michigan, Ann Arbor.

centages of those polled replying that it is "essential" or "important" that Americans "know about and understand the Holocaust."[3] Given the shockingly low levels of their own knowledge and understanding, how is it that these Americans—only 21 percent of whom were able to recognize that the "Warsaw ghetto" had some connection to the Holocaust—regard the Holocaust as "relevant" today and strongly hold to the opinion that Americans should know about it?[4] I do not want to lapse into an easy cynicism and suggest that they mean "other" Americans and not themselves, for I have no doubt that they include themselves in the picture. What kind of a picture is it, though, when people who know so little about something as momentous as the Holocaust express a view that indicates that they do indeed care a good deal about it? This question prompts a series of related questions: what do Americans mean by the Holocaust anyway, and how do they come to these meanings? What are their sources of information about the Holocaust, and what images do these sources project to them? How, in sum, do they come to know whatever it is they do know? These are the kinds of matters I wish to reflect on in this essay, but before proceeding to a consideration of how Americans have come to perceive and understand the Holocaust, I would like to draw attention to a few more general concerns.

To begin with, it is important to acknowledge that we possess a great amount of information about the fate of the Jews of Europe during the Third Reich. Indeed, the event that we have come to call the Holocaust is one of the most copiously documented crimes in history. For all of that, it continues to present massive problems to understanding. Why is that so?

In part, it is owing to the horrific nature of the Nazi assault against the Jews, an intended genocide whose scope and brutality surpass the limits of what most of us are capable of imagining. It is not easy for the mind to grasp the intentions behind this fury, just as it is not easy to understand the passions that drove it, the system that sustained it, and the people who served its terrifying and murderous ends. In saying as much, I do not want to suggest that there was anything essentially "unreal" or otherworldly about the Holocaust. It was all too real a historical event, but an event of such an unprecedented nature as to evade ready comprehension within the received categories of historical explanation. Beyond these problems of incomprehensibility, though, a second problem confronts us, and that has to do with how the memory of the Nazi crimes has been represented to us.

In fact, for most people a sense of the Nazi crimes against the Jews is formed less by the record of events established by professional historians than it is by individual stories and images that reach us from more popular writers, artists, film directors, television producers, political figures, and the like. We live in a mass culture, and much of what we learn about the past comes to us from those forms of communication that comprise the information and entertainment networks of this culture—novels, stories, poems, plays, films, television programs, newspaper and magazine articles, museum exhibitions, etc. It is not to detract in the least from the scholarly value of a work such as Raul Hilberg's magisterial study, *The Destruction of the European Jews,* to recognize that far more people are likely to learn about Jewish victimization under the Nazis from films like *Schindler's List* or from reading Anne Frank's *The Diary of a Young Girl* or Art Spiegelman's *Maus* than from reading Hilberg. Indeed, in a popular culture it is critical to recognize that historical memory is determined chiefly by popular forms of representation.

We also need to remember that, more than half a century after the liberation of the death camps, we lack anything like a consensus on what the Holocaust was and how it is to be understood and remembered. In its oldest and most normative conception, for instance, the Holocaust signifies the death of some six million Jews in Nazi-occupied Europe.[5] Simon Wiesenthal and those who follow his lead on this issue, however, challenge this figure and advocate a much wider conception of the victims of the Nazi crimes. They point to some eleven million dead.[6] This discrepancy in numbers is no small matter, for it reflects a major conceptual difference in what the Holocaust was and who is to be included among its victims—only the Jews or all of those who perished under the Nazi tyranny, including Polish political prisoners, Soviet soldiers, gypsies, homosexuals, the handicapped, the mentally ill, Jehovah's Witnesses, and others.

One would think that six decades after the end of World War II this basic question would be settled, but in fact it has not been. Nor has there been consensus on any of a number of other related issues. Indeed, any comparative study of the histories of World War II in different countries will quickly show that national myths and reigning ideologies have shaped the memory of the war years in diverse and often sharply contrasting ways.

Over the longest period of time visitors to Poland and the remains of the Auschwitz camp system would find that the presentation of the main camp had been organized along lines meant to serve a largely Polish national interest. Auschwitz, in this rendering, was projected as a crucial memory site of the martyrdom of the Polish nation, and only recently and rather incidentally is it also shown to be a place where over a million European Jews were destroyed.[7] Moreover, the numerous crucifixes that a visitor will see at Auschwitz-Birkenau and other former Nazi death camps mark these places symbolically as Christian burial sites. The fact that it was Jews who comprised the largest number of victims—90 percent of those murdered at Auschwitz-Birkenau were Jews—may not be at all apparent to people who visit these former killing centers and do not bring such knowledge with them.

And Poland is by no means a singular instance of this phenomenon. For decades the Russians resisted any proper acknowledgment of the Jewish dead at places like Babi Yar and instead have commemorated, without distinction, all of those who fell as "victims of fascism" during what they call the Great Patriotic War. The French have long postponed a national reckoning with their Vichy past and only now seem to be prepared to confront some of the ugly facts of active French collaboration with Nazi rule. To this day Germans debate whether the crimes committed by their countrymen two generations ago constitute a unique chapter in history or are to be compared with other acts of barbarism and mass murder in the twentieth century. For those in Germany who pursue this latter course, the aim is to "normalize" the Nazi crimes by situating them within a broad-based history of brutality and mass murder, a move that has the effect of dissolving the uniquely criminal features of German National Socialism within the abstract conceptual frameworks of "totalitarianism," "fascism," and the like. Meanwhile, as that debate among historians continues, there is a new and heightened emphasis on the role of Germans who resisted the tyranny of the Third Reich, and also on those, especially in the eastern parts of the country, who perished under allied bombing raids or were expelled in large numbers from their homes and lands. Such examples represent the shifting dynamics of historical memory across geographical contexts; in sum, national, cultural, ideological, religious, and political interests have shaped and continue to shape the ways in which the history of World War II and the crimes against the Jews have been presented to diverse publics.[8] Far from there being anything like a shared memory of the Holocaust, therefore, we find a multiplicity of historical memories and often a clash among them.

American culture, itself a dominant shaper of popular images, has not been exempt from the tendencies just described. Indeed, it is almost certainly the case that the future memory of the Holocaust will be determined to a large extent by America's role, along with that of Israel, Germany, and Poland, in projecting particular views of World War II and the Holocaust.

In what follows I shall aim to identify some of the sources that contribute to the ongoing process of imagining and presenting the Holocaust along specifically American lines.

One could approach a study of this kind in several different ways. A chronological study, for instance, would show when public attention to the Holocaust began to develop in this country, how it has waxed and waned over time, and how it has been affected by other contemporaneous events. Another way to proceed would be to conduct an institutional study, which would emphasize such matters as the building of American Holocaust museums and study centers, the development of school curricula and college-level courses on the Holocaust, the establishment under President Carter of a United States Presidential Commission on the Holocaust, the observance of Yom HaShoah and official American Days of Remembrance, synagogue- and church-sponsored liturgical programs on the Holocaust, academic conferences and publications, and other institutionalized forms of public memory.

For present purposes, however, I want to direct attention not so much to chronological and institutional forms of mediation but to typological ones. By typological I refer to that essential and still evolving "cast of characters"—victims, perpetrators, bystanders, and so forth—who form the core of the Holocaust "story." The focus of what follows, therefore, will be largely on the development of narrative forms of remembrance, both verbal and visual, and, in particular, on certain paradigmatic changes that help to guide the ways people in this country have come to conceive of the Holocaust. As we shall see, the matter of who precisely is to be regarded as a Holocaust "victim," "perpetrator," "survivor," and so on is by no means clear or simple but is dependent on a complex range of cultural attitudes, political ideologies, religious values, and the like. To identify and explain these contemporary influences on our sense of the past is a major aim of this essay.

One can begin with the term *Holocaust* itself. Although it is widely used today, the fact is that those Jews who suffered in the ghettos and camps of Nazi-occupied Europe did not think of themselves as victims of a "Holocaust." Nor did most of them employ such terms as *Hurban* or *Shoah*, which today sometimes alternate with *Holocaust* in popular usage. Rather, in referring to their fate in the immediate postwar years, they typically spoke about the "catastrophe," or the "recent Jewish catastrophe," or the "disaster." These more or less general terms remained dominant through the late 1940s and into the early 1950s, when *Holocaust* or *The Holocaust* gained currency and took on the connotations it has largely retained until today.[9] While it is far from clear that he actually coined the phrase, the writer Elie Wiesel had a prominent role in popularizing *The Holocaust* as the term of choice to designate the Nazi assault against the Jews. In Wiesel's usage and, following him, that of countless others, *The Holocaust* has been intended as an exclusive term to point to the sufferings and intended genocide of European Jewry. As already noted, however, there are others who have preferred to widen the application of the term *Holocaust* so that it includes all of those who perished at the hands of the Germans and their allies.[10]

The debate between those who reserve the term specifically and exclusively for the Jewish victims of Nazism and those who opt for much wider inclusion of victim populations is an ongoing one that takes place at the highest levels of scholarly and political authority. It is a debate of great consequence, for in terms of projecting an image of what the Holocaust was— a separate "war against the Jews," in Lucy Dawidowicz's formulation, or a part of World War II less specifically conceived and carried out—much depends on the numbers employed and the sense of the past that these numbers imply. Following Simon Wiesenthal, for instance, President Carter, speaking on Holocaust Remembrance Day in Washington in 1979, referred to eleven million victims of the Holocaust, among them six million Jews and five million non-Jews.[11] More recently, the language of "Holocaust" has been used by those who want to draw public attention to the crimes, abuses, and assorted sufferings that mar the quality of social life in today's America. In the passionate debates that are under way about abortion, for instance, one frequently encounters terms like "the abortion Holocaust," the "killing centers" where a "genocide" is being carried out against unborn baby "victims." Following this turn—and it is characteristically American in its intent to be broadly inclusive—*Holocaust* or *The Holocaust* is in the process of being transformed from a proper noun to a common noun, a semantic switch that signifies an important conceptual and ideological transformation as well. As a result, language that hitherto has been employed to refer essentially to the Nazi crimes against the Jews is now frequently applied to social ills and human sufferings of a diverse kind.

There are those who oppose this tendency and also those who favor it. The Israeli historian Yehuda Bauer has spoken out strongly against it, arguing that in the process of becoming Americanized, the Holocaust is in danger of becoming de-Judaized. As Bauer puts it, "In the public mind the term 'Holocaust' has become flattened," so that "any evil that befalls anyone anywhere becomes a Holocaust." Bauer recognizes that the semantic extension of the term *Holocaust* is accompanied by a cognitive shift, resulting in what he fears will be a "total misunderstanding" of the historical event that the term was originally meant to designate. What underlies this development? Its causes are various, but, in Bauer's view, much of it relates to those people who were charged with the responsibility of creating the United States Holocaust Memorial Museum in Washington, D.C. They were faced with a difficult dilemma, moreover, one of a specifically American kind: "It was unclear how the uniqueness of the Holocaust and its universalist implications could be combined in a way that would be in accord with the American heritage and American political reality."[12]

Bauer did not spell out what constitutes "the American heritage," but anyone familiar with the ideological tendencies that inform American political culture would be able to fill in for him. It is part of the American ethos to stress goodness, innocence, optimism, liberty, diversity, and equality. It is part of the same ethos to downplay or deny the dark and brutal sides of life and instead to place a preponderant emphasis on the saving power of individual moral conduct and collective deeds of redemption. Americans prefer to think affirmatively and progressively. The tragic vision, therefore, is antithetical to the American way of seeing the world, according to which people are meant to overcome adversity and not cling endlessly to their sorrows. Because Americans are also pragmatic in their approach to history, they are eager to learn what "lessons" can be drawn from the past in order, as many are quick to say, to prevent its worst excesses "from ever happening again."

The Holocaust has had to enter American consciousness in ways that Americans could readily understand within their own terms. These are terms that individualize, heroize, moralize, idealize, and universalize. It is through such cognitive screens as these that human behavior is apt to be refracted within American cultural productions. They have helped to shape the ways in which the Nazi Holocaust of European Jewry has been represented in this country on the popular level. In addition, "politically correct" attitudes and other ideological fashions of the moment also play a role in influencing how we read the past, including the years of destruction that characterize the Nazi era in Europe.

While significant attention has been focused on the Holocaust in recent years, we would do well to remind ourselves that during the war itself and for a number of years afterward the fate of Europe's Jews under Hitler was not a preoccupation within American political and cultural life. Consider American films on the subject. According to Ilan Avisar's important study

Screening the Holocaust, Hollywood produced some five hundred narrative films on the war and war-related themes during the years 1940–45. "In examining this harvest," Avisar writes, "we find striking avoidance of any explicit presentation of the Jewish catastrophe during the course of the war. *The Great Dictator* (1940) was a remarkable exception. . . . [Otherwise], Hollywood completely ignored the contemporaneous, systematic extermination of European Jewry."[13] Furthermore, Avisar notes, it was not until 1959, in filming the diary of Anne Frank, that Hollywood "addressed itself directly to the Nazis' genocidal treatment of the Jews."[14]

It is a matter of no small interest that it was the figure of Anne Frank that helped to break the relative silence within American culture about Jewish fate under Nazi tyranny. Anne Frank's diary was a popular success from the start, and to this day it can be taken as paradigmatic of the American reception of the Holocaust. First published in English translation in 1952, *The Diary of a Young Girl* remains one of the best-known and best-loved stories of World War II. The book was turned into a popular play by Frances Goodrich and Albert Hackett and produced on Broadway in 1955; four years later it was screened as an equally popular full-length film. The book, the play, and the film remain in circulation to this day, so much so that it is fair to say that more Americans are familiar with Anne Frank's story than with any other single narrative of the war years. *The Diary of a Young Girl* is widely read in American schools, and American youngsters regularly see the stage and film versions of the diary as well. Their teachers encourage them to identify with Anne Frank and to write stories, essays, and poems about her.[15] Some even see her as a kind of saint and pray to her.[16] For a stretch of time during their early adolescent years, many American girls view her story as their story, her fate as somehow bound up with their fate. For millions of young Americans, therefore, the Holocaust is first made known and is vividly personalized through the image of Anne Frank.

What is it that defines her image for people in this country, and why have they come to cherish it so? There is a vague understanding that Anne Frank was a Jew and for this reason was also a victim, but the stage and film translations of her diary do not make her appear "too Jewish," nor do they make her status as a victim too unbearably harsh. It is notable, for instance, that at no time during the play does a Nazi soldier or Gestapo agent ever appear on the stage. The play has its anxious moments, to be sure, but these are never fixed visually on those who actually pursued Anne Frank and her family in their hiding places and made them into victims. Rather, anxiety builds toward a fate that is carefully kept hidden from the audience, which is spared any direct confrontation with Nazi violence. Consequently, one can leave the theater feeling somehow uplifted by Anne Frank's story rather than deeply disturbed.

The early reviews of the Broadway production of the diary register these feelings in unambiguous ways. Writing in the *New York Herald Tribune* (October 6, 1955) about the play's debut at the Cort Theater, Walter Kerr had this to say: "Nearly all of the characters in 'The Diary of Anne Frank' . . . are doomed to death. Yet the precise quality of the new play at the Cort is the quality of glowing, ineradicable life—life in its warmth, its wonder, its spasms of anguish, and its wild and flaring humor." Writing in the *New York World Telegram and Sun* (October 15, 1955), William Hawkins concurred: "Producer, playwright, director, and actors have united to make a truly uplifting adventure out of as terrifyingly sordid a situation as it is possible to find in history. . . . One leaves the theater exhilarated, proud to be a human being." John Beaufort, the reviewer for the *Christian Science Monitor* (October 15, 1955), wrote of *The Diary of Anne Frank* as "an exquisite play which endows the deeper grief of its subject with a shining and even triumphant humanity." He went on to say that the play "moves one as readily to laughter as to tears. . . . The spirit of man, including his comic spirit, is by no means extinguished." Richard Watts, Jr., the reviewer for the *New York Post* (August 26, 1956), saw the play as "an inspiring drama, not a wrathful one. [The play] makes audiences feel that inspiration, that pride in mankind's potential courage, as members of the human race and not of any particular branch of it. To that extent, it is universal in interest, though its main characters are Jewish."[17]

These reviews, and numerous others like them, reveal clearly enough the terms in which Americans of the mid-1950s were prepared to confront the Holocaust: a terrible event, yes, but ultimately not tragic or depressing; an experience shadowed by the specter of a cruel death but at the same time not without the ability to inspire, console, uplift. In our own day, among those who come to know Anne Frank through the pages of her diary or the stage or screen versions of it, responses are remarkably similar to those cited above. The emphases typically fall on the cheerful, lovable, and transcendent aspects of Anne Frank's story—on the young girl's intelligence and warmth, humor and buoyant spirit, courage and determination—and not on her horrible ending. The contemporary American literary scholar and theologian Harry James Cargas has recently written about Anne Frank in terms that hardly differ from those of the 1950s: "This compassionate child, never forgetting to go beyond herself, to see the miserable condition of others rather than to wallow in her own situation as many of us might have done, despite all, evinced hope. Each time I read the Diary I am uplifted. Anne's spirit gives me hope. Each time I read the Diary I cannot help but feel that this time she'll make it, she'll survive."[18]

She did not survive, as we know, but went to a miserable death in Bergen-Belsen before she was yet sixteen years old. Nevertheless, the survival fantasy that is triggered in Cargas's encounter with Anne Frank is common among American audiences. Who, after all, wants to stare into the abyss and discover only blackness? Few people have the nerves to sustain so dark a vision of life. Consequently, Americans are typically given stories and images of the Nazi Holocaust that turn upward at the end rather than plunge downward into the terrifying silences of a gruesome death. The stage production of *The Diary of Anne Frank* ends with Anne's voice repeating what has become her signature line, informing us, as if from the heavens, "In spite of everything, I still believe that people are really good at heart." To which her father replies, humbly and affectionately, "She puts me to shame." Following these words the curtain comes down, ending Anne Frank's story not on a disconsolate note but an uplifting one.[19]

Optimistic and affirmative endings are an important component of what has been called American "civil religion." Consider the following passage, taken from a once widely circulated solicitation letter from the United States Holocaust Memorial Museum, as one more example of this tendency:

> Visitors will learn that while this is overwhelmingly a story about the extermination of the Jewish people, it is also about the Nazis' plans for the annihilation of the Gypsies and the handicapped, and about the persecution of priests and patriots, Polish intellectuals and Soviet prisoners of war, homosexuals and even innocent children.
>
> Then, finally, when breaking hearts can bear it no longer, visitors will emerge into the light—into a celebration of resistance, rebirth, and renewal for the survivors whether they remained in Europe, or as so many did, went to Israel or America to rebuild their lives. And having witnessed the nightmare of evil, the great American monuments to democracy that surround each departing visitor will take on new meaning, as will the ideals for which they stand.[20]

The topographical reference that gives rise to this note of American triumphalism is an important feature of the overall message that the United States Holocaust Memorial Museum means to convey. The museum is advantageously situated just adjacent to the National Mall in Washington, D.C. The Washington Monument and the Jefferson Memorial are nearby and easily visible. These national monuments have the effect of reestablishing museum visitors in the familiar and consoling realities of American space, and in so doing they can also have the effect of telling them that the exhibits they just saw, for all of their horror, signify an essentially European event. To identify it as such is not to diminish the significance of the Holocaust for Americans, but to mark it as an alien experience, one that took place far from America's shores and even farther from the American spirit of fair play, decency, and justice for all. It is imperative, therefore, that some means to return people to this spirit be built into how the Jewish catastrophe in Europe is to be presented to the citizens of this country. In conformity with this need, the letter from which I have quoted above concludes by urging all of us to remember "the six million Jews and millions of other innocent victims who died in the Holocaust" and, at the same time, to "also remember and renew our own faith in life . . . in civilization . . . in humanity . . . and in each other."

Given the story it tells in powerfully graphic fashion, however, the Washington Holocaust Memorial Museum is not and cannot be a pleasurable museum to visit. Its aim, which it carries out effectively, is to educate the American public about a historical experience of an excruciatingly painful kind, so much so that it would be the rare visitor who would emerge from this place unmoved. The emotional, moral, and pedagogical impact the museum makes is undoubtedly powerful. While one cannot say exactly what people take away with them and retain, the following account, which concludes an article by Estelle Gilson describing her own visit, may be representative of the responses of numbers of those who come:

> Do I think the United States Holocaust Memorial Museum will protect Jews in the future? Highly unlikely. Will it protect other minorities from genocide? Not likely. But it does what the United States does best. It informs. It bears witness to the Holocaust's existence, and provides a warning to whomever wishes to learn from it, that those who would dehumanize people in order to destroy them dehumanize themselves as well.
>
> To have walked through this exhibition alongside fellow Americans— Caucasian Americans, African Americans, Hispanic Americans, Asian Americans, and yes, Jewish Americans—all in their bright summer tourist garb, left me feeling strangely comforted and surprisingly proud.[21]

Comfort and pride are no part of what one typically feels upon leaving the remains of the Nazi camps in Poland or Germany or upon concluding a visit to Yad Vashem in Israel. Why, therefore, are such feelings evoked at the United States Holocaust Memorial Museum? The answer probably lies less in what is shown in this place and not in the others than in the site itself and the democratic ideals that America's capital exemplifies. America has its problems, but these problems do not begin to resemble those that overtook the countries of Europe during the period of the Third Reich or that might one day overtake a country as small and vulnerable as Israel if it ever drops its defensive guard. If one is to subject oneself to a serious confrontation with the history of the Nazi Holocaust at all, therefore, it is probably somewhat easier to do so at the National Mall in Washington, D.C., than it is anywhere else in the world.

The United States Holocaust Memorial Museum annually draws exceptionally large crowds, and everything about it suggests that for years to come it is destined to be a powerful instrument for educating millions of Americans and others about the Holocaust. Exactly what its pedagogical mission should look like, however, remains an ongoing source of discussion. Michael Berenbaum, who served as the museum's project director during the planning and construction stages and, for a time, was also director of the museum's research institute, took issue with Bauer, arguing that "the Holocaust is only 'Americanized' insofar as it is explained to Americans and related to their history with ramifications for future policy. The study of the Holocaust can provide insights that have universal import for the destiny of all humanity. A national council funded at taxpayers' expense to design a *national* memorial does not have the liberty to create an exclusively Jewish one in the restricted sense of the term, and most specifically with regard to audience."[22]

Expanding on the connection between a museum's presentations and its audience, Berenbaum wrote that, as the United States Memorial Council took up its task of telling Americans about the Holocaust, it realized that "the story had to be told in such a way that it would resonate not only with the survivor in New York and his children in San Francisco, but with a black leader from Atlanta, a midwestern farmer, or a northeastern industrialist." Connecting such a diverse audience to history, Berenbaum noted, means connecting them to the past in a way that "inform[s] their current reality," including what he calls their current "social need."[23] The social needs of Americans vary, and it is hard to imagine narrating any story of the crimes of the Nazi era that will remain faithful to the specific features of European-based historical events of two generations ago and, at the same time, address a multiplicity of contemporary American social and political agendas. Berenbaum's formula for resolving such potential problems was to recognize that while the Holocaust was a unique event, it carries universal implications. That is no doubt the case. His successors at the U.S. Holocaust Memorial Museum, now and in the future, will need to develop their own understandings of this formula in such a way as to make sure that the "uniqueness" of the Holocaust does not yield some of its priority as historical fact to what is taken to be its wider metaphorical ramifications for today's American visitors. For if the Washington museum ever adopts a broadening of its mission that declares "the museum's ultimate goal [is] an 'en-masse' understanding that we are not about what the Germans did to Jews but what people did to people,"[24] then it will cease to be a museum primarily devoted to educating the public about the Nazi Holocaust and become something else.

We need not wonder what this "something else" might look like, for it is already upon us, not at the Holocaust Memorial Museum in Washington, D.C., but at the Simon Wiesenthal Center's Museum of Tolerance, which has locations in Los Angeles and elsewhere. The mission of the Los Angeles museum is twofold: to inform visitors about the history of racism and social prejudices in America and to represent what the museum calls "the ultimate example of man's inhumanity to man—the Holocaust."[25] Both are noble aims, but by situating the Holocaust within a historical framework that includes such quintessentially American experiences as the Los Angeles riots and the struggle for black civil rights, both of which are prominently illustrated, the Museum of Tolerance relativizes the catastrophe brought on by Nazism in a radical way. America's social problems, for all of their gravity, are not genocidal in character and simply do not resemble the persecution and systematic slaughter of Europe's Jews during World War II. To mingle the victims of these very different historical experiences, therefore, is ultimately to broaden the conceptual base of the Nazi Holocaust to the point where it begins to metamorphose into that empty and now all but meaningless abstraction: "man's inhumanity to man."

This tendency to relativize and universalize the Holocaust has been a prominent part of the American reception of Holocaust representations from the start. It is strong today and seems to be growing, especially within those segments of American culture that are intent on developing a politics of identity based on victim status and the grievances that come with such status. The rhetoric of "oppression" has become a commonplace of con-

temporary American political, academic, and artistic discourse, and its ex-
ponents frequently take recourse to the signs and symbols of the Nazi
Holocaust to describe what they see as their own "victimization" within
American society.

In line with this tendency, consider the work of the feminist artist Judy
Chicago. Chicago (née Gerowitz), who claims descent from twenty-three
generations of rabbis but who, despite this proud lineage, acknowledges
that, until the age of forty-five, she knew virtually nothing about either Judaism or the Holocaust, has given us a large and ambitious art installation
entitled the *Holocaust Project,* which combines her own work in several media with the work of her husband, the photographer Donald Woodman.
The *Holocaust Project* had its opening at the Spertus Institute of Jewish Studies in Chicago in the fall of 1993 and traveled for shows at the Rose Art Museum at Brandeis University, the Los Angeles campus of the Hebrew Union
College, and elsewhere. As with this popular artist's other work, the *Holocaust Project* predictably drew sizable crowds and a good deal of media attention. Those who do not actually get to see the photo-paintings, tapes-
tries, and stained glass productions that make up this exhibit have access to
Chicago's work through an illustrated, oversized volume, also entitled
Holocaust Project. The book carries colored plates of the artwork along with
numerous preliminary sketches, historical and contemporary photographs,
excerpts from the artists' readings, and a detailed and highly revealing personal journal that Chicago kept as she set out to educate herself about the
Holocaust.[26]

Her search, which she describes as one in quest of her latent Jewish self
as well as of knowledge about the Nazi crimes, was intensive and demanding. It extended over a period of six or seven years and took Chicago and
Woodman on trips to numerous sites in Europe where the Holocaust had
been enacted as well as to Israel, where many of the survivors had emigrated. The couple visited former camp sites and other places of wartime
interest in France, Germany, Austria, Czechoslovakia, Poland, Russia,
Latvia, and Lithuania. Journal entries, drawings, and photographs illustrate
this ambitious itinerary and make clear that Chicago's search was not just
for knowledge in the cognitive sense but, more passionately, for an emotional sense of the "Holocaust experience." To make this "experience" her
own, as it were, Chicago did some things that go well beyond ordinary
tourist behavior. During a visit to the former Natzweiler/Struthof concentration camp in France, for instance, Chicago lay down on one of the long
iron shovels that had been used to feed the bodies of victims into the

flames of the crematorium oven and had herself photographed in this corpselike pose. A large black-and-white picture of her stretched out and seemingly entering the mouth of the oven is printed in the text of the *Holocaust Project,* accompanied by this brief explanatory note: "When I lay on the shovel that carried bodies into the crematorium, I realized that, had I lived in Europe during the war, this would probably have happened to me. (Donald is too young.)"[27]

This revelation is accompanied by numerous others recorded in the artist's journal, which indicate that the more she learned about the Holocaust, the more she learned about herself as a person, a woman, and a Jew. For instance, following her simulated ride into the crematorium oven, she traveled with her husband to Nuremberg, where it is borne in on her that she is in Germany, "where it began." They go off to a restaurant, "an old beerhall-type place," and chat away as they eat, "probably because we were afraid of the anguish we felt: the pain of *being* in Germany as Jews and letting ourselves know, feel, and experience this place, like no other place, where the Holocaust was born." It appears that in this German beerhall she experienced another revelation, this one confirmed by some reading she had been doing in the writings of Elie Wiesel: "The more I understand, the less I understand. I turn again and again to Wiesel for help, even though I don't always agree with what he says. But one remark of his was quite illuminating in terms of my inability to understand the perpetrators. I have written that I cannot inflict pain knowingly on others because I am a feminist and a conscious woman, and then I came upon Wiesel's statement that 'the Jews were told they were forbidden to diminish freedom. *They were forbidden [by Scripture] to inflict pain.*' Thus I find that I have carried a dual commandment, as a *feminist* and as a *Jew.* What an interesting revelation!"[28]

To someone who claims family descent from so lofty a figure as the Vilna Gaon, this sudden rush of Jewish knowledge, for all of its belatedness, must have been both confirming and inspiring. Yet it is hardly a singular insight, for the text of the *Holocaust Project* includes other "revelations" of this order, some suggesting a close connection between "the oppression of women" and "the oppression of Jews," others, in line with this linkage, indicating that the Holocaust may have been "a direct outgrowth of the patriarchal mind," still others linking the Holocaust to "the vulnerability of all human beings and, by extension, of all species and our fragile planet as well."[29] At one point, taking issue with Wiesel's claim that the Holocaust was a singular event in history, Chicago comes to the conclusion that, far from being unique, the Holocaust has to be understood as "*an aberration in*

the history of human cruelty. The Nazis went too far, much too far, but there
have been many, many cruel events in history."[30]

The culmination of the author-artist's growing wisdom about the Holocaust is reached when she concludes that it is futile to pin the blame for the
Nazi crimes on any one group in particular. In her own words, "Everyone
runs around trying to affix blame: The Germans did it; the French collaborated; the Poles were complicitous; the Americans and other Allies were indifferent. The list continues, trying to assign blame for something for
which no one is to blame, but for which all human beings are responsible.
*As a species, we are responsible for what we've done to each other, the Earth, and
its creatures.* The Holocaust can be seen as the logical outgrowth of the rule
of force, dominance, and power. It doesn't even matter which gender did it,
though it falls on men."[31]

In translating these hard-won, self-empowering insights into her art,
Chicago is guided by a point of view that, as she says, sets her and her husband apart from most of the members of "the Holocaust community."
Chicago favors "a more comprehensive approach," one that situates the
Holocaust as one "victim experience" among many, and that finds the root
of all of these in "the injustice inherent in the global Structure of patriarchy
and the result of power as it has been defined and enforced by male-domi-
nated societies."[32] Having sighted the enemy and given him his proper
name, the artist then set out to make his violence graphic.

There is not room enough here to comment on all of the pieces that
comprise the *Holocaust Project,* but suffice it to say that Judy Chicago's artwork itself reflects these emphases and understandings. One finds images
of Nazi brutality side by side with images of slavery, atomic warfare, animal
vivisection, and evil-looking gynecologists. Women are everywhere
abused, attacked, tormented. And there are other victims as well whose sufferings draw Chicago's sympathies: her "Pink Triangle" depicts both the
torture and the solidarity of male homosexuals (as a special effect, their
plight is set against a photographed background of pansies), and "Lesbian
Triangle" does more or less the same for women homosexuals. A large
tapestry entitled "The Fall," conceptualized along the lines of a "battle of
the sexes," depicts naked women being attacked by knife-wielding men
while other women are being burned alive. In this same piece, a black slave
ploughs furrows into the weeping earth-mother; a gaunt Jesus-like figure
hangs helplessly in the background; other men wield bloody swords or feed
people into the flaming ovens; and still others flay the hides of pigs and
women hung side by side on a rack. In the middle of all of this torment is

a reworking of Leonardo's "Vetruvian Man," which, an explanatory note tells us, is meant to show that the Holocaust had its true origin in "that moment in human history when men consolidated patriarchal power through force."[33] In Chicago's conception of history, all of our later troubles, including those brought on by the Nazis and their allies, have their root in the overthrow of matriarchy by cruelly aggressive, domineering men.

It is this tone and these understandings that inform the *Holocaust Project* from start to finish—or almost to the finish. The last piece, "Rainbow Shabbat," is a departure from all that precedes and is intended to close the exhibit on a prayerful note, "an invocation for human awakening and global transformation," as the artist puts it.[34] A large stained glass production, "Rainbow Shabbat" depicts twelve people around a sabbath table. At one end of the table there stands a woman, covered in a *tallit,* blessing the candles. At the other end, a man, also in a *tallit,* is depicted blessing the wine. And between these two seated around the table are representatives of the world's people: an Arab in kaffiyeh headdress, a Christian minister or priest with a large crucifix dangling on a chain beneath his clerical collar, Vietnamese, blacks, women, children, assorted whites. It is significant that the ten people around the sabbath table all face away from the man and toward the woman, for it is through her and not him that the world will find whatever renewal and redemption may be possible. The faces of these sabbath celebrants are expressionless but, inasmuch as they all have their arms about one another and seem to fall within the embrace of the praying woman's outstretched arms, we are given to understand that all is now well with the world or soon will be. Rainbow colors fill out the table scene from top to bottom, and on flanking side panels a large Jewish star, also surrounded by these bright colors, is inscribed with words that end the *Holocaust Project* on a prayerful note: "Heal those broken souls who have no peace and lead us all from darkness into light."[35]

It would be easy to see the *Holocaust Project* as one giant cliché from start to finish and dismiss it without further ado. Conceptually and visually, it is an atrociously flawed work of art serving an ideologically driven, weak-minded reading of history. It would be a serious mistake, however, to ignore Chicago's version of the Holocaust because in what makes it so miserably bad, it represents a number of trends that inform the American cultural and political mood today. And in no small measure, it is these trends that contribute to the shaping of American understandings of and attitudes to the Holocaust. In turn, the evolution of a certain "Holocaustal" cast of mind in American society carries no end of troubles with it.

As Philip Rieff, Christopher Lasch, and other serious social thinkers have told us, we are in an age that is marked by narcissistic indulgences of a relentless sort. In such a time, everything is drawn back to the self and its desires, the self and its needs, the self and its pains. Combine this extreme emphasis on subjectivity with the steady thrusts of an increasingly intrusive political correctness and an aggressive feminism of the most narrow kind, and you get productions like the *Holocaust Project,* according to which the genocidal crimes of Hitler's Germany are reduced to the deeds of a vicious "patriarchy" and Nazi victims are equated with monkeys in an animal laboratory and women during virtually every waking moment of their lives. Given the actual levels of atrocity that were enacted in Nazi-dominated Europe two generations ago, it is nothing short of perverse for an American artist to validate herself as a victim in these terms today; but in a culture that seems to encourage and reward victimhood status, it is no longer seen as being especially perverse. And so we have proliferating images of the Holocaust serving as ready-at-hand emblems of accusation in contemporary debates about AIDS, abortions, child abuse, gay rights, the rights of immigrant aliens, and so on. In fact, these are all matters of legitimate and serious social concern, but through analogizing them with the Nazi destruction of Europe's Jews, nothing but the sensational is added to the public discussion of what truly ails American society. And while the sensational is guaranteed to draw attention, it obfuscates and obscures more than it enlightens.

It also tends to make people lose their hold on reality. Listen to Judy Chicago one last time as she contemplates painting a rape scene for one of the panels of her *Holocaust Project.* "I am exhausting myself and depleting all my life's energy in fighting for the truth to be seen and heard. . . . I need to rest before I begin the rape image. Not only is it an intense, painful image, but it makes me very anxious. I keep thinking: am I going to get raped after I do this image: . . . But of course, I have no choice—so I'll just have to hope that art won't translate into life."[36] In this imaginary world, Holocausts threaten from every corner, and all are victims or potential victims. In more or less the same psychological register, even though with an eye on a different enemy, listen to the evangelist Pat Robertson: "Just what Nazi Germany did to the Jews, so liberal America is now doing to evangelical Christians. . . . It's no different; it's the same thing. It is happening all over again. It is the Democratic Congress, the liberal-biased media, and the homosexuals who want to destroy all Christians. It's more terrible than anything suffered by any minority in our history." As Robertson made this speech over his Christian Broadcasting Network, we learn that "footage of Nazi atrocities against the Jews appeared on screen."[37]

How, one wonders, does Robertson's audience respond to rhetoric of this kind? Will most recognize it as trumped-up, a form of religio-political hysteria, and, as such, seriously out of line with reality, or will they be prone to believe it? Does Robertson himself believe it? We do not know, anymore than we know how much of a genuine belief Judy Chicago has staked in her own seriously skewed version of the Holocaust. What we do know is that if people are exposed long enough to images of atrocity, they will no longer remain fully thinking people, capable of recognizing differences and making distinctions between one order of human experience and another. Given the penchant among growing numbers of Americans to proclaim themselves "victims," one must wonder if the spread of Holocaust images through the various layers of our culture may not be having such a self-deluding effect.

What has been suggested above about the representation of Holocaust victims within American popular culture applies as well to other types associated with the Holocaust. Raul Hilberg, one of the preeminent historians of the Nazi period, clearly had been thinking typologically when he entitled his 1995 book *Perpetrators, Victims, Bystanders*.[38] It has been generally understood that these three—in Hilberg's words, "a variety of perpetrators, a multitude of victims, and a host of bystanders"[39]—made up the essential core of the Holocaust in its time. In more recent years, however, as thinking and writing about the Nazi crimes have taken a figurative turn, there has been a substantial augmentation of this core and also a shift of emphasis within it. I refer especially to the emergence of the "survivor" and "rescuer" as prominent and popular types, along with the "liberator," the "resister," the "second-generation survivor," and the Holocaust "revisionist" or "denier." Interest in all of these has broadened the focus of the Holocaust "story" and influenced the point of view from which it is both narrated and received. In order to appreciate fully what Americans have come to know about the crimes of the Nazi era and how they have come to know it, therefore, one would have to look carefully at all of those whose actions and interactions collectively define the Holocaust for American audiences.[40] While this is not the place to carry out such a comprehensive task, I do want to examine the prominence that two of these types have enjoyed of late, namely the "survivor" and the "rescuer." To focus these observations, I turn to Steven Spielberg's hugely successful film *Schindler's List* and to the nature of the response to it among American filmgoers and critics.

For a number of years following the end of World War II, little public attention was paid in this country to those people who had managed to survive the Nazi assault against European Jewry and resettle in the United States. Their status was that of the "DP," the "immigrant," the "war refugee," or the "greenhorn," and attitudes toward them were hardly adulatory. Generous-hearted people did what they could to help these newcomers adjust to their new circumstances in America and rebuild their lives here; others more or less ignored them. To be sure, it was not difficult to recognize the pain that these Jewish refugees had suffered in Hitler's Europe, but war always brings on suffering, and the war to defeat Hitler was truly a terrible war. Besides, there was little point in keeping one's wounds open now that the war had been won. Throughout the late 1940s and well into the 1950s, a prevalent attitude was to put all of "that" behind one and get on with life. The age of the "survivor" had clearly not yet arrived.

Here is how William Helmreich, who has written an informative book about the experiences of Holocaust survivors in America, describes the situation in the immediate postwar years:

> For some Americans there seemed to be an inability to listen to the tales of woe recounted by the refugees. Most immigrants quickly learned not to talk about the war, often rationalizing their reluctance by saying that the stories were too horrible to be believed. Americans frequently responded to such stories with accounts of how they too had undergone privation during the war, mostly food rationing. Moritz Felberman [a survivor] was told by his aunt: "If you want to have friends here in America, don't keep talking about your experiences. Nobody's interested and if you tell them, they're going to hear it once and then the next time they'll be afraid to come see you. Don't ever speak about it."[41]

For some two decades or so following the end of the war, many of the "refugees" from Hitler's Europe probably did not often "speak about it," even in the privacy of their family homes. Just when this period of relative muteness ended is hard to say with any precision, but beginning in the middle to late 1960s and carrying up to the present day a radical change of attitude has taken place, so much so that today the "survivor" is a much honored figure and, in some instances, enjoys something close to celebrity status. The writer Elie Wiesel has played an important role in this regard, as have others. The result is that those who formerly had been regarded as "war refugees" have given up that unenviable status and taken on a new symbolic importance as "Holocaust survivors." As "survivors," these aging men and women are frequently sought as platform speakers at Yom HaShoah commemorative programs and other public occasions during the year, and sizable audiences are likely to turn out to hear them tell their tales. "Survivor" memoirs have been published in large numbers and now constitute a significant subgenre of Holocaust literature. In addition, the Fortunoff Video Archives at Yale University and other institutions have been engaged in ambitious efforts to interview these aging "witnesses" and record their stories on tape while it is still possible to do so.[42] In short, the "survivor" now enjoys a greatly heightened public profile and carries about him or her an aura that solicits honor, respect, fascination, and no small degree of awe. Leon Uris has recently summed up these attitudes by stating the case forthrightly: "These men and women are to be looked upon with wonderment."[43] And so, increasingly, they are.

Schindler's List, dedicated as it is to narrating the story of eleven hundred Jews rescued from what doubtless would have been a gruesome death, is a film that celebrates "survivors." As such, it builds upon a momentum within segments of American culture, and especially American Jewish culture, that has developed over the last number of years. As indicated by the subtitle of William Helmreich's book—*Against All Odds: Holocaust Survivors and the Successful Lives They Made in America*—many of those who survived the ghettos, camps, and assorted hiding places of Nazi-occupied Europe have done well in this country, and in their latter years they have dedicated themselves energetically and successfully to seeing to it that their own stories and the wrenchingly painful story of their era are preserved for future generations. Without the extraordinary commitment of these people, there would be no United States Holocaust Memorial Museum, no video archives for Holocaust testimony, no endowed chairs at American colleges and universities for the teaching of the Holocaust—and no *Schindler's List*. Their success in these respects is truly remarkable. The catalog of the Association of Holocaust Organizations, for instance, lists over one hundred Holocaust institutions throughout the United States and Canada, all of which are dedicated to educating the public about the Holocaust. These places exist largely because Holocaust survivors in North America have seen to it that they exist. Their mission, simply stated, is to carry on in perpetuity the memory work of a traumatized generation of European Jews who, in the short space of a generation, have transformed themselves from their once lowly status into unprecedented positions of influence and respect. Abandoning the reticence that marked their situation in the immediate postwar years, they have gained their voice and are not reluctant to use it when the need arises. No one who recalls the Bitburg affair in the spring of 1985 will soon forget that it was a "survivor" who faced off against the president of the United States and, with all of the world's television cameras recording the moment, "spoke truth to power." Who but Elie Wiesel—a figure who has come to symbolize the moral authority of his generation—would have dared publicly to tell the president of this country that it was "not [his] place" to travel to Germany to join Prime Minister Kohl for ceremonies at the military cemetery at Bitburg?[44] That moment epitomized an important development among survivors that had been growing steadily within the public culture of American Jewry, a development of newly found strength, self-confidence, and self-assertion. It is a development that has found its way into American culture at large and may have reached its high point during the 1994 Academy Awards ceremony when Branko Lustig, himself a survivor, and Steven Spielberg stepped before a vast and inordinately appreciative television audience and, in the name of the "survivors" as well as in the name of "the six million," accepted their Oscars as producer and director of *Schindler's List*. In so doing, they were emphatic that this generation of Holocaust "survivors," which knows itself to be the *last* of its kind, will not depart without leaving behind its mark for this and future generations. In no small measure, that determination is what is symbolized through the creation of the Washington Holocaust Memorial Museum and other institutions of its kind around the country.[45]

As *Schindler's List* makes clear, if we are in the age of the "survivor," we are also in the age of the "rescuer." For along with a high degree of public attention being cast on the "survivor," we have seen and continue to see the elevation through the popular media of "righteous gentiles," "helpers," "liberators," "rescuers," and "saviors." These are the people who helped the "survivor" to survive, and so they, too, are increasingly looked upon with a degree of wonderment, in their case wonderment accompanied by appreciation for their courage and conviction. These people are now frequently regarded as the "moral heroes" of the Holocaust, the ones who managed to exemplify virtue during a time when basic human goodness was otherwise hardly to be found. Those who speak of them unfailingly revert to such religious or quasi-religious metaphors as "the light that pierced the darkness," "the righteous," "the just," "the good Samaritans," and so on. In a time when many feel the need to locate a moral counterweight to the overwhelming darkness and terror inherent in the Holocaust, the "helpers" and "rescuers" are the ones who supply images of "light," "hope," "affirmation," and "goodness." In this regard, it is notable that the United States

Holocaust Memorial Museum is situated on Raoul Wallenberg Place, a designation rich in symbolic implication and one that helps to "balance" the horrors awaiting visitors inside the building with a sense of righteousness duly honored on the outside.

Thanks to Steven Spielberg's film, the Swedish hero Wallenberg is now joined by the German Oskar Schindler as another one of the "righteous among the nations." Moreover, the attention now focused on Schindler's wartime deeds has had the effect of renewing or creating interest in the stories of others who acted similarly: Aristedes de Sousa Mendes, Sempo Sugihara, Hermann Graebe, Miep Gies, Andre Trocme and the people of Le Chambon, the Danes, and so forth. Each of these put his or her life at risk to help protect and save Jews during the war, and while their numbers are not huge, their actions were clearly exemplary. The question that stands before us with respect to the "rescuers," therefore, is not one of their inclusion or exclusion from narrative accounts of the Nazi era but chiefly one of proportion: how central or peripheral are these "moral heroes" of the Holocaust to the larger history of the Holocaust?

Schindler's List answers this question in a way that moves "rescuers" like Schindler from the margins to the precise center of events. In doing that successfully, Spielberg has in effect repositioned the terms of the Holocaust "story" away from those advanced by Hilberg and others—the Holocaust composed essentially of "perpetrators," "victims," and "bystanders"—and placed the emphasis squarely on "rescuers" and "survivors." *Schindler's List*, after all, is a Holocaust film that focuses chiefly on the Jews who do *not* die at the hands of the Nazis but who, on the contrary, are actually saved by a Nazi who undergoes a moral conversion to goodness. If, as claimed by some, Spielberg's film is to be regarded from this point on as the "definitive" Holocaust film, and if, as claimed by others, it may actually do more to educate vast numbers of people about the history of the Holocaust than all the academic books on the subject combined, one has to recognize that it has achieved these ends as the result of a paradigm shift of significant proportions. In this film mass audiences are exposed to a version of the Holocaust that originates in long-standing American preferences for "heroes" and "happy endings," preferences that *Schindler's List* satisfies through its artful employment of tried and true Hollywood conventions of cinematic storytelling. To say as much is not to call into question Spielberg's achievement with *Schindler's List*, which is considerable, but it is to point out the fact that this is a film that presents a characteristically American way of reading and resolving an extreme history.

As for its impact, there was an extraordinary amount of interest in *Schindler's List,* revealing both laudatory and highly critical attitudes. No less a personality than President Clinton "implored" people to see *Schindler's List,* and other political figures, including governors of California and New Jersey, likewise gave the film their public endorsement and promoted it as a primary source of historical information and moral education. Especially in light of its overwhelming success at the 1994 Academy Awards, where it garnered no less than seven Oscars, *Schindler's List* has been still more lavishly acclaimed as a "great film," "a masterpiece," "an astounding achievement." In the *New Yorker,* Stephen Schiff declared it "the finest fiction feature ever made about the century's greatest evil. . . . It will take its place in cultural history and remain there." Terrence Rafferty agrees with this evaluation and has called Spielberg's film "by far the finest, fullest dramatic film ever made about the Holocaust." Jeffrey Katzenberg, at the time head of Walt Disney film studios, remarked that *Schindler's List* "will wind up being so much more important than a movie. . . . It will affect how people on this planet think and act. . . . It will actually set the course of world affairs." If not at quite this level of hyperbole, many others have weighed in with similar accolades.[46]

At the same time, the film has had its critics, some of them passionately opposed to what Spielberg has wrought. In the *American Spectator,* James Bowman denounced *Schindler's List* as a film that "cheapens and trivializes the enormity of the Holocaust" and offers "no sense whatever of the political realities that allowed such things to happen." J. Hoberman, film critic of the *Village Voice,* found the film "sentimental," too much of a "feelgood" movie, and therefore bound to encourage attitudes of "complacency" in viewers. Donald Kuspit sees *Schindler's List* as "stereotypical," the work of an artist who simply does not "understand" the history of the Holocaust: "*Schindler's List* is a triumph of simplemindedness—always Spielberg's strength." Claude Lanzmann, the creator of *Shoah,* has been harshly critical of Spielberg's film, denouncing it as one that is essentially false to the essential facts of the Holocaust: "To tell the story of the Holocaust through a German who saved Jews can only lead to a distortion of the truth, because for the overwhelming majority of Jews things like this did not happen."[47]

While critical opinion on the film is clearly divided, there is no question that Spielberg's cinematic statement is a major one and that from this point on *Schindler's List* is destined to play an influential role in determining how millions of people in this country and elsewhere will come to remember and understand the Nazi Holocaust. In light of this prospect, one is moved to ask: what version of the Holocaust does this film project? In particular, what images of Germans and Jews does Spielberg present in *Schindler's List?*

The fundamental dramatic confrontation in the film is not one between Jews and Germans but one between an evil German (Amon Goeth, the commander of the Plaszow labor camp) and a German who comes to exemplify righteous behavior (Oskar Schindler). As the movie progresses, the face-off between these two intensifies and takes on allegorical dimensions, and in the balance of the outcome there hangs the fate of the Jews. Otherwise, the Jews in *Schindler's List* are weakly imagined figures, for the most part either passive victims of random atrocity or venal collaborators with their persecutors. In just about all cases they appear as nondescript, anonymous figures or are presented in stereotypical fashion, the men among them associated with money deals and other sorts of scheming and the women as temptresses and seductresses. Itzhak Stern, the only Jewish character developed at any length, is an inflexible, soulless type, whose expression throughout the film rarely changes from that of the professional bookkeeper that he is. In just about every other respect, the Jews in *Schindler's List* are irrelevant to the major drama of the film, the battle between Oskar Schindler and Amon Goeth, the chief embodiments of "good" and "evil." In the contest between them, it is Schindler, of course, who prevails and who, at film's end, is the recipient of the Jews' gratitude, respect, and love.

This ending takes Schindler and the Jews through two major rites of passage, both of which have about them an aura of the morally sublime, if not indeed of the sacred: presenting him with a gold ring, the *Schindlerjuden* in effect "marry" themselves to this man out of heartfelt gratitude for his righteous deeds, which alone kept them from becoming Nazi victims; and in the final cemetery scene the same Jews, now elderly "survivors," pay their respects to the memory of their savior through the ritualistic placing of tokens of honor and love on his grave. Both scenes convey feelings of affection, respect, and reconciliation, and most filmgoers doubtless will be moved to respond to these with similar feelings of their own. In addition, it is noteworthy that both scenes project Schindler as a figure defined by overtly Christian symbolism—in the first, he holds forth in a dramatic speech that recalls Jesus' Sermon on the Mount; and in the second, the camera pans lovingly over the crosses in Jerusalem's Latin Cemetery, coming to rest on the gravesite where Schindler himself is buried.[48] These two scenes bring to culmination and closure the career of a man who may have been a morally flawed character in many other respects but who is nothing short of a saintly hero with respect to the Jews. One wants to identify with such a person, who has managed to transcend the baser qualities of his personality and behavior and come to exemplify virtue through his good deeds. Thus, although audiences might leave the movie theater with a strong lump in their throats, most are likely to feel somehow ennobled as a result of seeing this film.

As the Holocaust enters American public consciousness through *Schindler's List,* therefore, it may have the effect of dislodging earlier and more difficult feelings of shame and guilt that typically accompany reactions to images of the persecution and mass slaughter of Europe's Jews. As in the long and disturbingly powerful scene that depicts the clearing of the Kraków ghetto, Spielberg does not shy away from portraying brutality and bloodshed, but he places the responsibility for such atrocity on Nazi types who are little more than psychopathic thugs. The political dimensions of Nazi behavior go altogether unexplored in *Schindler's List;* in their stead one encounters raw sadism of an extremely personal rather than systemic kind. Identification with a character like the vicious Amon Goeth, who incarnates the murderous passions of a limitless evil, is out of the question for most filmgoers, who are far more likely to align themselves sympathetically with the "good" German, Oskar Schindler, the "rescuer" of the Jews. At film's end, an unrepentant Goeth goes to his death on the gallows, Schindler goes to his eternal rest as a man of honor, and the *Schindlerjuden* survive to strike out for a new life as settlers in Palestine.

What version of the Holocaust, then, does *Schindler's List* present? A recognizably American one, by which I do not mean a historically "false" one but rather one that interprets history along lines that Americans seem to require or at least instinctively prefer. Michael Andre Bernstein, writing in the *American Scholar,* correctly observes that by concentrating "on a small group of Jews who survived and on the good German who aided them rather than on all the millions who did not live and the millions of Germans and German sympathizers who did nothing to help," Spielberg satisfies "a characteristic American urge to find a redemptive meaning in every event."[49] That urge is not felt in such films as Alain Resnais's *Night and Fog* and Claude Lanzmann's *Shoah,* nor does one find it satisfied in the Auschwitz memoirs of such European writers as Primo Levi and Jean Améry. By contrast, it is on a note of redemptive promise that American productions on the Holocaust are likely to end. To reach such endings, however, it is necessary that a new paradigm of narrative construction be advanced, one focusing prominently on the more "affirmative" figures of the Holocaust story, notably "survivors" and "rescuers." *Schindler's List* is the most recent and also the most powerfully articulated example of this paradigm shift, but it is hardly alone. For increasingly one finds a desire for a greater degree of "balance" in representing the Holocaust, a "balance" that might be achieved by modulating somewhat an emphasis on the Jewish victims and their German torturers and murderers and focusing a new kind of attention on the "righteous gentile" or "rescuer."

Within the American context, this search within the darkness and evil of the Holocaust for figures of luminosity and goodness seems to be part of a larger cultural quest for religious meaning, or what today is loosely called "spirituality." As Eva Fogelman remarks in her *Conscience and Courage: Rescuers of Jews during the Holocaust* (1994), "People in the 1990s are hungry for role models," for inspiring examples "of moral courage during an immoral time." Her book is but one of many that identifies these role models with the "rescuers," whom she does not hesitate to define as the "spiritual heirs to the *Lamed Vav*—the thirty-six people of Jewish tradition whose sole task it is, in every generation, . . . to do good for their fellow men."[50] André Schwarz-Bart revived popular interest in the figure of the *Lamed-Vav* in his novel *The Last of the Just* (1959), although as he presents it, this tradition reached its point of exhaustion during the time of the Holocaust. In an effort to revive it, Marek Halter's 1994 film, *Tzedek,* presents the stories of thirty-six righteous gentiles who rescued Jews. Numerous other books and films do the same: in addition to Fogelman's *Conscience and Courage,* notable titles include Gay Block and Malka Drucker's *Rescuers: Portraits of Moral Courage in the Holocaust* (1992), Peter Hellman's *Avenue of the Righteous: Portraits in Uncommon Courage of Christians and the Jews They Saved from Hitler* (1980), Douglas K. Huneke's, *The Moses of Rovno: The Stirring Story of Fritz Graebe, A German Christian Who Risked His Life to Lead Hundreds of Jews to Safety during the Holocaust* (1985), Samuel P. Oliner and Pearl Oliner's *The Altruistic Personality: Rescuers of Jews in Nazi Europe* (1988), Mordecai Paldiel's *The Path of the Righteous: Gentile Rescuers of Jews during the Holocaust* (1993), Eric Silver's *The Book of the Just: The Unsung Heroes Who Rescued Jews from Hitler* (1992), Nechama Tec's *When Light Pierced the Darkness: Christian Rescue of Jews in Nazi-Occupied Poland* (1986), and many others of a similar kind.[51] In addition to these, at least half a dozen books on Raoul Wallenberg have appeared since the early 1980s, and titles on Oskar Schindler have reached American bookstores.[52]

Eva Fogelman is hardly alone, therefore, in wanting "to give altruism back its good name."[53] Among those involved in shaping the configurations of Holocaust memory, a new accent on the "positive" is notable, so much so that *Moment* magazine could actually publish an article entitled "Is Elie Wiesel Happy?"[54] Other, less bizarre indicators likewise point to a new interest in the "positive" or "good" aspects of the Holocaust. In 1984, the United States Holocaust Memorial Council sponsored a major conference entitled "Faith in Humankind: Rescuers of Jews during the Holocaust." Other, smaller conferences have since been held elsewhere on the same theme. The Altruistic Personality Project has done programs and sponsored publications of a similar nature, and projects such as Friends of Le Chambon, Thanks to Scandinavia, and Tribute to the Danes direct attention to regional rescue efforts.[55] Seen within this context, Steven Spielberg's film, far from being exceptional in its focus on "rescue," is the culmination of a development in Holocaust narrative that has been building momentum for a number of years now. In Eva Fogelman's view, it is not difficult to explain what it is that accounts for this development: "The brutal testimony of the Eichmann trial set off an urgent quest for evidence of human kindness during the war. People around the world needed to feel that the heart of man was not unrelievedly black. Rescuers were discovered."[56]

Within the American discourse on the Holocaust, Jewish scholars and artists as well as Jewish organizations have figured prominently in advancing this discovery, none more energetically than Rabbi Harold N. Schulweis. In 1963, on the heels of the Eichmann trial, Schulweis founded the Institute of Righteous Acts at the Judah Magnes Museum in Berkeley, California. Some twenty years later he went on to establish the Jewish Foundation of Christian Rescuers (Eva Fogelman served as its first director), which is now an integral part of the Anti-Defamation League's International Center for Holocaust Studies. In addition to his work in establishing these institutions, Schulweis has written about the desirability of directing public attention to the deeds of the "righteous." He is the author of forewords to the books of Douglas Huneke, Samuel and Pearl Oliner, and Mordecai Paldiel mentioned above, and the afterword to Carol Rittner and Sondra Myers's *The Courage to Care: Rescuers of Jews during the Holocaust* (1986). In addition, he has published several separate articles on "rescuers" and devotes a full chapter to them in his *For Those Who Can't Believe* (1994).

Through all of these writings, Schulweis has been concerned with how the Holocaust is being represented to diverse audiences in America: "How we interpret the Holocaust holds serious consequences for the character and morale of our children, not only for the Jewish child but for the non-Jewish child as well. . . . How effective, how constructive has been our way of relating this great atrocity? . . . It may be that we have unintentionally transmitted a morale-breaking pessimism in dwelling solely on the tragic past."[57] Schulweis has consistently argued that in transmitting knowledge of the Holocaust, nothing must be done, on the one hand, to mitigate the severity of the Nazi crimes against the Jews and, on the other, that everything must be done to identify and call attention to those good people who put themselves at risk to protect Jews whose lives were imperiled. In his own words, "In remembering the cruelty and barbarity of the Holocaust, we must not forget the moral heroes of conscience. In an era of the anti-hero, the heroes of conscience must be exalted."[58] Rabbi Schulweis is inclined to look upon memory as a "healing art," one characterized by the imperative to establish "balance" in what is recalled and represented. In this view, memory is most meaningful when it is dedicated to the purposes of "moral education." Consequently, in recounting the story of the Holocaust, Rabbi Schulweis argues that we face a question that is fundamentally ethical in its thrust: "How are we to remember without destroying hope?"[59]

In answering this question, Schulweis has developed both a pragmatic and a didactic approach to history and memory, one that seeks to interpret the Holocaust in ways that are fundamentally constructive. "Memory," he writes, "contains an ambiguous energy. It can liberate or enslave, heal or destroy. The use of memory carries with it a responsibility for the future." Thus, "it is to the moral act of remembering that we must be dedicated. How are we, as moral educators, to make memory the father of conscience and of constructive repentance?" His answer, not surprisingly, is to look to the "righteous among the nations" as a positive counterweight to what is otherwise an overwhelmingly negative and depressing record of villainy. "There is a moral symmetry in man," Schulweis insists, and to help restore it, we must become newly attentive to the voices of heroism: "The world is hungry for moral heroes . . . heroes whose altruism is lived out in action; models of exemplary behavior who realize our abstract ideals, human beings to be emulated." Hence, the discovery and promotion of Oskar Schindler and other "rescuers."[60]

These figures serve as a bridge in advancing the aims of Jewish-Christian dialogue in America, but beyond this pragmatic purpose they have reached a level of importance in Schulweis's thinking that elevates their goodness to a theological principle. "Where was Adonai in Auschwitz?" Schulweis asks. "Where was the power and mystique of Adonai within the hell of the Holocaust?" While other religious thinkers have raised similar questions about God's absence or presence in the Nazi death camps, it would be rare to find among them many who answer as Schulweis does:

> Where was Adonai in the Holocaust? Adonai was in Nieuvelande, a Dutch village in which seven hundred residents rescued five hundred Jews. . . . Adonai was in Le Chambon-sur-Lignon, whose citizens hid and protected five thousand Jews. . . . Adonai was in the rat-infested sewers of Lvov, where Polish sewer workers hid seventeen Jews. . . . Adonai was in Bulgaria . . . in Finland. . . . Adonai was with the Italian troops stationed in the southwestern half of Croatia in Yugoslavia, Greece, southern France, Albania.[61]

The list goes on and on, an "affirmative" antiphony to that strain of severe religious doubt, if not outright theological despair, that has entered the post-Holocaust religious consciousness of so many other writers. One recalls the broken, stuttering prayer that concludes Schwarz-Bart's *The Last of the Just:* "And praised. *Auschwitz.* Be. *Maidanek.* The Lord. *Treblinka.* And praised. *Buchenwald.* Be. *Mauthausen.* The Lord. *Belzec.* . . ."[62] As already noted above, Schwarz-Bart comes to the melancholy conclusion that the Nazi assault against the Jews was so overpoweringly destructive as to bring an end to the ancient Jewish tradition of the Just. By contrast, Schulweis not only revives this tradition but, on the basis of its Christian exemplars—multiplied many times thirty-six—actually presumes to locate God *within* the Holocaust. How he manages to do so other than rhetorically is not clear from his writings, in which he asserts a bold theological truth-claim but offers little compelling evidence to substantiate it. The absence of proofs aside, however, his position is significant for what it illustrates. For in his insistence that Nazi villainy be "balanced" by Christian "heroes" who incarnate "hope" and "goodness," Schulweis inscribes a new and characteristically American script for narrating the story of the Holocaust, one that has yielded a large and still growing corpus of "rescue" literature and film, of which Spielberg's *Schindler's List* is, for the moment, the culminating expression.

The reception of Spielberg's film clearly indicates that a great many people respond enthusiastically to narrative employments of the Holocaust that restore what Schulweis calls "the moral symmetry of man." In his own writing about the film, Schulweis has argued that if *Schindler's List* "has become the defining symbol of the Holocaust, it is . . . not because of its artistry alone, but because it enables the viewer to enter the dark cavern without feeling that there is no exit. 'How far that little candle throws its beam.' Memory of the Holocaust is a sacred act that elicits a double mandate: to expose the depth of evil and to raise goodness from the dust of amnesia."[63] In Schulweis's own writings, as well as in the work of others who have followed his lead, the accent falls preponderantly on the side of "goodness." His colleague Eva Fogelman, also arguing for a restoration of "moral symmetry," puts it this way: "Every child knows the name of Hitler, but how many know the name of Raoul Wallenberg?"[64]

The fact is that in the American population at large and not only among children, pitifully little is known about either Hitler or Wallenberg.[65] But even if it were the case that knowledge of the former ran deep and knowledge of the latter was all but absent, the case for "balance" would not be convincing. There was not nor can there be any "symmetry" in the historical weights of Hitler and Wallenberg, or Hitler and Schindler, or Hitler and the good people of Le Chambon. The deeds of the righteous are assuredly worthy of remembrance, but by placing them on an almost equal level with the deeds of Hitler and encompassing both within a "double mandate" of Holocaust memory, one reshapes the history of the Holocaust in ways that obscure how truly horrendous the Holocaust actually was. It is no part of Schulweis's intention to bring about such a consequence; indeed, he has declared himself emphatically on this point time and again. Nevertheless, the inevitable end point of his moral "art of memory" is clear: by projecting "rescuers" as central figures in narrative accounts of the Holocaust—as if the morality of Wallenberg or Schindler truly were on a par with the evil of Hitler—he changes the core of Holocaust remembrance in ways that will almost certainly vitiate any sober understanding of the deeds of the murderers and the sufferings of their victims.

As a consequence of such a change, religious faith may revive for some and the tenor of Jewish-Christian dialogue in America may improve for others, but for most, I fear, the exaltation of the "righteous" may, over time, foster a greater complacency about the most harrowing history of this past century. Those who advocate "balance," therefore, also need to keep proportion in mind—that is to say, the lineaments of historical reality itself. The Israeli writer Aharon Appelfeld has written on this matter in a way that restores some much-needed perspective: "During the Holocaust there were brave Germans, Ukrainians, and Poles who risked their lives to save Jews. But the Holocaust is not epitomized by the greatness of these mar-

velous individuals' hearts. . . . I say this because survivors sometimes feel
deep gratitude to their rescuers and forget that the saviors were few, and
those who betrayed Jews to the Nazis were many and evil."[66]

Appelfeld's view is not shared by all, however, and, especially in the
growing body of "rescue" literature, it is likely to be challenged by those
who wish to retrieve some remnant of moral idealism from a history of
mass murder. As already demonstrated, this tendency has been growing
stronger in recent years, although within American responses to the Holocaust one can trace it back to earlier decades, when the horrendous character of the Nazi genocide appeared simply too much for some to bear. One
hears the keynote to a religious counter-response, for instance, in Father
John A. O'Brien's foreword to Philip Friedman's *Their Brothers' Keepers*, the
first book in English on Christian "rescuers." O'Brien begins soberly
enough, as the following words reveal: "The story of Hitler's efforts to solve
the 'Jewish problem' in Germany and in all the countries which fell under
the yoke of the Nazis, by the simple expedient of exterminating them, . . .
is a ghastly and shocking tale of brutality, torture, and murder, which in de-
liberate, systematic savagery on a grand scale is probably unsurpassed in all
the annals of human history. From such a rehearsal readers instinctively recoil, for it does not make pleasant reading." O'Brien is correct on both
counts: the story of the Nazi crimes against the Jews is one of unparalleled
horror and, if presented in terms that do not mitigate its ghastliness, most
people may indeed recoil from it. Recognizing as much, American representations of the Holocaust, from the time of *The Diary of Anne Frank* in the
late 1950s to the appearance of the *Holocaust Project* and *Schindler's List,* seek
ways to "balance" a history of unbearable suffering with affirmative images
of hope. Thus, memory of Anne Frank's hideous fate in Auschwitz and
Bergen-Belsen is softened by her transcendent "message of faith in humankind"; the "victims" portrayed in Judy Chicago's *Holocaust Project* are
not only the European Jews who were slaughtered by the millions two generations ago but a much vaster and more generalized collective of suffering
humanity, animal life, and the earth itself; and the Jews of Kraców and
other European cities and towns who were rounded up and deported to
their deaths in the Nazi killing centers of Poland are rendered as background figures in *Schindler's List* in favor of a small number of Jews who
owe their lives to a "good" Nazi who turned out, against all expectations,
to be their savior. In these and so many other instances, one sees an American memory of the Holocaust evolving that shows us "victims" but *also*
"survivors," "perpetrators" but *also* "rescuers," "bystanders" but *also* "liber-

ators." Such a "balanced" portrait is intended to restore "the moral symmetry of man" and enables American educators to teach what is commonly called "the lessons of the Holocaust" to diverse and sundry audiences. In place of the scandal that, now and forever, should accompany any encounter with the unprecedented evil of the Nazi crimes against the Jews, we see the emergence of moral leveling agents of various sorts—the "righteous among the nations," the "rescuers," the "bearers of light in a time of darkness"—through whom Schulweis finds a way to a renewed faith in Adonai and O'Brien finds a means to celebrate Christian virtue: "It is needed to balance the degradation and baseness of the Jew-baiters with the gallantry and heroism of the Jew-aiders. . . . [*Their Brothers' Keepers*] shows that nineteen centuries of Christian teaching were not without results. So deeply had the fundamental law of the Christian religion, the duty to love one's neighbor, been woven into the warp and woof of the Christian conscience that thousands in all lands defied the sternest edicts and threats of the Gestapo and sheltered Jews. . . . They proved that they *were* their brothers' keepers and that not in vain had Jesus of Nazareth related the parable of the Good Samaritan."[67]

To which the ghost of Anne Frank replies, just before the final curtain falls, "Whatever happened to shame?"

Notes

1. These studies, the first of which appeared in 1993, have been published by the American Jewish Committee in the series Working Papers on Contemporary Anti-Semitism. Titles include "What Do Americans Know about the Holocaust?" (1993); "What Do the British Know about the Holocaust?" (1993); "What Do the French Know about the Holocaust?" (1994); "What Do Australians Know about the Holocaust?" (1994); "Current German Attitudes toward Jews and Other Minorities" (1994); and "Holocaust Denial: What the Survey Data Reveal" (1995); they are available from the American Jewish Committee, 165 East 56th Street, New York, NY 10022-2746.

2. Jennifer Golub and Renae Cohen, "What Do Americans Know about the Holocaust?" Working Papers on Contemporary Anti-Semitism, American Jewish Committee, 1993, 13.

3. Golub and Cohen, "What Do Americans Know," 38–40.

4. Tom W. Smith, "Holocaust Denial: What the Survey Data Reveal," Working Papers on Contemporary Anti-Semitism, American Jewish Committee, 1995, 31.

5. The exact number of Jews killed is not known and probably never will be known precisely. Raul Hilberg has placed the figure at 5.1 million; Lucy Dawidowicz estimated it at 5,933,900; Martin Gilbert, at 5.75 million; the *Encyclopedia of the Holo-*

caust states a minimum figure of 5,596,000 and a maximum of 5,860,000; and Wolfgang Benz sets the minimum at 5,290,000 and a maximum of over six million. As previously unavailable archival materials in the former Soviet Union are made known to scholars, these figures are likely to be revised and, from early indications, probably upward. Some of these figures and an informed explanation of how they have been reached can be found in Franciszek Piper, "The Number of Victims," *Anatomy of the Auschwitz Death Camp*, ed. Yisrael Gutman and Michael Berenbaum (Bloomington: Indiana University Press, 1994), 61–76.

6. In Yehuda Bauer's view, the Wiesenthal position is seriously flawed historically as well as conceptually: "It is apparently no less a man than Simon Wiesenthal . . . who has invented the '11 million' formula that is a key slogan in the denial of the uniqueness of the Jewish experience. Wiesenthal is going around campuses and Jewish congregations saying that the Holocaust was the murder of 11 million people— the six million Jews and five million non-Jews who were killed in the Nazi camps. In purely historical terms this is sheer nonsense. The total number of people who died in concentration camps during the war period—excepting Jews and Gypsies—was about half a million, perhaps a little more. On the other hand, the total number of non-Jewish civilian casualties during the war caused by Nazi brutality cannot be less than 20–25 million. . . . Probably some 2.5 million Soviet POWs died in special camps that were not part of the concentration camp system (though some thousands were shipped to concentration camps and murdered there)." Yehuda Bauer, "Whose Holocaust?" *Midstream*, November 1980, 43.

7. See Teresa Swiebocka, ed., *Auschwitz, A History in Photographs* (Bloomington: Indiana University Press, 1993); the essays printed in this volume reflect a significant change in Polish thinking about Auschwitz.

8. Among other works on the construction of national memories of World War II and the Holocaust, see Peter Baldwin, ed., *Reworking the Past: Hitler, the Holocaust, and the Historians' Debate* (Boston: Beacon Press, 1990); Saul Friedlander, *Memory, History, and the Extermination of the Jews of Europe* (Bloomington: Indiana University Press, 1993); Charles S. Maier, *The Unmasterable Past: History, Holocaust, and German National Identity* (Cambridge: Harvard University Press, 1988); Judith Miller, *One, by One, by One: Facing the Holocaust* (New York: Simon and Schuster, 1990); and Henry Rousso, *The Vichy Syndrome: History and Memory in France since 1944* (Cambridge: Harvard University Press, 1991).

9. For an early but still useful study of terminological origins and changes, see Gerd Korman, "The Holocaust in American Historical Writing," *Societas* 2, no. 3 (1972): 251–70; see also Zev Garber and Bruce Zuckerman, "Why Do we Call the Holocaust 'The Holocaust'? An Inquiry into the Psychology of Labels," *Modern Judaism* 9 (1989): 197–212.

10. Zev Garber and Bruce Zuckerman advocate a broader conception of what the "Holocaust" was and are open to the same historical criticism that Bauer levels at Simon Wiesenthal: "[The Holocaust] becomes a warning of what too easily can happen at any time, at any place, with anyone in the role of victim or victimizer. This is the way 'The Holocaust' should be characterized and especially how it should be taught. . . . The 'six million' figure, often invoked in characterizations of 'The Holocaust,' points up the problem of stressing uniqueness and chosenness over commonality. The truth is that eleven million people were killed by the Nazis in the con-

centration camps. Nearly half of these are excluded in most characterizations of 'The Holocaust,' and this seems to imply that Gentile deaths are not as significant as Jewish deaths." "Why Do We Call the Holocaust?" 208. The authors cite no sources to corroborate their reference to "eleven million" people killed in the concentration camps and probably look to Wiesenthal as their authority on this matter.

11. See "Address by President Jimmy Carter," printed in President's Commission on the Holocaust, *Report to the President,* September 27, 1979, http://www.ushmm.org/research/library/faq/languages/en/06/01/commission/ (consulted October 15, 2007).

12. Bauer, "Whose Holocaust?" 42.

13. Ilan Avisar, *Screening the Holocaust: Cinema's Images of the Unimaginable* (Bloomington: Indiana University Press, 1988), 96–97.

14. Avisar, *Screening the Holocaust,* 116.

15. See Anna Steenmeijer, ed., *A Tribute to Anne Frank* (Garden City, NY: Doubleday, 1971).

16. Reverential attitudes of this kind appear in letters to Otto Frank by young women correspondents; the letters, unpublished, may be found in the archives of the Anne Frank Foundation in Amsterdam.

17. For more on the reception of Anne Frank's diary in its book and stage versions, see Alvin H. Rosenfeld, "Popularization and Memory: The Case of Anne Frank," in *Lessons and Legacies: The Meaning of the Holocaust in a Changing World,* ed. Peter Hayes (Evanston, IL: Northwestern University Press, 1991), 243–78.

18. Cited in Dienke Hondius, "The Holocaust and Us," *Reconstruction* 2, no. 3 (1994): 95.

19. Frances Goodrich and Albert Hackett, *The Diary of Anne Frank* (New York: Random House, 1956), 174.

20. Undated, four-page letter of solicitation from Miles Lerman, chairman, United States Holocaust Memorial Museum.

21. Estelle Gilson, "Americanizing the Holocaust," *Congress Monthly,* September–October 1993, 6.

22. Michael Berenbaum, *After Tragedy and Triumph: Essays in Modern Jewish Thought and the American Experience* (Cambridge: Cambridge University Press, 1990), 22.

23. Berenbaum, *After Tragedy and Triumph,* 20.

24. "Crowds Strain U.S. Museum on Holocaust," *New York Times,* December 23, 1993. The quoted words are attributed to Naomi Paiss, onetime director of communications at the museum.

25. These aims are set forth in a Simon Wiesenthal Center–Museum of Tolerance promotional brochure.

26. Judy Chicago, *Holocaust Project: From Darkness into Light,* with photography by Donald Woodman (New York: Penguin, 1993).

27. Chicago, *Holocaust Project,* 36.

28. Chicago, *Holocaust Project,* 37; brackets in the original text.

29. Chicago, *Holocaust Project,* 9–10.

30. Chicago, *Holocaust Project,* 19.

31. Chicago, *Holocaust Project,* 62

32. Chicago, *Holocaust Project,* 27, 31.

33. Chicago, *Holocaust Project,* 90.

34. Chicago, *Holocaust Project*, 138.

35. Chicago, *Holocaust Project*, 139.

36. Chicago, *Holocaust Project*, 132.

37. Quoted in "ADL Hits Christian Fundamentalists," *The Forward*, June 10, 1994.

38. Raul Hilberg, *Perpetrators, Victims, Bystanders: The Jewish Catastrophe, 1933–1945* (New York: HarperCollins, 1992).

39. Hilberg, *Perpetrators, Victims, Bystanders*, ix.

40. The American Jewish Committee studies referred to in note 1 indicate that Americans acquire their information about World War II and the Holocaust chiefly from television programs. It is not uncommon today for popular television and radio talk shows to "debate" the reality of the Holocaust by featuring a "revisionist" and a "survivor" presenting what is commonly understood to be their respective "views." These programs reach large audiences, who seem drawn by the sensational and the controversial, but to what effect, we do not know. Inasmuch as these popular "debates" pit neo-Nazi "deniers" against Jewish "survivor/witnesses," they recapitulate the fundamental aggression of the Holocaust itself.

41. William Helmreich, *Against All Odds: Holocaust Survivors and the Successful Lives They Made in America* (New York: Simon and Schuster, 1992), 38.

42. The Fortunoff Video Archives for Holocaust Testimonies at Yale University has been engaged in filming the testimonies of Holocaust survivors for a number of years and is a major resource of its kind. At least two books have already been produced on the basis of these archival holdings: Lawrence Langer, *Holocaust Testimonies: The Ruins of Memory* (New Haven: Yale University Press, 1991) and Shoshana Felman and Dori Laub, *Testimony: Crises of Witnessing in Literature, Psychoanalysis, and History* (New York: Routledge, 1992). In addition, Steven Spielberg has established a foundation whose purpose is to record and videotape the testimonies of tens of thousands of Holocaust survivors.

43. Leon Uris, foreword to Ernst Michel, *Promises to Keep* (New York: Barricade Books, 1994), xiii.

44. For more on the Bitburg affair, see Geoffrey Hartman, ed., *Bitburg in Moral and Political Perspective* (Bloomington: Indiana University Press, 1986).

45. With assistance provided by some of these institutes, much work has been done over the years in introducing the Holocaust into the curricula of American secondary schools, and a number of states now mandate that such study be required of all of their students. In Michigan alone, for instance, over one hundred schools have adopted a well-regarded text on the Holocaust produced by Sidney Bolkosky, Betty Rotberg Ellias, and David Harris, *Life Unworthy of Life: A Holocaust Curriculum* (Farmington Hills, MI: Center for the Study of the Child, 1987). Other states employ other texts, not all of which stand up as well to critical scrutiny. In this regard, see Lucy Dawidowicz's "How They Teach the Holocaust," *Commentary*, December 1990, 25–32.

46. Stephen Schiff, "Seriously Spielberg," *New Yorker*, March 21, 1994; Terrence Rafferty, "A Man of Transactions," *New Yorker*, December 20, 1993; the Katzenberg encomium is quoted in the Schiff article.

47. James Bowman, "Lost and Profound," *American Spectator*, February 1994; J. Hoberman, "Spieilberg's Oskar," *Village Voice*, December 21, 1993; Donald Kuspit, "Director's Guilt," *Artforum*, February 1994; and Claude Lanzmann, "The Twisted Truth of *Schindler's List*," *Evening Standard* (London), February 10, 1994.

48. Since the appearance of the film, Oskar Schindler's grave in the Latin Cemetery of Jerusalem has become a popular site for pilgrims visiting Israel. In addition, tourists can visit Poland on monthly tours called "Oskar Schindler's Poland." See Jack Schneidler, "The Ghosts of Poland's Past," *St. Petersburg Times,* October 9, 1994.

49. Michael Andre Bernstein, "The *Schindler's List* Effect," *American Scholar* 63 (1994): 429–32.

50. Eva Fogelman, *Conscience and Courage: Rescue of Jews during the Holocaust* (New York: Anchor Doubleday, 1994), xix, 3.

51. A lengthy and critically perceptive review of the literature on "rescuers" is David Gushee's "Many Paths to Righteousness: An Assessment of Research on Why Righteous Gentiles Helped Jews," *Holocaust and Genocide Studies* 7 (1993): 372–401.

52. See, for instance, Elinor J. Brecher, *Schindler's Legacy: True Stories of the List Survivors* (New York: Penguin, 1994).

53. Fogelman, *Conscience and Courage,* xix.

54. Yosef Abramowitz, "Is Elie Wiesel Happy?" *Moment,* February 1994, 32–37, 78. The article is accompanied by photographs of Wiesel kissing his wife, bantering with a friend, and, to really make its point in unambiguously American fashion, posing with a baseball. It includes lines like these: "Elie Wiesel has not merely survived, he has triumphed. And if he would pause long enough to consider it, he might even say he's happy" (32). Anyone who has read Wiesel's brooding and deeply melancholy novel, *The Forgotten* (1992), will have a hard time imagining its author as the same person profiled as "happy" in Abramowitz's article.

55. See Dennis Klein, "The Exceptional Intervention," *Dimensions* 3, no. 3 (1988): 3.

56. Fogelman, *Conscience and Courage,* 301.

57. Harold M. Schulweis, "The Bias against Man," *Dimensions* 3, no. 3 (1988): 4, 5.

58. Harold M. Schulweis, *For Those Who Can't Believe* (New York: HarperCollins, 1994), 150.

59. Schulweis, "The Bias against Man," 5.

60. Schulweis, "The Bias against Man," 4, 6, 8.

61. Schulweis, *Those Who Can't Believe,* 148–49.

62. André Schwarz-Bart, *The Last of the Just,* trans. Stephen Becker (New York: Atheneum, 1961), 374. For a brief but illuminating history of the Jewish folk legend of the "just men," see Gershom Scholem, "The Tradition of the Thirty-Six Hidden Just Men," in *The Messianic Idea in Judaism and Other Essays on Jewish Spirituality* (New York: Schocken, 1971), 251–56.

63. Schulweis, *Those Who Can't Believe,* 157.

64. Fogelman, *Comcience and Courage,* 303.

65. The authors of "What Do Americans Know about the Holocaust?" and "Holocaust Denial: What the Survey Data Reveal" are in agreement about the knowledge level of Americans regarding the Holocaust and conclude that it is generally "shallow, incomplete, and imperfect." In their informed view, "Holocaust ignorance is widespread." Smith, "Holocaust Denial," 3, 22.

66. Aharon Appelfeld, *Beyond Despair* (New York: Fromm, 1994), xiii.

67. John A. O'Brien, foreword to Philip Friedman, *Their Brothers' Keepers* (1957; New York: Holocaust Library, 1978), 7–8.

Jedediah Smith Redwoods State Park, California, 1986. Courtesy of Bill Aron.

Before "The Holocaust": American Jews Confront Catastrophe, 1945–62

Hasia R. Diner

In the decade and a half following the end of World War II, that global conflagration which brought about the death of one-third of the Jewish people and the destruction of much of European Jewish communal life, American Jewry found many times, places, and modes of expression to articulate its intense reactions to that calamity. While historians may find it difficult, if not nearly impossible, to re-create the ways in which individual Jews talked about this catastrophic event in their homes or how they incorporated direct references and analogies to it into the discourse of their private spheres of everyday life, Jewish institutions—synagogues, schools, summer camps, publishing houses, magazines, and newspapers—left an easily recoverable paper trail that reveals a community that felt itself obliged to remember and commemorate. These formal institutions of American Jewish life, spanning a spectrum of ideologies and political positions vis-à-vis the concerns of the day, wove the details of the catastrophe into their rhetorical repertoires and used references to it to shape their political projects.

The ways in which they "used" the calamity of European Jewry, referred to consistently in the copious material produced in Yiddish as the *hurban,* or destruction, reflected the concerns and sensibilities of their times. From the perspective of the early twenty-first century with its ubiquitous invocations of the Holocaust and the widespread, highly public impress of that European event on the American landscape, the postwar references and performances of American Jews may seem oblique and wan. Such compar-

This essay was originally presented on March 17, 2004, at the Jean and Samuel Frankel Center for Judaic Studies, University of Michigan, Ann Arbor.

isons, however, should be seen as ahistorical and lacking sensitivity to the project that confronted American Jewry in the years after the war.

At the most simple level of analysis, the postwar memorial texts reflected the concerns, language, and sensibilities of the postwar period, while the memorial activities that predominated a half century later took on the vocabulary and values of a very different time. The two Jewries differed in so many other ways that looking for consistency in Holocaust memorial practice would be akin to looking for consistency in their treatment of gender issues.

The Jews of the United States emerged in 1945 from the trauma of World War II confronting a new reality. The United States had become the only large, organized, functioning center of Jewish life as a result of the brutal liquidation of six million Jews in Europe. The memorial texts and performances that American Jews created for their schools, synagogues, and community centers, as well as those that they crafted to share with their non-Jewish neighbors, represented experiments in expression.

These postwar American Jews had to create a culture of commemoration from scratch in the context of a global Jewish world that through the early 1960s lived with the aftershocks of the catastrophe. They had no precedent or example to follow as they took the first steps toward creating ceremonies, texts, graphic images, and music to remember what had just transpired. At school, synagogue, and community board meetings, they struggled to find the best, most appropriate, and most effective means by which to remember the victims, confront the perpetrators, and salvage the lives of the survivors. They made direct linkages between the memorial objects and practices that they fashioned and some of the political events that continued to rattle world Jewry as a result of Nazi brutality. As such, comparisons between the Holocaust projects of the early twenty-first century and those of the mid-twentieth century do little to further historical understanding of how a group of people—American Jews—at a particular moment—the years 1945 through 1962—went about the process of shaping their public to an event—the mass murder of six million European Jews—that affected them deeply but which few of them had lived through.

In the years from the cessation of hostilities and the defeat of Nazi Germany in 1945 until 1962 when the capture, trial, and execution of Adolf Eichmann made the Holocaust a matter of broad political commentary beyond the confines of the Jewish community, the Jews of the United States created works of liturgy, pageantry, drama, imaginative literature, sermons, pedagogical material, graphic arts, and scholarship to describe the catastrophe that had so recently engulfed their people. The testimonies of those who had endured the Nazi onslaught found their way into the pages of Jewish publications, onto the airwaves of Jewish radio programs, and into books, including those designed to memorialize the towns and regions of Europe where Jews once lived but no longer did. American Jews from across the political, denominational, class, and geographic spectrum wrote about the tragedy of European Jewry and its implications for the Jews of the United States, in newspapers, magazines, newsletters, books, articles, press releases, and the publications of Jewish organizations, written in English, Yiddish, and Hebrew. They used the mass media, radio and television, to broadcast to themselves and to their American neighbors aspects of their recent tragic history.

In the process of creating a series of texts, both in print and on the air, in which they described themselves to other Americans, they felt impelled to invoke the mass murder of the Jews of Europe. Although they themselves had lived so far from the scenes of suffering, they used the details of those horrific years to narrate their own American story. They also used imagery of the Nazi horrors to make a number of political points about their place in America, about the Jews as a global people, and about America as a civilization, which they, at one and the same time, embraced but sought to change. Their uses of the details of the slaughter, as specific fact and as analogy, went beyond the boundaries of the Jewish community. Their rhetorical repertoire of those years as they addressed the larger American public, including those who held the reins of power as well as the general public, included references, direct and indirect, to the Nazi assault on European Jewry.

In the late twentieth century Americans, Jews and non-Jews, became familiar with and accustomed to films, books, plays, museums, memorial markers, and other kinds of cultural works dealing with the Holocaust. The terminology of the Holocaust entered the contemporary lexicon and came to be used by advocates of many causes for a multitude of political and cultural purposes. Within the ranks of American Jewry, the Holocaust served as a powerful icon representing group membership, and leaders of nearly all Jewry's many segments marshaled it in hopes of achieving some particular end. What came to be called "Holocaust consciousness" continues in the first decade of the twenty-first century to function as a key element in the culture of American Jews, intended for general consumption as much as for identity-building enterprises within.

An American Jewish culture, shaped, in part, by this Jewish tragedy and current political concerns, emerged in the immediate years after World War II, especially in the 1950s. In politics, religion, the arts, philanthropy, and pedagogy, postwar American Jews set the terms for the contemporary memorial culture. From the late 1940s through the early 1960s, when the term *Holocaust* had not yet become the conventional way to name this tragedy and when American Jews did not see it as history but as the past present, they began the process of creating a culture of memory, which has grown with time but which has not changed substantially.

Yet, according to the regnant scholarship and indeed to a broad American Jewish consensus, none of this happened. Historians and other commentators, from within the Jewish world and from without, have with near-unanimity agreed that American Jews, in the aftermath of the war, did not articulate any deep sense of anguish nor engage in acts of public mourning. They did not, according to this unquestioned assumption about the past, use the Holocaust in the 1950s in the pursuit of their political and social agenda, except, according to one group of historians, to invoke the horrors of Nazism in order to fit into the culture of cold war American anticommunism. In particular, the leaders of the major defense organizations twinned the evils of Nazism and Communism, creating, these historians have asserted, a rhetorical trope depicting a generalized kind of totalitarianism without specifically Jewish victims, a move that allowed American Jews to participate in the anticommunist frenzy of the postwar period.[1]

The silence of American Jews, their unwillingness, disinterest, or inability to talk about the Nazi catastrophe in their communal institutions and in the rhetoric they crafted for the broader American public, functions as one of the key "truths" of the overall narrative of American Jewish history. Scholars have attributed great significance to the fact that postwar American Jews did not include the Holocaust in their communal culture. That silence, they have claimed, revealed much about the particular political position and cultural project of American Jewry.

Few have found this silence particularly impressive. Statements about American Jews' refusal to memorialize the European catastrophe or their embarrassment about invoking it in public have been cast in decidedly negative terms, laden with direct or implied condemnations of those who went about their lives in the emerging affluence of the 1950s without any nod whatsoever to the recent horrors. The assertion that postwar Jews kept silent, speaking only privately and furtively about the tragedy, is not just a scholarly paradigm but also a broadly accepted communal belief spanning otherwise deep political divides within the American Jewish world.[2]

Were it in fact true that American Jews in the postwar period failed to remember, recall, and invoke the European tragedy of their people, they would indeed merit the opprobrium of later generations. Had they not fused the legacy of that event with a series of political actions, later generations would be justified in viewing the behavior of their predecessors of a half century earlier as tellingly significant.

But the widely accepted belief that a culture of memorialization did not develop in the postwar period and the sweeping interpretations attached to this belief have been built on sand. The conclusions of historians, as well as popular beliefs, rest on little evidence—in stark contrast to the troves of empirical data to be found in archives, newspapers, and other primary sources, which historians, at least, must consult before interpreting what happened and how.

American Jews, in fact, as creators of texts and leaders of institutions, produced a large corpus of projects in nearly every medium available in those years referring to, representing, and lamenting the horrors of the Nazi era. In these works, in words and images, in artistic endeavors and political projects, they made amply clear that Jews had been the victims, that the Germans had perpetrated a crime upon the Jewish people, the chief victims, although millions of others had suffered as well, and that the implications of the slaughter had left an indelible mark on world Jewry. Every segment of Jewish opinion or ideology, every language group—Anglophones, Yiddish-speakers, and committed Hebraists—used its tongue of choice to articulate its anguish and its sense of the obligation to remember. While each group expressed its feelings differently and derived particular lessons from the horrors, they agreed on what had happened—the Germans and their allies had slaughtered millions of Jews, about one-third of the Jewish people—and that that wholesale liquidation destroyed full communities and cultures and violently brought into being a new era in Jewish history.

How can we account for the vast chasm between the reality that American Jews created a staggeringly large repertoire of works invoking the catastrophe and the thrust of scholarship and commentary maintaining that such acts of memorialization never took place? What forces have operated to blind historians to the existence of such material, available in plain sight, ready to be analyzed?

The fullest explanation of the disjunction between the easily retrievable evidence and the prevailing orthodoxy, which takes for granted that such sources do not exist, requires two scholarly projects. One, the larger, must uncover, array, and analyze the broad range of Jewish texts created in the period 1945 to 1962 that fully or partially dealt with the European catastrophe. These texts include those constructed of words to be read or heard in American Jewry's three languages, English, Yiddish, and Hebrew, directed at adults and at children. Some texts that depicted the concentration camps and ghettoes, the victims and the villains, used graphic images, ink on paper, paint on canvas, black-and-white photographs, stained glass, marble and granite, while yet others relied upon music, composed for use in synagogues, community centers, schools, and concert halls. All these must be displayed and analyzed as evidence to demonstrate that America's Jews in the postwar era did not feel obliged or able to refrain from paying respect to their recent calamity. The second aspect of the project asks why this body of material disappeared. Why did historians from within and without the Jewish world, from the Left and from the Right, as well as communal activists, construct the truth of American Jewish postwar "Holocaust avoidance"? This second focus, then, must probe the historiography and the evolution of the communal commentary and explain how and why a particular rendition of the past—one that in fact deviated radically from the empirical evidence—triumphed in airbrushing out of existence the cultural works of American Jewry in the crucial years between the end of World War II, with its ghastly revelations, and the execution of Adolf Eichmann in 1962.

Experiments in Expression

American Jews in these years produced a mountain of texts highlighting the European Jewish calamity. Some circulated exclusively, or nearly so, within the confines of the Jewish world. While they would have eluded the eyes of non-Jews, they infused American Jewish life. Because writers, journalists, radio program producers, and performers created much of this material in Yiddish, the memorial culture served a distinctly inner Jewish purpose. These years saw a massive journalistic outpouring in the Yiddish press, in Yiddish memoirs, fiction, and essays, all consumed by a Yiddish-reading public. The late 1940s saw the first publication of *yizkor bikher*—memorial books—compiled by both the survivors of the calamity and their compatriots who had left their towns and cites before the storm. Published by committees of those who had experienced the *hurban* themselves and those who had sat out those grim years in the United States, Canada, South America, South Africa, and Palestine, the memorial books of the postwar period included vignettes of life before the catastrophe, black-bordered pages listing the names of the murdered, as well as photographs of notable places that had been leveled and of the men and women who had lived there and went to their deaths at the hands of the Nazis. These volumes circulated almost exclusively among Jews with ties to the particular place being memorialized. But Jewish books that circulated nationally, like the *American Jewish Yearbook*, published by the American Jewish Committee, and the *Jewish Book Annual*, listed the names of newly published *yizker bikher* and thus disseminated information about the memorial projects to American Jews who otherwise might not even have known the names of the towns being mourned.

Although written in English, some Holocaust texts functioned exclusively within the boundaries of the American Jewish world. Starting immediately at the end of the war, Holocaust material found its way into prayer books and material fashioned for synagogues, Jewish community centers, Jewish youth organizations, and religious schools. A good deal of this material served a memorial purpose. As liturgy or pageantry, as physical marker or printed memorial book, these documents recalled to memory the Jewish people slaughtered by the Germans and their allies. They resembled Jewish memorial materials created out of other earlier catastrophes in Jewish history, and invoked images and metaphors of the Jewish past of suffering and bravery.[3]

At the same time, though, American Jews created texts for the consumption of a broader audience, including non-Jews as well as Jews. Books of fiction and nonfiction, which were published by mainstream publishing houses and marketed and distributed like other books, made it possible for the idiom of the destruction to filter into the larger American world. A few examples of this will have to suffice. In 1954, Viking, one of the country's largest and most prestigious publishers, brought out Irving Howe and Eliezer Greenberg's *A Treasury of Yiddish Stories*, which bore the dedication "To the Six Million." To Greenberg and Howe the history of Yiddish literature as represented by these stories could not be disassociated from the fact that "the world of the East European Jews came to its end in the ashes of Maidenek and Auschwitz—at the time and place, that is, when Western civilization collapsed," nor, they declared, could the stories be read without an awareness that "Zionism and Socialism came to attract the best young minds; and then came the century of Maidenek and Auschwitz." For each short story written by a victim of the Nazi horror, Howe and Greenberg duly noted the horrific fate of the author.[4]

Philip Bernstein, like many rabbis of the postwar period, wrote brief introductions to Judaism for lay audiences, Jews and non-Jews. He peppered his *What the Jews Believe,* published by Farrar, Straus and Young in 1951, with dozens of references to the Holocaust. In describing the fall holiday of Sukkot, for example, he noted that "the Nazis, according to the survivors of the concentration camps, derived exquisite joy from cruelty." Yet, Bernstein wrote, survivors he encountered at a displaced persons camp in Babehausen, Germany, told him that they found ways to celebrate. Bernstein described a memorial service at Feldafing, another DP camp, where "nearly every worshipper grieved for the loss of most of his family. The rabbi, himself a mourner, offered no easy consolation." And in praise of American Jewry and its response to the catastrophe, Bernstein detailed its financial assistance, which in 1948 saw the United Jewish Appeal raise more money than the Red Cross. The purpose of the money—"to save the survivors of the Nazi onslaught"—made it clear that in Bernstein's mind the events of the Nazi era had become inextricably bound up with the project of explaining "what the Jews believe."[5]

More dramatically, Leon Uris's blockbuster novel *Exodus* dominated best-seller lists for weeks, reaching a far larger public. While the book focused on the struggle of the Jews in Palestine for a state of their own, it also devoted attention to the experiences of the death camp survivors, whose blistering encounters with "the memories [that] would never leave" transformed them into recruits for the nationalist enterprise. Much of the *Exodus* narrative emerged from the memories of Dov Landau, who, sitting in a displaced persons camp in Cyprus, asked himself, "When had he been outside of barbed wire? It was so very long ago it was hard to remember. Barbed wire, guns, soldiers—was there a real life beyond them?" From this point on the novel needed Dov's story of the dehumanization of the Jews in sites of Nazi brutality in order to tell that of the heroic battle for the Jewish state. As Uris told his millions of readers about Dov, "As he looked at his arm with the blue tattooed number he relived the grotesque second when the doors of the gas chamber were flung open. Time and time and time again he saw his mother and his sister Ruth being removed from such a chamber at Treblinka. Time and time again he held that flickering candle close to the smothering bodies in the bunker in the Warsaw ghetto. . . . Over and over again he saw the skulls the Germans used as paperweights as his mother and his sister."[6]

Texts like these operated in a twofold manner, addressing both Jews and non-Jews in the same document, and linked private Jewish mourning with the larger reading public. They demonstrated that Jews, creating cultural works in the postwar period, did not necessarily shy away from invoking the European calamity, even when those books were issued by major publishing houses.

While much of the material produced in the decade and a half after the end of World War II served to recall and to remember, other texts on the Holocaust served more complicated, political ends linked to the exigencies of the postwar moment. American Jews produced vast amounts of Holocaust-related material to help raise money for refugees and assist in their resettlement, to pressure the governments of the United States, the Federal Republic of Germany, and other European nations to provide financial restitution and reparations to the Jewish victims of the Nazi crimes, to monitor the resurgence of Nazism in Germany and elsewhere in the world, to ensure that Nazi perpetrators were brought to justice, to facilitate family reunification and the return of Jewish children who had been placed in Christian institutions to save them and who had not yet been restored to their families, even ten years after the war, and finally to support the creation and sustenance of Israel. American Jews spent the decade and a half following the end of World War II picking up the pieces in the wake of the Holocaust, and in doing so told and retold what happened. They did not fail to note how much this event represented a tectonic shift in Jewish history. For example, every volume of the *American Jewish Yearbook* published in these years told in great detail about projects and programs of American and world Jewry vis-à-vis the political aftershocks of the Holocaust. These annual reference works, which the American Jewish Committee sent gratis to public officials around the country, described pointedly how the destruction of European Jewry had created a set of political crises—in the United States, Western Europe, Eastern Europe, South America, and Israel— and the reference books, dry as they might seem from their covers, made abundantly clear to anyone who read them, that into the early 1960s the Holocaust continued to reverberate in the lives of the Jewish people.[7]

Additionally, as American Jews participated in some of the momentous events of the late 1940s, 1950s, and early 1960s, most notably the flowering of the American civil rights movement and the frightening unfolding of the cold war, they produced and used texts that foregrounded the cruelties of the Nazis and their systematic slaughter of the Jews of Europe. As they confronted a series of political events in the United States, for example, the battle over prayer in public schools and the nagging issue of the need to reform immigration policy, American Jewish organizations and publications invoked events in Europe in the 1930s and 1940s as relevant metaphors and analogies.

Assembling this material has been for me an exhilarating detective process and one that is far from complete. Seeking the ways American Jews referred to the Holocaust in these years and invoked it for one purpose or another has taken me into nearly every possible corner of the American Jewish world of the middle of the twentieth century. It has allowed me to look into the texts and practices of Orthodox, Conservative, Reform, and Reconstructionist Judaism. It has brought me into Hebrew, Yiddish, and English materials created by secular as well as religious groups, intellectuals and communal workers, pedagogues and youth group leaders. I have looked at material from the American Jewish Left and the Zionist movement, as well as that produced by establishment groups like the American Jewish Committee. I have looked at national and local bodies, at individuals acting on their own and those representing formal organizations and institutions. Let me offer just a few examples of the places where American Jews talked about, performed, and used the Holocaust in these years.

American Judaism of the late 1940s, 1950s, and early 1960s functioned as a complex of denominations, synagogues, and seminaries. This era in fact represented the high point of synagogue affiliation, and although many rabbis and intellectuals decried what they considered the shallowness of the "religious revival" of these years, much of organized American Jewish life revolved around the congregations. These years saw the creation of new texts linking the practice of the Jewish religion to the horrors of Nazi Germany. In 1948, the Reconstructionist movement published its first high-holiday prayer book, while the Conservative movement issued its in 1951. Both *mahzorim* used the Yom Kippur martyrology liturgy to memorialize the Jews who perished in Europe. In the Reconstructionist *mahzor,* the editors, who considered themselves free to tamper with traditional texts, replaced the conventional Hebrew words of the *eleh ezkerah* (these I shall remember), a lengthy paean to ten rabbis tortured and executed by the Romans for their refusal to obey a ban on the teaching of Torah and the ordaining of disciples, with a poem by Hannah Senesh, a young Hungarian Jewish woman who had emigrated to Palestine but then parachuted back into Hungary as a soldier. Captured and killed by the Nazis, Senesh and her poetry lived on in this prayer book. Additionally a "Tribute to the Martyrs of the Bialystok Ghetto" became part of the Yom Kippur prayer cycle in the Reconstructionist text.[8] The Conservative *mahzor,* in a way typical of the movement's attitude toward liturgical innovation, kept the *eleh ezkerah* but in English appended a poetic reading, "To Our Six Million."[9]

In the fall of 1958, proponents of modern Orthodoxy, associated particularly with Yeshiva University, launched a new publication, *Tradition: A Journal of Orthodox Jewish Thought,* edited by Norman Lamm. Lamm justified the enterprise ("The Need for Tradition") with its double meaning in terms of "changes on the world scene that have caused, particularly in America, a perceptible reorientation vis-à-vis Orthodoxy in the total Jewish community. The horrors of the Hitler era have profoundly shaken man's confidence in the beneficent use of the power he has gotten. The creation of the State of Israel has done more than give all Jews a collective pride in their people. It has also given them a sense of rootedness in the long history that gave birth to the little bit of Middle Eastern geography." Not only did *Tradition* present itself as growing out of a new Jewish world shaped by the Holocaust, but it filled its pages with articles, book reviews, and references to the Nazi horrors. As befitted an Orthodox journal that took Jewish law as fundamental, it notified its readers of rabbinic rulings that reflected Jewry's ongoing encounter with the Holocaust. In 1960, for example, it reported on a *halakhic* ruling involving human skin. *Tradition* told of "a *Kohen* [a member of the priestly class] who has received books from Germany which are bound in the skin of concentration camp victims." The ruling, delivered by Rabbi Moshe Feinstein and discussed in the journal, stated emphatically that the recipient "may not bring them into his home because he is not permitted to defile himself by contact with any part of a corpse. He is also not permitted to sell them to anyone. He must bury the binding because it is part of a human body."[10]

Within the world of Orthodox Judaism, the sermon was a relatively recent innovation. Historically the absence of English-language sermons functioned as a hallmark of traditional congregations. In the 1940s, American Orthodox congregations began to incorporate what they previously viewed as a modernist deviation, and in the middle of World War II the Rabbinical Council of America began to publish annual collections of exemplary holiday and Sabbath sermons delivered by its members. Distributed presumably so other rabbis could draw on this material for their own sermons, the sermon anthologies referred repeatedly to the details of the recent calamity. Rabbi Solomon Roodman referred to it in his Purim *drash* (homily) of 1957, "Why the Jew Laughs," noting that "the most trenchant example of the true spirit of Jewish humor and unyielding faith which it motivates was confirmed by the many discoveries made in the ghettoes and extermination centers of Nazi Europe. Search teams which had visited those areas after the Nazis were brought to their knees discovered thousands of capsules containing manuscripts left by the victims of Nazidom." In a 1952 Passover sermon, "Here the Child Asks," Rabbi Moses Mescheloff stated: "The ancient Talmud legend of the salvation of the Jewish children is more than a hoary episode out of the past of our people. We, we in our own time have witnessed its repetition. Is it not the identical act that the Nazis committed against our youth? Did not the Nazis pursue our youth bereft of parental protection throughout Europe seeking their extermination? Did not our children hide in forests and caverns to escape their brutal persecutors? . . . With my own eyes have I seen such children. There are tens of thousands of them in Israel this very day. There are those with blue tattoo marks, mementos of the concentration camp, and those who escaped even this stamp of modern Egypt. They have been gathered together out of the impossible, impassable wastelands in Europe . . . brought back to Israel."[11]

The Reform movement did not issue new prayer books in these years, but in 1948, when the Hebrew Union College opened its School for Sacred Music, the first school founded in the United States to train cantors, it declared that its creations grew out of the movement's awareness that "the disappearance of the great centers of Jewish culture and learning in Europe during the occupation by the Nazi horde has posed many serious problems for world Jewry. . . . Among other things, the inspiration for Jewish sacred music has dried up in Europe, and we must look to other centers of Jewish life to fill the void."[12] This creative use of the destruction reverberated in Reform congregations through the 1950s. In 1957, Rabbi Louis I. Newman of New York's Reform congregation Rodeph Shalom published a book of plays and cantatas that he had written and staged in his congregation. *Pangs of the Messiah: A Play of World War II* won second place in a national contest sponsored by AZA (Aleph Zadik Aleph), the B'nai B'rith Youth Organization. It explored the reactions of a group of Jews in the eastern war zone as the Nazis entered their town. The trapped Jews debate among themselves what to do—to fight, to submit, to pray—in the face of the Nazi menace; the play comes to a close with an impassioned oration of the rabbi, who links the particular Jewish crisis faced by his townspeople with some universal human dilemmas: "Every people, all humanity must learn to be its own Messiah. . . . And we . . . are the people who must labor also for the coming of the Messianic days. The torments and horrors we are enduring—these may truly be the pangs of the Messiah." Another play in the Newman anthology, *Ein Breirah: No Alternative,* declaimed that "out of the camps of desolation, the flaming Ghettos of the cities, was born the saga of fortitude unto death." Newman's member chorus then sang the "Song of the Partisans," a "Vilna Ghetto song."[13]

The linking of the *hurban* with the practice of Jewish ritual took place outside of strictly denominational projects. In 1957, for example, Meyer Waxman, Sulamith Ish-Kishor, and Jacob Sloan collaborated to produce a gift book, *Blessed Is the Daughter,* for girls on the occasion of their bat mitzvah. The book graced the shelves of Jewish bookstores and was widely advertised in Jewish magazines. In it the authors depicted the cycle of the Jewish year. They included "The Day of Carnage," that is, the tenth day of the month of Tevet, a day that linked the beginning of the siege of Jerusalem by the Babylonians in 588 B.C.E. to the slaughter of six million Jews by the Nazis during the Second World War. The destruction of the great eastern and central European Jewish civilizations was the culminating tragedy of the process begun by the Babylonians 2,600 years ago. The text describing *Assarah be'Tevet* included a photograph of the Israeli chief rabbi, Dr. Isaac Herzog, planting the first tree in the Forest of the Six Million Martyrs. For Simhat Torah, the fall holiday marking the end of the liturgical year and the start of a new cycle of the reading of the Torah, Waxman and the other editors offered a story, "The Last Dance," depicting the last Simhat Torah in Warsaw, which came from an already published Holocaust memoir, the diary of a young boy, Hillel Seidman. They also included a reading about two girls, Chajke and Frumke, who served as couriers for the Jewish underground, their life stories drawn from Emmanuel Ringelblum's "monumental contemporary record" of the Warsaw ghetto, published by McGraw-Hill; a portrait of Hannah Senesh; and a historical account of the "Catastrophe in Europe" when "six million Jews of Europe—more than one-third of all the Jews in the world—had been slaughtered by the Germans under Hitler." Finally, despite the brevity of the volume and the festive occasion for which the authors intended it, they also included a poem by Marie Syrkin, an American Zionist leader, "The Silent Army," focusing on the newly created State of Israel, in which she exhorted a solemn host of six million to "bear the flame" of fighting for the Jewish state.[14]

A few more random examples of Holocaust memorialization from the enormous corpus will have to suffice here, perhaps as tantalizing foretastes of what will be a book-length study. Songbooks, designed for youth group and Jewish community center song sessions, routinely included songs like

"Ani Ma'amin" and "The Song of the Partisans," music associated with the ghettoes and concentration camps. All the songsters made clear in introducing the songs that the words and music had been drawn from the Jewish repertoire of the Nazi era. Ruth Rubin's *A Treasury of Jewish Folksongs* (1950) included these same songs of the partisans, described them in detail, and placed them in their Holocaust-era context. In her introduction she told her readers—and singers—that "in the dark years of the Nazi domination of Europe, a host of songs arose that record the heroic struggle of the Jewish people against the German overlord."[15]

In 1954, a number of popular books on American Jewish history appeared that connected the history of American Jews with the recent calamity. Elma Ehrlich Levinger's *Jewish Adventures in America: The Story of 300 Years of Jewish Life in the United States*, for example, found multiple ways to link the story of the catastrophe with her larger, celebratory narrative. In a biographical treatment of the philanthropist Nathan Straus, for example, she noted: "He gave large sums for the relief of those who suffered from the First World War. His death spared him the knowledge of the horrors of the Hitler persecution and of another conflict even more terrible than the last." She devoted a lengthy section to the efforts of American Jews to rescue the Jews of Europe as the shadow of Nazism fell over them—"American Jews to the Rescue"—and an equally full one to the postwar philanthropic juggernaut of American Jews. "There had never been such an appeal before." Likewise, she described Rabbi Stephen Wise as someone "who lived to see the persecution of Hitler which doomed six million Jews to death." Her popular historical account of American Jewry made it clear that in the mid-1950s, in a book published by a Jewish publishing house and intended for a primarily Jewish readership, American Jewish history, however upbeat and positive, could not be disassociated from the history of an era in which "six million Jews, not only those of German birth but . . . from German-conquered territory, perished in cattle cars, in concentration camps and crematoria."[16]

When American Jewry celebrated its tricentenary in 1954, it also took steps to commemorate the Holocaust. That year a committee formed in New York to create a Passover reading, entitled "A Seder of Remembrance." Initiated by the American Jewish Congress, the committee, which was headed by the writer and communal activist Rufus Learsi, became independent, and over the next few years annually distributed thousands of copies of the English and Hebrew text through Jewish community councils, synagogues, and other organizations. The committee also placed full-page copies of the bilingual text in dozens of American Jewish newspapers around the country every spring in anticipation of Passover. Dedicated to the memory of "the six million of our brothers of the European exile," who had been slaughtered "by a tyrant, more wicked than the Pharaoh who enslaved our forefathers in the land of Egypt," the short piece described the Nazis as "the evil ones," whose brutality "defamed the image of God in which man was created." The seder night had particular resonance for creators of this and other Holocaust texts. On the first night of Passover 1943, the "remnants of the Warsaw Ghetto" had risen up "to slay their oppressors as they were about to be slain." The reading, which was much used, judging by the large number of letters sent to the committee, depicted the survivors of the concentration camps and ghettos as people who emerged from their trauma still able to envision a day "when justice and brotherhood would reign among men."[17]

In a not dissimilar vein, Louis Ruchames, a Reform rabbi who was Hillel director for western Massachusetts, and a historian who specialized in African American history, addressed the Grand Street Boy's Club during Negro History Week in February 1955. Its members were men who had grown up on New York's Lower East Side, moved away, done well, and maintained a lively interest in the "old neighborhood." Ruchames spoke to them in part to mark the tercentenary of Jewish settlement in America, choosing as his topic "Parallels of Jewish and Negro History." His speech, later republished in the *Bulletin of Negro History*, commented on the imperative that "we Jews" must understand the "problems which have confronted the Negro." To Ruchames the parallel suffering that linked the two peoples had very immediate resonance, since "in our day, the lesson that men have had to relearn in every generation, that the rights of all men are inter-related, that no minority group is safe while others are the victims of persecution[,] has been seared into our minds and hearts through the burning flesh of six million of our brethren in Europe."[18]

Ruchames's words straddled the Jewish and the non-Jewish world. Delivered to a Jewish audience to mark Negro History Week and the festivities of the tercentenary of Jewish settlement in North America, the speech then became an article for consumption by an audience composed primarily of African American readers. He, like the creators of the seder reading, effortlessly linked the utterly Jewish with the universal in the same text and evinced no embarrassment in making the Nazi holocaust a central element in Jewish self-consciousness.

In the mid-1950s, when Ruchames served as the Hillel rabbi at Smith

College, Jewish students at the elite women's school transformed a radio play, *The Ballad of the Warsaw Ghetto,* originally broadcast on the "Eternal Light" series sponsored by the Jewish Theological Seminary, into a cantata with words, music, and modern dance. After arranging for the presentation of *The Ballad of the Warsaw Ghetto* to the other students at Smith College, Ruchames presented the cantata at other Hillel chapters and B'nai B'rith lodges in a dozen small and medium-sized towns around Massachusetts. Here too, then, a text that memorialized the Nazi catastrophe served Jewish and non-Jewish audiences and demonstrated not the unwillingness of American Jews to present themselves through the medium of the Holocaust but their sense of urgency to do exactly that.

Finally, from April 10 to April 14, 1957, the American Jewish Committee sponsored a series of meetings, symposia, and lavish dinners at New York's Waldorf-Astoria Hotel to mark a half-century of its particular brand of Jewish advocacy, one that emphasized the mobilization of gentile Americans' goodwill, eschewed militant and overt calls to Jewish self-interest, and stressed behind-the-scenes negotiations. At the opening banquet, with Christian clergymen, government officials, presidents of major universities, and Secretary-General of the United Nations Dag Hammarskjold in attendance, the committee's former president Joseph Proskauer sounded the dominant tone of the jubilee meeting. "Our ethos," he stated, has been to foster "useful, valid, scholarly research into those causes which have operated to make Catholics murder Protestants, Protestants murder Catholics, and both, in turn, from time to time, murder Jews, until we saw its culmination in the Hitler holocaust." Proskauer referred to various kinds of group hatred, but only one form, anti-Semitism, he argued, fostered hatemongers to cross conventional barriers and only it culminated in a "holocaust." Otto Kleinberg, a professor of psychology at Columbia University and formerly head of UNESCO's Division of Applied Social Science (and a refugee from Nazi Germany), called on America to solve its race problem, in part, to allow it to forge positive relationships with the newly emerging nations of Africa. He explained the need for this in light of the fact that "at the time of World War II and preceding it, the internal situation in Germany made a very big difference to its relationship to the outside world. The German treatment of Jews and other minorities modified and transformed the relationships of Germany with the other countries." Kleinberg, who knew Nazism firsthand, asserted: "We, of course are not in anything like as serious a situation as Germany was [but] we do . . . face this problem of strengthening democracy at home in order to create a truly democratic

alliance abroad." Numerous other speakers invoked the Nazi nightmare. Israel's ambassador to the United Nations, Abba Eban, forcefully recalled
that only "ten years ago . . . we stood in anguish before the martyred graves
of six million of our kinsman"—"never in all recorded history had any
family of the human race been overwhelmed by such a tidal wave of grief
and havoc as that which engulfed the Jewish people in the . . . Second
World War." Finally, the assembled dignitaries heard the American Jewish
Committee's resolutions to mark this anniversary, one of which acknowledged the "vast changes that have taken place in the structure of Jewish
communities" since 1906, particularly "as a result of the holocaust of the
Hitler period," in which "the great historic Jewish communities of Europe
have been decimated." Other resolutions called upon West Germany to
make good on its restitution promises and to check the troubling rise of
"ultra-nationalistic and chauvinistic" groups, warning that "further political developments in West Germany will be subject to the test of history."
A resolution on Israel, about whose establishment the American Jewish
Committee had long been ambivalent, declared that "the State of Israel
was established nine years ago under the aegis of the United Nations. It has
become a place of refuge for hundreds of thousands of victims of Nazi . . .
persecutions."[19]

These scattered references are a handful of examples of how American
Jews used and referred to the Holocaust in the years before the mid-1960s.
Knowing that behind them there exists a trove many times larger of words,
objects, and performances that invoked the memory of the slain Jews and
that sought to remedy some aspect of its cataclysmic impact leads us to the
second part of this project, to explore the inability of historians and later
commentators to confront this material.

Erasing the Evidence

Scholars from a number of "schools" and cultural orientations have helped
create and sustain the scholarly "truth" that American Jews refrained from
thinking about or invoking the Holocaust in the postwar years. One group,
primarily on the left, claims that the late-twentieth (or early twenty-first)
century American Jewish emphasis on the Holocaust has been constructed
to serve a series of fundamentally conservative, and in their assessment, ne-
farious purposes. For example, Norman Finkelstein's *The Holocaust Industry*
has lambasted American Jews, their communal organizations, and leaders
for investing, "too much public and private resources . . . in memorializing

the Nazi genocide." He has claimed, furthermore, that "much of the output is worthless, a tribute not to Jewish suffering but to Jewish aggrandizement," seeing it as "crass exploitation," a way to push the world to support Israel, whom he considers unworthy of support or recognition.

His argument, like those of other critics of contemporary Holocaust culture, pivots on a perception of history, one that posits that in the postwar period Jews, like other Americans, "paid the Nazi holocaust little heed." Because of the "conformist policies of the American Jewish leadership and the political climate of postwar America," American Jews "hewed closely to official US policy," which emphasized the fostering of cultural assimilation. Since he believes that Israel did not then play an important role in American Jewry's political agenda, Finkelstein concludes that it had no need to use Holocaust imagery. Rather, he sees the period after the end of World War II as one in which Jews emphatically chose to de-emphasize the Holocaust because of the emerging struggle between the United States and the Soviet Union. Finkelstein gives particular weight to the fact that, "with the inception of the Cold War" in 1949 and West Germany's emergence as an American ally in the anticommunist struggle, Germany could not be vilified as the perpetrator of the horrendous crimes that had taken place under Hitler. American Jews collaborated with the U.S. government in its courting of Germany, and in failing to name Germany as the culprit.[20]

Finkelstein's analysis may be the most extreme in this current, but it is in accord with the sentiments expressed earlier by other critics of the uses of the Holocaust by American Jews. Tim Cole, in *The Selling of the Holocaust* (1999), depicted the postwar period as one in which "those Jewish survivors who arrived in Britain, Israel, Canada and the United States tended to remain silent about their experiences," since "silence was a shared reaction." After all, Cole claimed, the Jews who lived in those places and who greeted the refugees believed it would be "detrimental to the best interests of Jewry" to memorialize the Holocaust or draw attention to its horrors. It would have been a shameful "perpetual reminder . . . that the Jews are a helpless minority whose safety and very lives depend upon the whim of the people among whom they live or the governments who control their destinies." That, he understood, they did not want.[21]

In the same year that Cole's book appeared, the University of Chicago historian Peter Novick created a stir with his study *The Holocaust in American Life*. His attack on contemporary Holocaust uses was anchored in his belief that from 1945 to 1967 American Jews did not want to appear "out of step with other Americans." Thus, "in matters having to do with Germany there was a virtual taboo on mention of the Holocaust," and not until the watershed moment of the Six Day War of June 1967 did American Jews link images of the Nazi cataclysm with the fate of Israel. Novick postulated that among American Jews, only those on the left willingly championed the memory of the Holocaust since they did not, by definition, participate in the anticommunist rhetoric. For others, engagement with the tragedy existed only "around the kitchen table." Where and when American Jewish publications and mainstream organizations did invoke images of Auschwitz or Nazism, they did so only to engage in the dominant anticommunist rhetoric of the postwar era, linking developments in the late 1940s and 1950s in the Soviet Union with the history of Jewish suffering under Hitler. Novick, as well as those who praised his book and cited his work as authoritative, asserted that when American Jews elided Nazism and Communism in their publications and speeches, they erased the specifically Jewish dimension of the Holocaust.[22]

Novick, Cole, and Finkelstein all agree that 1967 provided the pivotal moment when events in Israel changed the American Jewish political agenda and reshaped the ways in which American Jews presented themselves to the American public. In that newly constructed agenda, according to this group, the Holocaust emerged from obscurity to play a key role. American Jews, their leaders and organizations, exhumed the Holocaust to appeal to the world's sense of guilt and win support for Israel among those with power and influence in America. For Finkelstein, in particular, the fact that Israel and its interests pushed the Holocaust to the center of American Jewish consciousness made Holocaust observance particularly suspect. American Jews began to claim the Holocaust, these historians assert, for narrow, chauvinistic, and nonhumane purposes, a claim ultimately that had nothing to do with the victims of the Nazi genocide and everything to do with a particular political agenda of some three decades later.

None of these books rests on a solid base of empirical evidence, systematically and broadly gathered. This absence of data points to the linkage between their "scholarship" and their political agenda, one that is harshly critical of what they find offensive, inappropriate, and misguided in contemporary Holocaust performances, let alone unaesthetic. They seek to show how the culture of Holocaust memory from the late 1960s on reflects what they consider to be the reactionary political project of American Jews, including a defense of Israel's occupation of Palestinian lands, as well as what they view as an increasingly conservative Jewish stance on American domestic issues, particularly vis-à-vis African Americans and affirmative action. For Novick, the catapulting of the Holocaust to the top of the American Jewish rhetorical repertoire reflects the decline of any other kind of meaningful form of Jewish identity. As he sees it, religion and ethnic identity, particularly in the form of Jewish secular culture, have dried up as sources of meaning to American Jews, so organizations concerned with the crisis of Jewish continuity turned to the Holocaust as a surefire way to trigger feelings of Jewish solidarity, particularly among the young.[23]

Ironically, these moral evaluations of the political posture of American Jewry did not require these scholars to mount a historical argument. If they found what American Jews did in the 1970s and beyond to be politically or culturally problematic, they could have denounced them without seeking to find historical evidence to contextualize them in their books to make that point. Their criticisms would have stood or fallen on their own strengths and intellectual merits.

Yet history plays a key role in these books. They derive much of their punch from the "fact" that in the 1950s American Jews allegedly avoided and were silent about matters surrounding the destruction of European Jewry. The authors, Novick, Finkelstein, and Cole, whose links to an American Jewish mainstream are weak or nonexistent, ironically benefited from the fact that Jewish communal activists and historians had actually constructed the same scenario beginning two to three decades earlier. As far back as the late 1960s, internal critics of the Jewish "establishment," young people in the main, began to complain that their parents, literally and figuratively, had withheld from them knowledge of the Holocaust and that the previous generation had explicitly avoided talking about the European tragedy in order to strike a bargain with 1950s American culture. For example, writing in a symposium on Peter Novick's book, the historian Eli Lederhendler looked back to his own activist days "twenty-five years ago." He reported how he, as a young "active promoter of Holocaust consciousness," had confronted a Jewish educator—presumably older than himself—who had "offered his opinion in print that it was unwise to 'overdo' the curricular treatment of the Holocaust." Lederhendler then "entered the fray with a response in which I argued that American Jewry had not yet begun to 'confront' the Holocaust."[24]

Lederhendler's brief reminiscence points to the emergence of a new, confrontational, generationally differentiated debate within American Jewry in the late 1960s that made the Holocaust a matter of communal controversy. Young Jews who lived through the 1960s brought to the Jewish world a new consciousness, a product of their particular generation, shaped in large measure by the civil rights struggle, the movement against the war in Vietnam, the campus revolutions, and assertions of black pride and cultural separatism. Young Jewish participants in these movements applied the vocabulary of the movements to the Jewish communities in which they lived.

In the broadest sense these young activists questioned the basic premise on which they believed the Jewish communities functioned. They described in books, articles, manifestos, newsletters, and alternative newspapers what they saw as an ugly communal truth, one that showed how their parents' institutions, practices, and ways of thinking embodied all that was shallow, compromising, and wrong with America and its Jews. In their critique of the suburban congregations that had come to dominate the Jewish landscape, the affluence of the Jewish community, and its escalating levels of acceptance, disaffected youth—and the scholars who emerged from that Jewish countercultural groundswell—focused on what was wrong with American Jewry.

Whether those influenced by the Jewish counterculture turned to heightened levels of religious orthodoxy, more militant forms of Zionism, more demonstrative public assertions of Jewish distinctiveness, greater involvement in the campaign for Soviet Jewry, the creation of Jewish feminism, or the founding of *havurot* (extrasynagogal religious fellowships), they shared the assumption that what had preceded them had been obsequious, devoid of intense Jewish content, and collaborative with the mainstream culture.

The critique of the established community and, specifically, the argument that it had prevented the growth of a memorial culture united Jews along a wide political spectrum. It put Meir Kahane and his far right Jewish Defense League with Jews for Urban Justice, a progressive organization on the left. Both not only used Holocaust imagery for very different political purposes, but critiqued the community's leaders for suppressing any meaningful and deep confrontation with that history. Across the political spectrum, they challenged the communal leadership, infusing their rhetoric with graphic Holocaust images. The rage they expressed focused on contemporary issues, but segued easily into historical diatribes, claiming that in the face of the Nazi menace American Jews did little and in the aftermath of the catastrophe went about their business as though nothing cataclysmic had occurred.

Kahane, in his manifesto *Never Again*, claimed: "Millions in Europe went to their gas chambers and crematoria, and we knew of it. We knew of it and were worse than silent, for he who knows of horror and limits himself to tepid, useless, respectable, occasional efforts is worse than the one who knows and does nothing." Kahane realized that his words would offend and upset many in the "Jewish establishment," a phrase he invoked repeatedly. "Why raise such a painful subject? That which was done is done and buried and what can be gained by going back over this most terrible of Jewish historical periods?" In answering his own question, he made clear that the leadership that attacked him "still shepherds us and still speaks in our name and gives us guidance." His Jewish Defense League would do what had not been done by those responsible for the "moral bankruptcy" of the American Jewish community. It would make sure that "Jewish heroes and martyrs" would "be brought to the attention of Jewish youngsters." It would sponsor "in-depth study of the Holocaust, the Jewish partisans and resistance in Nazi Europe," and it would create programs of Jewish self-defense, overtly based on the truth that "the death of six million Jews has in no way lessened the thirst of the world for Jewish blood," a point that the leadership of the community refused to acknowledge as it continued its morally suspect assimilationist behavior.[25]

At the other end of the political spectrum, *The Freedom Seder: A New Haggadah for Passover,* edited by Arthur Waskow and published in 1969, also merged Holocaust imagery with biting attacks on prevailing Jewish practices. It offered a reading from Emmanuel Ringelblum's Warsaw ghetto diary and the *Ani Ma'amin,* neither which would have been out of place in American Jewish texts of the time or of the previous two decades. But it went on to offer a frontal attack on the politics of American Jewry. "In America," the Haggadah declaimed, "we" (presumably American Jews) "have been both coerced and cajoled into abandoning the prophetic legacy," while, "for the sake of a mess of pottage, they" (presumably the leadership) "have abandoned their birthright in the Prophets and the Covenant." "Our people," the seder participant was instructed to intone, "have been frightened into allowing themselves to be purchased, and they have been purchased at such affluent prices that they have forgotten to be angry." That amnesia, the editors predicted, would come with a price, because "we know the cost of hushing; we counted it in millions dead. So we shall choose the risks of freedom." One contributor to the *Freedom Seder* worked out this theme further in an editorial note about "what's wrong with the American Jewish establishment." Its sin was that it had "completely lost track of what being Jewish is—in the pursuit of safety and material gain. . . . American Jewish life is largely geared toward defense and chauvinistic fund-raising." In "the willingness of the Jewish Establishment to compromise their own ethical/moral posture for the sake of what they think is the best interest of Israel," it had adopted the position "Don't rock the boat or give the (goyishe) Establishment any trouble or they'll pull the rug out from under Israel." On the following page the text quoted Adolf Eichmann: "I sat at my desk and got on with my job."[26]

In these works challenging the American Jewish status quo, Holocaust imagery played a pivotal role. Not that it had not been present before in art, sermons, liturgy, ceremony, and communal rhetoric, but now it came to be a central device of the rising generation, the "new Jews" who hoped to create from scratch novel forms of Jewish communal rhetoric and practice. As they saw it, much of what had come before them, that which had been produced by the "Jewish establishment," had no resonance in part because it lacked sting. They considered much of American Jewish culture of the 1950s as thin and weak, without the intensity that they believed Judaism and Jewish life needed. They took upon themselves the challenge of critiquing the American Jewish status quo and made Holocaust imagery part of that challenge.

Their assessment of American Jewry dismissed as trivial the texts, practices, artifacts, and ceremonies that their parents had created to remember the Jewish victims of the Nazi era. They devalued the postwar doings of the organizations that had monitored Nazi war crimes trials and reported them in detail in the press, that had pressed Germany to make reparations and root out resurgent Nazism, and that had called on the U.S. government to support Israel as a place of refuge for survivors. Indeed, the young people of the late 1960s, at the time and later, as they went on to write their own books and create new forms of Holocaust observance, played a crucial role in erasing from public consciousness all that had been said, done, written, and created about the catastrophe in the period from 1945 to 1962.

The process of erasing early American Jewish cultural and political action about the Holocaust and its victims continued apace in the work of scholars who in the 1970s began to write the history of American Jewry. Many historians of the Jewish experience in America, some of them religiously observant individuals, deeply involved in the inner life of the Jewish communities where they lived, and enthusiasts for Israel, in fact provided the imprimatur of scholarly authenticity for assertions that Novick and Finkelstein were to make in the late 1990s.

Work that might be considered "insider" writing about American Jewish history falls into two broad categories: first, key works in the field of

American Jewish history and culture, and second, memoirs by American Jewish intellectuals and activists written at the end of the twentieth century but looking back to the postwar era. Both kinds of sources assert, directly and indirectly, that the Holocaust was not part of the expressive repertoire of American Jews in the fifteen years after the end of World War II, and that only the Israeli victory in 1967 brought the Holocaust out of historical hiding.

A few examples from historical scholarship of the 1990s will demonstrate the currency of this thinking and the degree to which it represents an academic and communal assumed truth. Until the 1990s no historian studying American Jews actually tackled the postwar period. In the 1970s and 1980s, the few works of history that dealt with this era treated it as contemporary studies and painted it with broad brushstrokes. Scholars like Henry Feingold and Arthur Goren made almost no reference to the ways in which American Jews in those years had remembered the Holocaust and its victims, concentrating instead on suburbanization, the decline of anti-Semitism, upward mobility, and the like. Where these historians dealt with cultural matters, they focused instead on the great success of American Jewish novelists and dramatists in creating works that explored Jewish themes for American audiences.[27]

By the 1990s, though, American Jewish historians did in fact begin to pay attention to the postwar period, and in their treatment of that era they played a pivotal role in excising the history of Holocaust commemoration as a factor in American Jewish life and culture. In 1992, the American Jewish Historical Society sponsored the publication of a five-volume history of Jewish life in the United States. The fifth volume, which spanned the years from 1945 through the 1980s, written by Edward Shapiro, not only ignored anything that had been created before 1967 to recall the lives of the Jews of Europe who perished at the hands of the Nazis, but stated that "for the first decade and a half after the end of World War II, Jews were reluctant to discuss the Holocaust." With no empirical data at his command, with no evidence drawn from archives or published primary sources, Shapiro wrote categorically: "During the 1950s, Jewish communities did not sponsor Holocaust commemorations, the Jewish lecture circuit did not feature speeches on the Holocaust. . . . and there was little public discussion among Jews regarding the fate of European Jewry." This assertion, since then recycled by other historians, including Finkelstein and Novick, means that that which had taken place did not in fact occur. Shapiro additionally offered a number of explanations about what finally shook American Jewry out of its muteness. None proved to be as important in his view as the Six Day War, a lightning bolt that allowed "repressed memories of the Holocaust" to spring "out in the open."[28]

The same year that Edward Shapiro made his pronouncement, Howard Sachar, in a one-volume history of American Jews, made the same point. While offering a few examples from the late 1940s, he saw the 1950s as the era of silence, one in which the difficulty of confronting the theological implications of the extermination of European Jews "inhibited Jewish writers and philosophers, no less than Jewish communal leaders, from coming to grips with the Holocaust." In Sachar's analysis, the "economic and political advancement" enjoyed by American Jews and the "preoccupation with the birth and growth of Israel" pushed the European catastrophe to the margins of public consciousness, from which it reemerged with vigor after 1967.[29]

It would not be interesting or useful to cite and quote from every work that has advanced this paradigm.[30] Let me, instead, cite a few examples to indicate how widely this thinking pervades the field, how little evidence supports it, and how scholars from within the world of American Jewish history or, Jewish history more broadly, have concurred with the analysis that fundamentally indicts American Jews for failing to put the Holocaust into the foreground of their communal culture in the 1950s.

Two works from 1997 illustrate this point. First, Gerald Sorin's *Tradition Transformed* emerged as probably the best one-volume history of American Jews, one that has been widely adopted for use in undergraduate courses. Sorin leaned heavily on Edward Shapiro's *A Time for Healing* to fashion his final chapter, which deviates not at all from Shapiro's analysis. If anything, he exceeded him in condemning postwar American Jews for their failures to engage in acts of public mourning or make use of the Holocaust in their communal culture. He claimed that American Jewish culture of the 1950s was based on a "conspiracy of silence," with survivors who refused to talk and American Jews who refused to listen collaborating in a project that would last until the 1970s, when "the consciousness of its [Holocaust's] enormity and the struggle with its meaning took a place as one of the pillars supporting identity." The "historical amnesia" of the 1950s persisted until the "Six Day War . . . ended the silence."[31]

Second, in 1997, Stuart Svonkin published *Jews Against Prejudice*, one of the first book-length historical works on American Jewish political culture of the 1950s. Here is a study of how American Jewry's "big three" defense organizations (the American Jewish Committee, the American Jewish Congress, and the Anti-Defamation League) created a role for Jews in the arena of liberal politics. Svonkin focused on tendencies to universalize rather than particularize, to create programs and texts to fight prejudice in general rather than anti-Semitism. In particular, Svonkin assumed that the defense agencies had no reason to single out the European Jewish catastrophe. The era, he asserted, ended in the late 1960s. Citing and quoting Shapiro, Svonkin attributed the silence of the organizations to the fact that "American Jews seemed to have been reluctant, or unable, to come to terms with the mass destruction of European Jewry." Both Sorin and Svonkin saw the 1950s as the nadir of Holocaust consciousness, a period in American Jewish history when outside pressures, particularly the cold war and the desire of Jews to participate in the bounty of suburban affluence, as well as their own shame and embarrassment at having a mournful history, closed off the wellsprings of any kind of commemorative memorial culture.[32]

One final example from the early twenty-first century demonstrates the hardiness of the paradigm. In 2001, in a series of lectures at the University of Washington, Alan Mintz, a professor of Jewish literature at the Jewish Theological Seminary, explored the contours of Holocaust memory in the United States. He focused on the role of American popular culture in general in spreading a distinctively American set of images and tropes. He categorically dismissed anything American Jews produced in the 1950s, a decade that amounted to a "celebration" of American liberalism, "at which the Holocaust and everything we now associate with it were not welcome guests." Mintz acknowledged that at the immediate end of the war movie theater newsreels made it impossible to avoid the subject in all of its gruesomeness, but "an acute awareness of the Holocaust was not part of the American Jewish experience during the first two decades after the event because it impeded this process of Americanization." Jews were "too deeply engaged in the energetic enterprise of entering American society and seizing the opportunities offered to them to be available to make the subversive sadness provoked by the Holocaust." Mintz wrote his book after the publication of *The Holocaust in American Life,* which he praised, noting that its "most valuable sections . . . deal with the forties and fifties and the role of the Cold War" in making Holocaust silence the norm in American Jewish culture.

Mintz, like all those who have endorsed this narrative, had little empirical evidence. Although he suggested in a footnote that "there is much work to be done in fleshing out our picture of the late forties and fifties," he like Sorin, Shapiro, Novick, and Finkelstein, among others, relied on inherited communal memory, rather than consulting the massive amount of empirical material available from this period. In accepting this assumption, historians from across the political spectrum, with very different positions vis-à-vis Judaism and Jewish culture, have met and shared in the erasure of history.[33]

In this they have joined with a number of scholars and communal leaders who have invoked their own memories of the period before 1967 to prove just how much has changed since that watershed moment. They have told their personal stories along the lines of this narrative trope, which has dominated the scholarship. In so doing, these memoirists demonstrate that despite available empirical evidence to the contrary, the truth of Holocaust erasure in the 1950s functions as more than the construct of historians. It exists as the overarching orthodoxy. Arthur Hertzberg, rabbi, historian, Jewish communal activist, wrote in *A Jew in America* (2002) that the "measure of how much the times were changed was the suddenly revived memory of the Holocaust" in the 1970s. Before that moment "American Jews did not want the mass murder in Europe to be much mentioned in public." He recalled how he had spoken from the pulpit about the Warsaw ghetto uprising, and "the father of a young woman whose Bat Mitzvah was being celebrated that Sabbath went to the board of the synagogue to complain that I had ruined a happy family occasion by bringing up so sad a topic." Besides the analytic problem of conflating one person's reaction—the complaining father—with all of American Jewry (we do not learn how the board reacted), Hertzberg's anecdote stands in sharp contrast to the bat mitzvah gift book, for example, with pages and pages specifically dedicated to telling the story of the six million, the Rabbinical Assembly *mahzor* with its Yom Kippur dirge "To the Six Million," and the large numbers of articles that have appeared in *Conservative Judaism*, the movement's magazine, to indicate that the denomination had incorporated the tragic events into its religious projects.[34]

Political scientist Daniel Elazar, an American-born scholar who emigrated to Israel and wrote extensively on American Jewish communal politics, reminisced about his years in Habonim, the Labor Zionist youth movement. Remembering the postwar period from the vantage point of 1993, he noted that the Holocaust was rarely mentioned in the activities of the group. He recalled that Americans who had fought in the Abraham Lincoln Brigade on the Republican side of the Spanish civil war were their heroes, while the partisans and ghetto fighters were not.[35] Peter Novick, in fact, cited this particular memory of the early 1950s as evidence for his argument.

While it is obvious why Novick found this statement appealing, it is harder to explain why Elazar remembered the past the way he did, since his memories conflict with material in the Habonim archives, including handbooks for group leaders and counselors and descriptions of programs from both summer camps and city clubs showcasing the Holocaust. The summer camps, in particular, used the destruction of European Jewry as a way to mark the summer fast day of Tisha be-Av, a moment in the liturgical year that recalls the Babylonian and Roman destructions of the Temple in Jerusalem.

Habonim in fact published in 1957 a history of its camping activities, *Adventures in Pioneering,* in which graduates of its various camping programs enumerated how they, as staff, had grafted Holocaust imagery onto Tisha be-Av programming or, as campers, had experienced the heightened emotions of the day. One writer chronicling activities at Camp Kvutzah in California in 1956, wrote: "Our general camp theme was: 'Jewish Heroism through the Ages.' Through lectures, discussions, literary trials, models, games, and the arts, the children at camp became acquainted with the heroic moments in Jewish history beginning with our ancient struggles for freedom and independence down to the modern deeds of courage and valor of the defenders of the Warsaw Ghetto and of the Hagana."

Elazar, who remembered no Holocaust programming in his Habonim days—and Novick who accepted Elazar's memories—might have been interested in the ceremony staged at the movement's national convention in 1945 and then reprinted in its anniversary book in 1957. The 1945 gathering began with a poetic presentation of remembrance, "Hazkara," that evoked the "blood-soaked plains of Poland," the ghettoes and concentration camps, ending with a question, will "these dried bones yet live?"[36]

Lastly, in *Chutzpah* (1991), a memoir-manifesto dedicated to the premise that "American Jews need more chutzpah," or willingness to vociferously assert that "we are entitled to first-class status," Alan Dershowitz recounted his elementary and high school years at Brooklyn's Etz Chaim Yeshiva, where "many of our teachers—especially in our religious subjects—were right off the boat from the European displaced persons camps." Despite their experiences and those of "several of our classmates [who] had also experienced Hitler's concentration camps," the classrooms and playgrounds proved to be places where talk of those traumas never took place. Yes, he admitted, "it was in the air," but it never entered the realm of the concrete in terms of curriculum or conversation.[37]

Yet in a yearbook assembled by eighth graders in 1953 at a nearby school, not terribly different from Etz Chaim, the Yeshivah Flatbush, the children committed to writing exactly what Dershowitz—who would have been in the tenth grade that year—claimed only hovered amorphously in the atmosphere. In the yearbook, no doubt edited by teachers and approved by administrators, autobiographical pieces recounted the horrors of the Nazi era and tales of rescue and survival. One boy, Kenneth Wetcher, a sixth-grader, wrote in a short story, "I am the only child in my family. I was born, April 16, 1941. . . . At the age of one and one half, we went by cattle train from Russia to Poland. On the way soldiers made signs at us that they would slit our throats. In Poland many people hated Jews and threatened to kill us." Abraham Fuksman, "born May 1, 1940 in Barawich, Poland," told his teachers, schoolmates, and other adults who may have seen the yearbook, that at the time the Nazis started to attack Poland, "I stayed with my parents," but, "on the sixteenth month, my parents gave me away to a Christian woman in order to save me. . . . I did not know I was a Jew. . . . As soon as the war ended with a casualty list of over 6,000,000 people my mother and father came to take me back." Other Yeshiva Flatbush children used Holocaust imagery in their poems, drawings, and vignettes about Jewish holidays, particularly Hanukkah, Purim, and Israeli Independence Day. Where Dershowitz remembered his Etz Chaim days as devoid of Holocaust talk, the words on paper, penned by the children of the other Brooklyn Orthodox day school, cast grave doubt on those later memories.[38]

Clearly a large chasm separates how American Jews, academics among them, think about the postwar period and the actual data to be found in archives, publications, books, and articles. The former accept as true that American Jews could not, would not, and did not weave the images, words, and metaphors of the European destruction of the Jews into their communal culture in the first decade and a half after World War II ended, while the latter show otherwise. How can this disjunction be explained?

Perhaps in light of the time of Holocaust performance in recent decades, postwar references and invocations have seemed so paltry that scholars and activists have dismissed them from the historic record. In truth, the ways in which American Jews remembered the tragedy of the Nazi era earlier do pale when compared to such contemporary phenomena as the Holocaust Memorial Museum in Washington, D.C., movies like *Schindler's List* and *The Pianist*, and projects like the March of the Living, in which thousands of Jewish teenagers from around the world converge on Auschwitz on Yom Ha-Shoah (Holocaust Remembrance Day). They could easily help to excise from personal and communal memory what came before.[39]

Second, for communal insiders and critics of American Jewry alike, seeing Holocaust observance as a historically continuous phenomenon, which changed and grew over time, diminishes the significance of the June 1967 war. By looking at Holocaust observance as an evolving phenomenon that began immediately (and indeed grew out of wartime communal practices) after the end of the war, and then developed as writers of prayer books, compilers of songbooks, and creators of a range of other texts experimented with images and tropes, minimizes the role of Israel's victory in stimulating American Jewish consciousness. The idea that that event represented a momentous turning point in American Jewish political and cultural life has become thoroughly embedded in historical consciousness. To assert that it did not represent a watershed, that American Jews had found many times and places to remember the catastrophe before June 1967, then implies that modern American Jewish history need not be divided into a pre-1967 and post-1967 period.[40]

Even more important: since the late 1960s American Jewish engagements with the Holocaust have taken place in a very different kind of America. In that earlier era, American Jews stood alone as the creators of books, poems, paintings, musical compositions, prayers, magazine articles, public ceremonies, and other kinds of texts that spoke of gas chambers, crematoria, annihilations, liquidations, mass murders, genocides, and destructions of total communities and cultures. In those earlier years, immediately after the war and into the early 1960s American Jews had no "partners" or "competitors" in this kind of rhetoric.

Since the 1960s, a new tone and texture have come to dominate American public culture, one that venerates and validates discussions of group suffering. American Jews, who had earlier lamented in their particular ways the tragic fate of the six million, now did so alongside other Americans from other ethnic backgrounds who also created texts and practices that memorialized tragedy.

Additionally, after the 1960s, the language of "Holocaust" and the appearance of the word itself in capital letters came to be used to describe many other historical outrages and horrendous calamities against many other people. The tendency of many others to refer to their own "Holocausts" gave Jews in the United States a particular cultural project, designed to make sure that they did not lose that word and idea, that their very particular history would not be lost. The massive Holocaust memory project that American Jews launched in the 1970s, the development of programs designed to inspire "Holocaust consciousness," and the magnetic draw of the Holocaust in American popular culture well beyond the boundaries of the Jewish community, all have histories that grew out of the concerns and contours of late-twentieth-century America, a very different America from that of the years 1945 to 1962.

The differences between those two eras and the differences in the context of their Holocaust performances deserve to be studied in a comparative fashion. Whatever conclusions would emerge in such a study, it should not blind historians—as it has heretofore—to the efforts of American Jews, writers, teachers, summer camp counselors, rabbis, artists, as well as the consumers of these texts, to remember the six million. American Jews did not experience a period of amnesia, nor did they go about their postwar lives silent or impervious to the recent tragedy. They cobbled together a set of communal practices that reflected their sense of identity and deserve not to be airbrushed out of the historical record.

Notes

1. Michael Staub, *Torn at the Roots: The Crisis of Jewish Liberalism in Postwar America* (New York: Columbia University Press, 2002).

2. One of the few commentators to describe American Jewish interactions with the memory of the Holocaust in decidedly positive terms was Jacob Neusner, not a scholar of American Jewish history but of Talmud. Commenting on the 1950s, he wrote that it was not that people failed to "notice the absence of more than five million European Jews." Rather they did not manifest the obsession with it that came to characterize later American Jewish cultural tendencies. In the 1950s, Neusner, believed, much of what was performed vis-à-vis the European tragedy was imbued with an aura of "refinement, restraint, and dignity." Jacob Neusner, "How the Extermination of European Jewry Became the Holocaust," in *Stranger at Home: "The Holocaust," Zionism, and American Judaism* (Chicago: University of Chicago Press, 1981), 82–91.

3. See David Roskies, *Against the Apocalypse: Responses to Catastrophe in Modern Jewish Culture* (Cambridge: Harvard University Press, 1984).

4. Irving Howe and Eliezer Greenberg, *A Treasury of Yiddish Stories* (New York: Viking, 1954), particularly 12, 19, 67, 70, 72.

5. Philip S. Bernstein, *What the Jews Believe* (New York: Farrar, Straus, and Young, 1951), 40, 22, 31.

6. Leon Uris, *Exodus* (Garden City, NY: Doubleday, 1958). Much of Dov's confrontation with the memories of the Nazis and the death camps can be found in chaps. 22–26, pp. 117–54.

7. It would be impossible to list every reference to the Holocaust that appeared in the various volumes of the *American Jewish Yearbook*. Literally hundreds of references appeared in each volume, and well into the 1960s the writers and editors of the *Yearbook* demonstrated how much the event loomed in their consciousness as well as in

that of the women and men who were involved in the various projects around the world.

8. *High Holiday Prayer Book* (New York: Reconstructionist Foundation, 1948), 387–96.

9. United Synagogue of America, *High Holiday Prayer Book* (Hartford, CT: Prayerbook Press, 1951), 386.

10. Norman Lamm, "The Need for Tradition: The Editor's Introduction to a New Journal," *Tradition* 1, no. 1 (1958): 10; *Tradition* 3, no. 1 (1960): 80.

11. Rabbinical Council, *Manual of Holiday and Sabbath Sermons* (New York: Rabbinical Council Press, 1957), 137–38; Rabbinical Council, *Manual of Holiday and Sabbath Sermons* (New York: Rabbinical Council Press, 1952), 143–44 are two of hundreds of possible examples.

12. "Hebrew Union College–Jewish Institute of Religion." Nearprint Collection, Document Group 20, American Jewish Archives, Cincinnati.

13. Louis I. Newman, *Pangs of the Messiah and Other Plays, Pageants, and Cantatas* (New York: Bloch, 1957) 3, 27, 222.

14. Meyer Waxman, Sulamith Ish-Kishor, and Jacob Sloan, *Blessed Is the Daughter* (New York: Shengold, 1957), n.p., 86–87, 134–35, 136, 137, 151–52.

15. Ruth Rubin, *A Treasury of Jewish Folksong* (New York: Schocken, 1950), 12, 175.

16. Elma Ehrlich Levinger, *Jewish Adventures in America: The Story of 300 Years of Jewish Life in the United States* (New York: Bloch, 1954), 233–35, 238–40, 277.

17. "Seder Ritual," 1-50, American Jewish Historical Society.

18. *Bulletin of Negro History*, December 1955, 63–64.

19. *Proceedings of the Fiftieth Anniversary Observance of the American Jewish Committee: April 10–14, 1957: The Pursuit of Equality at Home and Abroad* (New York: American Jewish Committee, 1958), xi, 3, 27, 40, 133, 140, 141, 157, 199, 226, 228, 230.

20. Norman G. Finkelstein, *The Holocaust Industry: Reflections on the Exploitation of Jewish Suffering* (London: Verso, 2000), 4–8, 12–18, 42.

21. Tim Cole, *Selling the Holocaust: From Auschwitz to Schindler* (New York: Routledge, 1999), 2, 148.

22. Peter Novick, *The Holocaust in American Life* (Boston: Houghton Mifflin, 1999), for example, 91, 96.

23. Of the three only Novick made any attempt to provide documentation, but his references when studied closely show how his contemporary agenda shaped his scholarship. He made some superficial forays into the records of the American Jewish Committee, but did not survey even the entire corpus of material from that one organization. He saw random bits of American Jewish journalism, but with no thoroughness or consistency, and his lack of interest, indeed utter avoidance of sources coming from the world of Judaism—the religious sphere—as well Zionism, Jewish education, Jewish summer camping, as just a few examples, indicates that he engaged with a very superficial set of sources. He had no access to or interest in, it seems, any materials in Yiddish or Hebrew, nor did he survey the vast body of archival material on Jewish organizations' use of radio in the late 1940s and 1950s to refer to the horrors of the Holocaust. He made no use of even easily available material like the *American Jewish Yearbook*, the *Jewish Book Annual*, or scholarly publications like *Jewish Social Studies*, which abounded with references to the Nazi catastrophe and which did not require any knowledge of any other language.

24. Eli Lederhendler, "On Peter Novick's *The Holocaust in American Life*," *Jewish Social Studies* 7, no. 3 (2001): 161.

25. Meir Kahane, *Never Again! A Program for Survival* (Los Angeles: Nash, 1971).

26. Arthur I. Waskow, *The Freedom Seder: A New Haggadah for Passover* (Washington, DC: Micah Press, 1969), 17, 19, 54, 45–47.

27. Arthur A. Goren, "The Jews," in, *Harvard Encyclopedia of American Ethnic Groups*, ed. Stephan Thernstrom (Cambridge: Belknap Press of Harvard University Press, 1980), 592–98; Stanley Feldstein, *The Land I Show You: Three Centuries of Jewish Life in America* (Garden City, NY: Anchor Press, 1978), 416–71; Henry L. Feingold, *Zion in America: The Jewish Experience for Colonial Times to the Present* (New York: Hippocrene Books, 1974), 299–357. Feingold began his final chapter, "The American Jewish Condition Today," with a philosophic statement that indicated that the Holocaust had come to be a crucial element in American Jewish self-consciousness, "the touchstone of all contemporary sensibility" (299), but he did not historicize this statement and explore how American Jews went about the process of weaving it and images of it into their communal practices.

28. Edward Shapiro, *A Time for Healing: American Jewry since World War II* (Baltimore: Johns Hopkins University Press, 1992), 213–16.

29. Howard Sachar, *A History of the Jews in America* (New York: Knopf, 1992), 839, 844, 847.

30. Neusner, "Extermination of European Jewry," 84; Rona Sheramy, "Defining Lessons: The Holocaust in American Jewish Education," Ph.D. diss., Brandeis University, 2001; and Staub, *Torn at the Roots,* are a few examples of scholarship that have chipped away at the prevailing paradigm. Neusner's piece was an article with no documentation, Sheramy's is a dissertation that focuses on the uses of the Holocaust in American Jewish pedagogic material and has several chapters on the pre-1967 period, while Staub, although he has much material on the pre-1967 period and the invocation of the Holocaust, never strayed beyond a few sources, particularly *Commentary.*

31. Gerald Sorin, *Tradition Transformed: The Jewish Experience in America* (Baltimore: Johns Hopkins University Press, 1997), 194–95, 217.

32. Stuart Svonkin, *Jews Against Prejudice: American Jews and the Fight for Civil Liberties* (New York: Columbia University Press, 1997), particularly 180, 185–86; a number of other works on Holocaust memory and Holocaust memorial projects give some attention to efforts to commemorate the tragedy in the late 1940s but do not extend their analyses and consider the 1950s at all. See James Young, *The Texture of Memory: Holocaust Memorials and Meaning* (New Haven: Yale University Press, 1993), 287–90; Edward Linenthal, *Preserving Memory: The Struggle to Create America's Holocaust Museum* (New York: Viking, 1995), 5–9.

33. Alan Mintz, *Popular Culture and the Shaping of Holocaust Memory in America* (Seattle: University of Washington Press, 2001), 5–8, 187.

34. Arthur Hertzberg, *A Jew in America: My Life and a People's Struggle for Identity* (San Francisco: Harper, 2002), 403–4.

35. Daniel J. Elazar, "Detroit, the Early 1950s: 'Habonim Was Looked at a Bit Wild,'" in *Builders and Dreamers: Habonim Labor Zionist Youth in America,* ed. J. J. Goldberg and Elliot King (New York: Habonim Dror, 1993), 173.

36. David Breslau, ed., *Adventures in Pioneering: The Story of 25 Years of Habonim*

Camping (New York: Chay Commission of the Labor Zionist Movement, 1957), 98–100, 159–62.

37. Alan M. Dershowitz, *Chutzpah* (Boston: Little, Brown, 1991), 42.

38. *Yeshivah Yearbook: 1953* (Brooklyn, NY: Yeshivah Flatbush), 28, 30, 34, 36, in the possession of the author.

39. Irving Howe made a point in this vein in his autobiography, *A Margin of Hope*. When in the memoir he explored his own political and intellectual engagement with the Holocaust, he admitted that he did in fact react slowly, but "would add mildly that now, when incessant talk about the Holocaust risks becoming a media vulgarity, we may value silence a bit more than anyone could have supposed in earlier years." Howe in fact participated in 1950s remembrance inasmuch as his anthology of Yiddish short stories put the tragedy onto the front page. Irving Howe, *A Margin of Hope: An Intellectual Biography* (New York: Harcourt Brace Jovanovich, 1987), 247–48.

40. This point and the need to rethink the significance of 1967 has been made by Eli Lederhendler, *New York Jews and the Decline of Urban Ethnicity, 1950–1970* (Syracuse: Syracuse University Press, 2001). Here I need to plead a bit guilty myself. In my book *The Jews of the United States* (Berkeley and Los Angeles: University of California Press, 2004) I have built my final chapter around the date 1967.

Religious Identities in Public and Private

Havdallah, Henry S. Jacobs Camp, Utica, Mississippi, 1993. Courtesy of Bill Aron.

Rethinking American Judaism

Arnold M. Eisen

My aim in this essay is to report on research conducted, and on reflection undertaken, in the course of three related projects, research, and reflection that have thus far resulted in several publications but have not, until now, yielded a synthesis intended to bring the conclusions of the three together. One of the projects on which I shall report here, *Rethinking Modern Judaism* (1998), examines the patterns of Jewish religious practice and thought that have been evident in Central Europe, Western Europe, and America from the start of Emancipation until our own day.[1] A second study, *The Jew Within* (2000), completed along with the sociologist Steven M. Cohen, seeks to provide an account of current trends among moderately affiliated American Jews.[2] *Taking Hold of Torah* (1997) marshals scholarship in the service of a personal statement about the Jewish future that I hope will soon emerge in the United States.[3] One might usefully consider the three books as concerned with the past, present, and (desired) future of American Jewry, and in keeping with that schema, I shall begin this essay with the past: specifically, the "contract with modernity" (Jacob Katz's term) that was "signed" by Jews at the onset of Emancipation and which, I believe, continues to define and shape the conduct of their descendants in America today.[4]

The Impact of Emancipation

A major part of the "rethinking" that I urge upon my readers in the first book under discussion here involves the notion—common to many mod-

This essay was originally presented on March 24, 1999, at the Jean and Samuel Frankel Center for Judaic Studies, University of Michigan, Ann Arbor.

ern Jews and many scholars of modern Jewry alike, but in my view mistaken—that the attenuation of Jewish faith and observance over the past two centuries should be understood as the result of *Enlightenment*. According to this account, it was Jews' acquaintance with and internalization of a worldview dominated by science and rationality that led them far from Judaism. The process of disaffection was allegedly straightforward. Jews first adopted Enlightenment notions acquired in the course of education or exposure to the zeitgeist, with the result that they then (not surprisingly) lost traditional belief in God and revelation, and then—another inevitable consequence—quite naturally cast off or reduced observance of practices dependent on the religious authority in which they no longer believed. Practice expresses or enacts belief, in this view; belief is pictured as a realm largely set apart from other things, one in which particular ideas or truths are held to be self-evident until challenged by other beliefs, which supplant them. Jewish commitments were done in the light of reason.

The story that I wish to tell puts the emphasis instead upon *Emancipation*. It argues first of all that for the past two centuries Jews have for the most part navigated their way through modernity's unfamiliar terrain very much as we still do: not so much via altered *beliefs* as through eclectic patterns of *observance* and the varied, often individual sets of *meanings* discovered in those practices or associated with them. These observances and meanings, I believe, have been arrived at not only as a result of the very real and substantial intellectual upheaval that we call Enlightenment but also, and more decisively, as a result of the new sorts of selfhood and community that were demanded by the radically altered social, political and economic orders in which Jews were granted or promised new liberties. As Franz Rosenzweig put it, probing the motives for Jewish adherence to the commandments over the centuries, "Can we really fancy that Israel kept this Law, this Torah, only because of the one 'fact which excluded the possibility of delusion,' that the six hundred thousand heard the voice of God at Sinai?" Other, more tangible factors were involved, then and now, in the decision on behalf of observance. Other factors than nonbelief in revelation at Sinai have been involved, I shall argue, in the decision *against* observance.[5]

Practice cannot be separated from belief, of course. I remain very much a student of modern Jewish thought and not only of modern Jewish practice. But there exists no one-to-one relation between the two, I maintain, and practice certainly should not be seen as the mere enactment or expression of belief. Very often it is the other way around; and we can also point to occasions on which part of the attraction of a particular practice lies precisely in the fact that one can find it meaningful for a *variety* of reasons or in the absence of any reason whatever. Practice may be valued in part, too, because it helps one to avoid questions of meaning (and truth) altogether. All of these patterns, I suspect, are familiar from personal experience to contemporary Jews and gentiles alike.

In some cases, the relation between Emancipation and Jewish practice was quite direct. Newly centralized state authorities dictated what sorts of things Jews could and could not do if they wished to achieve or retain the rights of citizenship. Governments decided how rabbis should be educated, and what sorts of sermons they could preach. In other cases, newly coalescing societies exercised social pressure on Jews to adopt or discard particular ways of eating, dressing, walking, and speaking—all of which directly, and not at all by accident, impinged on religious observances that involved eating, dressing, walking, and speaking, and so impinged on the beliefs associated with those observances. Jews had to demonstrate attainment of *Bildung* if they wished to be accepted. They had to prove that they were *civilized* in order to enter civil society. Some Jews, of course, altered or omitted observances of their own accord, without direct outside pressure or dictation, because the practice in question no longer seemed to accord with their sense of who they were or wished to be, or did not suit the relation with non-Jewish neighbors that they sought or had achieved. Why separate milk from meat, Sabbath from weekday, if one did not wish to be distinguished as a Jew from "all the nations"—and dietary laws or Sabbath observance not only symbolized but *imposed* that unwanted distinctiveness?

The calculations involved in this distinction, which I call the politics of modern Jewish practice, of course varied enormously with time, place, and personal proclivity. But the *necessity* of the calculation, I believe, should not be in doubt. It points us to the fact that the theory and practice of modernity—the theory clearly articulated in works such as Kant's *Religion within the Limits of Reason Alone;* the practice imposed by a host of legislative acts and political leaders in Germany, France, England, and America— were often not at all neutral as regards the religious practices of the Jews. The latter constituted a religious minority who defied the logic of emergent modern nation-states both because they *were* a minority and because Judaism put the emphasis upon practice—inevitably particularist and distinctive—rather than upon theory (or spirit or intent), which claimed to be universal.

Recall Spinoza's famous tribute to the impact of circumcision as the eternal guarantor of Jewish distinctiveness at the close of chapter 3 of his *Tractatus*. "The sign of circumcision is, as I think, so important that I could persuade myself that it alone would preserve the nation forever."[6] The passage goes a long way toward explaining the animus against Judaism displayed in Kant's *Religion*, a central passage of which argues that Judaism could never be a true (i.e., rational) religion, suitable to a modern, ethical state, because it is comprised of statutes rather than teachings and because these statutes inevitably divide the Jews from the rest of humanity. Even the Ten Commandments, Kant argues, were "not so prescribed as to induce obedience by laying requirements upon the moral disposition," as Christianity did later on with its own ethical injunctions. The words of Moses were "directed to absolutely nothing but outer observance," and thus for Kant, "the proof that Judaism has not allowed its organization to become a religion is clear."[7] His indictment was powerful, and widely shared. Jews throughout the modern period, including American Jews in our own century, to varying but always significant degrees, have always had to decide, when considering a particular practice, whether they wished to challenge the reigning notions of modernity, society, religion—and themselves.

That is all the more true, I believe, because Kant and other theorists presumed a notion of *ritual* that was at odds with Jewish conceptions of observance. Indeed they bequeathed not only to religious practitioners but to modern scholarship about religion a notion of ritual as unthinking, rote behavior (consider our use of the adjective "ritualistic") and of tradition as (in Max Weber's memorable phrase in "Politics as a Vocation") "mores sanctified through the unimaginably ancient recognition and habitual orientation to conform."[8] Several scholars, most notably Mary Douglas and Jonathan Z. Smith, have drawn attention to the scholarly prejudice that is expressed in such conceptions of ritual and to the roots of this prejudice in Protestant polemics against Catholicism that were subsequently incorporated into Enlightenment polemics against religion as a whole.[9] I found it necessary to devote an entire chapter of *Rethinking Modern Judaism* to the adjustments that we need to make in such theories of ritual in order to give a fair scholarly reading of Jewish practice, which tended until the modern period to be perceived as *law* and which was often imposed upon everyday experience (diet, for example, or sexual relations) rather than set aside from it. Both aspects are problematic for the reigning theories of ritual.

My point here, however, is somewhat different. It is that Jews, whether acquainted with the scholarly literature on ritual or not, have been forced or pressured by the conceptions of ritual prevalent in the modern West not only to justify their retention of *particular* rituals inherited from Jewish tradition (the Sabbath, for example) but to justify their performance of *rituals as such*. Why engage in activity that is patently repetitive, bespeaks obedience rather than autonomy, interferes with spontaneous thought and devotion, and can only be reconciled with rational religion if it is understood as merely symbolic and instrumental? Modern Jewish thinkers from Moses Mendelssohn onward, seeking to provide meaning and motivation to Jewish practice, have had their work doubly cut out for them. "From Mendelssohn on," as Rosenzweig put it, "our entire people have subjected itself to the torture of this embarrassing question; the Jewishness of every individual has squirmed on the needle point of a 'why.'"[10] How to make rational—that is, universal—sense of age-old, highly particularist, often quite arbitrary, practice? Once more the issue persists, unabated, in twenty-first-century America.

Two enduring sorts of justification for practice, and the problems inherent in both of these, are of particular interest to me here.

First: Jewish thinkers have often followed Mendelssohn's lead in *Jerusalem* (1783) by offering *universalist* rationales for practices that are inherently and demonstrably *particularist*. The "eternal truths" taught Jews in the Torah, whether moral or metaphysical, are, according to Mendelssohn, only reminders of what Jews should really know through reason. All human beings have equal access to those truths. Judaism is distinguished only by its "historical truths" (e.g., Exodus or Sinai) and its "ceremonial scripts" (e.g., Passover, the Sabbath or dietary laws). The script is meant to point Jews toward eternal truths, or at the very least to stimulate reflection upon them. The many particular observances unique to Jews are thus in service to a small set of universal recognitions that are meant to be shared with all humanity.[11]

Mendelssohnian construals of observance have proven very popular among a great many rabbis, teachers, and parents over the past two centuries, spanning all the denominational divisions of Judaism. What is the meaning of Passover? It is, of course, the "festival of freedom." Why light Hanukkah candles? Because they summon Jews to resist tyranny and oppression. What is the meaning of the Sabbath? Creativity, morality, freedom, writes Mordecai Kaplan, founder of Reconstructionism, in *The Meaning of God in Modern Jewish Religion* (1937).[12] Why separate meat from milk? Because, according to Samson Raphael Hirsch, the first theoretician of Orthodoxy, in a book written exactly a century earlier, the division reminds us of the difference between human beings and other animals.[13]

The problems with such rationales should be obvious. For one thing, the reasons given for observance may be trite or unconvincing or even objectionable, which is in part why one major tendency in rabbinic thought is profoundly suspicious of the attempt to offer any "reasons for the commandments" whatever. After all, in the rabbis' view, the mitzvoth were binding on Jews whether they liked these particular reasons or not. Why endanger observance with bad reasons, or the notion that obedience was contingent on the provision of reasons found by the actor to be good? More important, and more specific to modern circumstances: Why should Jews observe practices *unique to Judaism*—sometimes at the cost of economic loss, unwanted distinctiveness from the larger society, or political reprisals—if the messages conveyed by these rituals are *entirely universal,* that is, available to everyone, whether they observed these practices or not? Why set oneself apart through observances that proclaim a truth that joins Jews to all others through the faculty of reason? In Mendelssohn's terms: Why employ the "ceremonial script" of the commandments, if all this "script" does is remind Jews of "eternal truths" about God and morality that God has made available, at least in principle, to *every* human being in every time and place, whether that person practices this set of symbolic observances, or a very different one?

But how could Jewish thinkers *not* offer such universal messages? Given that communal leaders could no longer *coerce* religious observance, but rather had to *persuade* Jews to undertake it, that persuasion could not but come in terms that Jews would find persuasive, and these terms would perforce tend to be drawn from the larger culture, not from Judaism. The problem seems as unavoidable as it is insuperable, a function both of the new ideas with which Jewish minds were furnished (Enlightenment) and of Emancipation, the loss of Jewish communities with "plausibility structures" able to offer counter-ideas that were equally convincing. It is no surprise that so many modern Jews have so often found the universalist rationales proposed for their particularist observance unconvincing. Indeed, I argue in *Rethinking Modern Judaism,* many Jewish thinkers, and not only "ordinary" Jews, have at times engaged in practices far "out in front" of their beliefs—with the beliefs struggling unsuccessfully, and rather noisily, to catch up.

In the absence of other reasons for observance—I come now to the second pattern of special interest here—the connection to *ancestors* has achieved a new prominence. A great many Jews in the modern period have felt a strong obligation to follow in the footsteps of their immediate and distant forebears. Indeed, this obligation has comprised a major part of what it has meant for them to be Jews. They feel called upon to observe commandments once observed by their ancestors, *not* in order to draw nearer to God by means of those observances—the traditional stance, articulated in countless Jewish rituals—but simply to draw near to *the ancestors themselves,* to walk in their ways and to draw inspiration from their memory. This activity, still very much evident in America today, is seen by Jews who perform it as growing out of and bearing witness to their deep-seated and inescapable relation to close or extended Jewish family members. The ancestors, as it were, demand reenactment of their own Jewish practices through their progeny's agency; and the connection to them effected by means of this practice becomes not nearly the *motive* but the *meaning* of what their descendants do Jewishly. In such cases, I believe, a strict dichotomy between "mitzvah" and "nostalgia" is patently inadequate. I refer to this pattern, not entirely facetiously, with the phrase "nostalgia as modern Jewish mitzvah."

My intention in doing so is not to stretch the concept of commandment so wide that it comes to include everything any Jew does, for whatever reason. But neither should we restrict the notion of mitzvah to behavior undertaken by Jews in obedience to commandments believed to have been given by God to Moses at Mount Sinai. Traditional literature on revelation and mitzvah allows far more latitude than this to both terms, and modern Jewish practice in my view demands it as well. Ethical obligations, for example, have always constituted a major portion of the commandments, and became for many Jews over the past two centuries the principal, or even the sole, means of acting out the duties incumbent upon them. Their Judaism was one of "ethical monotheism," whether or not they believed that the ethical obligations were revealed, or that reason, if the source of that obligation, is divine. Kaplan, to cite another example, probably spoke for many millions of modern Jews when he "reconstructed" Judaism as a "civilization" and "revalued" the commandments as "folkways" that he believed commanded Jews even though they did not emanate from a personal, divine Commander—but rather from the collective wellspring of the Jewish nation. A similar sense of obligation has impelled Jews to contribute to the revival and protection of Israel or the rescue of Jews from Ethiopia and the former Soviet Union. The source of obligation in all three cases is not the covenant of Sinai; but neither is it completely unrelated to that covenant.

It has, of course, not been clear to many modern Jews (nor is it clear in

many of the leading works of modern Jewish thought) how particular observances actually derive from the will of the ancestors, anymore than it is
clear how they derive from the will of God. Nor is it clear to me, as I study
the modern Jewish search for authority, that those who conduct the search
really want the quest to be successful. They may well be far more comfortable with the stance of perennial *searcher,* the self-description of *journey* and
quest, than they would ever be with the notion of arrival. The latter would
presumably include a definition of authority to which the Jews who held it
would have to be obedient, and a commitment that they would have to regard as final. Both of these cut against the grains of moderns committed to
autonomy, exploration, and fulfillment. It is sometimes better not to find
what one is seeking.

Moreover, the student of contemporary American Judaism is confronted with the paradox that many "ordinary" Jews, as well as Jewish
elites (rabbis and theologians), have seemed to replace "God" or "revelation" as the ultimate authority to which they appeal with the far more ambiguous "god-term" of *tradition.* They have done so at the very same moment that they have become aware, thanks to historical consciousness,
that "tradition" they invoke is not entirely a given but is, at least in part,
the result of their own construction and selection. The paradox is perhaps
most apparent in Kaplan, who in effect urged countless practices on his
readers with the argument that "this is what Jews do, and have always done
and so should continue to do in order to find 'salvation' i.e. self-fulfillment
as Jews," at the same time as he urged them to "revalue" the meanings associated with those practices. The point is evident in a variety of other
thinkers as well. Indeed, widespread awareness of these dilemmas among
contemporary Jews prompts knowing laughter at jokes such as the one
about the elderly member of the congregation who reports to a questioning
newcomer that the tradition in their congregation has always been that
people *stand* for the recital of the Shema. A second veteran congregant dis-
agrees, however. His countertradition holds that people in their synagogue
have always *sat* for the Shema. The two finally agree that the real tradition
of the congregation, what people have in fact always done, is to *argue* about
whether they should stand for the Shema or sit.

Why should we perform a particular observance, then, or do so in a particular way? Because "tradition" suggests or requires it, or at least *our* tradition does, or *one* of our traditions does. This rationale, too, is unconvincing
when subjected to the scrutiny of historical criticism. But it is no less inescapable for that—and its failings, like those of other rationales, may not

in the end matter all that much, if Jews are doing what they do for other reasons, anchored more in private satisfactions, and in vague yearnings for continuity with the past, than in either communal loyalties or obedience to God.

The Journey of the Sovereign Self

That is certainly what Steven Cohen and I discovered in our interviews with "moderately affiliated Jews"—the group comprising the bulk of American Jewry, who are neither among the most active 20–25 percent of the population (as measured by a diverse set of indicators) nor among the least active 20 percent, those unaffiliated all their lives, at the other end of the spectrum. We call the work "The Jew Within" in recognition of the finding that, to an ever larger degree, the discovery and construction of Jewish meaning in America (as of ultimate significance more generally) occur in the private sphere. American Jews, we found, enact and express their decisions about Judaism primarily in the intimate spaces of love and family, friendship and reflection, the spaces in which contemporary Jews are in their own eyes "most themselves," rather than in the public sphere of organizational life, support for Israel, or the various political, philanthropic, and social causes in which they are (less and less) involved. It is primarily in private space and time that American Jews define the selves who they are and want to be.

We probed these private spaces by means of in-depth interviews, usually lasting three to four hours, which gave the Jews we met the chance to say, in their own words and with due respect for the complexities involved, just what they do and do not find meaningful in the Jewish lives they lead. We presented these Jews, in the terms they themselves used frequently, with the chance to "tell their personal stories," to recount their personal journeys, and we discovered in the process that these personal stories and journeys, rather than any received creed or communal discipline, are at the heart of our subjects' self-identity as Jews.

I will dwell briefly on three of our principal findings, all of them directly related to the account of modern Judaism that I have provided above.

First: in keeping with the theory and the practice of modernity, and in conformity with the pattern discerned among Americans of all faiths by Robert Bellah and his coauthors in *Habits of the Heart* (1985), the "first language" spoken by our subjects is very much one of profound individualism.

Community—though a buzzword in our interviews, a felt need, even a real hunger for some—is a "second language" subordinate to the first.[14] The Jews we met, like the Christians studied by Bellah and other researchers, do not speak it as often or as well. Indeed the language of self remains predominant even among the most Jewishly active members of our sample. They told us repeatedly that they decide week by week, year by year, which rituals they will observe and how they will observe them. They constantly reconsider which organizations and charities they will join or support, and to what degree; which beliefs they will hold; which loyalties they will acknowledge. The self is and must remain autonomous and sovereign, in this view of things. The only meanings it holds for observance are those that it has supplied, in a personal construction built out of the manifold repertoire available.

"Each individual has to decide the proper way to serve his religion," said a teacher in Queens. (All names cited in this study are fictitious.) "My way is not right or wrong," he continued, "it's just my way." Irv, a salesman in Queens, added that Judaism must be strictly nonjudgmental. "I don't have any problem with what anybody does [as far as Jewish observance is concerned], as long as they don't tell me what I have to do. So, if you want to be involved in something that's very dear to your heart, that's fine, but don't sit there and tell me about something that is clearly an option in life, that I have to be doing it, and should be doing it, because I am [Jewish]." Sam expressed a strong sense of "extra responsibility for other Jews," on the grounds that "you have to take care of your own first." But he has little interest in the synagogue and none whatever in secular Jewish organizations. Irv refuses to believe that his religion is the right one and all of the others, wrong. "It is what you make of it, what you want to do with it, and that is how it should be."

Virtually all our interviewees articulated this sovereignty in relation to the practices of Jewish tradition. They reserve the right to decide what and how they shall perform Jewish practices, and to a person prefer home rituals—which take place on their own "turf," and are enacted with others who are close to them personally—to public observances performed in a way, and with a group, over which they have little control. Sarah, a computer programmer who lives in Berkeley, likes to conduct her own seders so she can set both the guest list and the content of the ritual. "It turned out that it was just easier for me to do it myself, because then I could get the Haggadahs that I wanted to use." She has had trouble finding a synagogue she likes because "nothing really seemed to [suit her], either they're too much or too little." Edward, a Chicago lawyer, put the matter most succinctly. "I elect to observe [Judaism] as I elect to observe it. If something is potentially annoying, I avoid it."

American Jews simply will not undertake rituals with which they are uncomfortable, or associate with anyone who challenges the Jewish choices they have made. Seventy-four percent of the participants in a national survey conducted for our study, comprising a representative sample of American Jewish adults, agreed with this statement: "I have the right to reject those Jewish observances that I don't find meaningful." Tony, an engineer who lives in suburban Boston, told us that Passover is the most meaningful holiday to him, in part because it carries memories of seders conducted by his grandfather. He and his wife will have two seders this year, he will attend services at Passover, he is in synagogue nearly every Sabbath, but he has "tremendous difficulty with High Holidays services. Sometimes I go to hear Kol Nidre. This year I didn't. My wife and son went. My wife said, 'Aren't you going?' I said: 'I can't do it.'"

The sovereign Jewish self, however, does not merely carry on the archetypical pattern of modernity: individual autonomy replacing inherited collective authority; achieved identity in place of ascribed identity; secular rebellion against the sacred. The Jews we met all seek an abiding significance in their lives that goes beyond daily activities and the limits of their own reason or mortality. They readily discussed their highly personal searches for transcendent meaning and confessed, to a degree that surprised us, that they believe in and converse with God. What is more, they reported a strong desire to find their personal sense of direction and ultimate purpose largely or entirely in the framework of *Jewish* practices and beliefs. They are not leaving faith behind in favor of secular national or communal loyalties, as many of their parents and grandparents had done. Nor are they leaving particularist Jewish loyalties behind in favor of universal commitments, as others of their ancestors had done. They are in fact profoundly dissatisfied with secular affiliations and in search of decidedly spiritual meaning. Far from embracing the universal, they take the existence of "multiple lifeworlds" for granted, and proclaim the value of "local narratives" and not merely of global truths.

This is, to be sure, a variant on the modern story—the self after all remains sovereign; individual autonomy remains uncompromised; modern institutions and patterns of thought by and large remain unchallenged—but the variant is no less significant than the source from which it springs. We seem to be seeing a "postmodern" variant on the "modern" Jewish self, one with far-reaching consequences for the fate of the "modern" and the "Jewish" from which it derives.

The character of the uneasy peace made by our interviewees with the assumptions of modernity is perhaps most visible in the contradiction between two deeply held notions about what it is to be a Jewish self. On the one hand, as we have seen, they proclaimed without cease their sovereign right, and that of their children, to *choose* at every moment whether and how to be a Jew. There were no good Jews and no bad Jews. No one had the right to tell any other Jew what he or she had to do or believe in order to be a Jew. On the other hand, this was so because our subjects maintained that the fact of birth as a Jew, being the child of at least one Jewish parent, meant that one was a Jew forever after regardless of what one did or believed, with the possible exception of outright conversion to another faith. One's children and grandchildren would be Jewish forever after for the very same reason. Identity is thus both "ascribed" and "achieved," chosen by the individual and a fact that long precedes and survives choice. It is a matter that can just as easily or legitimately be sloughed off as affirmed, and yet is also (though our interviewees never used the word) *in the blood.* Tribal loyalties, duties owed the Jews, are explicitly repudiated, but the echoes of tribalism remain pronounced.

By far the most meaningful aspect of Jewish identity for the American Jews we interviewed is the connection that Judaism effects between them and their ancestors and descendants; by far the most meaningful activity in which they engage as Jews is the *performance of rituals at home with their families.* Sociologists Marshall Sklare and Joseph Greenblum observed a generation ago that there is a pronounced "political" character to this preference. Home observance by definition takes place in private rather than public space. As undertaken by American Jews, it also usually transpires in private time (the evening) rather than in time that conflicts with work or other social obligations. The collision with the gentile sphere is thereby minimized, as is the risk that observance will threaten gentile acceptance. What is more, Jewish practice is focused on children, which means that one can explain the activity to others, and to oneself, as something less than a statement about one's own adult identity. One is not affirming ethnic distinctiveness or religious truth by lighting the candles or saying the blessing over the wine, but merely passing on a tradition, helping to bring the family together. All of this, I think, remains very much the case for the Jews we interviewed.[15]

However, it is no less significant, and probably more so, that home and family comprise the *content* as well as the site of all that the Jews we interviewed find most meaningful. One sits with one's children at a Passover seder and tells stories not only about the collective ancestors who, according to the Torah, left Egypt so many centuries ago, but also about the immediate ancestors who sit around the seder table now or who did so in years past. Tensions with parents and other family members were described to us as a major part of the meaning (not entirely positive, but always highly charged) of the occasion. Memories of parents and grandparents who presided at previous seders were recounted to us in loving detail, even in portions of the interview that had no apparent connection with ritual observance. Nostalgia—connection to ancestors—is for these Jews very much what their Judaism is about.

"Pesach is my favorite holiday," reported Molly, a physician in Boston, using the Hebrew word for Passover. "I look forward to it for ages." Her husband has accumulated many different Haggadoth, and each year they construct a service drawn from several of them, mixing Hebrew with English and old passages with new. This year each person invited to the seder was asked to write a midrash on a particular passage. "Children wrote stories, and we read them. Adults did it. . . . It was really fun." When the babysitter took the children out to McDonald's last year during the holiday, "I was beside myself. . . . She just didn't get it." Molly does not have a kosher home, but McDonald's during Passover was out of the question. In recounting the meaning of the holiday, she did not mention the universalist themes of freedom and oppression that, as we learned elsewhere in the interview, first captured her husband's interest in the holiday. We suspect these themes are important to Molly as well. A less acceptable "meaning" would have precluded observance of the holiday that now matters so much to her. But family seems a far more immediate and important source of meaning. Molly perhaps articulated another when she answered the question, "What do you like about being Jewish?" by noting the pleasure she derives from "feeling part of a community that was both recognizable but also never felt very mainstream." She enjoys learning about Jewish "writings people have studied for thousands of years, and I can read them and think about them as well."

Universal and particular join here in a way that Molly finds meaningful and nonthreatening. She enjoys the fact that she can and does eat at McDonald's throughout the year, but can choose not to do so at Passover. The holiday helps to remind her and her children of the degree to which they belong to America, but also stand apart as members of a people that has existed for a very long time in many different societies and cultures. Passover is thus very much about freedom and identity for her, two of its traditional themes, but in a personal way that is very much wrapped up in her immediate experience, in memories of her grandparents and in celebration with her children.

The connection between observance and transmission from ancestors to descendants received its most vivid expression in our interview with a woman who told us that her mother had recently called—soon after the death of her husband, our subject's father—to request that her daughter take the Sabbath candlesticks that she had inherited from her own mother decades earlier. When our interviewee, call her Suzanne, readily agreed to do so, her mother clarified that she was not simply asking her daughter to take the candlesticks but to use them. "I know," Suzanne replied, to which her husband said, more or less, "Are you nuts? You never set foot in a synagogue. We never observe the Sabbath in any way. We only had a seder, or lit candles on Hanukkah, when our kids were little. We don't any longer. And you're going to light Sabbath candles every week?" "Don't you understand?" Suzanne answered him. "This has nothing to do with God or Judaism. These were my mother's candlesticks. She inherited them from her mother, and lit them as her mother had before her. I will do it too, and hope my daughter will use them after me."

Other interviewees reported arriving at the same lesson, if less dramatically. Sabbath meals, Passover seders, building a sukkah—all allow for a *depth* of personal experience, and a *range* of personal meaning, when enacted with family in keeping with the practice of remote or immediate ancestors, which are precluded by the more rigid, and inevitably collective, character of synagogue services or organizational activity. The rewards and attractions to the self are commensurate.

I don't mean to suggest that other meanings of observance are entirely irrelevant. Passover is valued in part as the festival of freedom. The Sabbath is valued in part because its bestowal of rest to all creatures seems an act of compassion, and its promise of rest to human beings a guarantor of dignity. But these themes are mentioned only rarely in our discussions, and seemed far less important to our interviewees than the family. Had the repertoire of meanings available for observance been uniformly objectionable, we suspect that no amount of potential family togetherness would have made observance attractive; but that is not a problem. Particularist meanings to the Sabbath, for example, have long since been replaced by universalist messages. This leaves participants free to impose their own meanings—and family, present together around the Sabbath table in a way marked off from the rest of the week, stands in the foreground.

This brings me to the third aspect of Jewish meaning among moderately affiliated American Jews on which I want to report: our subjects' relation to God and the synagogue. Once again we encounter a striking paradox. The Jews we met overwhelmingly believe in God. Some spoke about their relation to a personal being of the sort we find in the thought of Martin Buber, an "I-Thou" presence who comforts them and provides meaning to life, but does not directly command or judge them or rouse fear or punish them.[16] "God is . . . an angel on my shoulder. God is something like a best friend. A day doesn't go by when I don't have a literal conversation with God about something." Others think of God as a force, or set of forces, such as we find described in the thought of Mordecai Kaplan: not a personal being, but aspects of the universe that move it in the direction of order and truth, and provide a "ground" for ethics.[17] "There are times when I think of God as being the best that all of us can be, in a humanistic, secular sense. In a sense I believe in a primal force—a spirit that causes things to happen, that sets the world in motion." They are also surprisingly content with, and even fondly attached to, their synagogues, despite or because of the fact that they attend them only irregularly. But they told us time and again that they do not come to synagogue expecting to find God there, or stay away because they do not. God and synagogue both loom large in their experience as Jews, but they described no strong or straightforward relationship between the two.

In part this is because the words in the prayer book simply do not very much interest the Jews to whom we spoke. Whether Orthodox, Reform, Conservative, or Reconstructionist, the liturgies describe a God in whom the Jews we met do not believe. The God of the prayer book, we might say, is "too Jewish." Only one or two of the more than fifty Jews we interviewed expressed belief in a God who had revealed the Torah at Sinai, or had vouchsafed a unique destiny to the Jewish people, or would send a Messiah at the end of days to redeem the Jews and return them to the Land of Israel. It is no surprise, then, that they have no enthusiasm for, or relation to, the words of the prayers.

Yet this does not translate into a lack of enthusiasm for the synagogue, because the latter supplies an encounter with tradition and an experience of community, which *do* exercise a very powerful attraction. God can be, and is, encountered in a variety of settings, unlike community—familiar faces, networks of friends, people who call on one for help. One has to step out of the home, out of the self, to find it. The experience is welcome, so long as autonomy is not compromised. Music in the service creates and enhances the sense of community, all the more if the words to the melodies are in Hebrew, and if both melody and words are redolent of generations past. This is true whether or not one actually understands the words, or can carry a tune. Tradition, imbibed in this way outside the home, reinforces what goes on in the home. It is seen by adults and children alike as an extension of private commitments, shared with people in an extension of private space. Indeed, we were told time and again by Jews who attend services that synagogue offers them a time for self: precious space for quiet moments of introspection, away from daily routine and apart from the demands of family members who have often enough been left at home. Rabbis are regarded positively when they contribute to the spiritual nurturing for which our Jews search; but can also impel Jews away from the synagogue, or Judaism as a whole, by embodying the opposite of what particular Jews happen to be seeking. Programs of adult education offered by the synagogue, if conducted at a high intellectual level, were uniformly praised by our respondents. They enhance commitment without compromising autonomy.

Wade Clark Roof, in his studies of American Christians of the baby boomer cohort (*Generation of Seekers*, 1993),[18] found a similar alienation from the received tenets of the religious tradition, and a similar predilection for personal faith arrived at as the fruit of personal journey. The language reported from his interviews is likewise individualist, utilitarian, and psychological rather than normative or collective. One informant makes it clear that he is in church because he likes it and believes it is good for him, while the majority of Roof's respondents, even those classified as conservative, agreed that religion is "something you do if it meets your needs." Majorities also agreed that one can be a good Christian without attending church at all. The sentiment would have been applauded by the Jews we interviewed, and was in fact echoed in their own comments about the synagogue. The latter must serve the journey, be seen as an enlarged sphere of self and family, in order to secure the loyalties of The Jew Within. If not, the synagogue will suffer the fate of public commitments—Israel, federation, Jewish peoplehood—to which this generation of American Jews, relative to its parents' generation, feels decidedly less loyalty and connection.

Revitalizing Tradition and Community

The enthusiasm expressed by moderately affiliated Jews for home observance and for synagogues that offer the experience of tradition and community is even stronger, as we would expect, among Jews more committed
to observance, individuals who also tend to be better educated in the details and varieties of Jewish tradition. It also seems to be the case, however,
that the challenges American Jews face in maintaining and extending their
Jewish commitments are part and parcel of the modern situation, and so
will not easily or entirely be overcome. Many are shared with other ethnic
and religious traditions. No quick fix is available. Neither assimilation nor
intermarriage will end or greatly diminish any time soon, and Jews will certainly not be motivated to make Judaism a more central and substantial
part of their lives by preying on guilt about the numbers killed in the Holocaust or haranguing people about ethnic or religious obligations that they
no longer recognize. However, a variety of evidence accumulated in recent
years suggests that there is a strategy that proves effective in motivating
Jewish commitment: provision of experiences of compelling meaning and
palpable community. Both are in short supply among Jews, who inhabit a
particularly mobile, individualist, and secular niche of contemporary
America. Both can be made available in Jewish settings such as camps,
schools, synagogues, Jewish Community Centers, and Israel.

The vision of Jewish meaning and community that I have proposed
takes account of, though it does not surrender to, the sovereign self and its
personal quest for meaning, just as it presumes, but tries to work around,
the breakdown of integral Jewish communities. Any meaning proposed to
contemporary American Jews for their acceptance will have to demonstrate
its relevance and its adequacy to their experience in the variety of settings
where life is lived: family and politics, faith and ritual, professional and
personal roles. Any community proposed for their affiliation will have to
be voluntarist rather than coercive, fragmentary rather than totalistic, pluralistic rather than claiming exclusive purchase on the good and the true. I
have set forth this vision in some detail in *Taking Hold of Torah,* and will not
attempt to summarize it here. Suffice it to say that I define Jewish community as a group of Jews joined to one another by tangible bonds of obligation and engaged in serious dialogue with Jewish history and traditions.
Setting forth a vision such as this one is, of course, far easier than accom-
plishing it when the logic of Emancipation and the assumptions of En-

lightenment still militate strongly against increased Jewish commitment by large numbers of American Jews.

My point, however, reinforced by linking this book to the other two, is to emphasize possibilities as well as constraints—itself a major "rethinking" for scholars and leaders of American Jewry too often given over to a relentless pessimism where the future is concerned. Political considerations of the sort I have described remain paramount in Jewish decision-making about ritual. Universalist rationales continue to be less than convincing reasons for undertaking particularist observances. Nostalgia continues to be a major, and sometimes trivializing, aspect of Jewish practice. Nonetheless, community is perhaps more a felt need than ever before, now that voluntarism is utterly taken for granted; Jews are scattered far from family, friends, or Jewish neighborhoods; and many are discontented with the isolation that besets them and their children. Meaning is also perhaps a more precious good than ever before, now that the secular culture is perceived by many Jews as unable to provide either ethical guidance or a sense of ultimate purpose. God is not dismissed out of hand by Jews with higher degrees. Family, while often the springboard in the search for both meaning and community, is not of itself taken to be an adequate answer to the search. American society, finally, seems more amenable than before to expressions of distinctiveness, as American culture seems more open than before to expressions of faith. Jewish feminists at one end of the continuum marking participation in the trends and institutions of the surroundings, and ultra-Orthodox Jews at the other end, both testify to the success of their movements and to the changing possibilities for distinctive Jewish practice in America, as well as to various ways in which Jews have taken advantage of these possibilities to mark their belonging as well as their apartness.

The time has thus proven propitious for Jewish educators, leaders, and institutions who have been able to offer more of an answer to the personal quest on which so many Jews in America seem embarked. This has particularly been the case where they have been able to provide experiences of compelling meaning and palpable community *together.* Many of their efforts have already met with success, thereby challenging the notion that success is impossible, and offering testimony that a "rethinking" of American Judaism is under way in other venues than the academy.

Notes

1. Arnold M. Eisen, *Rethinking Modern Judaism: Ritual, Commandment, Community* (Chicago: University of Chicago Press, 1998).

2. Steven M. Cohen and Arnold M. Eisen, *The Jew Within: Self, Family, and Community in America* (Bloomington: Indiana University Press, 2000).

3. Arnold M. Eisen, *Taking Hold of Torah: Jewish Commitment and Community in America* (Bloomington: Indiana University Press, 1997).

4. Cf. Jacob Katz, *Out of Ghetto* (New York: Schocken, 1978).

5. Franz Rosenzweig, "Teaching and Law" (originally published in "The Builders"), in *Franz Rosenzweig: His Life and Thought*, ed. Nahum Glatzer (New York: Schocken, 1976), 239.

6. Benedict Spinoza, *A Theologico-Political Treatise*, trans. H. M. Elwes (New York: Dover, 1951), 56.

7. Immanuel Kant, *Religion within the Limits of Reason Alone*, trans. Theodore M. Greene and Hoyt H. Hudson (New York: Harper and Row, 1960), 116–17.

8. Max Weber, "Politics as a Vocation," in *From Max Weber*, ed. Hans Gerth and C. Wright Mills (New York: Oxford University Press, 1969), 78–79.

9. Mary Douglas, *Natural Symbols: Explorations in Cosmology* (New York: Pantheon, 1982), 1; Jonathan Z. Smith, *To Take Place: Toward Theory in Ritual* (Chicago: University of Chicago Press, 1987), 98–103.

10. Rosenzweig, "Teaching and Law," 238.

11. Moses Mendelssohn, *Jerusalem*, trans. Allen Arkush (Hanover, NH: University Press of New England, 1983). See especially part 2.

12. Mordecai M. Kaplan, *The Meaning of God in Modern Jewish Religion* (New York: Reconstructionist Press, 1967).

13. Samson Raphael Hirsch, *Horeb: A Philosophy of Jewish Law and Observances*, ed. and trans. I. Grunfeld, 2 vols. (London: Soncino, 1962).

14. Robert Bellah et al., *Habits of the Heart: Individualism and Commitment in American Life* (Berkeley and Los Angeles: University of California Press, 1996).

15. Marshall Sklare and Joseph Greenblum, *Jewish Identity on the Suburban Frontier: A Study of Group Survival in the Open Society*, 2d. ed. (Chicago: University of Chicago Press, 1979), 57.

16. See Martin Buber, *I and Thou*, trans. Walter Kaufman (New York: Charles Scribner's Sons, 1970).

17. See Kaplan, *Meaning of God*.

18. Wade Clark Roof, *Generation of Seekers: The Spiritual Journeys of the Baby Boom Generation* (San Francisco: Harper San Francisco, 1993).

Temple Beth Zion, Boston, 2004. Courtesy of Bill Aron.

American Judaism in Historical Perspective

Jonathan D. Sarna

Thirty years ago, when I first became interested in American Jewish history, I mentioned my interest to a scholar at a distinguished rabbinical seminary, and he was absolutely appalled. "American Jewish history?" he growled. "I'll tell you all that you need to know about American Jewish history: The Jews came to America, they abandoned their faith, they began to live like goyim, and after a generation or two they intermarried and disappeared." "That," he said, "is American Jewish history; all the rest is commentary. Don't waste your time. Go and study Talmud."

I did not take this great sage's advice, but I have long remembered his analysis, for it reflects, as I now recognize, a long-standing fear that Jews in America are doomed to assimilate, that they simply cannot survive in an environment of religious freedom and church-state separation. In America, where religion is totally voluntary, where religious diversity is the norm, where everyone is free to choose his or her own rabbi and his or her own brand of Judaism—or, indeed, no Judaism at all—many, and not just rabbinical school scholars, have assumed that Judaism is fated sooner or later to disappear. Freedom, the same quality that made America so alluring for persecuted faiths, also brought with it the freedom to make religious choices: to modernize Judaism, to assimilate, to intermarry, to convert. American Jews, as a result, have never been able to assume that their future, as Jews, is guaranteed. Each generation has had to wrestle anew with the question of whether its own children and grandchildren would remain

This essay was originally presented on March 8, 2003, at the Jean and Samuel Frankel Center for Judaic Studies, University of Michigan, Ann Arbor.

Jewish, whether Judaism as a living faith would end and carry on as ancestral memory alone.

Many readers surely recognize this assimilationist paradigm. It is a close cousin to the secularization thesis that once held sway in the study of religion. In American Judaism, it might be called "the myth of linear descent," the belief that American Jews start off Orthodox, back in the immigrant generation, and each subsequent generation is a little less Jewish in its observance until that inevitable day when a descendant intermarries and ends up marching down the aisle of a church. We can all point to families where this has actually happened: the Gratz family, the Schiff family, the Warburg family. It has happened too in many lesser-known Cohen, Levi, and Israel families throughout the United States.

"Will the Jews continue to exist in America?" Rabbi Arthur Hertzberg asked almost half a century ago. "Any estimate of the situation based on an unillusioned look at the American Jewish past and at contemporary sociological evidence must answer flatly—no . . . History, sociology, and the emptiness of contemporary Jewish religion all point in the same unhappy direction."[1] Actively by choice, or passively through inaction, assimilation has been widely assumed to be unavoidable. My field of American Jewish history, if not a complete waste of time, is viewed as a foredoomed enterprise.

Yet the history of American Judaism, at least as I have come to understand it while researching *American Judaism: A History* (Yale University Press, 2004), is in many ways a response to this ongoing fear that Judaism in the New World will wither away. Over and over again, I found Jews rising to meet the challenges both internal and external that threatened Jewish continuity, sometimes, paradoxically, by promoting radical discontinuities. Casting aside old paradigms, Jews transformed their faith, reinventing American Judaism in an attempt to make it more appealing, more meaningful, more sensitive to the concerns of the day. They did not always succeed, as the many well-publicized accounts of eminent Christians whose parents, grandparents, or great-grandparents turn out to have been Jews amply attest. But the story of American Judaism, at least as I recount it, is still far from the stereotypical story of "linear descent." It is, instead, a much more dynamic story of people struggling to be Americans and Jews, a story of people who lose their faith and a story of people who regain their faith, a story of assimilation, to be sure, but also a story of revitalization.

Let us consider a few examples. In the 1820s, some highly motivated and creative young Jews in the two largest American communities where

Jews lived, New York and Charleston, moved to transform and revitalize their faith, somewhat in the spirit of the contemporaneous Second Great Awakening. They hoped, in so doing, to thwart Christian missionaries, who always insisted that in order to be modern one had to be Protestant, and they sought most of all to bring Jews back to active observance of their faith. They felt alarmed at the spirit of Jewish "apathy and neglect" that they discerned all around them. Chronologically, their efforts paralleled the emergence of the nascent Reform movement in Germany, where Jews, "convinced of the necessity to restore public worship to its deserving dignity and importance," had in 1818 dedicated the innovative Hamburg Temple. Their efforts also paralleled developments in Curaçao, where in 1819 more than one hundred Jews, unhappy with their cantor and seeking a new communal constitution "in keeping with the enlightened age in which we live," had separated themselves from the organized Jewish community rather than submit to its authority. In both of these cases, revealingly, government officials had intervened and effected compromise.[2] In America, where religion was voluntary and established religious leaders could not depend upon the government to put down dissent, innovators faced far fewer hurdles.

The young people in New York, "gathering with renewed arduor [*sic*] to promote the more strict keeping of their faith,"[3] formed an independent society entitled Hebra Hinuch Nearim, dedicated to the education of Jewish young people. Their constitution and bylaws bespeak their spirit of revival, expressing "an ardent desire to promote the study of our Holy Law, and . . . to extend a knowledge of its divine precepts, ceremonies, and worship among our brethren generally, and the enquiring youth in particular." Worship, they insisted, should be run much less formally, with time set aside for explanations and instruction, without a permanent leader and, revealingly, with no "distinctions" made among the members. The overall aim, leaders explained in an 1825 letter, was "to encrease [*sic*] the respect of the worship of our fathers."[4]

In these endeavors, we see all of the themes familiar to us from the general history of American religion, not only in that era but in many other eras of religious change including our own: revivalism, challenge to authority, a new form of organization, antielitism, and radical democratization. Given the spirit of the age and the fortunate availability of funding, it comes as no surprise that the young people plunged ahead, boldly announcing "their intention to erect a new Synagogue in this city," which would follow the "German and Polish minhag [rite]" and be located "in a more convenient situation for those residing uptown."[5] On November 15, 1825, the new congregation applied for incorporation as B'nai Jeshurun, New York's first Ashkenazic congregation.[6]

In Charleston, where a far better-known schism within the Jewish community occurred, one finds several close parallels to the New York situation. Again the challenge to the synagogue-community came initially from young Jews, born after the Revolution. Their average age was about thirty-two, while the average age of the leaders of the Beth Elohim congregation approached sixty-two. Dissatisfied with "the apathy and neglect which have been manifested towards our holy religion," somewhat influenced by the spread of Unitarianism in Charleston, fearful of Christian missionary activities that had begun to be directed toward local Jews, and, above all, like their New York counterparts, passionately concerned about Jewish survival, forty-seven men petitioned congregational leaders to break with tradition and institute change.[7]

Two-thirds of the Charleston reformers were native-born, and most were people of comparatively modest means who participated in local civic affairs. According to one account, almost three-quarters of them were not paying members of the synagogue. In Charleston, as so often in the history of American Judaism, change was stimulated by outsiders. The reforms in traditional Jewish practice that the reformers sought to introduce, moreover, were far more radical than anything that had been called for in New York. They advocated, among other things, an abbreviated service, vernacular prayers, a weekly sermon, and an end to traditional free-will offerings in the synagogue. When, early in 1825, their petition was dismissed out of hand, they, anticipating the New Yorkers by several months, created an independent Jewish religious society, the Reformed Society of Israelites for Promoting True Principles of Judaism according to its Purity and Spirit—a forerunner of American Reform Judaism.[8]

This is not the place for a full-scale discussion of how young Jews in New York and Charleston transformed American Judaism and helped to shape the pluralistic, competitive model of Judaism that we know today. What is important, for our purposes, is that Jews who formerly had not been interested in Jewish religious life became interested in the 1820s, and that Jewish life, as a result of their efforts, became stronger and more diverse. We have independent confirmation of some of these trends from Rebecca Gratz of Philadelphia, the foremost Jewish woman of her day and a perceptive observer: "Our brothers have all become very attentive to shool [synagogue] matters," she wrote in an 1825 family letter; "they rarely omit attending worship. We all go Friday evening as well as on Saturday morn-ing—the [women's] gallery is as well filled as the other portion of the house."[9] Note that in this revival, as in all subsequent ones, women num-bered significantly among those affected by the new religious currents.

The 1820s marked the first revitalization of Judaism that I know of in America, stimulated by young, native-born men and women concerned that Judaism would not survive unless they initiated change. But it was cer-tainly not the last. I have written elsewhere about the immensely influen-tial American Jewish awakening of the late nineteenth century. This revival was spawned not by East European Jews but by American-born Jews like Cyrus Adler and Henrietta Szold on the East Coast and Ray Frank on the West Coast, along with others who grew alarmed at evidence of assimila-tion in American Jewish life: religious laxity, intermarriage, interest in Eth-ical Culture, and the like. Spurred also by the growth of anti-Semitism in this era, they created what they called alternately a "revival," an "awaken-ing," and a "renaissance." If I may be permitted to quote myself:

> A major cultural reorientation began in the American Jewish commu-nity late in the 1870s and was subsequently augmented by mass immi-gration. The critical developments that we associate with this period—the return to religion, the heightened sense of Jewish peoplehood and particularism, the far-reaching changes that opened up new opportuni-ties and responsibilities for women, the renewed community-wide em-phasis on education and culture, the "burst of organizational energy," and the growth of Conservative Judaism and Zionism—all reflect differ-ent efforts to resolve the "crisis of beliefs and values" that had devel-oped during these decades. By 1914, American Jewry had been trans-formed and the awakening had run its course. The basic contours of the twentieth-century American Jewish community had by then fallen into place.[10]

The late nineteenth century awakening does not fit into the standard para-digm of American Jewish history. Central European Jews, all of us were taught, assimilated out of existence: how, then could they have staged a re-vival? Rather than exploring this paradox (or altering the paradigm), most accounts of American Jewish life simply ignore these developments alto-gether and focus on East European Jewish immigration instead.

For me, however, the late-nineteenth-century awakening illustrates a major theme in American Judaism: the fact that repeatedly, down to our very own day, American Jews have creatively *adapted* their faith to their new environment. Reshaping Judaism in response to challenges from within and from without, they have time and again revitalized their faith, strengthening it, sometimes in surprising and unexpected ways that have brought Jews back into synagogues and produced children more religiously knowledgeable and observant than their parents. The fear that Judaism would not survive unless it changed certainly underlay many of these developments. But, in retrospect, the many creative responses to this fear, the innovations and revivals promoted by those determined to ensure that American Jewish life would continue and thrive, seem to me of far greater historical significance.

Judaism and Religious Pluralism

Another theme that I find central to the history of American Judaism is the fact that, for the major part of American history, Judaism has been the nation's largest and most visible non-Christian faith. Every Jew, every synagogue, every Jewish organization, periodical, and philanthropy has served as a conspicuous challenge to those who sought to define the nation (or its soul) in restrictively Christian terms.

From their very first steps on American soil, back in 1654, Jews extended the boundaries of American pluralism, serving as a model for other religious minorities and, in time, expanding the definition of American religious liberty so that they (and other minorities) might be included as equals. Recall that Peter Stuyvesant, the dictatorial director-general of New Netherland and himself an elder of the Reformed Church and the son of a minister, sought to compel the Jews to depart. His mission was to establish order among the citizenry, to combat "drinking to excess, quarreling, fighting and smiting." Seeking to promote morality and social cohesion, he looked to enforce Calvinist orthodoxy while rooting out nonconformity.[11]

This explains why Stuyvesant sought permission from Amsterdam to keep the Jews out. The Jews, he explained, were "deceitful," "very repugnant," and "hateful enemies and blasphemers of the name of Christ." He asked the directors of the Dutch West India Company to "require them in a friendly way to depart" lest they "infect and trouble this new colony." Revealingly, he warned in a subsequent letter that "giving them liberty we cannot refuse the Lutherans and Papists." Decisions made concerning the Jews, he understood, would serve as precedents and determine the colony's religious character forever after.[12]

Largely for economic reasons (as well as the fact that Jews numbered among its principal shareholders), the Dutch West India Company turned down Peter Stuyvesant's plea. They ordered him to permit Jews to "travel," "trade," "live," and "remain" in New Netherland, "provided the poor among them shall not become a burden to the company or to the community, but be supported by their own nation." After several more petitions, Jews secured the right to trade throughout the colony, serve guard duty, and own real estate. They also won the right to worship in the privacy of their homes, which, according to some accounts, is more than the Lutherans were permitted to do.[13]

The opening of the colony to Jews, just as Stuyvesant feared, soon determined policy for members of the colony's other minority faiths as well. "We doubt very much whether we can proceed against [these faiths] rigorously without diminishing the population and stopping immigration which must be favored at a so tender stage of the country's existence," the directors admonished in 1663 after Stuyvesant banished a Quaker from the colony and spoke out against "sectarians." "You may therefore shut your eyes, at least not force people's consciences, but allow every one to have his own belief, as long as he behaves quietly and legally, gives no offense to his neighbor and does not oppose the government."[14] Under the British, who took New Amsterdam in 1664 and renamed it New York, this policy was maintained. In the 1740s, the city boasted houses of worship for Anglicans, Dutch Calvinists, French Huguenots, German Lutherans, Presbyterians, Baptists, Quakers, and Jews.[15]

Following the American Revolution, Jews once again played a role in ensuring that religious liberty was not restricted to Christians alone—sometimes, as in New York, simply by being present. It is probably no accident that New York, the most religiously pluralistic of the new states, was the first to grant "free exercise and enjoyment of religious profession and worship, without discrimination or preference" to all its citizens, Christian and non-Christian alike. Pennsylvania's new constitution was more restrictive, requiring officeholders to "acknowledge the Scriptures of the old and new Testament to be given by divine inspiration." But after several widely publicized petitions from Jews, that clause was dropped in 1790. The U.S. Constitution, of course, followed the most liberal state precedents, and, thanks to Charles Pinckney of South Carolina (another state with a visible Jewish community), it explicitly included the words "no religious test shall ever be required as a qualification to any office or public trust under the authority of the United States." Revealingly, the only petition concerning religious liberty that reached the federal Constitutional Convention, meeting in Philadelphia, also came from a Jew, Jonas Phillips, who memorably declared that "the Israeletes [*sic*] will think them self happy to live under a government where all Relegious societys are on an Eaquel footing."[16]

A Virginian who called himself a "Social Christian" probably reflected the views of many dissenters when he publicly opposed the granting of full equality to non-Christians. "The bulk of this community are Christian," he observed, "and if there be a few who are Jews, Mahomedans, Atheists, or Deists amongst us, though I would not wish to torture or persecute them on account of their opinions, yet to exclude such from our publick offices is prudent and just; to restrain them from publishing their singular opinions to the disturbance of society, is equally sound policy and a necessary caution to promote the general good; nor is it sinful or tyrannical to compel them to pay towards the support of religious worship, though they do not join it." That view, however, did not prevail, even in the "Social Christian" home state of Virginia. Instead, in 1786, the General Assembly of Virginia finally enacted the bill for religious freedom proposed by Thomas Jefferson seven years earlier: "That no man shall be compelled to frequent or support any religious worship, place, or ministry whatsoever, nor shall be enforced, restrained, molested, or burthened in his body or goods, nor shall otherwise suffer, on account of his religious opinions or belief; but that all men shall be free to profess, and by argument to maintain, their opinions in matters of religion, and that the same shall in no wise diminish, enlarge, or affect their civil capacities."[17]

The famed correspondence between Jews and George Washington went even further in defining the place of Judaism in the new nation. The address of the "Hebrew Congregation in Newport" to the president, composed for his visit to that city on August 17, 1790, following Rhode Island's ratification of the Constitution, paralleled other letters that Washington received from religious bodies of different denominations and followed a long-established custom associated with the ascension of kings. Redolent with biblical and liturgical language, the address noted past discrimination against Jews, praised the new government for "generously affording to all liberty of conscience and immunities of citizenship," and thanked God "for all of the blessings of civil and religious liberty" that Jews now enjoyed under the Constitution. Washington, in his oft-quoted reply, reassured the Jewish community about what he correctly saw as its central concern—religious liberty. Appropriating a phrase contained in the Hebrew congregation's original letter, he characterized the United States government as one that "gives to bigotry no sanction, to persecution no assistance." He described religious liberty, following Thomas Jefferson, as an inherent natural right, distinct from the indulgent religious "toleration" practiced by the British and much of enlightened Europe, where Jewish emancipation was so often linked with demands for Jewish "improvement." Finally, echoing the language of the prophet Micah (4:4), he hinted that America might itself prove something of a promised land for Jews, a place where they would "merit and enjoy the good will of the other inhabitants; while every one shall sit in safety under his own vine and fig tree and there shall be none to make him afraid."[18]

Bigotry and persecution, of course, did not thereafter miraculously disappear. American Jews continued to have to fight for their religious rights well into the twentieth century, and manifestations of anti-Jewish prejudice have continued to the present day. But important changes nevertheless took place. Slowly, America came to understand itself in broader and more inclusive religious terms that pushed beyond the perimeters of Christianity. Abraham Lincoln's memorable phrase in the Gettysburg Address, later incorporated into the Pledge of Allegiance, was "nation under God." Thanks to the efforts of interfaith organizations around World War II, terms like *Judeo-Christian* came into vogue. Will Herberg, in a best-selling book published in 1955, described a "tripartite scheme" of American religion: "Protestant-Catholic-Jew." All of these terms signified Jews' newfound acceptance in the world of American religion, their emergence, in less than two hundred years, from a curiosity into America's "third faith." No longer were they grouped, as they had been in the colonial mind, with exotic religions and nonbelievers, as in the well-known colonial-era phrase "Jews, Turks, and infidels." Instead, by the late twentieth century, they emerged as acknowledged religious insiders.[19] The fact that Connecticut senator Joseph Lieberman (an Orthodox Jew), Vermont governor Howard Dean (the husband and father of Jews), and Massachusetts senator John Kerry (the grandchild of Jews) have all run for the presidency surely testifies to the enormous transformation that America has experienced over the past 350 years (even the past 50!).

"Only in America," the journalist Harry Golden proclaimed in a best-selling book of that title published in 1958. Senator Joseph Lieberman echoed that comment when Al Gore nominated him for the vice presidency in the 2000 election. While something of an exaggeration—Jews have also been nominated for and attained high office in countries stretching from Austria to Singapore—"only in America" reflects a widely felt sense that the history of Judaism in the United States is both special and distinct: "America," as the saying goes, "is different." And in many ways it *is* different. Discrimination and persecution, the foremost challenges confronting most diasporic Jews through the ages, have in America been far less significant historical factors than democracy, liberty of conscience, church-state separation, and voluntarism. Emancipation and enlightenment, central themes of Jewish history in Europe, have also been far less central to the history of the Jews in the United States. That, incidentally, is why historians of modern Judaism from Heinrich Graetz onward have had trouble with American Judaism: it does not fit neatly into the field's established rubrics. Expulsions, concentration camps, and extermination, of course, have never been part of American Jewish history. By contrast, in America, as nowhere else to the same degree, Judaism has had to adapt to a religious environment shaped by the denominational character of American Protestantism, the canons of free market competition, the ideals of freedom, and the reality of diversity. What is distinctive in American Judaism is largely a result of these factors.

Religious Diversity within American Judaism

Let me say a further word concerning the subject of diversity, a third theme in my history of American Judaism, and one, to my mind, that has been absolutely central almost from the very beginning. In the seventeenth and eighteenth centuries, every known colonial American Jewish community included both Sephardim and Ashkenazim, and was comprised of Jews who came from widely scattered backgrounds. By 1790, the United States census recorded Jews who had been born in England, France, Germany, Holland, Poland, Portugal, and the West Indies, as well as in the American colonies, a mix that mirrored the composition of the late-colonial Jewish community as well.[20] The Sephardic form of Judaism predominated, as it always had in North America, but from the early eighteenth century onward the preponderance of colonial Jews were actually Ashkenazim or people of mixed background. Within every community, even within many individual families, a full gamut of religious observances and attitudes could be found, a spectrum ranging all the way from deep piety to total indifference. In the years following the American Revolution, Jacob Rader Marcus found that "there were almost as many Judaisms as there were individuals."[21] In matters of religious practice, as in so many other aspects of life during the early republic, individual freedom reigned supreme, setting a pattern that would govern American Jewish life forever after.

Jewish life in America became even more diverse following the migration of tens of thousands of Central European Jews from Bavaria, Western Prussia, Poland, and Alsace between 1820 and 1880. During that time, America's Jewish population ballooned from about 3,000 to around 250,000. Immigrants spread out across the length and breadth of the country, reaching all the way to California. Already by the Civil War, the number of organized Jewish communities with at least one established Jewish institution had reached 160, distributed over thirty-one states and the District of Columbia. Jews moved into every region of the country and lived in more than one thousand American locations during this period, wherever rivers, roads, or railroad tracks took them. Like the bulk of immigrants to America's shores, then and later, they pursued opportunities wherever they found them.[22]

During this era, the diversity of American Jewish life was often reflected in the diversity of American synagogues, each committed to a different *minhag,* or rite, such as the German rite, the Polish rite, the English rite, and so forth. By the Civil War, every major American Jewish community had at least two synagogues, and larger ones, like Philadelphia, Baltimore, and Cincinnati, had four or more. Jewish leaders regularly expressed impatience with all these divisions and pressed for unity. They argued that what Jews held in common was far more important than the liturgical differences that divided them, and they condemned the situation in cities like New York where five or more Jewish rites competed. But since similar divisions characterized any number of American religious groups—French Catholics and Irish Catholics worshiped apart; so did Lutherans of different backgrounds, and in one Cincinnati county there were four different Baptist churches reflecting four different points of origin—arguments for unity frequently fell on deaf ears. In some Jewish circles, in fact, the smorgasbord of worship choices even drew praise, perhaps a reflection of new marketplace values. "The Israelites living here come from various countries," one immigrant wrote back to his relatives in Bamberg approvingly. "Everybody can choose freely where or in which synagogue he wants to be enrolled."[23]

Actually, numbers of Jews chose not to enroll in any synagogue whatsoever. In America, unlike in Germany, the state placed no pressure on Jews to affiliate with a religious community, and in any case, thousands of Jews had settled in remote areas where no synagogues could be found. Even in Cincinnati, where four synagogues did exist by midcentury, 22 percent of the city's Jews were estimated to be unaffiliated. Nationally that figure stood much higher. According to the 1850 census, only 35 percent of America's Jews could even be accommodated within America's synagogues: there were but 17,688 seats for some fifty thousand Jews (and some of those seats regularly sat vacant).[24] Discounting the smaller congregations that the census missed, and the young children who would have been left at home, it seems reasonable to assume that as many as half of America's Jews were unaffiliated at midcentury. Jewish leaders took this to be a matter of grave concern.

Diversity, many at the time believed, posed a threat to the longtime viability of the American Jewish community. They looked to unify Jews through an overarching authority ("chief rabbi"), a conference of rabbis, or perhaps a unified prayer book, what Isaac Mayer Wise called *Minhag Amerika*. Without unity and centralized authority, they warned, Judaism would decline. Like so many before and after them, they feared that America would prove to be a land that was good for Jews but bad for Judaism.

Paradoxically, though, diversity triumphed, for mid-nineteenth-century Jews pursued three different strategies to try to ensure Judaism's survival. Some argued that Jews themselves needed to be "regenerated" through greater emphasis on Jewish education and the strengthening of Jewish religious life. Others insisted that Judaism as a religion was at fault and needed to be "reformed." Still others felt that community and kinship, rather than rituals and faith, should form the new basis for Jewish life; they sought to unite Jews around ties of peoplehood.

The first strategy, perhaps best articulated by the great Orthodox Jewish leader Isaac Leeser, advocated tradition in an American key. He called for greater emphasis on Jewish education, decorum, aesthetics, an English-language sermon, but nothing that deviated from Jewish law. Years after he himself had passed from the scene, those whom he influenced continued to pursue the goal of an Americanized traditional Judaism, insisting that Judaism's future depended upon the education and uplifting of American Jews rather than upon any fundamental changes to Judaism itself. A later generation would call this modern Orthodoxy.[25]

The second strategy, made famous by the great Reform Jewish leader Isaac Mayer Wise, presumed that Judaism itself needed to change in order for it to survive. Reformers urged Jews to abandon rituals that seemed incompatible with modernity and to adopt innovations that promised to make Judaism more appealing and spiritually uplifting, like shorter services, vernacular prayers, organ music, and mixed seating. "We hold that all such Mosaic and rabbinical laws as regulate diet, priestly purity, and dress originated in ages and under the influence of ideas entirely foreign to our present mental and spiritual state," the famed 1885 Pittsburgh Platform of Reform Judaism declared. "Their observance in our days," it continued, "is apt rather to obstruct than to further modern spiritual elevation." Reformers advocated thoroughgoing reforms—the removal of what they saw as Judaism's accumulated "defects and deformities"—to keep Judaism alive and lure young Jews back to the synagogue.[26]

The third strategy aimed at preserving Judaism in America rejected the synagogue altogether and focused on ties of peoplehood as the unifying element in Jewish life. This idea found its most important institutional expression in the Jewish fraternal organization B'nai B'rith (literally, "sons of the covenant"), established in 1843. The preamble to the order's original constitution carefully avoided any mention of God, Torah, ritual commandments, or religious faith, but stressed the importance of Jewish unity: "B'nai B'rith has taken upon itself the mission of uniting Israelites in the work of promoting their highest interests and those of humanity." While synagogues divided Jews and alienated some of them altogether, B'nai B'rith argued that fraternal ties—the covenant *(b'rith)* that bound Jews one to another regardless of religious ideology—could bring about "union and harmony."[27]

The three strategies put forth to save American Judaism, in addition to being three means of achieving a common preservationist end, also reflected deep uncertainty surrounding the central priorities of American Jewish religious life. Which of their core values, Jews wondered, should be priority number one: (1) to uphold and maintain Judaism's sacred religious traditions, (2) to adapt Judaism to new conditions of life in a new land, or (3) to preserve above all a strong sense of Jewish peoplehood and communal unity? Many Jews, traditionalists and reformers alike, actually cherished all three of these values. The history of American Judaism is replete with oscillations back and forth among these priorities, a reflection of tensions, deeply rooted within Judaism itself, between the forces of tradition and the forces of change, between those who supported compromise for the sake of unity and those who insisted upon firmness for the sake of principle.

Religion and Identity Politics

Looking back, these tensions may be seen to have been highly beneficial. Proponents of different strategies and priorities in American Jewish life checked each other's excesses. Together they accomplished what none might have accomplished separately: they kept American Judaism going. But it is important to recognize, at the same time, that this benefit came at a steep price. Often, and even to this very day, American Jewish religious life, because of its great diversity, has seethed with acrimonious contention, the unseemly specter of Jews battling Jews.

With so many bitter divisions in Jewish life—between the different religious movements and among them; between Jews of different backgrounds and ideologies; between in-married Jews and intermarried Jews; matrilineal Jews and patrilineal Jews; straight Jews and gay Jews; born Jews and converted Jews; American Jews and Israeli Jews; committed Jews and indifferent Jews—some have questioned whether Jews can remain a united people at all in the twenty-first century. Knowledgeable observers have foreseen "an unbridgeable schism" in Jewish life, "a cataclysmic split," "the bifurcation of Jewry." Well-regarded volumes on contemporary Judaism carry titles like *A People Divided* and *Jew vs. Jew*.[28]

Issues like patrilineal descent, the ordination of openly gay rabbis, the sanctioning of same-sex marriages, and the ordination of women feed the "culture wars" within American Judaism. Ugly local disputes, many of them involving Orthodox efforts to find accommodation for their religious needs and lifestyle choices, also publicly pit Jews against one another, sometimes even in court. Some Orthodox Jews, in response to these developments, question whether rabbis should perform marriages between Orthodox and Reform Jews. Some Reform Jews, in response to these same developments, question whether intermarriage with a liberal non-Jew is not preferable to marrying an Orthodox Jew. Even the Torah itself no longer provides a basis for Jewish unity. Once, synagogues across the spectrum of Jewish life used the same Torah text and commentary, a volume edited in England by the American-trained chief rabbi Joseph H. Hertz. In the twenty-first century, Reform, Conservative, and Orthodox Judaism each offer congregants their own movement's text and commentary on the Torah and view those produced by the other movements with disdain.[29]

For all of these dangers, however, Jewish unity is far from dead. In fact, as America moves back to the center politically, signs within American Judaism suggest a parallel return to the "vital center" and a shift away from the divisive struggles of earlier decades. Independent day schools, transdenominational high schools, nationwide programs of adult Jewish learning, the revitalized Hillel programs on college campuses, the Birthright Israel travel initiative, and an array of other local and national activities aimed at revitalizing American Judaism all look to bring Jews of different religious persuasions together. Threats to the State of Israel and fears of rising world-wide anti-Semitism likewise promote a sense among American Jews that they need to find ways to communicate and cooperate with one another across the various religious streams, distances and differences notwithstanding. The question, not so different from the one facing Jews in the mid-nineteenth century, remains where to compromise for the sake of unity and where to stand firm for the sake of principle.

A recent book entitled *One People, Two Worlds: A Reform Rabbi and an Orthodox Rabbi Explore the Issues That Divide Them* (2002) captures this dilemma. Its two authors, rabbis who stand on opposite ends of the Jewish spectrum, prove by the very act of communicating with one another that "discourse among Jews can be civil even when disagreements exist." Yet the controversy generated by the book also demonstrates the fragility of these efforts, for the Orthodox coauthor, at the behest of his fervently Orthodox colleagues, withdrew from a seventeen-city speaking tour on which he and his Reform counterpart were set to dialogue jointly on stage. This mixed message of communication and cleavage reflects, perhaps even more than the authors intended, the parlous tension between "compromise" and "principle," "one people" and "two worlds." The fate of American Judaism—whether its adherents will step back from the edge of schism or fall into it—hangs perilously in the balance.[30]

With so many questions and issues and tensions confronting them, it comes as no surprise that Jews today feel bewildered and uncertain. Should they focus on quality to enhance Judaism or focus on quantity to increase the number of Jews? Embrace intermarriage as an opportunity for outreach or condemn it as a disaster for offspring? Build religious bridges or fortify religious boundaries? Strengthen religious authority or promote religious autonomy? Harmonize Judaism with contemporary culture or uphold Jewish tradition against contemporary culture? Compromise for the sake of Jewish unity or stand firm for cherished Jewish principles?

Simultaneously, indeed, Jews witness two contradictory trends operating in their community, assimilation and revitalization. Which will predominate and what the future holds nobody knows. That will be determined day by day, community by community, Jew by Jew.

Regularly, American Jews hear, as I did at the start of my career from a scholar at a distinguished rabbinical seminary, and as other Jews did in colonial times, and in the era of the American Revolution, and in the nineteenth century, and in the twentieth century, that Judaism in America is doomed, that assimilation and intermarriage are inevitable. Should high rates of intermarriage continue and the community grow complacent, that may yet prove true.

But history, as we have seen, also suggests another possibility: that today, like so often before, American Jews will find creative ways to maintain and revitalize American Judaism. With the help of visionary leaders, committed followers, and generous philanthropists, it may still be possible for the current "vanishing" generation of American Jews to be succeeded by another "vanishing" generation, and then still another.

"A nation dying for thousands of years," the great Jewish philosopher Simon Rawidowicz once observed, "means a living nation. Our incessant dying means uninterrupted living, rising, standing up, beginning anew." His message, delivered to Jews agonizing over the loss of six million of their compatriots, applies equally well today in the face of contemporary challenges to Jewish continuity. "If we are the last—let us be the last as our fathers and forefathers were. Let us prepare the ground for the last Jews who will come after us, and for the last Jews who will rise after them, and so on until the end of days."[31]

Notes

1. Arthur Hertzberg, *Being Jewish in America* (New York: Schocken, 1979), 82, 85. For his later view, see his article in *Encyclopedia Judaica Yearbook, 1990–1991*, reprinted in Jonathan D. Sarna, *The American Jewish Experience*, 2d ed. (New York: Holmes and Meier, 1997), 350–55.

2. W. Gunther Plaut, *The Rise of Reform Judaism: A Sourcebook of Its European Origins* (New York: World Union for Progressive Judaism, 1963), 31; Michael A. Meyer, *Response to Modernity: A History of the Reform Movement in Judaism* (New York: Oxford University Press, 1988), 53–61; Isaac S. Emmanuel and Suzanne A. Emmanuel, *History of the Jews of the Netherlands Antilles*, 2 vols. (Cincinnati: American Jewish Archives, 1970), 1:306–27, esp. 319.

3. *National Advocate* (New York), December 5, 1825, 2.

4. Joseph L. Blau and Salo W. Baron, *The Jews of the United States: A Documentary History, 1790–1840*, 3 vols. (New York: Columbia University Press, 1963), 2:542–45; *Christian Inquirer*, September 17, 1825, 151.

5. David de Sola Pool, *An Old Faith in the New World: Portrait of Shearith Israel, 1654–1954* (New York: Columbia University Press, 1955), 437.

6. Israel Goldstein, *A Century of Judaism in New York: B'nai Jeshurun, 1825–1925* (New York: Congregation B'nai Jeshurun, 1930), 54–55; the original spelling of the congregation's name was "B'nai Yeshiorun."

7. Robert Liberles, "Conflict over Reforms: The Case of Congregation Beth Elohim, Charleston, South Carolina," in *The American Synagogue: A Sanctuary Transformed*, ed. Jack Wertheimer (Cambridge: Cambridge University Press, 1987), 282; Blau and Baron, *Jews of United States*, 2:554.

8. L. C. Moise, *Biography of Isaac Harby* (Charleston: n.p., 1931); Lou H. Silberman, *American Impact: Judaism in the United States in the Early Nineteenth Century* (Syracuse: Syracuse University Press, 1964); James W. Hagy, *This Happy Land: The Jews of Colonial and Antebellum Charleston* (Tuscaloosa: University of Alabama Press, 1993), 128–60; Meyer, *Response to Modernity*, 228–33; Gary Phillip Zola, *Isaac Harby of Charleston, 1788–1828* (Tuscaloosa: University of Alabama Press, 1994), 112–49.

9. David Philipson, *Letters of Rebecca Gratz* (Philadelphia: Jewish Publication Society, 1929), 75–76.

10. Jonathan D. Sarna, *A Great Awakening: The Transformation That Shaped Twentieth-Century American Judaism and Its Implications for Today* (New York: Council for Initiatives in Jewish Education, 1995), 7.

11. Oliver A. Rink, "Private Interest and Godly Gain: The West India Company and the Dutch Reformed Church in New Netherland, 1624–1664," *New York History* 75 (July 1994): 245–64; Henry H. Kessler and Eugene Rachlis, *Peter Stuyvesant and His New York* (New York: Random House, 1959), 66; Patricia U. Bonomi, *Under the Cope of Heaven: Religion, Society and Politics in Colonial New York* (New York: Oxford University Press, 1986), 25.

12. Samuel Oppenheim, "The Early History of the Jews in New York, 1654–1664," *Publications of the American Jewish Historical Society* 18 (1909): 4, 5, 20.

13. Oppenheim, "Early History," 8–37; Joyce D. Goodfriend, *Before the Melting Pot: Society and Culture in Colonial New York City, 1664–1730* (Princeton: Princeton University Press, 1992), 11, 84; James Homer Williams, "An Atlantic Perspective on the Jewish Struggle for Rights and Opportunities in Brazil, New Netherland, and New York," in *Jews and the Expansion of Europe to the West, 1450–1800,* ed. Paolo Bernardini and Norman Fiering (New York: Berghahn, 2001), 369–93.

14. E. T. Corwin, ed., *Ecclesiastical Records of the State of New York,* 7 vols. (Albany, 1901–16), 1:530.

15. All of these houses of worship were portrayed in David Grim, *Plan of the City and Environs of New York as they were in 1742–1744* (New York, 1813).

16. Jonathan D. Sarna and David G. Dalin, *Religion and State in the American Jewish Experience* (Notre Dame, IN: University of Notre Dame Press, 1997), 63–75; Philip B. Kurland and Ralph Lerner, *The Founders' Constitution,* 5 vols. (Indianapolis: Liberty Fund, 1987), 4:638.

17. Sarna and Dalin, *Religion and State,* 68–69.

18. Blau and Baron, *Jews of United States,* 1:8–11; Sarna and Dalin, *Religion and State,* 79–82. The editor of Jefferson's papers suggests that Jefferson may even have drafted Washington's reply to the Jews of Newport. See Julian P. Boyd, ed., *The Papers of Thomas Jefferson,* 21 vols. (Princeton: Princeton University Press, 1950–74), 19:610n; for Jefferson's views on toleration, Charles B. Sanford, *The Religious Life of Thomas Jefferson* (Charlottesville: University of Virginia Press, 1984), 27.

19. Mark Silk, "Notes on the Judeo-Christian Tradition in America," *American Quarterly* 36 (spring 1984): 65–85; Will Herberg, *Protestant-Catholic-Jew: An Essay in American Religious Sociology,* rev. ed. (New York: Anchor, 1960).

20. Ira Rosenwaike, "An Estimate and Analysis of the Jewish Population of the United States in 1790," *Publications of the American Jewish Historical Society* 59 (1960): 23–67.

21. Jacob R. Marcus, *United States Jewry, 1776–1985,* 4 vols. (Detroit: Wayne State University Press, 1989–93), 1:610–13.

22. Rudolf Glanz, "The Spread of Jewish Communities through America before the Civil War," *YIVO Annual* 15 (1974): 7–45; Rudolf Glanz, "Where the Jewish Press Was Distributed in Pre–Civil War America," *Western States Jewish Historical Quarterly* 5 (1972): 1–14; Uriah Z. Engelman, "Jewish Statistics in the U.S. Census of Religious Bodies (1850–1935)," *Jewish Social Studies* 9 (1947): 130.

23. Abraham J. Karp, "Overview: The Synagogue in America—a Historical Typology," in Wertheimer, *The American Synagogue,* 5; Linda K. Pritchard, "The Spirit in the Flesh: Religion and Regional Economic Development," in *Belief and Behavior: Essays in the New Religious History,* ed. Philip R. Vandermeer and Robert Swierenga (New Brunswick, NJ: Rutgers University Press, 1991), 97; Blau and Baron, *Jews of United States,* 3:810.

24. Steven G. Mostov, "A 'Jerusalem' on the Ohio: The Social and Economic History of Cincinnati's Jewish Community, 1840–1875," Ph.D. diss., Brandeis University, 1981, 150; Engelman, "Jewish Statistics," 129.

25. Lance J. Sussman, *Isaac Leeser and the Making of American Jewry* (Detroit: Wayne State University Press, 1995) is the standard biography.

26. James G. Heller, *Isaac M. Wise: His Life, Work and Thought* (New York: Union of American Hebrew Congregations, 1965), and Sefton D. Temkin, *Isaac Mayer Wise: Shaping American Judaism* (Oxford: Littman Library, 1992) are the best biographies. On Reform Judaism, see Meyer, *Response to Modernity;* the Pittsburgh Platform is reprinted there on pp. 387–88.

27. Edward E. Grusd, *B'nai B'rith: The Story of a Covenant* (New York: Appleton-Century, 1966), 20; cf. Deborah Dash Moore, *B'nai B'rith and the Challenge of Ethnic Leadership* (Albany: SUNY Press, 1981).

28. Jack Wertheimer, *A People Divided: Judaism in Contemporary America* (New York: Basic Books, 1993), xiii; Reuven Bulka, *The Coming Cataclysm: The Orthodox-Reform Rift and the Future of the Jewish People* (Oakville, Ontario: Mosaic, 1984), 13; Irving Greenberg, *Will There Be One Jewish People in the Year 2000?* (New York: National Jewish Resource Center, 1985); David Vital, *The Future of the Jews: A People at the Crossroads?* (Cambridge: Harvard University Press, 1990), 101.

29. Samuel G. Freedman, *Jew vs. Jew: The Struggle for the Soul of American Jewry* (New York: Simon and Schuster, 2000); Debra Nussbaum Cohen, "Are the Jewish People Splitting Apart?" www.jewishaz.com/jewishnews/971003/split-sb.html (consulted October 15, 2007).

30. Ammiel Hirsch and Yosef Reinman, *One People, Two Worlds: A Reform Rabbi and an Orthodox Rabbi Explore the Issues That Divide Them* (New York: Schocken, 2002); Samuel G. Freedman, "They Canceled Dialogue," *Jerusalem Report,* December 16, 2002, 54.

31. Simon Rawidowicz, *Studies in Jewish Thought,* ed. Nahum N. Glatzer (Philadelphia: Jewish Publication Society of America, 1964), 223; Marshall Sklare, *Observing America's Jews* (Hanover, NH: University Press of New England, 1993), 262–74.

Three Generations, Borough Park, New York, 1975. Courtesy of Bill Aron.

From Fluidity to Rigidity: The Religious Worlds of Conservative and Orthodox Jews in Twentieth-Century America

Jeffrey S. Gurock

Conservatism and Orthodoxy in America, circa 2000

By the close of the century, it had become clear that most Conservative and Orthodox Jews in America were living increasingly within two very different religious worlds. More than any other time in their history in this country, the minority of America's Jews who attended Orthodox synagogues—from the *shtibls* of Brooklyn to the affluent congregations of suburbia—adhered to the requirements and demands of Jewish law with ever intensifying punctiliousness.[1] Conversely, Conservatism's larger contemporary rank and file, while affirming the importance of Judaism in their lives, did not view the strictures of halacha (Jewish law) as essential to their religious existence. The 1990 American Jewish population survey, for example, revealed significant gaps in religious observance and synagogue attendance between these two religious groups. Whereas 64 percent of all self-described adult Orthodox Jews reported that they always maintained separate meat and dairy dishes in their homes—a sure sign of adherence to kashruth—only 18 percent of Conservatives did so. Regarding Sabbath observance, 54.4 percent of Orthodox Jews refrained from "handling money on the Sabbath," while only 13 percent of Conservatives were thus constrained. More than half of the Orthodox adults surveyed attended synagogue "once a week or more." Only one in eight of their Conservative counterparts were similarly disposed.

This essay was originally presented on March 16, 1998, at the Jean and Samuel Frankel Center for Judaic Studies, University of Michigan, Ann Arbor.

The 1990 survey also suggested that the future would witness Orthodox and Conservative laypeople drifting even further apart in their religious lifestyles. Orthodox "baby boomers"—people then in their late forties and early fifties—who presumably were in community leadership positions even as they were raising the next generation of youngsters—were more punctilious in their observances and commitments than the overall Orthodox group. Nearly eight of ten of these middle-aged people attended synagogue once a week or more, and more than eight of ten of them always used separate dishes and refrained from using money on Saturday. Concomitantly, Conservative "baby boomers" were keeping the Sabbath, following kosher laws, and going to services to almost the same degree and at the same rate as were all other Conservative adults.[2]

For all the punctiliousness of this Orthodox profile, there still were American Jews who identified themselves as Orthodox but who did not live in accord with that denomination's teachings. For example, as late as 1986 an Orthodox rabbi who had served congregations in Youngstown, Ohio, and Providence, Rhode Island, could point out that in America's smaller cities, "religious observance and knowledge" among members of Orthodox synagogues "are in a sorry predicament." It was his unhappy lot to minister to "non-practicing" Jews, "who almost always view . . . faith in sociological and ethnic terms."[3]

Meanwhile, if Orthodoxy still had its soft underbelly of graying nonobservant constituents,[4] Conservatism had its own committed cadre of those who adhered to traditional practices, and perhaps did so with a zeal comparable to that of their Orthodox counterparts. As of 1986, some 20 percent of the Conservative group regarded Sabbath, kashruth observance, and weekly synagogue attendance as essential religious values. They were reading Jewish law differently than their Orthodox counterparts; but their conclusions led them as well to assertively observe the traditions. Still, on balance, the denominations' rank and file lived more and more their separate Jewish lives.

The rabbis who served these two very disparate communities were raised and educated within these very different religious environments. Among the younger men and women ministering to Conservative congregations—those ordained circa 1985 to 1990—close to 70 percent hailed from homes that were affiliated with the Conservative movement. There they received their earliest training and indoctrination within congregational Talmud Torahs or religious schools. Unlike prior generations—about which we will have much to say later—almost none of these rabbis (3 percent) came from Orthodox homes. The close to one-third of younger rabbis who did not come from within the United Synagogue community had been raised mostly within Reform or unaffiliated families.[5] And if by 1998, approximately 10 percent of the rabbis who served in Conservative synagogues were ordained at "Yeshiva University or other Orthodox seminaries," these colleagues were among the more senior members of the Rabbinical Assembly. Certainly, none of the approximately 16 percent of the women serving in United Synagogue pulpits were trained at Yeshiva's Rabbi Isaac Elchanan Theological Seminary (RIETS).[6]

There are no quantitative studies of the younger men who served in American Orthodox pulpits. Nonetheless, several reasoned statements can be made about the emerging and future leaders of that denomination based on an examination of the family and educational backgrounds of the some 144 men who were honored at a 1993 RIETS quadrennial *Khag Ha-Semicha* (ordination celebration). What can be said about RIETS' rabbis certainly holds true for the more sectarian elements within the Orthodox community.[7]

The typical early 1990s graduate of RIETS was a scion of an Orthodox Jewish family who, in many instances, might have been the son or grandson of a rabbi trained at the same school or at a European yeshiva. He was, likewise, the product of the extensive network of North American Orthodox day schools and received informal educational training and direction in that movement's youth groups and summer camps. His road to the rabbinate led him to Yeshiva's undergraduate schools, which, along with a year or two of study in an Israeli yeshiva, prepared him for his ordination training.

There were, of course, some notable exceptions to this pattern, exceptions of which RIETS was enormously proud. Some of their younger rabbis were Jews from nontraditional backgrounds who found Orthodoxy as maturing adults.[8] A few other idiosyncratic types were young men who had begun their rabbinical training at the Jewish Theological Seminary (JTS) and who transferred to Yeshiva. In prior generations, as we will presently discuss, Yeshiva students frequently "checked out" to JTS for careerist or for ideological reasons.[9] Now, it seemed that a few more traditionally minded fellows from Morningside Heights who were unhappy with the ideological direction JTS was taking, or were desirous of RIETS' more intensive style of traditional learning, were enrolling at the Orthodox institution.[10]

In any case, with the exception of the erstwhile JTS men and the handful of *Baalei Teshuvah* (the newly observant) who made RIETS their home, most contemporary RIETS graduates possessed little formal exposure to the religious world of Conservative (or Reform) Judaism. Those trained in the sectarian yeshiva world, it may be reasonably assumed, had even fewer interdenominational contacts. Similarly, contemporary Conservative rabbis testified to very few experiences where they studied formally with those destined to be their Orthodox rabbinical counterparts. Both denominations' rabbis, much like their congregants, live in different religious worlds.

The majority of Conservative and Orthodox Jews who stayed within their own specific religious spheres also prayed in very different types of synagogues. The more liberal denomination's religious rite and scene has been aptly characterized as reflecting the "triumph of egalitarianism." Even in those Conservative congregations that were not served by a woman rabbi or cantor, women enjoyed almost the same set of synagogue privileges as did men. As of 1997, almost all United Synagogue affiliates counted women in the minyan (83 percent), permitted women to lead the services (78 percent), and allowed women to read from the Torah (82 percent), and "Bar and Bat Mitzvah celebrants [were] treated the same way."[11]

None of these signs of egalitarianism were visible in the rites of even the most avant-garde Orthodox synagogues.[12] Whereas 79 percent of Conservative synagogues had a woman serve "as a president of the congregation during the past 15 years,"[13] only a handful of Orthodox synagogues had placed a female in such a position of lay authority. And, while some Orthodox feminists had articulated, as a point of advocacy, the possibility that a woman might someday be ordained as an American Orthodox rabbi, no Orthodox rabbinical training institution had shown any interest in encouraging such a development.[14] In the meantime, the "problem" or phenomenon of mixed seating in Orthodox synagogues—an issue that plagued Orthodox leadership for generations—had virtually disappeared from the scene.[15] Likewise, if many Orthodox synagogues, not unlike their Conservative counterparts, once habitually conducted late Friday night services for their rank-and-file members, more recent gatherings in Orthodox synagogues after Friday sundown have often been designed "to make Friday Night Shabbes," as an outreach device for the unaffiliated.[16] For more than two out of three Conservative congregations at the end of the twentieth century, the late Friday night service was basic.[17]

Even as most Conservative and Orthodox laity, rabbis, and synagogues were going their own separate religious ways, a few spokesmen on the periphery of their respective movements were drawn together by their own sense of gender egalitarianism, Judaism, and the demands of halacha. In

1983, the Union for Traditional Judaism (UTJ) was founded by more traditional elements formerly associated with the Conservative movement and JTS who opposed the ordination of women even as they felt that the halacha permitted greater female participation within the synagogue than that offered by the usual Orthodox synagogue.[18] A minority of Orthodox rabbis who supported "separate and somewhat equal" Women's Tefillah groups and other Orthodox feminist manifestations within their synagogues communicated and worked with UTJ people. Still, while these "Open Orthodox" spoke of their comfort with UTJ people, they also wanted that splinter group to clearly dissociate itself from Conservatism. For in general, all Orthodox rabbis disdained Conservatism's theology even as they differed among themselves on the question of associating with the liberal movement's advocates on nonreligious, communal issues.[19]

When Conservative and Orthodox Jews Had Much in Common

For the greater part of the twentieth century, the lines of demarcation and the points of differentiation separating these two Jewish expressions and distinguishing their adherents were not so readily apparent. To begin with, until very recently most members of both Orthodox and Conservative synagogues honored in their breach the basic demands of Jewish law. As our prime example, neither group's rank and file was particularly punctilious in its observance of the laws of Sabbath. And their Americanized synagogues, be they named Conservative or Orthodox, whether affiliated with either the United Synagogue or the Orthodox Union and the Young Israel, accepted that reality as a religious fact of life and attempted to work with, and around, that basic deviation from tradition.

Nonobservance of the Sabbath—a very useful metaphor for irreligiosity—was already evident within the community that attended, with ever decreasing frequency, the immigrant synagogues of the downtown districts. Hebrew poet Ephraim Lisitsky accurately remembered the ghetto scene when he wrote: "in the Jewish Quarter through which [the Sabbath Queen] had just passed they trampled with weekday shoes the train of her bridal gown." In his immigrant neighborhood in Boston, he noted matter-of-factly, "very few Jews observed the Sabbath."[20]

Christian muckraker Ray Stannard Baker had a similar impression of what he called "the disintegration of the Jews." He talked of a conversation with a Russian Jew who related that "from the moment I entered the shop my religious interest began to decline . . . I ceased going to the synagogue first only on week days, later on Saturday as well."[21] Two concomitant sociological surveys of downtown New York Jews provide evidence that this Jew who strove to advance at religious costs was far from alone. A 1912 study showed that only one-quarter of Jewish workers did not labor on the Sabbath. A year later, in 1913, another report revealed that nearly 60 percent of the stores in a Jewish area of the Lower East Side were open on Saturday.[22]

It must be understood that those who worked and did not pray in the synagogue on the Sabbath were, in the majority, not "free thinkers" who opposed Orthodox teachings. These same people were not against the existence of synagogues, and they certainly identified with the faith of the past on the High Holidays. Their problem was not so much with Orthodoxy's dogmas but rather with its inability and unwillingness to integrate the traditions with their new ambitions and lifestyle. It was not only their pursuit of affluence that moved them away from observance. Many of those who had begun to succeed economically, and who did not have to work, saw the Sabbath as a day for shopping and recreation. If, as one historian has put it, "Hester Street storekeepers shamelessly exhibited their wares on the Sabbath," they did so to attract Jewish customers. The Yiddish theaters were also open on Friday night and for Saturday matinees, attracting hordes of "Orthodox" Jews.[23]

Stannard Baker's colleague, Hutchins Hapgood, reported on this interesting slice of immigrant religious life.

> The Orthodox Jews who go to the theater on Friday, the beginning of Sabbath, are commonly somewhat ashamed of themselves and try to quiet their consciences by a vociferous condemnation of the actors on the stage. The actor, who through the exigencies of his role, is compelled to appear on Friday night with a cigar in his mouth, is frequently greeted with hisses and strenuous cries of "Shame, shame, smoke on the Sabbath!" from the proletarian hypocrites in the gallery.[24]

Some of these theatergoers purchased their tickets before the Sabbath to assuage their consciences. There were others who attended shows after services. Then there were those Orthodox Jews who frequented religious services on Saturday with very different types of tickets in their hands. In describing the Lower East Side as "one of the biggest communities in the world filled with Jewish establishments [where] observing the Jewish Sabbath [is] more in the breach than in practice," a downtown synagogue leader unhappily observed that "the most visible sign of Sabbath observance, perhaps, is the stream of hundreds of Jews entering a synagogue, with a ticket of admission, the price of which was probably paid on Saturday."[25]

Observance of the Sabbath both within the Jewish general public, and among synagogue-goers, decreased further as those of East European stock acculturated further and moved away, starting as early as 1900, from the ghettos to second settlement areas. Once again, it should be noted that there were communities of Sabbath-observing Jews who successfully relocated out of downtown to new neighborhoods and who retained their fidelity to halachic practices. For example, in the Williamsburg, Brooklyn, of the 1910s, Sabbath-observing families were certainly as much the rule as the exception. According to one observer of that neighborhood's scene, a "representative" family in the vicinity was headed by a father who "did not let a day pass without praying with the *Minyan* at the synagogue" and by a mother whose "house was a model of *Kashruth* [where] the Sabbaths and holidays were celebrated with the proper ceremonies."[26]

Concomitantly, in Manhattan's affluent and acculturated Yorkville and West Side pious synagogue leaders and worshipers could be found spending Saturday afternoon immersed in the study of rabbinic texts. Significantly, their children were more accustomed either to playing baseball in the streets on the day of rest or to attending matinees with previously purchased tickets. But, even as these family and synagogue elders struggled with their youngsters' slow, incremental drift away from their values, they could not help but notice that their own synagogues were also home to board members who were either oblivious to, or unconcerned with, halachic strictures. When, for example, Mordecai Kaplan founded the Jewish Center in 1917, he counted among his lay leaders habitual Sabbath-desecrators who had a large stake in synagogue life. The vice president of his center's Building Committee openly let it be known that on at least one occasion, "he was called to the telephone" when he returned home from the synagogue and "rushed downtown to the Hotel Biltmore for a meeting." Indeed, Kaplan also related that at one memorable meeting held, not incidentally on a Saturday afternoon in a quasi violation of the spirit of the Sabbath, a supporter of his who never attended Sabbath morning services because he was at his office, was so moved by the rabbi's message that he attempted "to hand a thousand dollar bill to the committee right out of his pocket." It remained for the synagogue's president, himself a devout Sabbath observer, to remind his colleague curtly that "we don't take money on the Sabbath."[27]

Beginning in the 1920s, second-generation Jews of East European heritage were once again on the move away from old neighborhoods and old
ways. In the new settlement areas on the outskirts of cities, where they
would remain until the end of the Second World War, synagogue-goers
continued their tradition of noncommitment to Sabbath observance. As in
the past, economic constraints and pursuits led those who belonged to synagogues to work on the Sabbath. Herbert S. Goldstein described this situation in his 1936 radio address to the Orthodox Union, in which he declared
that "most of my brethren who have broken Jewish unity did so because of
the desire for social prestige or on account of the pressure of economic conditions." Defining those negligent in their observances as definitely within,
and not without, his Orthodox community, Goldstein asserted that "just
because a Jew thinks he is forced to give up this or that part of his faith is
no reason for his retreating completely from the banner of tradition."[28]

That same year, a rabbi of a United Synagogue congregation in Wilkes-
Barre, Pennsylvania, reported that in order to attract "a considerable number of men to Sabbath services," he had to make sure that all devotions
were completed by 11:00 a.m. "In the whole congregation of about 250
families, there are not one-half dozen men who are not compelled to go to
business on Saturday." This rabbi's willingness to move rapidly through the
services had much to do with the reality that his congregants were also not
particularly interested in attending Friday night services after a long week
of work and before going off to their jobs the next morning. Indeed, a few
years earlier, in surveying some forty-six colleagues nationwide, he discovered that in so many places congregants, "tired from a day's business and
anticipating the Saturday business for which they prepare much of the
week," were happier sitting next to the radio on Friday night. For this generation of Jews, the Yiddish theater was passé, and the television had yet to
be available.[29]

A sister United Synagogue congregation in Brooklyn did not change the
time or abridge the length of Saturday morning services to accommodate
workers. Prayers began "at 8:45 a.m. and extend[ed] to about noon." It remained to worshipers themselves to find moments for Sabbath devotions
within their Saturday business day. All members of the synagogue, it was
reported,

> with some exceptions, leave on time, but all do not arrive on time.
> Some even straggle in about a half-hour or so before the conclusion of
> the service. Some attend to their mundane business after services. Oth-
> ers transact their business during the services.

Many of these worshipers showed no compunction about violating the Sabbath in getting to services. Adumbrating travel patterns that would become the norm in America after the Second World War, "some come to the synagogue," it was found, "by subway or automobiles. Even some Bar Mitzvah boys are brought to the synagogue by automobiles."[30] This rampant nonobservance among members of Orthodox synagogues did not sit well with one lay leader of the Orthodox Union who traveled the country in 1940. Bert Lewkowitz took a jaundiced view of "Jews who do not observe the Sabbath, who do not take their children to any Hebrew school and do not give them a Jewish home atmosphere [but] consider themselves Orthodox Jews because they have a seat on the High Holidays in an Orthodox Synagogue."[31] Still, there coexisted in this heterogeneous third-settlement congregation members and worshipers who were "devout, observing Jews to whom the service is sacred and to whom the synagogue is the house of God."[32]

A halfhearted revival of Judaism took place in the United States after the Second World War. Then it became a good American value in new suburban neighborhoods for second- and third-generation Jews to affirm religion through affiliation with a Jewish house of worship. It was also important to Jews who feared assimilation to varying degrees and abhorred intermarriages of all sorts, to identify themselves and their children with the touchstone institution, the synagogue, in their religiously mixed neighborhoods. In this environment, Jews joined suburban Orthodox, Conservative, and Reform synagogues en masse, with the United Synagogue experiencing the most dramatic growth.[33]

However, interest in religious observance in no way paralleled increased levels of affiliation. The same Jews who, for example, joined Conservative congregations because they liked its modern and yet traditional service, did not feel obliged to attend these devotions on a regular basis. One early 1950s survey that the United Synagogue conducted determined quite plainly that "two-thirds of members did not attend even late Friday evening services regularly and attendance at Saturday morning and holiday services was negligible." Indeed, this report highlighted that "synagogue leaders lead their members in not attending services."[34] Not incidentally, as of 1950, it became permissible under Conservative construction of Jewish law for congregants who lived distances from the synagogue to drive their automobiles to and from services. From that point on, the rabbinic way was there for those who wanted to observe the Sabbath according to Conservative strictures, but apparently the lay will was still not there. This unhappy set of circumstances caused one Rabbinical Assembly member to lament to his colleagues that "one cannot serve a congregation at any time without being depressed and disheartened by the widespread disintegration of Sabbath observance among our people."[35] It was, to some observers' minds, as if families availed themselves of the total panoply of Conservative congregational social, recreational, and cultural activities that brought Jews together, but they stayed away when it came time to pray, except on the High Holidays. In fact, one United Synagogue leader spoke sadly of "stately synagogues filled often with the heavy emptiness of empty pews."[36]

It was not solely economic exigencies that kept Jews away from Sabbath services. Now it was also a question of whether Jews would rather go to synagogue or stay at home—maybe in front of their small, flickering television sets. The Sabbath was becoming, in the words of one Conservative rabbi, "the recent addition to the American Jew's fast-growing list of expendables." As of 1953, 57 percent of Conservative synagogue leaders surveyed reported that they had no "Friday night observances" in their unkosher homes.[37]

These dismal statistics were a source of little satisfaction or consolation to suburban-looking Orthodox officials of the 1950s–1960s. For in many ways, their situation among postwar Jews was even worse. Not only were they often losing the battle for members against their Conservative and Reform counterparts, but most of those who chose to affiliate with their Americanized synagogues continued to be nonobservant. Essentially, Orthodoxy's and Conservatism's suburban rank and file shared most of the same religious values.[38]

Like their Conservative brethren, Orthodox Jews worked on the Sabbath. As before, "the businessman's observance of the Sabbath is a vexing problem," reported the president of a fledgling Orthodox synagogue in New Rochelle, New York. "The retailer is liable to suffer tremendously by having his store closed on . . . the busiest day of the week." Many of those who did attend services drove to synagogue on the Sabbath. The only real difference between them and their Conservative fellow suburbanites was that Orthodox worshipers drove without the approval of their rabbis and sometimes, more observant worshipers censured them. Some guilt-ridden Orthodox drivers "appease[d] their guilt by parking . . . [their] car[s] a few blocks away." Others hid their violations "out of respect for the orthodoxy of the older members."[39]

Some postwar Jews belonged simultaneously to both the Conservative and the Orthodox congregations in their vicinity and blurred further the denominational lines. In Milwaukee a sociologist found that almost 15 percent of the members of that community's Orthodox synagogue also "re-tain[ed] membership" in either a Conservative or Reform congregation.[40] Concomitantly, a Boston-based observer had his own problems defining who was Orthodox and who was not. "Some Jews," he noticed, "go to non-orthodox temples but try to keep *Shabboth* [*sic*] and *Kashruth*. Others attend orthodox *shools* [*sic*], but drive there on *Shabboth*." Maybe, he suggested, the best practical definition of an "orthodox Jew is one who believes in the Divine origin of the Torah, tries to learn more about it and to observe the *Mitzvoth* and precepts more fully and who affiliates with an orthodox syn-agogue."[41]

A contemporary young Orthodox rabbi defined the nonobservant com-ponent similarly, even as he defined them as solidly within the Orthodox camp. In his view,

> we must include in the category of orthodox Jew the one who, while of lesser or negligible observance in personal life, retains spiritual alle-giance to traditional Judaism. He is not a *practicing* Jew [emphasis his] but rather a *preferring* [my emphasis] Jew.

For this suburban-based rabbi, Orthodoxy's communal agenda was to try to find ways of convincing those who strayed to return to traditional forms of behavior. However, in the 1950s–1960s Orthodoxy was only mar-ginally successful in such forms of spiritual retrieval work.[42]

Even as much of Orthodox life during the 1950s–1960s was character-ized by rampant nonobservance, two important, albeit minority, segments of that community were showing signs of profound and consistent com-mitment to Orthodox teachings and practice. In time, these staunchly ob-servant Orthodox Jews would increase in numbers and change their de-nomination's profile and outlook. The first group was composed of native-born and third-generation Jews who had managed somehow to maintain their fidelity to the fundamental strictures of halacha even as they acculturated and rose economically in America. Their immigrant grandparents, as we have shown, were dedicated to preserving the Sabbath and other traditional observances while they resided on the Lower East Side or within other downtown urban enclaves. Their parents, as we have also noted, continued to keep the fires of Orthodox practice alive through the interwar period, sometimes with the help of many friends and neighbors, in settlements like Williamsburg. Elsewhere in the metropolis, they were an observant Orthodox minority in places like Manhattan's affluent West Side or the Bronx's Grand Concourse. And observant Orthodox Jews constituted the very smallest of minorities in many cities and regions beyond the metropolis.[43] In the postwar era, this generation was continuing their family and halachic traditions either in new urban neighborhoods, or they, too, joined the move to suburbia.

Such was essentially the case with the so-called "representative" Williamsburg family we identified previously, whose religious saga in America is worth further examination. It will be recalled that the immigrant parents had successfully relocated from Manhattan to Brooklyn with their commitments intact. Their "good and upright" second-generation children remained in Williamsburg until the early postwar period.[44] Then a decline in real estate values, the physical deterioration of the neighborhood, and the change in the racial composition of Williamsburg, as well as their own economic mobility, all conspired to cause them to seek new places to live. Actually, in this family's case, it was a third generation of observant Jews—the now-grown grandchildren of the immigrants—who moved first. Their positive experiences inspired their own, somewhat reluctant, parents to consider leaving the old neighborhood behind.[45]

A married daughter eventually settled in Far Rockaway, a community that earned for itself, by 1960, the proud reputation as a "Torah-Suburb-by-the-Sea." It boasted of being home to some four to five thousand "observant Jews . . . in the 35–45 age range . . . part and parcel of the American milieu [who] migrated to Far Rockaway from such nurturing grounds of American Jewish Orthodoxy . . . as Manhattan's Lower East Side, Washington Heights and Brooklyn's Williamsburg and Boro Park."[46]

A married son chose to build his home in Boro Park, another community "worlds apart in [its] outlook and in [its] conception of Jewish values, as well as in their practices and observances" from other American Jews. In that neighborhood, residents observed the uncommon American sight of "grocery stores, barbers, bakers, tailors, sporting 'Shomer Shabbos' signs in droves along . . . [the] main business thoroughfares."[47]

This Williamsburg family—and its Manhattan, Bronx, and Long Island counterparts too—were able to perpetuate their religious values over several generations in good measure because of their conscious opting for a degree of preventive socialization for their children, especially for their sons. The interwar period witnessed the growth of a modest string of day schools and yeshivas primarily in New York, especially in Brooklyn and usually for boys,[48] that effectively complemented the informal educational messages and values that were inculcated at home. In an era where most American

Jewish youths—including those from Orthodox families—received, at most, a Talmud Torah education, these special children were provided with many of the tools to emerge potentially as a distinguishable elite of observant and committed second- and third-generation American Jews. Such realities were clearly implicit in the Williamsburg family's experience.[49]

While these Orthodox Jews continued to make their way within early postwar America, a second group of even more committed Orthodox Jews was just arriving on these shores. This breed of self-segregating newcomers began settling here in the mid-1930s. Refugees first from Hitler's terror and later from Stalin's tanks sought this country because the Europe of which they were once a part had been, or was in the process of being, destroyed. These were the Jews who during the period of mass migrations had heeded the words of those East European rabbis who had declared America off-limits to those who wished to serve God properly. Now here, brought to America by the tragedies of their times, they began, under the guidance and leadership of their erstwhile rebbes, rabbis, and *roshei yeshiva*, to attempt to reconstruct the religious civilization they had seen burned before their eyes. Interestingly enough, many of the Hasidic sects that made up a goodly part of this new migration found their first American homes in Williamsburg as that neighborhood deteriorated and changed. In time, elements of that community would spread out within Brooklyn to Boro Park and beyond, again following in the footsteps of the aforementioned Americanized, observant group. Other Lithuanian "yeshiva world" types would settle early-on in their own closed, suburban, almost rural communities such as Lakewood, New Jersey. Concomitantly, Washington Heights in Manhattan became a center for German refugee Orthodoxy. Over succeeding decades, into the 1970s, these sectarian groups' influence and impact would be increasingly felt within both the larger Orthodox group and American Jewry in general. In the 1950s, however, they still constituted a committed minority within a predominantly nonobservant American Orthodox majority.[50]

An Era of Denominational Fluidity, 1900–1960

If, for most of the twentieth century, the designation "Conservative" or "Orthodox" Jew did not denote fundamental differences in religious behavior among so much of American Jewish laity, much the same can be said about the labels used to describe the congregations they infrequently attended and the rabbis they rarely heeded. Although we will soon speak of

United Synagogue congregations as opposed to Orthodox Union synagogues, and of rabbis trained at JTS as distinct from those who were ordained at its competitor, RIETS, we will also see immediately that the terms
Conservative and Orthodox synagogue—and sometimes even the titles
Conservative and Orthodox rabbi—obscure, rather than clarify, our understanding of the intricate textures of American Jewish religious life from
1900 through at least the 1960s.

The earliest synagogues for the masses of less-than-observant synagogue-goers date back to the turn of the twentieth century on the Lower
East Side and in Philadelphia. There, rabbis-in-training at the JTS organized
modern Orthodox services under the auspices of the Orthodox Union,
which was then tied closely to that rabbinical training institution. The Jewish Endeavor Society reached out to their community with Saturday afternoon services, directed at those who were working Saturday morning or
were attending matinees early Saturday afternoon. Their orthodoxy was ev-
idenced by their strict segregation of the genders during prayer, their use of
the siddur and their performance of the entire *mincha* service, which included the reading of the Torah. Their weekly English-language sermons,
their supplementary English prayers, and, as important, their myriad of ancillary American social and educational events on both Saturday evening
and during the week, punctuated their modernity.[51]

Essentially, these experimental synagogues foreshadowed in staffing
and in organizational affiliation a type of American Orthodox synagogue
and rabbi that existed well into the 1950s. For close to fifty years, young
men graduated from JTS who perceived themselves as Orthodox rabbis and
were accepted as such in established Orthodox Union (OU) congregations
in second- and third-settlement areas. These congregations adhered strictly
to Orthodox practices—most notably they were congregations with *mechitzas* or balconies—even as they offered congregants all sorts of modern
ancillary activities. The young Mordecai M. Kaplan, arguably the first of
that type, was called to Kehilath Jeshurun's (KJ) pulpit in 1903. His erstwhile student and future nemesis, Herbert S. Goldstein, followed him to
that synagogue in 1913, only to leave to establish his Institutional Synagogue in Harlem in 1917. Kaplan's colleague, Elias L. Solomon, served as En-
glish-speaking rabbi at KJ from 1917 to 1923. Each of these men worked har-
moniously with that idiosyncratic East European rabbi Moses S. Margolies,
who, though a leader of the rejectionist Agudath ha-Rabbanim, agreed
with, or at least acceded to, the seminarians' efforts to modernize that congregation. Their neighbor in Yorkville, Moses Hyamson—not a JTS gradu-

ate, but rather a seminary faculty member—ministered to Orach Chaim from 1913 to his death in 1949. Outside New York, Samuel Rosenblatt (JTS '25) was rabbi of Baltimore's Beth Tefilo for more than thirty years. He received his call in 1929 in no small measure due to the intercession with congregational leaders of JTS graduate Goldstein, then president of the OU. (It also helped that his father was the renowned cantor Yossele Rosenblatt.) And about the time Rosenblatt was settling in Maryland, Samuel Benjamin (JTS '19) was appointed to the Hebrew Institute of University Heights (Bronx, N.Y.)[52]

The Young Israel (YI) movement was fired with a mission similar to the Endeavorers, and its initial personnel were also comparable to the JTS. When it was established in 1913 on the Lower East Side, JTS students were among the founders of this Orthodox synagogue movement, which had the approbation of their teacher Mordecai M. Kaplan. In the 1920s–1930s, the YI, known for its modern Orthodox services, American social events, and Endeavorer-like late Friday night "forums"—not services—expanded its network of some twenty-five congregations into New York's outer boroughs and into five other cities nationwide. In this interwar period, the YI slowly lost its JTS connection. The few affiliates that engaged rabbis in this largely lay-led movement took on graduates of RIETS and not JTS. Still, this Orthodox network continued to reach out to Jews of all commitments.[53]

At the same time that the OU and the YI began their efforts among the less than observant, the United Synagogue of America started in 1913 to address these same groups of Jews in the same types of neighborhoods. As this national synagogue body grew from 22 affiliates at its founding to approximately 130 by 1920 and to 229 at that decade's end, there began to emerge within their midst many congregations that foreshadowed in mission, ritual, and leadership "much of the Conservative synagogue's religious program of today." Ensconced in the better-built neighborhoods on the fringes of interwar cities, these congregations offered second-generation Jews a sociologically sophisticated mixture of liturgical traditionalism and innovation even as they projected a deep understanding of the personal, economic, and family needs of potential congregants. For example, when founded in 1922, the Jamaica Jewish Center of Queens featured "family pews," English preaching, a mixed choir of boys and girls, and confirmation services on Shavuoth, even as the synagogue promised to maintain daily morning and evening services "when a permanent house of worship is established." Just as important, it conducted two Friday night services, one at sundown year round, the other at 8:00 p.m., during the "short" fall and winter months. The later devotions seemingly accommodated commuters who could not return in time from their inner-city places of work to attend sundown services.[54]

In Boston, Conservative rabbi Herman Rubenovitz instituted a more liberalized synagogue ritual when he prevailed upon his board, as early as 1914, "to introduce the use of the organ and mixed choir at our services on Sabbath and holidays [even as] . . . the traditional Hebrew prayers were to be maintained." Rubenovitz thus established a pattern of ritual behavior that would long predominate among Conservative congregations throughout New England.[55]

Meanwhile, in Cleveland in 1921, innovative rabbi Solomon Goldman pushed liturgical and ideological limits further still. In the Cleveland Jewish Center, where family pews and late Friday night services were de rigueur, Goldman shortened the Sabbath service and eliminated ritual elements that smacked of "antiquarianism" and "Orientalism." As important, he used his pulpit to promulgate his affinity for the incipient Reconstructionist ideology of his mentor, Mordecai M. Kaplan.[56]

Of course, when these congregations and other similarly disposed, full-fledged United Synagogue Conservative synagogues were not calling Jews to pray, they offered potential members a panoply of child-centered, family-oriented leisure time activities within their synagogue centers even as they cast all of these developments within the mold of traditional Jewish ideas and concepts.

While these rabbis and their synagogues surely adumbrated the Conservative movement of today, they were far from totally representative of the United Synagogue or of the Rabbinical Assembly of their day. Throughout the 1920s and 1930s, leading synagogues and significant spokesmen for these national religious organizations readily and repeatedly defined themselves as "modern Orthodox," and they were seen as such both within their communities and on the national scene. Each of their experiences, histories, and biographies underscores the fluidity of denominational allegiances and demonstrate how difficult it was to characterize a synagogue or rabbi as "Conservative" or "Orthodox" during the entire interwar period.

There was, to begin with, the Young Israel of Brooklyn, "organized in 1918 [as] the second organization of the Young Israel movement," which joined the United Synagogue a year later and was a member as late as 1929.[57] A neighboring Brooklyn Orthodox synagogue, Shomrei Emunah, which rented space to the Young Israelites when they first established themselves in that borough, was also a member of the United Synagogue through the 1920s. Though nominally a member of JTS's congregational body, Shomrei Emunah was hardly loyal to that institution. If anything, it was proud of the praise Yeshiva officials lavished upon it in 1923 as a "congregation [that] is leading all congregations in New York and the country over in its sincere devotion to our Yeshivah [sic]."[58] Then, there was the Washington Heights Congregation, founded in 1914 and led initially by Rabbi Moses Rosenthal, a young JTS graduate who a year earlier had helped establish the Young Israel downtown. This congregation earned, early on, the approbation of downtown Orthodox spokesman, Judah David Eisenstein, who in the late 1920s would himself move up from the Lower East Side and affiliate with the uptown group. As he saw it, the services were conducted in strict Orthodox manner, though some modern features were introduced, such as sermons in English and congregational singing. In short, it was "American Orthodox."[59]

In 1919, the Washington Heights Congregation secured the services of JTS graduate Rabbi Max Drob, who ministered to the congregation until 1927 while serving as president of the Rabbinical Assembly, supposedly the Conservative movement's rabbinical body. But Drob defined himself as Orthodox and punctuated that belief with public statements worthy of any good Young Israelite, a movement he lauded as "the only group of young people that has made its religious yearnings vocal . . . and it has come out unequivocally for traditional Judaism."[60]

In one particularly forceful Young Israel–like statement, Drob averred that his Orthodoxy held that "traditional Judaism can be promulgated only in synagogues that are outwardly as well as inwardly beautiful . . . where decorum and order prevail . . . [and] where modern methods of teaching and preaching prevail." As significant, Drob asserted unqualifiedly, that when the "United Synagogue was founded . . . it did not sanction the innovations made by some of its constituent synagogues." He was no friend of Solomon Goldman–style innovations.[61]

Essentially, while in Washington Heights, Drob and Rosenthal followed in the footsteps of the young Kaplan, Goldstein, and Solomon, except that their synagogues paid membership dues to the United Synagogue and the Yorkville synagogue was linked to the OU. Moreover, in all major respects, the Washington Heights Congregation resembled the Orthodox Jewish Center, whose founding rabbi, Kaplan, and lay leadership were deeply involved with the United Synagogue. The West Side synagogue would remain with that congregational union well into the 1920s and into the tenure of Leo Jung, Kaplan's successor.[62]

The young Louis Finkelstein followed literally in Solomon's steps. In 1919, upon graduation from JTS, he replaced his fellow JTS alumnus at Congregation Kehilath Israel, an Orthodox synagogue in the South Bronx. Solomon had just accepted KJ's call, and he would serve that Yorkville OU congregation for five years while he was president of the United Synagogue. During Finkelstein's own twelve years in Crotona Park, he supervised a modern Hebrew school, inaugurated Young Israel–like Friday night forums, and oversaw the construction of a community center for a myriad of purely social activities. With all these modern innovations, this United Synagogue affiliate adhered strictly to Orthodoxy during services. Women were segregated in the balcony, and the time, order, and schedule of prayers was not changed. In fact, Finkelstein undoubtedly endeared himself to the most traditional elements in his synagogue when he earned *semicha* from Moses Hyamson at JTS. (We will discuss the larger significance of this particular type of rabbinical training track later on.) Finkelstein's career in an Orthodox synagogue ended in 1931 when he accepted a full-time position teaching Talmud at JTS. Kehilath Israel officials understood his decision. During the depression, they were hard pressed to pay his salary.[63]

New York was not the only place where JTS rabbis led modern Orthodox synagogues affiliated with the United Synagogue. During the 1920s and early 1930s, Temple Beth-El of Dorchester, a Boston suburb, conducted Orthodox services and many traditional religious programs under the leadership of JTS graduates David A. Shohet and Harry M. Katzen. The so-called Fowler Street synagogue was "practically never closed" with its "*Beth Hamidrash* . . . filled with *minyanim*" for daily worship and with various study groups of Talmud." Beth-El boasted of a "*Chevrah Shas* [that] meets every evening for the study of the Talmud," a "*Chevrah Mishnayoth* [that] meets every morning for the study of the daily '*Perek*,'" and a "*Chevrah Ein Yaakov* . . . for the study of the haggadic [*sic*] portions of the Talmud." In keeping with the religious culture of the past, the rabbis spoke Saturday morning in Yiddish, "excepting at Bar Mitzvah occasions when the sermon was delivered in English or in Hebrew." On the [High] "Holidays, the rabbi preached the first day in English, the second day in Yiddish." As significant, in keeping with the realities of congregant life there was a Saturday morning minyan that began at 6:30, convenient for those people who worked on the Sabbath.

Rabbi Shohet's credentials among Boston's most traditional Jews were especially impressive since he had come to America and to the JTS with *semicha* already conferred upon him by Rabbi Yom Tov Lippman of

Dinaburg (Dvinsk, today Daugavpils), Rabbi Reuven David Burstein of Kamenetz-Litovsk and his own father, Rabbi Nathan Shohet, also of Lithuania. But it was Shohet's successor, Harry Katzen, who received the greater degree of public approbation from the larger Orthodox community that had no linkage whatsoever with JTS. In June 1932, for example, Rabbi Yaakov Ruderman, then head of the Cleveland yeshiva and soon to lead the Ner Israel Rabbinical College of Baltimore, joined Katzen in his congregation's celebration of its Chevrah Shas, having completed its study of the Talmud. Only six months later, the congregation was the site of the installation of Rabbi Joseph B. Soloveitchik as "head of eleven united Orthodox synagogues in Boston."[64]

Shohet's and Katzen's close friend and colleague, Louis Epstein, rabbi from 1918 to 1925 in neighboring Roxbury's Beth Hamidrash HaGadol, and then at Knesset Israel in the new Boston suburb of Brookline, spoke proudly of his efforts in promoting Orthodox synagogue life in his city. Epstein, one of the Rabbinical Assembly's most distinguished talmudists, who frequently addressed the very vexing communal problem of *agunot* with learned rabbinic discussions, boasted of early Orthodox training in the Slabodka yeshiva in Lithuania and in America at RIETS before earning JTS ordination in 1913. He clearly expressed his religious preferences when in 1925 he turned down an offer to lead Philadelphia's Conservative Har-Zion Temple. In a letter to its leaders, he stated clearly,

> I am not a conservative [sic] Rabbi; I am Orthodox, and I have been becoming more and more convinced that a man of my religious views is out of place at Har-Zion Temple. I would have insisted on a male choir, on the cantor facing the ark, on a solid program of religious education and on a strict observance of the Sabbath in connection with all synagogue activities.[65]

And then there is the most remarkable case of Morris Teller, the rabbi from 1916 to 1925 of Congregation B'nai Emunah, the United Synagogue congregation in Tulsa, Oklahoma.[66] Among those who supported his stances and status were members of the same family that was deeply involved in the backing and running of RIETS, the JTS's traditional opponent and competitor. Many years later, Teller would recall that seminary president Cyrus Adler was very anxious to capture this Orthodox congregation for the United Synagogue fold. Adler felt that this young man's "traditionalism and tactfulness" would overcome the prejudices of some members who "would have preferred a Yeshiva-trained rabbi." Teller was a very good

find, especially "since in [his] religious conduct, [he] was virtually Orthodox." More importantly, he had the backing of local oil magnates Samuel
and Marion Travis, nationally known Orthodox philanthropists. Their
largesse had just contributed, in no small measure, to the installation of
their brother-in-law, Dr. Bernard Revel, in 1915 as president of RIETS, with
the mission of creating within that yeshiva a modern Orthodox rabbinical
training program. While Revel was beginning his herculean efforts, they
were comfortable turning to a JTS rabbi. Indeed, to insure that others in
Tulsa would be as accepting of Teller as they were, they approached Adler
with an intriguing plan; an idea that would, in its own way, undercut
Revel's own efforts.[67]

In April 1917, Travis wrote to Adler that "a recent Seminary graduate
. . . was doing excellent work and that the Congregation was delighted with
him." Still, Travis believed that the community would have been even happier with their rabbi if he possessed traditional *semicha*. Backing up his
words, Travis offered to fund a scholarship program at JTS to provide select
students "with additional instruction in Talmud and Codes." In this way,

> the Seminary would be helping those young men who had the inclina-
> tion to devote themselves to Jewish law, and that the country would
> gradually receive a group of men with modern education who at the
> same time would be recognized by the orthodox communities as com-
> petent to give decisions on questions of Jewish law.

After some debate within the JTS faculty, the Travis-Adler plan to re-
move "this detriment to our [JTS] graduates" was accepted, and a
"sufficiently intensive" course in Talmud and Codes was implemented to
permit the awarding of *hatarat hora'a*. As it turned out, Teller did not avail
himself of that opportunity. Louis Finkelstein, as previously noted, was the
first JTS man to earn *semicha*.[68]

No one questioned the commitment to Orthodoxy of the Young Israel
of Brooklyn, nor of Leo Jung's Jewish Center, nor for that matter of the
Bronx congregation that Louis Finkelstein served, even if they did affiliate
with the "Conservative" congregational movement. But Orthodox eye-
brows might have been raised about the fidelity to traditional practice of
those other "modern Orthodox" United Synagogue members and their rabbis. Questions could even have been raised about Morris Teller, the Travises'
favorite. To begin with, although Max Drob defined himself as Orthodox
and for eight years served in a New York congregation that strictly segregated the genders, prior to coming to Washington Heights, Drob had min-

istered in Syracuse and Buffalo in Americanizing congregations where mixed seating was the vogue. Interestingly enough, when Drob left Washington Heights in 1927 he moved comfortably over the Harlem River to the [Grand] Concourse Center of Israel, where he would officiate for the final twenty-two years of his life in a mixed-seating congregation.[69]

In Dorchester's Temple Beth El women sat in a separate balcony. But that congregation, under Shohet and Katzen, deviated from Orthodox practice through its very popular "late Friday evening services" held during the winter several hours after sundown "Kabbolath Shabbes" prayers. At that later service, so reminiscent of Conservative synagogues of the time, the traditional prayers were recited and the bilingual "rabbi and invited guests" delivered sermons and lectures in English.[70]

Louis Epstein came to Roxbury having already initiated late Friday night services in a Dallas congregation, Shearith Israel, after convincing local Jewish entrepreneurs "to close the business hours . . . at 6 o'clock to release the tired storekeeper for religious services [later] that night."[71] He maintained that tradition as an Orthodox rabbi in New England, while also permitting mixed seating in his congregation.[72]

When Teller arrived in Tulsa, he found that the Travis family and the community they led had already made their own idiosyncratic compromise in seating arrangements. Marion Travis would explain years later,

> My brothers who were ultra-orthodox were against men and women sitting together or for women sitting downstairs. But some of the wives of members refused to sit in the balcony. Compromise being the art of the possible, we tried to make everyone happy. We, therefore, wound up with men and women sitting on one side of the building in family pews, and the men alone sitting on the other side, with a high curtain between the two sides down the center aisle.

Teller had no problem with that arrangement, and most of the Travises liked his own modern initiative of late Friday night "assemblies." For several years in the early 1920s a number of congregants, including David Travis, who "were critical of the interpretation of Orthodoxy by B'nai Emunah and believed in a more strict and closer following of the tenets of Judaism," seceded and formed their own Orthodox synagogue. But they returned to B'nai Emunah in 1925, and David Travis was elected president of the reunited congregation, before Teller departed for a higher-paying position in Chicago.[73]

Boston appears to have been the only locale where concerted efforts were made to undermine the credibility and positions of JTS-trained rabbis. There, the synagogue policies that Shohet, Katzen, and Epstein championed, albeit more traditional than their putative Conservative colleague, Herman Rubenovitz, did not sit well with some elements of Boston's Orthodox community. Though the visiting Orthodox luminaries who appeared in Dorchester in the early 1930s, including the young rabbi Joseph Soloveitchik, gave their own tacit approval to what that congregation was doing, members of the Chevrah Shas of Boston did not. Frequently during the 1920s, these rabbis complained to JTS officials about what Epstein called "the undermining influence there that has so far practically ruined Orthodox Judaism in the eyes of the more decent Jews." Shohet complained about "the pressure brought about by the Yeshiba [sic] and the 'Orthodox' Union, which is trying to create an anti-Seminary sentiment in Boston," even as he asserted that he "held the balance of power between all elements, the Lomdim, Maskilim, Modernists, Young and Old, Men and Women . . . [in making] the Congregation . . . the leading Orthodox synagogue in Boston." Yet, despite these annoying fulminations, JTS-trained rabbis maintained their positions as Orthodox rabbis within their local interwar community.[74]

Perhaps the Orthodox Union did not more roundly condemn nontraditional synagogue practices because many of its own affiliates, both south of the Mason-Dixon Line and even in its heartland of New York, seated men and women together during prayers, or the sexes were not separated by a *mechitza*. These congregations, like their United Synagogue counterparts and competitors, also routinely conducted the late Friday night service. In Atlanta, for example, in 1932 Congregation Ahavath Achim, under the leadership of Rabbi Harry Epstein, began conducting late Friday night services that permitted members, as one student of that congregation has put it, "to attend the synagogue after work or before the theater." At these devotions, designed "to bring about greater interest and added inspiration," women were allowed to come down from the balcony and to sit across the aisle from men. Together, they experienced, with the help of a choir, an innovative service, "complete with songs, prayers, English readings and of course, an English language sermon." Epstein's model for these initiatives may well have been Tulsa's B'nai Emunah, that noteworthy United Synagogue affiliate, where he had served for a year as Teller's successor. But Epstein's allegiances were with the Orthodox Union. Perhaps his disinterest in the United Synagogue was due to the fact that this modern Orthodox rabbi had had no real contact with JTS. Epstein had come first to

Tulsa and then to Atlanta after having received *semicha* in Palestine subsequent to studying at RIETS, at Chicago's Hebrew Theological College, and in Lithuania. Epstein and his congregation were more than acceptable to the OU. By the mid-1930s, Epstein was a member of the OU's national executive committee.[75]

An Atlanta- and Tulsa-style Union affiliate could also be found in Birmingham, Alabama. Temple Beth-El joined the Orthodox Union in 1908 soon after its founding some six months earlier. Its forty-four original members had broken with their old-line Orthodox synagogue, K'nesset Israel, because they were "dissatisfied with the strict doctrine of the synagogue and wished a more liberal policy of worship." In the congregation's early years, "liberalization" meant men and women sitting together. By the 1930s, it also meant the institution of the Beth El Forum, discussion club meetings after short and late Friday evening services. Abraham Mesch, a Palestinian-trained rabbi who was ordained by Chief Rabbi Abraham Isaac Kook, was the champion of this program, which reportedly attracted hundreds of people to the congregation. During the early years of his tenure, Beth El also began talking about installing an organ in the sanctuary for use on the Sabbath as well as instructing the cantor to face the congregation and not the Holy Ark. Still, Beth El long maintained "very cordial relations" both with Knesset Israel and with the national Orthodox Union.[76]

For interwar Bronx congregations like the Kingsbridge Heights Jewish Center and the Mosholu Jewish Center, mixed seating and late Friday night services were basic to Orthodox synagogue ritual and life. Both of these congregations favored a type of religious activity highly reminiscent of what then existed in Tulsa and Boston except that these modern Orthodox synagogues affiliated with the Orthodox Union and not the United Synagogue. In Kingsbridge Heights, for example, men and women sat together both in the main sanctuary and in the balcony. At the same time, a few miles over in the North-Central Bronx, Mosholu Jews were comfortable during the year with seating patterns reminiscent of Atlanta, where men and women sat across an aisle from one another. On the High Holidays, however, men and women sat together in the main sanctuary. Apparently, the large number of Jews who frequented the synagogue only during the High Holidays preferred, or maybe insisted upon, this mode of operation. Habitual synagogue attendees were drawn to that synagogue's late Friday night services, the most popular and attractive service of the week.[77]

Where was RIETS and its graduates as JTS men served in all of these United Synagogue and Orthodox Union pulpits and ministered to the masses of less-than-fully-observant East European Jews and their children? As the interwar period opened, Bernard Revel was only beginning to mold the type of student who conceivably could compete against JTS graduates. The ideal Yeshiva product was to be deeply grounded in the world of Talmudic erudition and committed to the strictures of the *Shulkhan Arukh,* and at the same time be a well-spoken English preacher, aware of and comfortable with the American world around him and sensitive to the social and religious needs of the nonobservant community that he would serve. Revel's own family in Tulsa probably would have been very pleased to have such a candidate serve their community, rather than turn to a JTS man. But we can conjecture that, so early on in 1917, that type of Americanized and sophisticated rabbi had not yet emerged from Yeshiva. It also seems, from Travis's offer of scholarship money to JTS, that the family was not totally convinced that Revel could achieve his revolution in Yeshiva education.[78]

Only in the 1920s did a small cadre of rabbis emerge from RIETS ready to challenge JTS rabbinic hegemony and in some instances to take Orthodox pulpits away from the United Synagogue and move them into the Orthodox Union. The selection in 1923 of Joseph H. Lookstein as assistant rabbi (to the East European Rabbi Margolies, known as "Ramaz") at Kehilath Jeshurun was probably the earliest impressive sign that Yeshiva was coming of age as a trainer of Americanized rabbis. Prior to Lookstein, it will be recalled, this Americanizing Orthodox congregation had turned to JTS graduates Kaplan, Goldstein, and Solomon to speak and minister to the younger generation in their own language. Now a RIETS man fit the bill.[79]

Yeshiva, and for that matter the Orthodox Union, was also pleased when their rabbis succeeded JTS men in congregations that had formerly affiliated with the United Synagogue. In 1930, for example, Irving Miller succeeded JTS graduate Norman Salit at Far Rockaway's Shaarey Tefila, a congregation that had been founded twenty years earlier "largely through the assistance and counsel of Rev. Dr. Mordecai M. Kaplan." Shaarey Tefila enrolled in the Orthodox Union that same year. In 1932, five years after Max Drob left the Washington Heights Congregation for the Grand Concourse, RIETS graduate Sol B. Friedman assumed the pulpit of a congregation that had just then joined the Orthodox Union. In 1937, a few years after Louis Finkelstein left the Bronx's Kehilath Israel for a full-time position at JTS, Yeshiva man Asher Siev took over his Orthodox pulpit and immediately moved that synagogue into the Orthodox Union.[80]

Evidently, in these Orthodox congregations members were somewhat more comfortable with the rabbis trained at Yeshiva, so long as they had the right social graces. The Washington Heights Congregation said as much when they set out searching for "a cultured, optimistic, zealous rabbi [with] . . . a sense of humor" to lead a congregation that was "marked by a trend to firmer Orthodoxy." It is also true that often RIETS men were willing to accept lesser salaries than JTS graduates, a consideration of no small moment in the depression era.[81]

Jewish Theological Seminary graduates were certainly mindful of their competitor's successes. As early as 1929, a Rabbinical Assembly Placement Committee would report to its membership that

> we are no longer the only institution in American Jewry that claims to supply English-speaking rabbis to congregations in the traditional fold. There is no record of how many of our congregations have been lost to men of other institutions . . . but the number would seem from personal observation high, particularly in the metropolitan districts. . . . A determined effort should be made to create new fields for Seminary men.[82]

However, despite Yeshiva's demand that its graduates not accept posts in congregations that did not have *mechitzas*, when RIETS men occupied erstwhile United Synagogue pulpits where mixed seating obtained, they frequently did not move quickly, or at all, to change that particularly offensive pattern. Such was the case beginning in 1931 when Ben Zion Rosenbloom succeeded Seminary man William Malev at the Kingsbridge Heights Jewish Center. Under Rosenbloom's leadership, the congregation left the United Synagogue and joined the Orthodox Union. But under this Yeshiva graduate, its tradition continued of mixed seating and of late Friday night services that featured the Levinthal prayer book.[83]

Concomitantly, Yeshiva also had to cope with another, even more, vexing reality. Even as the Orthodox seminary was "winning" some pulpits for its graduates, an appreciable number of its students were leaving Yeshiva for rabbinical training and placement at JTS. They migrated, in many cases, essentially because upon ordination the seminary offered them the possibility of securing a more substantial rabbinical post than did Yeshiva. Of greatest significance to us is that many of these "careerists" did not perceive themselves as leaving the Orthodox community by going off to the seminary. (Others, to be sure, moved on to JTS because they felt an ideological and theological kinship for Conservative Judaism.) Many of those who studied in Morningside Heights in the 1920s–1930s have observed retrospectively that "Yeshiva's training was out of sync with the American marketplace." Under these conditions, the seminary would continue to train rabbis for the varying types of Conservative and Orthodox synagogues that served the masses of second-generation American Jews.[84]

All told, the terms Conservative and Orthodox synagogue—and sometimes even the titles Conservative and Orthodox rabbi—inadequately impose distinctive characterizations and categorizations on the interwar religious scene that are far more appropriate for the postwar and contemporary days. How close and how undifferentiated so many of these Americanized synagogues were then was probably summarized best in 1942 when an Orthodox Union vice president Rabbi David De Sola Pool wrote the following very candid assessment of his community and of "Judaism and the Synagogue" of his day:

> Today it is growing increasingly difficult to discern any essential organic difference between Orthodoxy and Conservatism. The main differentiae seem to be that Conservative synagogues permit men and women to sit together, and make more use of English in the services than do most Orthodox synagogues. Yet, some Orthodox synagogues use some English in their services and seat the sexes, if not together, at least on one floor. No logical or clear line can be drawn today between American Orthodoxy and Conservatism. . . . American Orthodoxy no longer mirrors East European life. It is adapting itself to the American environment. Innovations like the late Friday evening service or the removal of the women's gallery, or the confirmation of girls or a community *seder* . . . would have shocked the worshipers of a generation ago. Today such practices are accepted in numerous congregations.[85]

If, in the end, so many interwar synagogues and the rabbis who led them differed so little one from the other,[86] what ultimately moved individuals and families with their similar attitudes toward personal religious practice to affiliate either with "Orthodoxy" through its Union or "Conservatism" through the United Synagogue? In some cases, it was reportedly the locality's "conservative atmosphere and reverence for the past" that bolstered the Orthodox synagogue even if younger members might ride to synagogue on Saturday morning service, "but leave their automobiles a few blocks away out of respect for the orthodoxy of older members." Such was apparently the case in Charleston, South Carolina, where two Americanized Orthodox synagogues predominated through the close of the Second World War. The eventual rise in that town of an enduring United Synagogue presence during the late 1940s had much to do with the arrival of new settlers who were not bound by local traditions.[87]

Elsewhere, in a more idiosyncratic case, it was the prejudices and pro-clivities of a powerful East European rabbi that, ironically, helped the United Synagogue secure an early and enduring hold on the allegiances of so many second-generation Jews. In Philadelphia, Bernard Levinthal, a leader of the old-line Agudath ha-Rabbanim, jealously protected his pre-rogatives as that city's chief rabbi, centralized Orthodox synagogues under his suzerainty, and kept young RIETS men from assuming influential pul-pits for more than a generation. Yeshiva lore has it that Levinthal's personal agenda left Philadelphia wide open to JTS products and to the United Syn-agogue.[88]

In Detroit during this interwar period the masses of nonobservant Jews showed little interest in attending synagogues of all types, except during the Days of Awe. But when they were moved to attend, a combination of "nostalgia, and/or love for their parents [and] memories of their child-hood" directed them toward traditional forms of synagogue life. Thus, as late as the mid-1940s, Congregation Shaarey Zedek was the United Syna-gogue's sole representative in the entire Detroit area. And it was hardly a Conservative congregation. As one synagogue memoirist has aptly put it: "We were supposed to be Conservative but what we were was Orthodox." Not until 1931 did Shaarey Zedek even begin to alter its long-standing by-laws to permit mixed seating in the sanctuary even as it provided "for a sec-tion which was to be reserved for those who wished to follow the Orthodox tradition."[89]

Movement toward Rigidity, 1960–2000

In the years that followed the Second World War, there was no immediate dramatic shift in the religious outlooks of those who attended United Syn-agogue as opposed to Orthodox Union congregations. The change that did start almost immediately after the war was the beginning of a winnowing out of the Orthodox synagogue of so many nonobservant "diehards" and their comfortable relocation within what were becoming ritually distinc-tive, suburban Conservative synagogues. Increasingly, in this new Ameri-can era, third- and fourth-generation American Jews felt no guilt regarding their un-Orthodox behavior. Instead, they saw themselves as Conservative Jews, followers of a legitimate expression of middle-class Judaism that not only encouraged full family participation in synagogue rituals but offered many synagogue-centered ancillary activities. At the same time, when they prayed in their Conservative synagogues, they still felt very much in touch with ancient revered traditions, even if their Sabbath and Holiday devotions were accompanied by a mixed choir and maybe instrumental music.[90]

The beneficiaries of this newfound enthusiasm were, of course, the postwar generation of rabbis who were trained for the Conservative rabbinate at the Jewish Theological Seminary. They addressed the needs of the younger generation with a new aggressiveness. While many of the rabbis who emerged from Morningside Heights in the late 1940s and 1950s still may have hailed from Orthodox homes, this new cadre of leaders no longer spoke of themselves as "modern Orthodox rabbis." They were part of a growing and conquering Conservative movement.[91] These former Orthodox Jews would be joined eventually by younger colleagues who were reared in Conservative homes as the seminary succeeded in recruiting and training its own men for their suburban-based religious centers. These leaders were, likewise, neither constrained by their own—or by congregational—nostalgia, guilt, inertia, or inherent traditionalism that had characterized an earlier generation. They moved smartly to capture new communities for their movement.[92]

All told, the early postwar decades that witnessed United Synagogue affiliates increasingly display all the ritual and ancillary characteristics of today's Conservative congregations, saw that organization grow from approximately 350 members in 1945 to 800 twenty years later. By the mid-1960s, sociologists were comfortable speaking of the "victory of Conservatism" and of it having "achieve[d] primacy on the American scene."[93]

Postwar Orthodox leaders were not unaware that they were losing the numbers battle. Leo Jung said as much in 1959 when he candidly told the Orthodox Union that "the myth of an Orthodox majority" is "still to be found in some official and semi-official declarations or announcements." This "illusion" he declared, "is pernicious because it creates an optimism utterly unjustified by the circumstances." Contemporary impartial demographic studies only confirmed his impressions when they showed that in both Northeastern and Midwestern cities fewer than 20 percent of their Jewish populations defined themselves as Orthodox, including, of course, both the observant and nonobservant types.[94]

At the same time, both Jung and those who responded to his comments were also quick to assert that if Orthodoxy was destined to be a "minority" denomination, let it be at least a "respectable" minority. For one of Jung's interlocutors that meant tightening the definition of what made a synagogue Orthodox. Describing himself as a member of "a right thinking and just doing minority," this Syracuse, New York, layman pointedly suggested that

> instead of having 700 graduates . . . of Orthodox schools . . . who serve congregations concerning some of which there is doubt if they are conducted in accordance with the *Shulhan Arukh*, which prescribed the proper regulations for a synagogue—were it not better for us to have half that number, however, small but remaining bastions of traditional Judaism? Not synagogues erected by modern architects but such rather that as are planned by God-fearing men where the Jewish religion of two thousand years is truly lived.[95]

This newly expressed pride as a "minority" group that "no matter how small our numbers" possessed "inalienable rights" occasionally manifested itself in efforts to oppose or roll back the pervasiveness of mixed seating both within and without their movement. In one celebrated 1955 case in Mount Clemens, Michigan, and due to the almost fanatical efforts of a local lay leader, the Orthodox Union secured relief from that state's supreme court prohibiting the majority of Congregation Beth Tefilas Moshe's members from removing the *mechitza* from their synagogue. The Union was no less pleased with an out-of-court settlement in 1958 that two members of its Pacific Coast Region engineered. They convinced "a prominent North Hollywood congregation" to avoid "severing its ties with the Union of Orthodox Jewish Congregations of America and joining a deviationist movement." Elsewhere, in Cincinnati and Louisiana court cases, the Union was unsuccessful in keeping synagogues from removing their *mechitzas*. In each of these instances, they could not keep those individuals in erstwhile Orthodox congregations who wanted to sit in egalitarian settings from joining the Conservative synagogues down the block. Still, for Orthodox Union leadership "the attendant widespread publicity made great numbers of our people aware of the sharp line of demarcation dividing authentic Judaism from the deviationist ideology."[96]

The Orthodox Union's attempts during these national battles to draw its own lines in the denominational sand ultimately did not change the flow of Orthodox laypeople toward Conservative synagogues. But its new aggressiveness did have an impact upon those graduates of RIETS and other rabbinical schools who defined themselves as Orthodox but who served in mixed-seating congregations. Increasingly, they became men without a denomination as they struggled to keep congregants from joining neighboring Conservative synagogues even as, it has been observed, "Orthodox Jewish publications denominated those who defended the Orthodoxy of mixed seating as 'Conservative Jews' and ridiculed 'mixed seating Orthodoxy' as a contradiction in terms." In time, some of these congregations and rabbis gravitated toward the Conservative movement. Others decided to toe Orthodoxy's mark and installed *mechitzas*. Still others, particularly synagogues in the Midwest, labeled themselves "Traditional Synagogues" as a way of distinguishing themselves from their Conservative and Orthodox counterparts.[97]

If Orthodoxy seemed destined in the 1960s to be but a "respectable minority," what has changed the denominational picture over the more recent generation and contributed to the much-heralded resurgence of contemporary Orthodoxy in the most recent decades and even to polemical talk of that movement's coming hegemony in the twenty-first century?[98] Truth be told, contemporary Orthodoxy has not recaptured the hearts and souls of most American Jews. The winnowing of its once-majority nonobservant minions has continued apace. If anything, the 1970s–1980s witnessed a decline in the numbers of Jews who defined themselves as Orthodox or were members of Orthodox synagogues. As one analysis of the 1990 survey of the American Jewish population pointed out, despite all the publicity about Orthodox *Baalei Teshuvah* (Jews who "return" to Orthodoxy) swelling the most traditional ranks, "the major trend . . . has been the continual decline in the proportion of Orthodox among American Jewish adults, from 11% in 1971 to 6% in 1990." What changed is the intensity, level of commitment, and even rigidity of those who have proudly and assertively remained in Orthodoxy's camp.[99]

The committed cohorts who have led and taken part in Orthodoxy's very visible renaissance have emanated primarily from two complementary sources that I introduced earlier. The first major group is made up of the children and grandchildren of that small interwar contingent of native-born Jews who defined themselves as Orthodox and who held fast to traditional practice in both their homes and their congregations. One of the keys to their immediate ancestors' religious survival had been their affinity for day school or yeshiva education when it was unpopular. We had observed this outlook previously within the "representative" Williamsburg family that we profiled. In the last forty years, the numbers of such families have increased dramatically as this form of self-segregation has become widely accepted among the observant for both their sons and daughters. If anything, day-school education has become almost a sine qua non for full acceptance and comfort within the contemporary Orthodox synagogue. As one separatist Orthodox leader put it pointedly some years ago: "When I was a youngster [during the interwar period], it was very possible for someone to be an Orthodox Jew without continuing [intensive Jewish education] beyond elementary school. Today it is unthinkable that one can really be an Orthodox Jew unless he had at least graduated Yeshiva high school."[100]

The second highly observant cohort that has openly and aggressively demonstrated its commitment to Orthodoxy consists of refugee Orthodoxy's second and third generations. Beneficiaries too of intensive Jewish education, usually of a much more separatist sort, these are the now-grown children and grandchildren of the immigrants who fled to America from Germany and Eastern Europe during and after Hitler's reign. Their devotion to the maintenance of old-world Orthodoxy is as strong, if not stronger, than their parents' generation. The intensity of their commitment to the faith has had no small impact on the outlook of the observant day-school compatriots as they too understand their identities.[101]

Needless to say, American Orthodoxy's new core constituencies live religious lives that are very different both from their denomination's earlier majority of nonobservant members and from the religious behavior of most members of today's Conservative synagogues. To begin with, there is no question that Sabbath and Holiday services must be held only at sunset, the time to begin to scrupulously observe the holidays. Fortunately, many Orthodox Jews are affluent enough and are living in a tolerant enough society, that the demands of work and employment do not regularly test their faith.[102] In addition, there is also no question of how they should get to *shul* on the Sabbath. They walk to services from their homes that are often situated in suburban enclaves, in parts of towns that are increasingly inhospitable to nonobservant Jews. Moreover, for this younger generation, the synagogues they attend are not primarily ritual, commemorative, or memorial domains. Nor are they really centers for the intensification of Jewish identity. Rather, they are places where the already committed assemble, pray and study, helping them increase their familiarity with tradition beyond what they had learned of it in school.[103] Finally, to the extent that these Jews talk about socioreligious ancillary activities, their concerns are largely with *eruvim* (enclosures permitting carrying on the Sabbath), which permit parents to wheel baby carriages to services, thus enabling the Orthodox family to stay together while praying together, albeit on opposite sides of *mechitza*.[104]

Blessed with such committed groups of congregants, rabbis of today's strictly Orthodox congregations no longer feel the pressure to accommodate, or to turn a blind eye toward, the activities of the minority of graying nonobservant members. If they choose, these rabbis, if not their religious lay majority, can even establish the punctilious observance of mitzvoth as norms for full integration within their congregation. Of course they can engage in a myriad of outreach activities to bring the disaffected into their Orthodox fold. But here too, to become full-fledged members of the Orthodox group, these initiates must in time commit themselves to the increasingly rigid requirements of that most traditional American Jewish community.[105]

Conclusion: Contemporary Commonality?

Today, most Orthodox and Conservative Jews possess different religious values, belong to synagogues that are ritually distinctive, and are led by rabbis whose background, training, and orientation are fundamentally different. Still, notwithstanding these rigid lines of demarcation, some elements still remain on the margins of both movements, which, arguably, share similar religious outlooks and comparable commitments. If anything, those Conservative Jews who staunchly uphold halachic processes—as their movement defines them—and who, in their personal observances, regard the Sabbath, the maintenance of kashruth, and regular synagogue attendance as core religious values, have much in common with those within an identifiable Orthodox periphery who persistently test the elasticity of Jewish law in response to changing contemporary circumstances. Certainly those who are among the most traditional of Conservative Jews and those who champion what has been described as an Open Orthodoxy have much to say to each other and, from all accounts, are willing, at least, to dialogue with each other. As time goes on, it will be intriguing to observe and to report whether these groups find formal common cause in their religious quests and perhaps even find or create a unifying denominational identity.

Notes

1. It must be emphasized that notwithstanding the suggested commonalities within the Orthodox community from the *shtibls* to the suburban communities, in observing the Sabbath, adhering to kashruth, attendance at synagogue, etc.—behavior patterns that we are contrasting with Conservatives—there are major differences

among Orthodox groups on ideological and philosophical issues. So-called modern or centrist Orthodox differ from their more traditional, rightist, or sectarian counterparts—each one of these adjectives can be found in the literature—on the fundamental issues of the Orthodox Jew's place in and attitude toward the modern world. These differences manifest themselves in variant views on the value of secular education, the role of the modern state of Israel, the status of women, the possibilities for dialogue with Jewish religious leaders of differing stripes, etc. For a comprehensive articulation of the centrist position see Norman Lamm, *Torah U'Mada: The Encounter of Religious Learning and Worldly Knowledge in the Jewish Tradition* (Northvale, NJ: Jason Aronson, 1990). This position can also be followed through the pages of *Tradition: A Journal of Orthodox Thought,* particularly the years 1976–present. For alternative points of view, one can begin with criticism of Dr. Lamm's work and similar articles in journals like the *Jewish Observer.*

2. Extrapolated data from the Council of Jewish Federations 1990 National Jewish Population Survey. I am grateful to Professor Chaim Isaac Waxman for conducting these extrapolations for me. The interpretation of the data is mine.

3. Shmuel Singer, "Orthodox Judaism and the Smaller American Community," *Tradition* 22, no. 1 (1986): 59–63.

4. The definition of nonobservant Orthodox that was used so suggestively by Charles Liebman in his groundbreaking article "Orthodoxy in American Jewish Life," *American Jewish Year Book* 66 (1965): 34–36, may still apply to the older members of the Orthodox community. For them, the issues of nostalgia, family tradition, or simple discomfort within large, liberal Jewish settings may still keep them within the Orthodox community.

5. Aryeh Davidson and Jack Wertheimer, "The Next Generation of Conservative Rabbis: An Empirical Study of Today's Rabbinical Students," in *The Seminary at 100: Reflections on the Jewish Theological Seminary and the Conservative Movement,* ed. Nina Beth Cardin and David Wolf Silverman (New York: Jewish Theological Seminary, 1987), 33–46.

6. Jack Wertheimer, Project Director and Editor, *Conservative Synagogues and Their Members* (hereinafter *CSM*) (New York: Jewish Theological Seminary, 1996), 44.

7. The information used here to describe the background and early training of 1993 RIETS graduates is based on an analysis of the biographical forms filed by these graduates with Yeshiva University's public relations office as well as the press releases and local press accounts of the backgrounds of those honored. Though not every graduate filed a form or was publicly profiled, there does exist a critical mass of information to make the reasoned statements that follow. These sketches, forms, and reports are on file at Yeshiva University's public relations office. Additionally, for the best study of so-called transplanted Lithuanian "Yeshiva World" students of a generation ago, see William Helmreich, *The World of the Yeshiva: An Intimate Portrait of Orthodox Jewry* (New York: Free Press, 1982).

8. For an example of Yeshiva publicity about a so-called *Baal Teshuvah* who graduated from RIETS, see "Pascagoula Native is in Rabbinic Convocation," *Mississippi Press,* May 11, 1994, 22.

9. For a fuller examination of the history of Yeshiva students who ended up ma-

triculating at JTS, see Jeffrey S. Gurock, "Yeshiva Students at JTS," in *Tradition Renewed: A History of the Jewish Theological Seminary of America*, ed. Jack Wertheimer, vol. 1 (New York: Jewish Theological Seminary, 1997), 471–515.

10. "Eight Recently Ordained Bronx, N.Y. Rabbis to Participate Mar. 6 in Rabbinic Convocation," *NEWS RIETS* (Rabbi Isaac Elchanan Theological Seminary Press Release), February 9, 1994; author interview with Rabbi Douglas Lerea, a graduate of both JTS and RIETS rabbinical schools.

11. *CSM*, 16–17.

12. There is, to my knowledge, but one idiosyncratic Orthodox congregation, the Hebrew Institute of Riverdale, that permits mothers and fathers to ascend together to the bimah (altar) and to there offer a blessing of thanksgiving and separation upon the occasion of their son's bar mitzvah or daughter's bat mitzvah. That same congregation, and a few like-minded Orthodox synagogues, also allow (with their rabbi's approval) egalitarian megillah readings on Purim and on the Three Pilgrimage Festivals. But even the most avant-garde congregation does not permit women to be part of the minyan, lead services, or take part in the Torah reading, actions that to all Orthodox minds are clear violations of their understanding of halacha.

13. *CSM*, 16.

14. As of 1997, an American Orthodox woman, Haviva Krasner-Davidson, who attempted to apply for admission to RIETS, was reportedly soon to be ordained as an Orthodox rabbi in Israel. Additionally, Orthodox feminist Blu Greenberg and others have predicted that eventually a woman would be ordained as an Orthodox rabbi in America. However, there has been no movement within any recognized rabbinical training body toward that possibility. If anything, Orthodox feminist activities have been staunchly opposed by most Orthodox rabbis. At the same time, it must be noted that since the 1970s, Orthodox feminists have instituted what may be described as "separate and somewhat equal" women's tefillah groups. These groups have their own cadre of Orthodox rabbinical supporters who have placed their imprimatur on these gatherings. Interestingly enough, even as these groups and their rabbis have been tarred by the rightist opponents as being like the Conservatives, advocates of greater roles for women within Orthodoxy have been sure to place distance between themselves and Conservative Jews. For a basic description of contemporary Orthodoxy and feminism, see Jeffrey S. Gurock, "Orthodox Judaism," in *Jewish Women in America: An Historical Encyclopedia*, ed. Paula Hyman and Deborah Dash Moore (New York: Routledge, 1997), 1009–16.

15. According to Rabbi Raphael Butler, executive director of the Orthodox Union, there were by 1997 some seven congregations affiliated with the Union that did not have *mechitzas*. Three of these congregations lacked a *mechitza* in their main sanctuary and had a smaller *beth medrash* that had such a separation. Four others had no *mechitza* at all in their synagogues. Orthodox Union policy at that point was to continue to hold as constituent synagogues those seven congregations, with the understanding that they were moving toward installing a *mechitza* in their sanctuaries. There were a number of other self-defined Orthodox congregations in America that had no *mechitza* and that had shown no desire to move in that traditional direction. Such synagogues were afforded organizational services by the Orthodox Union, but were not, or were no longer, eligible as members. Discussions of these organizational

dynamics were contained in Orthodox Union board minutes that are held confidentially by that organization. Raphael Butler telephone conversation with Jacob J. Schacter, October 9, 1997.

16. See undated flyer circa November–December 1996 entitled "Friday Night Shabbat Experience: Friday Evening Service and Dinner," which offers the unaffiliated the chance to "Sing with us. Pray with us. Experience the beauty of our 'no-Hebrew necessary'" Beginners Service, which started at 6:45, two hours after sundown. Four large Manhattan-based Orthodox congregations endorsed this flyer. Comparable activities have taken place in other cities nationwide. It should be noted that these activities are separate from "Oneg Shabbat" activities in Orthodox synagogues, which are generally for the observant rank-and-file who may return to the synagogue for a lecture or discussion Friday night after welcoming the Sabbath at sundown.

17. *CSM*, 43. The typical, late-twentieth-century Conservative synagogue also stands out in other important ways, such as its use of instrumental music during Sabbath and holiday services and in its reading of the Torah on a triennial cycle, among other ritual practices. See *CSM*, 21.

18. Jack Wertheimer, *A People Divided: Judaism in Contemporary America* (New York: Basic Books, 1993), 154–56.

19. Avraham Weiss, "Open Orthodoxy! A Modern Orthodox Rabbi's Creed," *Judaism*, fall 1997, 409–21. Seemingly, the UTJ has moved increasingly away from its Conservative roots. In 1990, for example, its original name, Union for Traditional Conservative Judaism, was changed to its present name, reflecting its more traditional stance. See Wertheimer, *A People Divided*, 155.

20. Ephraim Lisitsky, *In the Grip of Cross Currents*, quoted in excerpt form in *How We Lived: A Documentary History of Immigrant Jews in America, 1880–1930*, ed. Irving Howe and Kenneth Libo (New York: Richard Marek, 1979), 96.

21. Ray Stannard Baker, *The Spiritual Unrest* (New York: Frederick A. Stokes, 1910), 117–18.

22. Moses Rischin, *The Promised City: New York's Jews, 1870–1914* (Cambridge: Harvard University Press, 1962), 146–47.

23. Rischin, *The Promised City*, 146. For an important, detailed examination of Jewish consumerism (including on the Sabbath and holidays) as a function of the acculturation of Jews, see Andrew Heinze, *Adapting to Abundance: Jewish Immigrants, Mass Consumption, and the Search for American Identity* (New York: Columbia University Press, 1990).

24. Hutchins Hapgood, *The Spirit of the Ghetto: Studies of the Immigrant Quarter of New York* (New York: Funk and Wagnalls, 1902), 125–26. See also on this subject pp. 92, 121–22.

25. Max Oxenhandler, "The Jewish Youth of the East Side," *Jewish Forum*, January 1923, 61.

26. George Kranzler, *Williamsburg: A Jewish Community in Transition* (New York: Feldheim, 1961), 17, 18, 214–15.

27. For a discussion of Sabbath observance patterns and nonobservance in these communities, see Jeffrey S. Gurock and Jacob J. Schacter, *A Modern Heretic and a Traditional Community: Mordecai M. Kaplan, Orthodoxy, and American Judaism* (New York: Columbia University Press, 1997), 91–92, 93, 115.

28. *Orthodox Union,* June 1936, 1.

29. Louis M. Levitsky, "The Story of an Awakened Community," *The Reconstructionist,* February 7, 1936, 9; "Conduct of Religious Services," *United Synagogue Recorder,* October 1927, 11.

30. Samuel P. Abelow, "Eastern Parkway in Jewish Life," *Jewish Forum,* September 1945, 199–200.

31. Bert Lewkowitz, "The Future of Judaism as a Layman Visions It," *Jewish Forum,* December 1940, 177; see also Meyer Waxman, "American Orthodoxy—the Fifth Unknowable," *Jewish Forum,* October 1924, 651.

32. Abelow, "Eastern Parkway," 199–200.

33. For contemporaneous accounts of the so-called Jewish revival see Nathan Glazer, *American Judaism* (Chicago: University of Chicago Press, 1957), 107–28; Will Herberg, *Protestant-Catholic-Jew: An Essay in American Jewish Sociology* (Garden City, NY: Doubleday, 1955); and Marshall Sklare, *Conservative Judaism: An American Religious Movement* (Glencoe, IL: Free Press, 1955). For statistics on the growth of the United Synagogue see Jack Wertheimer, "The Conservative Synagogue," in *The American Synagogue: A Sanctuary Transformed,* ed. Jack Wertheimer (Cambridge: Cambridge University Press, 1987), 123 (derived from the *Biennial Convention Reports of the United Synagogue of America* from 1952 to 1965). See also Simon Glustrom, "Some Aspects of a Suburban Jewish Community," *Conservative Judaism,* winter 1957, 26–32 for an on-the-scene and upbeat account of Conservative successes in a New Jersey suburb.

34. Emil Lehman, "The National Survey on Synagogue Leadership," *Proceedings of the 1953 Biennial Convention, United Synagogue of America* (November 15–19, 1953), 37. See also Wertheimer, "Conservative Synagogue," who also uses this survey, 131.

35. "Responsum on the Sabbath," *Proceedings of the Rabbinic Assembly* 14 (1950): 112–88.

36. *Proceedings of the 1953 Biennial Convention* (1953), 36–37, quoted in Wertheimer, "Conservative Synagogue," 132. Wertheimer should also be credited with making the point about synagogue members attending all activities except services. See Wertheimer, 132.

37. Lehman, "National Survey on Synagogue Leadership," 37. On the idea of the Sabbath as expendable and for references to the social dynamics of nonattendance at Sabbath services, see Samuel Penner, "The Seattle Plan," *Proceedings of the Rabbinical Assembly* 14 (1950): 193–94.

38. This commonality of values and levels of nonobservance were identified by some important sociological studies of the time. See for example, Marshall Sklare and Mark Vosk, *The Riverton Study: How Jews Look at Themselves and Their Neighbors* (New York: America Jewish Committee, 1957), 10–13. See also Sidney Goldstein and Calvin Goldscheider, *Jewish Americans: Three Generations in a Jewish Community* (Englewood Cliffs, NJ: Prentice Hall, 1968). This study of Providence, Rhode Island, conducted in 1962, found inter alia that the lines dividing the three religious divisions were increasingly becoming blurred, at least in the minds and behavior of native-born Jews. Although Orthodox Jews were more ritual-oriented, over two-thirds did not attend synagogue services at least once a month, and generational declines were noted in their adherence to traditional ritual practices associated with the home. See p. 231.

39. Bert Lescot, "Orthodoxy in Suburbia," *Jewish Forum*, February 1958, 21. On the issue of driving to synagogue on the Sabbath see also Julius M. Hurst, "Sabbath Riding," *Jewish Life*, September–October 1952, 36–37.

40. Howard W. Polsky, "A Study of Orthodoxy in Milwaukee: Social Characteristics, Beliefs and Observances," in Marshall Sklare, *The Jews: Social Patterns of an American Group* (1921; Glencoe, IL: Free Press, 1958), 328.

41. Philip K. Isaacs, "Orthodox Jewry in Boston: A Survey," *Jewish Life*, October 1958, 48.

42. Ralph Pelcovitz, "Who Is the Orthodox Jew," *Jewish Life*, November–December 1964, 16.

43. For a study of acculturated Orthodox Jews in interwar Yorkville and the West Side, New York, see Jenna W. Joselit, *New York's Jewish Jews: The Orthodox Community in the Interwar Years* (Bloomington: Indiana University Press, 1990). Unfortunately, this study that purports to examine the total Orthodox community in the city at that time does not delve in detail into the styles of Orthodox life in the Bronx or Brooklyn.

44. It should be noted that not all of this Williamsburg family's youngsters followed in their first-generation parents' footsteps. Though one son was inspired to keep the laws and to raise a family "in the spirit of our tradition," his brother felt much differently. By the late 1940s, he became, in the parlance of his religious brother, "A High Holiday Jew [who] . . . lives in a swanky neighborhood in Forest Hills," on the outskirts of suburbia. We might call this rebellious brother, and probably his descendants too, representative of postwar nonobservant Orthodox (or Conservative) Jews. See Kranzler, *Williamsburg*, 214–15.

45. Kranzler, *Williamsburg*, 215–19.

46. Michael Kaufman, "Far Rockaway—Torah Suburb by the Sea," *Jewish Life*, August 1960, 20.

47. Israel Tabak, "The Need for Jewish Missionaries," *Jewish Life*, June 1947, 34–35; Joseph Kaminetsky, "Boro Park," *Jewish Life*, October 1953, 18–23.

48. To be sure, elementary yeshiva education dates back to the founding of Yeshiva Etz Chaim on the Lower East Side in 1886. Secondary Jewish education began in 1915 with the organizing of the Talmudical Academy, again on the Lower East Side. In the period between 1917 and 1939, there was a modest growth of day schools in North America. According to one survey between 1917 and 1939, twenty-eight schools were founded, twenty-three of them in New York, and the remainder in Baltimore, Dorchester (Massachusetts), Union City (New Jersey), Montreal, and Toronto. By 1940, there were an estimated seven thousand youngsters attending such schools, most of which went up to the eighth grade. Of the twenty-eight schools, only eight were coeducational and one was for girls only. The New York neighborhoods that had these schools included Boro Park, Crown Heights, Williamsburg, Brownsville, and East New York (all in Brooklyn), Lower Manhattan and Yorkville in Manhattan and the East Bronx. On the origin and growth of these schools, see Alvin I. Schiff, *The Jewish Day School in America* (New York: Jewish Education Committee of New York, 1956), 28–46.

49. Kranzler, *Williamsburg*, 216.

50. On the transformation of Williamsburg into an immigrant, heavily Hasidic community, see Kranzler, *Williamsburg*, 25–44 and passim. See also, on the sociology

of that Hasidic community, Solomon Poll, *The Hasidic Community in Williamsburg* (New York: Free Press, 1962). On the changes that took place in Boro Park see Egon Mayer, *From Suburb to Shtetl: The Jews of Boro Park* (Philadelphia: Temple University Press, 1979). See also, on the history of the Lithuanian Yeshiva world in America, Helmreich, *World of the Yeshiva.*

51. For a history of the Endeavorers see Jeffrey S. Gurock, "Consensus Building and Conflict over Creating the Young People's Synagogue of the Lower East Side," in *The Americanization of the Synagogue,* ed. Norman J. Cohen and Robert Seltzer (New York: New York University Press, 1995), 230–46.

52. We know from Kaplan's own private writings that while he was a rabbi at Kehilath Jeshurun, he no longer considered himself an Orthodox rabbi. However, his public profile was compatible with Orthodoxy. On this and other aspects of his career in Yorkville, see Gurock and Schacter, *Modern Heretic,* chap. 3. That chapter also describes Kaplan's harmonious relationship with Ramaz in the Yorkville pulpit. For a biographical description of Goldstein's career see Moshe D. Sherman, *Orthodox Judaism in America: A Biographical Dictionary and Source Book* (Westport, CT: Greenwood Press, 1996), 79–81. For information on Rosenblatt's appointment to Beth Tefilo see Samuel Rosenblatt, *The Days of My Years* (New York: Ktav, 1976), 85–87 and passim. See also Gurock interview with Israel Miller, July 23, 1997 (author's possession). On Benjamin's short career at Hebrew Institute see *Who's Who in American Jewry,* vol. 3 (1938–39), 74. See also Gurock interview with Beatrice Friedland, July 23, 1997 (author's possession). Benjamin was rabbi in University Heights 1928–30. For a list of OU congregations in New York in 1930 see attachment to "Benjamin Koenigsberg to Friend, March 24, 1930," Koenigsberg Papers, Yeshiva University Archives.

53. On the history of the Young Israel, see National Council of Young Israel Organizations, *Annual Convention: 5694/1934* (brochure on file at the American Jewish Historical Society). Its brief descriptions of congregations noted only four rabbis in YI pulpits. See also "Constitution of Council of Young Israel and Young Israel Synagogue Organizations," ca. 1935, American Jewish Historical Society. On Kaplan's involvement with Young Israel's foundings, see Gurock and Schacter, *Modern Heretic,* 78–81.

54. Wertheimer, "The Conservative Synagogue," 119–20.

55. Herman H. Rubenovitz and Mignon Rubenovitz, *The Waking Heart* (Cambridge, MA, Nathaniel Dane, 1967), 34.

56. Jacob J. Weinstein, *Solomon Goldman: A Rabbi's Rabbi* (New York: Ktav, 1973), 13–14; Aaron Rakeffet-Rothkoff, *The Silver Era in American Jewish Orthodoxy: Rabbi Eliezer Silver and His Generation* (New York: Yeshiva University Press; Jerusalem: Feldheim, 1981), 112–14.

57. On the Young Israel of Brooklyn's affiliation, see National Council of Young Israel Organizations, *Annual Convention,* 48; United Synagogue of America, *Sixth Annual Report* (1919–20), 131, and *Fifteenth Annual Report* (1929), 15. See also *United Synagogue Recorder,* April 1923, 11.

58. *Congregation Shmorei Emunah Testimonial Dinner in Honor of Rabbi Dr. Harry I. Wohlberg, November 4, 1973* (Brooklyn: Shomrei Emunah, 1973), 1–5. This congregational journal claims that the congregation was a member of the Orthodox Union from its inception in 1907. They have no historical memory of their ever being part of the "Conservative" congregational group. However, they are listed as members of

the United Synagogue in its annual reports of 1919–20 and 1929. Moreover, the synagogue address and the official listed as president of the congregation in 1919 in the United Synagogue report are the same as the address and name listed in the congregational journal, lending credence to our description of them as United Synagogue members. I would date their official involvement with the Orthodox Union from 1930, when they are listed as a New York affiliate. See "Benjamin Koenigsberg to Friend, March 24, 1930."

59. On Rosenthal's early involvement with the Young Israel, see Gurock, "A Generation Unaccounted for in American Judaism," *American Jewish History,* December 1987, 247–59. On the history of this congregation, see Washington Heights Congregation, B'nai Yisrael. *Fiftieth Anniversary, 1914–1964* (New York: n.p., 1964), 1–2.

60. Max Drob, "A Reaffirmation of Traditional Judaism," *Jewish Forum,* October 1929, 420.

61. Drob, "Reaffirmation of Traditional Judaism," 416–20.

62. On early Jewish Center involvement with the United Synagogue, its self-definition as Orthodox, and its perception that the Seminary was an Orthodox institution, see Gurock and Schacter, *Modern Heretic,* chap. 6, especially pp. 116–21.

63. On the history and activities of Kehilath Israel during Finkelstein's tenure, see *United Synagogue Recorder,* October 1922, 11; January 1925, 30; October 1925, 25. On Finkelstein receiving Orthodox ordination at JTS, see Louis Ginzberg to Cyrus Adler, October 26, 1922, Adler Papers, Library of the JTS. See also undated interview with Louis Finkelstein, Majorie Wyler Papers, Ratner Center, JTS.

64. On the history, rabbis and ritual of Beth El, see *United Synagogue Recorder,* October 1925, 26; July 1928, 14. For biographical sketches of Shohet and Katzen, see their biographical forms in their respective alumni files at JTS. On public Orthodox activities during the early 1930s, see *Jewish Advocate* (Boston), June 24, 1932, pt. 3, p. 3; December 11, 1932, 1.

65. For information on Epstein's background, see his "Application for Admission to the Preparatory Course of The Jewish Theological Seminary of America" and his biographical fact sheet in his alumni file in the Library of the JTS. See also in that file the following letters that relate to the offer tendered to him by Har Zion: Cyrus Adler to Epstein, May 7, 1925, May 13, 1925; Epstein to Adler, May 11, 1925; Epstein to Mr. Cohen, undated [May 1925]. Interestingly enough, Epstein was also a candidate to succeed Mordecai Kaplan at the Jewish Center. See on that possibility Epstein to Adler, July 24, 1922, and Adler to Epstein, September 7, 1922. Both letters are in the aforementioned Epstein alumni file. On Epstein's advocacy of Orthodoxy in Brookline, see *Jewish Advocate* (Boston), November 12, 1925, 1; and January 13, 1927, 1.

66. It is uncertain when B'nai Emunah joined the United Synagogue and for how long it remained a member. The previously noted 1919–20 listing of United Synagogue affiliates does not list it as a member, nor does the 1929 listing. However, the *United Synagogue Recorder,* January 1924, 14, does note its congregational activities, as it did all of its members. There is no congregational history or memory of the synagogue belonging to the Orthodox Union until 1936, when it is noted in that body's journal *Orthodox Union,* November 1936, 3. We will discuss later the implications of congregations switching to the Orthodox Union in the 1930s. Also, Rabbi Arthur D. Kahn, telephone interview by the author, October 21, 1997.

67. *B'nai Emunah, Tulsa Oklahoma, 1916–1966* (Tulsa: n.p., 1966), 12, 28.

68. "To the Chairman and the Board of Directors of the Jewish Theological Seminary of America, April 29, 1917," Library of the JTS. For a discussion of this plan, see Gurock, "Yeshiva Students at JTS," 490–91.

69. For information on the upper New York State congregations that Drob served, see B. G. Rudolph, *From a Minyan to a Community: A History of the Jews of Syracuse* (Syracuse: Syracuse University Press, 1970), 84–85; Selig Adler and Thomas E. Connolly, *From Ararat to Suburbia: The History of the Jewish Community of Buffalo* (Philadelphia: Jewish Publication Society, 1960), 270–71. That Drob saw himself as an Orthodox rabbi despite his serving in a mixed-seating congregation is made evident by a letter Drob sent to Solomon Schechter in 1915, where he described congregational life at Buffalo's Temple Beth El. "It has always clung to the Orthodox ritual, and its adherence to the strict rules caused a secession almost fifty years ago resulting in the formation of the Reform Temple. . . . In short, we are doing our best to conduct the congregation as an Orthodox synagog [*sic*] on a modern basis." What Drob was undoubtedly referring to was his opposition to the efforts of his predecessor, Rabbi Jacob Landau, to shorten the services by reading only a portion of the Torah each week and by using the Jastrow prayer book. In other words, he proved his Orthodox mettle by opposing more dramatic changes. We will presently see this was a common stance by rabbis of that time. See Drob to Schechter, April 25, 1915, Drob file, Alumni Files, Library of the JTS.

70. *United Synagogue Recorder,* October 1925, 26.

71. *The Golden Book of Shearith Israel Commemorating the Congregation's Fiftieth Anniversary, 1884–1934* (Dallas: Shearith Israel, 1934), n.p. I have not been able to determine if Shearith Israel was, in the second decade of the century, a member of the Orthodox Union. It was not a member of the United Synagogue.

72. On the ritual at these Boston-area congregations, see Gerald Herbert Gamm, "Neighborhood Roots: Exodus and Stability in Boston, 1870–1990," Ph.D. diss., Harvard University, 1994, 237, 241, 313 and passim.

73. *B'nai Emunah,* 9, 22, 28. For discussion of Teller's search for a higher-paid job in Chicago, see Samuel Cohen to Morris Teller, October 5, 1925; Teller to Cohen, October 12, 1925; Teller to Adler, January 28, 1926, Teller file, Alumni Files, Library of the JTS.

74. See David A. Shohet to Cyrus Adler, May 25, 1925, Shohet to Samuel S. Cohen, August 2, 1925, Shohet to Israel Levinthal, September 2, 1930, Shohet file, Alumni Files, Library of the JTS. See also Louis Epstein to Cohen, July 1925, Epstein file, Alumni Files, Library of the JTS.

75. On the history of Ahavath Achim, including the reference to nonobservance patterns among members, see Michael J. Safra, "America's Challenge to Traditional Jewish worship: Changes in Atlanta's Synagogues, 1867–1972," B.A. Honors Thesis, Department of History and Frankel Center for Judaic Studies, University of Michigan, 1997, 64–65 which in turn relies upon Kenneth Stein, *A History of Ahavath Achim* (Atlanta: Standard Press, 1978), 44. For a biographical study of Harry Epstein, see Mark Bauman, "Rabbi Harry H. Epstein and the Adaptation of Second-Generation East European Jews in Atlanta," *American Jewish Archives* 42 (fall–winter 1990): 133–46. It is impossible to determine precisely when Ahavath Achim entered the Orthodox Union and when Epstein was first elected to its board. However, from

ephemeral documents—letterheads from the Orthodox Union as well as some pamphlets that they published—it is evident that by 1936–37, the synagogue and the rabbi were both active in that organization. A reference to that congregation appears in the *Orthodox Union,* November 1936, 3.

76. For a discussion of the history of Beth El and Knesset Israel see Mark H. Elovitz, *A Century of Jewish Life in Dixie: The Birmingham Experience* (Tuscaloosa: University of Alabama Press, 1974), 91, 93–95, 99, 163–64. It should be noted that by 1944, Rabbi Mesch was anxious to have the synagogue join the United Synagogue. And, in fact, in 1944 the congregation voted to belong to both national synagogue organizations.

77. It is uncertain precisely when each of these congregations joined the Orthodox Union. Both congregations were formed in the 1920s and, as we will later discuss, were served then by rabbis trained at the Jewish Theological Seminary. However, the congregations were never listed as members of the United Synagogue. A listing of Bronx synagogues affiliated with the Orthodox Union as of 1930 also does not list them as member institutions. However, references to these congregations as affiliates of the OU do appear in that organization's newspaper in the mid-1930s. See for example, *Orthodox Union,* November 1936, 2; January 1937, 2. See Gurock interview with Herschel Schacter, July 22, 1997; and Miller, interview, for discussions of ritual practices that obtained when these congregations were members of the Orthodox Union (in author's possession).

78. On Bernard Revel's transformation of RIETS from an East European transplant to its emergence as an American Orthodox yeshiva and seminary see Jeffrey S. Gurock, *The Men and Women of Yeshiva: Orthodoxy, Higher Education and American Judaism* (New York: Columbia University Press, 1988), 43–66. On the Travis family's relationship with JTS, see above.

79. On Lookstein's appointment and impact on Kehilath Jeshurun, see Joselit, *New York's Jewish Jews,* especially chap. 3, pp. 54–96.

80. *The Scroll of the Twentieth Anniversary Celebration, Congregation Shaarey Tefila, October 26, 1930* (Far Rockaway, NY: Congregation Shaarey Tefila, 1930), n.p.; Washington Heights Congregation, *Fiftieth Anniversary,* n.p.; Asher Siev, interview by the author, July 24, 1997.

81. Washington Heights Congregation, *Fiftieth Anniversary,* n.p.; Siev, interview. Like Finkelstein, Siev recalled that the congregation was often unable to pay rabbinic salaries during the 1930s.

82. "Report on the Reorganization of the Placement Committee," *Proceedings of the Rabbinical Assembly* 3 (1929): 123–24. See also on the problem of competition, Jacob Minkin to Cyrus Adler, November 13, 1929, Minkin files, Alumni Files, Library of the JTS.

83. On the patterns of synagogue life under Rosenbloom in Kingsbridge Heights, see Miller, interview, who succeeded Rosenbloom in 1941. According to Miller, that synagogue did not change its seating patterns until several years later, after the Second World War. As noted previously, the congregation was a member of the Orthodox Union as early as 1936. See *Orthodox Union,* November 1936, 3.

84. Gurock, "Yeshiva Students at JTS," 497–98.

85. David de Sola Pool, "Judaism and the Synagogue," in *The American Jew: A Com-*

posite Portrait, ed. Oscar Janowsky (New York: Harper and Brothers, 1942), 50–54. See also Lewkowitz, "Future of Judaism," 177. In reporting on his travels throughout the country, Lewkowitz observed that "men and women sit [together] in Orthodox as well as so-called conservative congregations."

86. Having identified the varying forms of synagogue life and ritual subsumed under the banners of both the United Synagogue and the Orthodox Union during the interwar period with an emphasis on how close many of these congregations were in outlook and staffing, it still remains to be determined how prevalent each of these styles were within their own "movements" and whether we can speak of a predominant type of synagogue during that era. For example, while it is clear that many Orthodox Union congregations had mixed seating and the late Friday night service—so common to the United Synagogue—the absence of any self-study or extant documentation from the Orthodox Union makes it impossible to determine how many of their synagogues displayed those "deviant" characteristics. De Sola Pool surely gives us the sense that such behavior obtained widely, but precisely how pervasive it was cannot be determined. The United Synagogue's self-studies during the early 1930s and the early 1940s seem to indicate that the majority of their congregations resembled in ritual the "deviant" Orthodox Union synagogues of their day and not the Conservative synagogues of the postwar and contemporary period. For example, the 1933 study evidences that close to 90 percent of the congregations surveyed had both the late Friday night service and the early Friday night service. Mixed seating seemed to be so universal within the United Synagogue that it was not even studied as part of the survey. More than 70 percent of these congregations conducted daily services, just like the Orthodox Union congregations. On the other hand, the use of organs during Sabbath and holiday services was very rare. Only 10 percent of congregations used such music on the holy days. While this study does mention the desire of some congregations to shorten the Sabbath service, there was no quantification offered of the degree to which they had moved away from the Orthodox ritual. This persistence of traditional forms of ritual behavior continued to characterize the United Synagogue congregations as late as the beginning of the 1940s. Then, a study revealed that 97 percent of its affiliates conducted late Friday night services and that 70 percent still conducted an early Friday night service. Similarly, it was noted that "in the overwhelming majority of cases, the traditional Schacharis (Saturday morning prayers) is conducted with almost no modification or change." And in "81% of the replies, the Torah reading is according to the annual cycle with the traditional number of men being called up to the Torah." Moreover, among its rabbis in the field, while there were some "requests for drastic revision of the prayer book, for the abbreviation of the service . . . , the majority of our men, however, ask for the retention of the traditional texts." What all this suggests is that the predominant type of Americanized synagogue during the interwar period serving the masses of nonobservant but traditionally oriented Jew may have been the one where men and women sat together and where late Friday night was prime time for synagogue attendance. But, in so many other ways, the congregations, be they Orthodox Union or United Synagogue, adhered to traditional patterns and strictures. See Morris Silverman, "Report of Survey on Ritual," *Proceedings of the Rabbinical Assembly* 5 (1933): 321–39; "Report of the Prayer Book Commission," *Proceedings of*

the Rabbinical Assembly 8 (1944): 151–56. See also Wertheimer, "The Conservative Synagogue," 120, for his observation on why the predominance of mixed pews was not studied.

87. Aaron Solomon, "Tradition in Charleston," *Jewish Life*, January–February 1957, 17–20. Charles Reznikoff and Uriah Z. Engelman, *The Jews of Charleston: A History of an American Jewish Community* (Philadelphia: Jewish Publication Society of America, 1954), 215–16, 237–38.

88. Bernard Levinthal's checkered career included his leadership of the Agudath ha-Rabbanim in 1904, condemning the seminary as a school incapable of producing Orthodox rabbis even as he sent his own son to that same school, and consistently implicitly encouraged its graduates to establish themselves in his own Philadelphia. This is truly worthy of further study. See my discussion of Levinthal in *American Jewish Orthodoxy in Historical Perspective* (Hoboken, NJ: Ktav, 1996), 26, 367.

89. On the history of Detroit Jewry and its synagogues, see Robert A. Rockaway, *The Jews of Detroit: from the Beginning, 1762–1914* (Detroit: Wayne State University Press, 1986); Sidney Bolkosky, *Harmony and Dissonance: Voices of Jewish Identity in Detroit, 1914–1967* (Detroit: Wayne State University Press, 1991), 98–99, 104–9; Eli Grad and Bette Roth, *Congregation Shaarey Zedek 5622–5742/1861–1981* (Southfield, MI: Congregation Shaarey Zedek, 1982), 56, 62; Ruth and Eiga Hershman, "Rabbi Abraham M. Hershman," *Michigan Jewish History*, June 1981, 16–32; Robert Rockaway to Gurock, November 24, 1997; Gurock phone conversation with Bolkosky, November 25, 1997. It should be noted that Shaarey Zedek, which dates itself back to 1861, is representative of a type of early United Synagogue of America congregation that was founded before the period of East European emergence from first-settlement neighborhoods. Apparently Shaarey Zedek began as a Central European synagogue—a breakaway from the Reform Temple Beth El—and later attracted East European Jews. It is also noteworthy that there was a small Young Israel presence founded in Detroit in 1925 that adhered to its more rigorous form of American Orthodoxy. See Bolkosky, *Harmony and Dissonance*, 105–6; *Inventory of the Church and Synagogue Archives of Michigan* (Detroit: Michigan Historical Records Survey Project, 1940), 34.

90. The early postwar decades witnessed a slow but steady increase in ritual innovations. By 1948, two-thirds of congregations had mixed choirs, and the vast majority had confirmation ceremonies for boys and girls. However, only 20 percent used organs on holy days and one in three congregations had bat mitzvahs. The mid-1960s and beyond would witness increased egalitarianism in the services and governance of Conservative synagogues. See Wertheimer, "The Conservative Synagogue," 130–32, 135–37, for a discussion of these innovations as a Conservative movement far different from Orthodoxy and more popular than the more traditional denomination emerged and flourished.

91. This understanding of the time for Conservatism efflorescence and achievement of numerical hegemony among the masses of Jews differs from the interpretations of Sklare and others who have seen Conservatism winning out over Orthodoxy numerically in the interwar period. It is suggested here that the periodization of their "conquest" of American Judaism is after World War II. It is then that the Conservative movement began to increasingly display the characteristics of service and ritual that would continue throughout the contemporary era. See Sklare, *Conservative Ju-*

daism, 66–128; Herberg, *Protestant-Catholic-Jew,* 186–95; and Glazer, *American Judaism,* 79–106, for examples of this older historiography. See also Gurock, "The Winnowing of American Orthodoxy" *Approaches to Modern Judaism* 2 (1984): 41–54, for an earlier critique of their periodization.

92. On the decline of men from Yeshiva and other Orthodox homes studying at the JTS and the emergence of rabbis from that institution who had grown up in the Conservative camp, see Gurock, "Yeshiva Students at JTS," 498–500.

93. For statistics on the United Synagogue's growth during this time, see Wertheimer, "The Conservative Synagogue," 123. For the sense that Conservatism was victorious by the mid-1960s, see Sklare, *Conservative Judaism,* 254.

94. Leo Jung, "A Plea to Organized Orthodoxy," *Jewish Forum,* February 1959, 6. For 1960s demographics, see Morris Axelrod, Floyd J. Fowler, and Arnold Gurin, *A Community Survey for Long Range Planning* (Boston: Combined Jewish Philanthropies of Greater Boston, 1967), 119; Goldstein and Goldscheider, *Jewish Americans,* 177; Albert J. Mayer, *Milwaukee Jewish Population Study* (Milwaukee: Jewish Welfare Fund, 1965), 48, quoted in Sklare, *Conservative Judaism,* 254.

95. Samuel Yalow, "A Righteous Minority and the Individual," *Jewish Forum,* June 1959, 93–94.

96. For an analysis of the importance of these court cases, see Jonathan D. Sarna, "The Debate over Mixed Seating in the American Synagogue," in Wertheimer, *The American Synagogue,* 381–86. To be sure, in the 1920s there had been the also celebrated case of the Cleveland Jewish Center–Solomon Goldman controversy over mixed seating and more. Still, Sarna points out, and I agree, that the 1950s cases had the "effect of solidifying Orthodoxy's position on this issue." See also *Report of the President Submitted to the Sixtieth Anniversary National Biennial Convention of the Union of Orthodox Jewish Congregations of America,* November 13, 1956, 8–10.

97. For examples of popular and scholarly literature defining Orthodoxy's position on mixed seating that was read by rabbis in the field, see Morris Max, "Mixed Pews," *Jewish Life,* October 1949, 16–22; Fabian Schoenfeld, "Review of *The Sanctity of the Synagogue,*" *Tradition* 2, no. 2 (1960): 340–41; and Norman Lamm, "Separate Pews in the Synagogue: A Social and Psychological Approach," *Tradition* 1, no. 2 (1959): 161–64; see especially 144 n. 3 for his comments on Orthodox rabbis who deviate from norms. See also Harold I. Levine, "The Non-observant Orthodox," *Tradition* 2, no. 1 (1959), 1–19, for more on defining rabbis of mixed seating congregations within and without Orthodoxy. Liebman's 1965 study of Orthodoxy pointed out that according to the OU, between 1955–1965 some thirty Orthodox synagogues that once had mixed seating installed *mechitzas.* Liebman noted that this was "the first break in a trend which had been moving in the opposite direction since the 19th century." This trend, as we have noted previously, would continue and accelerate in the succeeding decades. See Liebman, 56.

98. As early as 1971, Sklare, who had heralded the hegemony of Conservative Judaism during the postwar period, already remarked that "Orthodoxy has transformed its image from that of a dying movement to one whose strength and opinions must be reckoned within any realistic appraisal of the Jewish community." See Marshall Sklare, *America's Jews* (New York: Random House, 1971), 40. See also David J. Schnall, "Orthodoxy Resurgent," *Judaism* 30, no. 4 (1981): 460–63.

99. Bernard Lazerwitz, J. Alan Winter, Arnold Dashefsky, and Ephraim Tabory, "A Study of Jewish Denominational Preferences: Summary Findings," *American Jewish Year Book* 97 (1997): 115–29. For other studies that speak about the decline in Orthodox numbers but a rise in intensity of their commitment, see Daniel J. Elazar, "How Strong Is Orthodox Judaism Really: The Demographics of Jewish Identification," *Jewish Action,* spring 1991, 62–63; George Kranzler, "The Changing Orthodox Jewish Community," *Tradition* 16, no. 2 (1976): 61–67; Egon Mayer and Chaim I. Waxman, "Modern Jewish Orthodoxy in America: Toward the Year 2000," *Tradition* 16, no. 3 (1977): 98–109. These studies also suggest, if not predict, the rise of these committed Orthodox numbers in the future based on the higher birth rate of these people as compared with other American Jews. For a polemical contention that Orthodoxy alone will survive in the twenty-first century, see "The Future of American Jewry: Will Your Grandchild be Jewish?" *Washington Jewish Week,* May 22, 1997, 14, based on an Antony Gordon and Richard M. Horowitz Independent Survey (1994) of the National Jewish Population Survey. For a cogent refutation of this interpretation of the 1990 data, see Samuel Heilman, "Is the Future Really Rosy for Haredim?" *Jewish Week,* February 20, 1998, 30. This having been said, it should be reiterated that contemporary Orthodoxy is not devoid of its nonobservant or "nominal" components, although, as suggested at the outset of this paper, they tend to be older than most committed Orthodox Jews.

100. On the connection between day school education and belonging to the contemporary Orthodox community, see Mayer and Waxman, "Modern Jewish Orthodoxy," 99–100; Samuel C. Heilman and Steven M. Cohen, *Cosmopolitans and Parochials: Modern Orthodox Jews in America* (Chicago: University of Chicago Press, 1989), 195–97; William Helmreich, "Old Wine in New Bottles: Advanced Yeshivot in the United States," *American Jewish History,* December 1979, 243. To be sure, not all day school students come from observant homes. Moreover, there are subcategories of nonobservance in the day school community. Helmreich has identified cohorts who send their youngsters to day school who are Sabbath-observers, but who are not intensely engaged in the Orthodox resurgence. See on this Helmreich, "Trends within Contemporary Orthodoxy," *Judaism* 30, no. 4 (1981): 381–82.

101. On the impact the refugee Orthodox community has made on the larger Orthodox community in the realm of education, see Mayer and Waxman, "Modern Jewish Orthodoxy," 103; Kranzler, "Changing Orthodox Jewish Community," 66–67; Heilman and Cohen, *Cosmopolitans and Parochials,* 182–83. See also Haym Soloveitchik, "Rupture and Rapture: The Transformation of Contemporary Orthodoxy," *Tradition* 28, no. 4 (1994): 64–130; Isaac Chavel, "On Haym Soloveitchik's 'Rupture and Rapture . . . ,'" *Torah U'Mada Journal* 7 (1997): 122–36 and Soloveitchik's "Clarification and Reply," 137–49.

102. Jews today have a relatively easier time in balancing careers with Sabbath observance. See Chaim I. Waxman, "The Sabbath as Dialectic: The Meaning and Role," *Judaism* 30, no. 1 (1982): 37–44; Mayer and Waxman, "Modern Jewish Orthodoxy," 106–7.

103. On the sociology and anthropology of a representative Orthodox synagogue, see Samuel C. Heilman, *Synagogue Life: A Study in Symbolic Interaction* (Chicago: University of Chicago Press, 1973). See also Mayer and Waxman, "Modern Jewish Ortho-

doxy," 109, on the Orthodox synagogue as something other than a Jewish center, but rather as a place of learning for the committed.

104. See note 15, which indicates that there are today very few Orthodox Union congregations without *mechitzas*. See also, Lawrence H. Schiffman, "When Women and Men Sat Together in American Orthodox Synagogues," *Moment,* December 1989, 45–49, which speaks inter alia about the involuntary winnowing out of the Orthodox Union of congregations that did not have such partitions.

105. On the raising of the standards for full membership and comfort within the Orthodox synagogue see Waxman, "The Sabbath as Dialectic," 43–44; Heilman and Cohen, *Cosmopolitans and Parochials,* 183. Of course, accommodations are made for those people who are moving toward Orthodoxy. I am referring here to attitudes toward people who show no interest in becoming more observant.

Grandfather teaches grandson about the Torah, Los Angeles, 2002.
Courtesy of Bill Aron.

New Directions in Jewish Theology in America

Arthur Green

Theology has not been the creative forte of the Jewish people throughout most of the last century. We have been too busily engaged in the process of surviving to have had the energy to devote to sustained religious reflection. We have struggled to find our way as latecomers into modernity, to establish ourselves on new shores and amid unfamiliar cultural landscapes. We have survived an encounter with evil incarnate that cost us the lives of fully a third of the Jewish people, including an untold number of thinkers, teachers, and their students, Hasidic masters and disciples, many of whom in better times might have helped us to figure out the puzzles of Jewish theology. For the past fifty years the Jewish people as a body politic has been fully and single-mindedly engaged in the task of reconstruction, in our case meaning above all building the State of Israel as a secure national home for the Jewish people and securing emigration rights for Jews who chose to go there. Besides these monumental undertakings, all else seemed to pale.

Nevertheless, we have hardly been bereft of theologians and religious thinkers. In recent memory there have been two bursts of theological creativity especially worthy of note. One began in the late 1960s, when such thinkers as Emil Fackenheim, Richard Rubenstein, Arthur Cohen, and others began to integrate the lessons of the Holocaust into Jewish religious parlance. The other has taken place over the course of the past two or three decades and has more to do with both the recovery of religious language and the ways it may, must, or may not be updated in order to carry Jewry into the rather uncharted waters that lie ahead in what most seem to be-

This essay was originally presented on November 7, 1993, at the Jean and Samuel Frankel Center for Judaic Studies, University of Michigan, Ann Arbor.

lieve is a radically new era in the history of the Jewish people. Here the names of David Hartman, Irving Greenberg, Judith Plaskow, Arthur Waskow, Neil Gillman, and Eugene Borowitz all come to mind. Quite a rogues' gallery of thinkers for a people too busy to theologize!

But this latter crop of thinkers appears precisely—and hardly accidentally—at a time when I believe the Jewish people are ready for theology and, indeed, need it urgently. I breathe deeply, add a *barukh ha-shem,* and note that nowhere in the world are there persecuted Jews who need our help. With the possible exceptions of small communities in Syria and Iran, there is no one through whom North American Jews can live a vicarious Jewish life or for whose sake they can postpone thinking about the nature of their own Jewishness "because there are more urgent things to do."

Indeed thinking about our own Jewishness is precisely what we Jews need most to do. We need to define our goals for the continuity of Jewish life. What do we mean by a Jewish future in America? How much of Judaism, what sort of religious life, what kind of community can we imagine existing several generations into the future? How much of assimilation can we tolerate and still survive as a distinct culture? How will we believe in our Judaism, and what will be the important Jewish experiences we will share with our children? We need to create a vision of a contemporary Judaism that will attract the coming generations and articulate a meaning deep and powerful enough to help us withstand the tremendous assimilatory powers by which we are surrounded. If there is to be a future for Jewish life on this continent, I believe that the theologian will now have a great deal to do with it.

The following remarks are offered from a particular theological point of view; I do not present them as an objective description of a historical phenomenon called Jewish theology. They are, if you will, a theologian's rather than a historian's definition of the Jewish theologian's task. I see myself as a theologian in the tradition of an East European school of Jewish mystical theology, itself the heir of the kabbalistic and Hasidic traditions. The chief figures in this school (here identified as such for the first time) in the twentieth century were Judah Loeb Alter of Ger, author of the *Sefat Emet;* Abraham Isaac Kook, chief rabbi of Palestine during the British mandate; Hillel Zeitlin, teacher and martyr of the Warsaw ghetto; and my own teacher Abraham Joshua Heschel.

This school is defined by a sense that the starting point of theological reflection is the cultivation of inwardness and the opening of the soul to God's presence throughout the world. The members of this group may all be characterized as experientialist mystics. Each of them celebrates inward religious experience, his own as well as that provided by literary or historic example, as the primary datum with which the theologian has to work. Each in one way or another also points toward an ultimately unitive view of religious truth, a unity that transcends the borders of particularisms. They are all engaged in a search for Jewish expression of transcendent one-ness, such as might "broaden the bounds of the holy" to overcome even such seemingly intimate distinctions as those between the holy and the profane or between the divine, the natural or worldly, and the human realms.

This group of thinkers also has some other key elements in common. All are awed by the constantly renewing presence of God within the nat-ural world; they may in this sense be said to share a "Creation-centered" theological perspective. Their perspective is deeply immanentist: God is to be known by seeing existence through its "innermost point," by attaining an inward vision, or by addressing the questions of "depth theology." A certain crucial veil needs to be lifted in order to enable the mind to achieve a more profound (and essentially intuitive) view of reality. Their religion is in this sense universalistic, relating in the first instance to a divine reality that is not limited to the particular Jewish setting. Within the group there is an evolution to be traced on this question, from the *Sefat Emet,* still liv-ing within the Hasidic/mythical universe that sees only the Jewish soul as potentially aware of divinity, to the much greater universalism of a Heschel, who had full respect for the spiritual legitimacy of non-Jewish re-ligious life.

These East European spiritual teachers are all thoroughly comfortable with their Judaism, a garment that is completely natural to them. None of them is primarily a "defender" of the tradition, nor are any of them inter-ested in proving their own orthodoxy to others. They all see halacha as a natural part of the way Jews live, but they do not turn primarily to halachic texts as their source of spiritual nurturance. In this way they are to be dis-tinguished from another group of East European religious figures, the pan-halachists of the Lithuanian school, who proclaim halacha itself to be the only authentic expression of Judaism.

This group of Jewish mystical or experientialist theologians is also to be distinguished in the broadest terms from the German-Jewish theological developments of the nineteenth and twentieth centuries. The East Euro-peans published chiefly in Hebrew, secondarily in Yiddish, until Heschel brought their insights to America in expanded English translation. The

German-Jewish theological enterprise was conducted entirely in the German language. The difference, perhaps seemingly a superficial one, is related to two very major divergences:

1. The East Europeans wrote for people who knew Judaism deeply from within. There was no need here to explain basic Jewish terms, beliefs, attitudes. Even kabbalistic ideas, presented in a new way by Kook or Zeitlin, would fall on well-attuned ears. The German Jewish enterprise was a highly self-conscious one, always seeking to discover and describe the "essence" or "true spirit" of Judaism and explain it to an audience of non-Jewish as well as uninformed Jewish readers.
2. To do so convincingly (and there is much of apologetics in the air of German-Jewish thought), Judaism must be described and defended in terms set by the canon of German philosophical thought in the period, primarily Immanuel Kant and G. F. W. Hegel. Even Martin Buber and Franz Rosenzweig, who were in open existential rebellion against the overdomination of systematic philosophy, had their agendas largely set by the needs of that rebellion, by being overtly against Kant, as personified by Hermann Cohen, or Hegel, the subject of young Rosenzweig's doctoral dissertation and the address of the first portion of his *Star of Redemption*. The East Europeans, by contrast, were steeped deeply in the premodern Jewish religious sources and their classical idiom. When they did turn to such modern thinkers as Nietzsche or Bergson, they did so out of a sensed affinity between these writers and their own Jewish sources.

I begin my remarks with this excursus on spiritual lineage partly because I want to make it clear that I see theology as a significant undertaking only in a devotionalist context, that is, a context where prayer (in the broadest sense), a cultivation of interiority, and awareness of divine presence in all of life are given primacy. As this may be considered a somewhat odd or offbeat position among contemporary Jews, I begin by emphasizing its historic roots. In a broader sense, the views I articulate may be called neo-Hasidic. I believe that postmodern Jews' recovery of the kabbalistic-Hasidic tradition is a decisive event in our ongoing spiritual history, one that should have a great impact upon the future of Jewish theology.

Bearing this legacy in mind, I shall attempt that which the tradition in its wisdom so thoroughly avoids: a definition of Jewish theology and its task.

Each Jewish theology is a religious attempt to help the Jewish people under-
stand the meaning of Jewish life and Jewish existence out of the store of texts,
symbols, and historical experiences that are the shared inheritance of all Jews.

This definition seeks to emphasize several key points. It begins by understanding theology as a "religious" undertaking. This point is far from
obvious, especially in a world where theology too often dresses itself in academic garb and seeks a borrowed legitimacy from philosophy or social science. By "religious" in this context, I mean to say that theology emerges
from living participation in the life of the faith community. It seeks to give
expression in the language of that community to the essentially ineffable
experience of divinity and to articulate a series of beliefs around the relationships of God, world, and person. (In the case of Judaism, there is added
to this universal triad a second specifically Jewish three: God, Torah, and
the Jewish people.)

In order to do this, theology must have recourse to language. Herein lies
the first of many tensions that characterize the theological enterprise: the
mystic knows God mostly in silence. Surely the deep well of inner awareness in which the divine is to be found reaches far beyond the grasp of
words or concepts. Both personal experience and kabbalistic tradition
confirm this. Knowing full well the inadequacy of words and the mental
constructs they embody, the theologian has no choice but to become articulate. In this we are heirs to both the prophet and the mystical teacher who
rail against their inability to refrain from speaking. We continue to rail, and
continue to speak.

Our speaking is saved from *utter* inadequacy by our tradition of sacred
speech. God speaks the world into being, according to our Torah, an act
that is repeated each day, or perhaps even each moment, in the ongoing renewal of creation. We know that such divine speech is not in our human
language, nor is the cosmic speech-act anything quite like our own. Nevertheless, the claim that the God we worship is a God of words is of value as
we seek to use language to speak about the sacred. Our prayer book intro-
duces each day's verbal worship by blessing God, "who spoke and the
world came to be." Prayer is the bridge between the abstract notion of divine speech and the use of human words to speak of God. Let us say it in
the language of grammar: the divine first-person use of speech, God's own
"I am," is usually inaccessible to us except in rare moments. Our third-per-
son voice in theologizing—"God is"—rings hollow and inadequate. These
are brought closer by our willingness to use speech in the second person—

the saying of "You" in prayer, our response to the divine "you" we feel addressed to us—which redeems speech for us and brings the divine into the world of language.

This clearly means that theology is dependent upon prayer. Prayer is a primary religious activity, a moment of opening the heart either to be filled with God's presence or to cry out at divine absence. Theology comes later, the mind's attempt to articulate and understand something that the heart already knows. In defining theology as a "religious" activity, I mean to say that it grows out of a rich and textured life of prayer. The theologian's prayer life, which may be as filled with questioning, doubt, and challenge as it is with submission and praise, is the essential nurturer of religious thinking.

In Jewish terms, theologizing is part of the mitzvah of knowing God, listed by Maimonides as first among the commandments. Knowledge of God is the basis of both worship and ethics, according to many of the Jewish sages. The term *da'at* or knowledge, bears within it a particularly rich legacy of meaning. It is best translated "awareness," the intimate and consciousness-transforming knowledge that all of being, including the human soul, is infused with the presence of the One. This *da'at*, sometimes compared in the sources to the knowledge with which Adam "knew" his wife Eve, is far more than credence to a set of intellectual propositions. It is a knowing whose roots extend back in the Tree of Life, not just to the Tree of Knowledge. We know God out of a thirst that fills our whole being. Religious knowledge, not at all the same as "information about religion," never comes in response to mere intellectual curiosity.

But the language the Jewish theologian speaks is not one of words alone. The traditions of Israel are filled with speech-acts of a transverbal sort. These are epitomized by the sounding of the shofar, described by some sources as a wordless cry that reaches to those places (in the heavens? within the self? in the Self?) where words cannot penetrate. The same may be said of all the sacred and mysterious silent acts of worship: the binding of tefillin, the waving of the *lulav*, the eating of matzoth. All of these belong to the silent heart of the Jewish theological vocabulary. Each mitzvah, say the kabbalists, is a half-hidden way of pronouncing God's name. All this is part, indeed the very heart, of *language*.

In defining Jewish theology as an "attempt to help the Jewish people," I mean to say that the theologian has an active and committed relationship to the community. A Jewish theologian is a theologian who works with the Jewish people, not just with the symbolic vocabulary of the Jewish tradition. There is no Judaism without Jews, and that is no mere tautology. To be a Jewish theologian, especially in an age when the very future of our existence is threatened, is to accept the value of Jewish continuity and to direct one's efforts toward the building of a Jewish future. This does not mean that theology is to become the handmaiden of survivalism or that particular theological ideas are to be judged on their value for Jewish survival. The prophets hardly limited themselves in this way, nor should we. But it does mean that the theologian speaks out of the midst of a living community and addresses himself or herself in the primary sense to that community of Jews. If there are other masters to be served, as there always are (I think of such masters as pluralism, consistency, scholarly objectivity, political integrity, and so forth), let us remember that the Jewish people and its needs should come near the head of the line.

Here again I must refer to the particular tradition out of which I speak. In this tradition, Jewish theology has passed only in the last two generations from the hands of rebbes to those of their less-defined modern successors. The legacy of the Hasidic master is not yet forgotten here. He may be characterized as a latter-day descendent of the Platonic philosopher-king. Drawn by his own inclination to dwell exclusively in the upper realms of mystical devotion, he is forced by communal responsibilities to dwell "below," amid his people, and concern himself with their welfare. Cleaving fast to both realms at once, he thus becomes a pole or channel between heaven and earth. While the contemporary theologian should stay far from the pretense and pomposity that often result from such exaggerated claims of self-importance, he or she would do well to imitate the grave sense of communal as well as spiritual responsibility, and the link between these two, that went with the mantle of those who "said Torah." We too are saying Torah; in a certain sense, we bring Torah into being.

Jewish theology seeks to understand "the meaning of human life and Jewish existence." The questions faced by theology are universal. It exists in order to address itself to the essential human quest for meaning; while nurtured from the wellsprings of tradition, it grows most vigorously in the soil of personal religious quest. It wants to address issues of life and death, our origins in Creation, and the purpose of existence itself. Its answers will come in Jewish language, to be sure, and hopefully in rich and undiluted Jewish language. But it takes its place as a part of the human theological enterprise and is healthily nourished today as in all ages by contact with the best in philosophical, religious, and scientific thinking throughout the world. The American Jewish theologian who understood *this* best was

Mordecai M. Kaplan. He developed a theology in response to the finest Western social thought of his day, much as his German-Jewish counterparts did in response to idealist philosophy. A Jewish theology for today must stand in dialogue—mutual and unapologetic dialogue—with the best of theological understanding of religion, science, and the humanities in our own contemporary world.

Alongside its universal concerns, Jewish theology will also have to turn itself to the particular, seeking out the meaning of distinctive Jewish existence and the special contribution that the Jewish people has to offer. We have just lived through the most terrible age of martyrdom in Jewish history, and ours is a time when being a Jew can still mean the potential sacrificing of one's children's lives so that our people may live. At the same time, our community suffers terrible losses due to assimilation and indifference. In the face of this reality, the would-be theologian in our midst must offer us some reason why the continuation of our existence is religiously vital, even at such a terrible price. To do anything less would betray the trust we as a community place in the theologian. The Jewish theologian should have something to say to the large number of Jews, including many of our deepest seekers and most sensitive religious souls, who have turned away from Judaism and sought their spiritual nourishment elsewhere. To these Jews we should not offer condemnation—their souls are truly "babes captive among the heathen," to use a halachic phrase. Nor should we seek to "convince" them by vain arguments that Judaism is "better" or "more true" than other religions. Rather we should open to them an experiential path to return home. The Jewish theologian as one who articulates religious experience should not forget this audience.

"Texts, symbols, and historical experiences" are the quarry out of which a contemporary Jewish theology is hewn. We are a tradition and a community shaped by and devoted to a text. In the primary sense, "text" refers here to the written Torah, read and completed each year by Jews in an ever-renewing cycle of commitment. Whatever the origins of that text, the Jewish religious community has accepted it as holy. It may no longer stand as the authoritative word of a commanding God, but it remains the most essential sanctum of the Jewish people, a source of guidance, wisdom, and ancient truth. Our relationship to it may at times include protest and rebellion along with love and devotion. But it remains our Torah, and we remain its Jews. We can no more reject it and spiritually remain Jews than the fish can reject water, to use a classic image, or than the mature adult can reject his or her own legacy of memory, one that inevitably includes both joy and pain.

Many of our most important sources are written in the form of commentaries to this text. These the theologian must study, seeking to add his or her contemporary voice to this tradition. Here the Aggadic strand is particularly important. Jewish theology in its most native form is narrative theology. It tells our story. The theologian was originally one who "told the tale"—that of Creation, of Exodus, of Abraham and Isaac, or of Ruth and Naomi—and subtly put it into a distinctive theological framework. This method is ours to study and continue, as is amply demonstrated by the widespread renewal of midrashic writing in recent decades, a great sign of health within Jewish theological creativity. The contemporary Jewish theologian could do no better than to retell the tale or tell some new tales in his or her own way. Much of the best of Jewish theology in the twentieth century has been written by poets and novelists. I think of Paul Célan, Uri Zvi Greenberg, and Jacob Glatstein; of S. Y. Agnon, Franz Kafka, I. B. Singer, and Elie Wiesel; these offer significant humbling to those of us who call ourselves theologians.

Works of ancient Aggadah were reshaped by the kabbalists within their own systematic framework to create a profound sort of mystic speech. Study of this Aggadic-kabbalistic tradition and the search for ways to adapt it to contemporary usage is a key task of Jewish theology. The old Aggadic-homiletic tradition is reopened once again within Hasidism. Study of the creative use made of traditional sources by the Hasidic masters will serve as another important paradigm for contemporary efforts. The vast literature of Hebrew theological and moral treatises, a genre almost completely neglected other than by historical research, should also be important to the theologian. These too should be part of "text" in its broadest sense, as should be the artistic and musical creations of many generations and varied Jewish communities throughout the ages. All of them belong to what I mean by "text."

I have already mentioned symbols as forms of silent religious speech. Here I would like to digress in order to add a reflection on the power of religious symbolism as constituted in the language of the kabbalah. The kabbalists taught of the ten *sefirot*, primal manifestations of the endless One that encompasses all of being. Each of these ten is represented in kabbalistic language by one or more conventional terms and by a host of symbolic images. A certain face of the divine reality, to take one example, is conventionally called *hesed*, or grace. But in kabbalistic writings it is often referred to by such symbol terms as *morning, milk, Abraham, the right hand, the priest, love, south, lion (on the divine throne), myrtle twig*, and a host of other names. Each of these terms, when used in the kabbalists' symbolic reconstruction of the Hebrew language (for we are speaking of nothing less) has the same referent. What the kabbalist has in effect created is a series of symbolic clusters, and when any member of a cluster is invoked, all the others are brought to mind as well. I call this reconstruction, not deconstruction, of language. The clusters make for powerful new meanings of words and patterns of association. Meaning is thus greatly amplified and broadened, though within contours that remain quite clear to one who plays well at this symbolic keyboard. Kabbalah makes for an enrichment and amplification of meaning, not its breakdown.

It is particularly important that each of these clusters contains elements of both classically Jewish and *natural* symbols. The Bible saw the variety and splendor of creation as the great testament to God's handiwork. But nature was to a degree desacralized in later Judaism, which viewed study, religious practice, and reflection on Jewish sacred history as the chief areas where one should seek contact with God. The kabbalist greatly reinvigorates Jewish language by this symbolic resacralization of the natural world. Rivers, seas, seasons, trees, and heavenly bodies are all participants in the richly textured description or "mapping" of divinity, which is the kabbalist's chief task.

Jewish theology needs to find a way to repeat this process, to "redeem" the natural for our theology and to bring the religious appreciation of the natural world into central focus as an object of Jewish concern. We need to do this first and foremost for our own souls. We need to lead our religious parlance out of the ghetto that allows for the sacrality only of what is narrowly ours and allow ourselves to see again, to "lift up our eyes to the hills," to "raise our eyes to heaven and see who created these," opening ourselves anew to the profound sacred presence that fills all of being. We also need to do this as members of the human religious community, all of which is charged in our day with creating a religious language that will reroot us in our natural surroundings and hopefully lead to a deeper and richer appreciation—and therefore to less abuse and neglect—of our natural earthly heritage. In this area Jewish theology is lagging far behind the Jews, many of whom take leading roles in the movement for preservation of the planet but with little sense that Judaism has anything to offer to these efforts.

The Judaism of Kook, Zeitlin, and Heschel is one that had begun to undertake this task. All of them saw this world in its variety and splendor as nothing less than the multicolored garb of divine presence. For fifty years Judaism has, however, turned in other directions. Shaken to our root by the experience of the Holocaust, our religious language took the predictable route of self-preservation by turning inward, setting aside this universalist agenda as nonessential to our own survival. We needed in those postwar years to concentrate fully on our own condition, first in outcry and later in the rebuilding of our strength, especially through the creation of Israel and its cultural and religious life. Now that time has begun to work its inevitable healing on both mind and body, we find ourselves somewhat shocked and frightened by the rapid pace of this turn inward and the narrowing effect it has had on Jewish thought. In the face of these, we find ourselves turning back to the interrupted work of our nascent Jewish universalists and theologians of radical immanence, knowing that we need to resume their task.

The impact of these history-making decades is not lost, however. In adding "historical experiences" to the texts and symbols that comprise the sources of our Jewish learning, I mean to say that there has been a profound change wrought on the Jewish psyche by the events of this century. We are no longer able to ignore the lessons of our own historical situation, as Jews sought to do for so many years. Emancipation, Zionism, and persecution have all joined forces to drive us from that ahistorical plateau where the Jewish people once thought they dwelt in splendid isolation. We need a theology that knows how to learn from history, from our role among the nations, from our experiences both as victim and as conqueror. Without the ability to handle these real-life situations with moral integrity and strength, our Judaism of texts and symbols will become mere cant.

Finally, we need to insist in our definition that all these are "the shared inheritance of all Jews." Nothing in our tradition belongs to an exclusive group within the Jewish people. This includes groups defined by religious viewpoint; by national origin, by gender, and by all the rest. The legacy of Hasidism is too important to be left to the Hasidim alone; Sephardic ballads and Yemenite dance no longer belong to the descendants of those groups alone. Words like *halacha* or *yeshiva* should not be left to the Orthodox; they are the inheritance of all Israel. So are observances like dwelling in the sukkah, bathing in the *mikveh,* and dancing with the Torah. None of the legacy belongs exclusively to men, and none of it exclusively to women.

All of this should be sufficiently obvious not to need stating here, but that is unfortunately not the case. The theologian should be committed to the entirety of the Jewish people, more than to any subgroup or denomination within it. This will mean an ongoing devotion to the endless task of educating Jews—all kinds of Jews—and bringing them home to their roots in the people Israel. It is both a mitzvah and a privilege to participate in this task. For having a key role in it, the theologian should be grateful.

Identity Politics

Rabbi Laura Geller and Dr. Freda Furman, Los Angeles, 1980. Courtesy of Bill Aron.

Jewish Feminism Faces the American Women's Movement: Convergence and Divergence

Paula E. Hyman

The Jewish feminist movement has transformed the public space of American Jewry. Distinct from American feminism, the "Jewish feminist movement" does not consist of the totality of women of Jewish origin who are active in American feminism. Nor does it have a single address. Rather, it is a loose construct of Jewish women who have brought feminist insights and critiques into the Jewish community and into the field of Jewish studies in the American university. All have been influenced by the American women's movement, but all have dissented from some of its manifestations. It is the complex relation between specifically Jewish feminism and the American women's movement that this essay explores.

The impact of Jewish feminism is readily apparent in any investigation of American Jewish life. Formerly relegated to the home, to synagogue sisterhoods, and to their own philanthropic organizations, since 1970 women have emerged as spiritual leaders in the synagogue and as lay leaders and professionals in the organized Jewish community. The first woman rabbi was ordained in 1972; in about three decades there were hundreds of rabbis, graduates of Reform, Reconstructionist, and Conservative rabbinical schools, serving American Jewry. About 180 women cantors also serve in the American Jewish community.[1] Courses on the history of Jewish women and on women and Judaism have appeared on many American campuses, and gender has been tentatively incorporated as a category of analysis in Jewish studies courses. Although there were no women among the twenty-

This essay was originally presented on March 17, 1997, at the Jean and Samuel Frankel Center for Judaic Studies, University of Michigan, Ann Arbor.

five professors who established the Association for Jewish Studies in the late 1960s, women now constitute about 35 percent of its members and sponsor an active Women's Caucus. Even the conservative critic of many aspects of feminist ideology, Jack Wertheimer, in his thoughtful survey of the state of Judaism in America in the last half of the twentieth century, has noted feminism's considerable impact on the American Jewish community and the source of creativity it has been.[2]

Like Zionism, Jewish feminism emerged from an encounter of Jews who were deeply concerned with the fate of their group culture with secular Western culture.[3] The Zionist movement did not spring in an unmediated way from Jewish tradition; indeed, it initially inspired hostility from the leaders of Orthodox Jewry in both Western and Eastern Europe. It took secularized Jews, influenced by the rise of modern nationalism in the latter part of the nineteenth century, to found a Jewish nationalist movement that gave a radically modern form to traditional Jewish longings. Jewish feminism, too, did not spring in an unmediated way from Jewish tradition; indeed, it initially inspired, and continues to elicit, hostility from the leaders of Orthodox Jewry. It took secularized Jews, influenced by the rise of feminism in America in the 1960s, to establish a Jewish feminist movement that provided a radically modern form to strivings for gender equality. Here the parallel between Zionism and Jewish feminism founders because the strivings for gender equality did not find direct expression in the male-produced classical Jewish texts as the yearning for restoration in Zion had. Still, Jewish feminists asserted, from their first public efforts in the early 1970s, that the demands of feminism were fully consonant with Jewish experience in the modern era, with Jewish self-understanding, and with traditional Jewish concern for the status of women. The conditions of the late twentieth century had simply provided a new concept, that of gender equality, that undermined the misogyny and "separate but equal" approach that characterized many rabbinic attitudes toward women, attitudes shaped by the social and ideological contexts of premodern times.

A Jewish feminist movement is inconceivable without the emergence of a robust American women's movement by the end of the 1960s. The second wave of twentieth-century American feminism, often dated from the publication in 1963 of Betty Friedan's *The Feminist Mystique,* had been institutionalized with the establishment of the National Organization for Women. American feminism provided the ideological framework and the social format for Jewish feminism.[4] Young Jewish women were found in large numbers in places quickly penetrated by feminist ideas: the American university and the civil rights and anti-Vietnam movements of the 1960s.[5] Because of their middle-class incomes, small family size, and cultural valorization of education in the years following World War II, 1970 Jewish families provided their daughters with higher education to a much greater percentage than other white Americans. In 1970 more than half of American Jewish women of college age were enrolled in college.[6]

Many young Jewish women were introduced to feminist ideas on the campus, not in their college courses but in consciousness-raising groups that mushroomed in the first few years of the 1970s. These groups provided opportunities for women to share their experiences growing up female in the 1950s and 1960s and to read feminist literature ranging from Simone de Beauvoir's classic *The Second Sex* to the radical new literature produced by young Americans, such as Kate Millett's *Sexual Politics*, Shulamith Firestone's *The Dialectic of Sex*, and Robin Morgan's collection entitled *Sisterhood Is Powerful*.[7] All three were available by 1970. As the historian Hester Eisenstein has pointed out, in its early years American feminism focused on "the socially constructed differences between the sexes" as the "chief source of female oppression. In the main, feminist theory concentrated on establishing the distinction between sex and gender, and developed an analysis of sex roles as a mode of social control."[8] Liberation, then, necessitated severing the connection between gender and social function, the opening up of societal roles to all, irrespective of gender.

Despite the fact that Shulamith Firestone and Robin Morgan, as well as Betty Friedan, were of Jewish origin, none dealt specifically with Judaism or with the Jewish community. Betty Friedan asserted her Jewishness only a decade or so after the publication of her book, and in response to the United Nations' welcome of Yasir Arafat and her perception of the reemergence of anti-Semitism—a subject I will address further.[9]

This avoidance of Judaism was characteristic of American ideological and political culture of the time. Within feminism this reticence was reinforced by the presumption that gender trumped all other aspects of identity. American feminism proclaimed that all women were united, despite their differences of class, race, and ethnicity, because their gender invariably led to a subordinate status. Although many working-class and black women quickly dissented from a feminist agenda that overlooked their multiple allegiances and their solidarity with men of their own groups, Jewish women within the American feminist movement tended initially not to assert a Jewish dimension to their feminism or to bring the issue of gender equality to the Jewish community.

A specifically Jewish feminism emerged in America only when young women who had received a substantial Jewish education and participated actively in Jewish religious and cultural life concluded that they could not limit their feminist analysis to general American social conditions and institutions alone. Once they experienced the feminist "click," the realization that female inferiority was a cultural construct, that things did not have to be the way they were, Jewish women became acutely aware of the inequities women suffered in Jewish law, in the synagogue, and in Jewish communal institutions.[10] By 1974 articles analyzing the patriarchal nature of Judaism had appeared, a group called Ezrat Nashim had issued a call to the Conservative movement to count women in the minyan and to ordain women as rabbis, and the Jewish Feminist Organization had formed as a result of two successful conferences in New York City, held in 1973 and 1974 and attended by hundreds of women (and some men as well).[11] The conferences aimed to bring together secular and religious Jewish feminists to explore Jewish women's identities and needs. Speakers included Congresswoman Bella Abzug and Orthodox feminist Blu Greenberg. As was the case with the American women's movement, Jewish feminists focused on prescribed sex roles as a mode of social control—specifically the ways in which women had been excluded from education and positions of power because of their gender. They dedicated themselves to achieving equal access of women to the realms from which they had been excluded.

The Jewish Feminist Organization, which was formally founded in April 1974, articulated the double goal that became characteristic of Jewish feminism: to achieve "the full, direct, and equal participation of women at all levels of Jewish life—communal, educational, and political" and "to be the voice of the Jewish feminist movement in the national and international movement."[12] From its early days, then, Jewish feminists presumed that they had particular issues to advance in the women's movement.

There were many Jews who participated in the American women's movement but relatively few who identified in the early 1970s with specifically Jewish feminist groups. Many feminists, Christians as well as Jews, had determined that their patriarchal religions were simply a source of oppression and hence irrelevant to their lives. Those who sought a vehicle for their own spirituality often turned to Eastern religions, such as Buddhism, or to the goddess-worshiping Wiccan tradition.[13] Or they determined to take the theologian Mary Daly's advice and create new religious traditions based on their own experiences as women. In 1973, in her widely read book *Beyond God the Father: Toward a Philosophy of Women's Liberation*, Daly, who had been raised as a Catholic and taught at a Catholic college, formulated a rationale for a woman-centered spirituality that would undermine the hierarchic thinking characteristic of patriarchy, thereby providing the basis for human liberation. She called on women to refuse to be co-opted by institutions, like the church (and by implication the synagogue), "whose sexism is direct and explicit (e.g., written into rules and by-laws) but whose ideologies, policies, and goals are not defined exclusively or primarily by sexism." (For her, the Catholic Church oscillated between this level-two category and the level-one category of antiwoman institution "whose ideologies, policies, and goals not only are directly and explicitly sexist but even are exclusively and primarily defined by sexism.") Instead, she suggested that women could resist co-optation by recognizing "that our own liberation, seen in its fullest implications, is primary in importance." Liberation would include the formation of exodus communities of women, founded on a covenant of sisterhood, that leave behind "the false self and sexist society." Women had the option, in Daly's words, to give "priority to what we find valid in our own experience without needing to look to the past for justification."[14]

Jewish feminists as I've defined them could not follow Mary Daly. They felt that their Jewishness was a fundamental aspect of their identity that transcended traditional Judaism's assumptions about women and specific constraints on women's access to religious education and to agency within Jewish law. They could not define themselves solely through their feminist ideology and affiliations. As Judith Plaskow wrote in *Standing Again at Sinai*, the first systematic feminist Jewish theology, "the move toward embracing a whole Jewish/feminist identity did not grow out of my conviction that Judaism is 'redeemable,' but out of my sense that sundering Judaism and feminism would mean sundering my being."[15] As Plaskow's statement indicates, Jewish feminists could not turn their back on the Jewish past, finding validity in their own experience alone, when the impress of the Jewish past on their very identity was so strong.

There were American feminists with whom Jewish feminists felt a special kinship. In battling sexism within their tradition and in exploring feminist interpretations of classical texts, Jewish feminists shared many of the perspectives of Christian feminists. They were aware of Protestant denominations that had ordained women as ministers and were intrigued by Christian feminist exegesis of the Adam and Eve story. Reflective of this sympathy was the reprinting of Phyllis Trible's essay "Depatriarchalizing in Biblical Interpretation" in the first Jewish feminist collection of essays, *The Jewish Woman: New Perspectives*, published in 1976.[16]

But, as Plaskow indicated, their Jewish identity was rooted in Jewish historical experience and culture as much as in belief. Just as black feminists felt that their experience and culture as members of a racial minority could not be subordinated to their gender without denying their essential being, so Jewish feminists (though clearly not all feminists of Jewish origin) felt they could not deny the centrality of Jewishness in their identity. This connection to Jewish history and culture, however vague its content, was not limited to Jewish women who were religiously affiliated. As the editors of *Lilith,* the new Jewish feminist journal that defined its constituency as secular as well as religious feminists, wrote in their premiere edition in 1976, "As women, we are attracted to much of the ideology of the general women's movement; as Jews, we recognize that we have particular concerns not always shared by other groups."[17]

Aside from refusing to walk away from Judaism because it was a patriarchal culture, Jewish feminists also combated aspects of the American women's movement that they viewed as reflective of a tendency of some on the political left to delegitimate Jewish particularity and even to indulge in anti-Semitism. Jewish feminists sought recognition of their particularity within the American women's movement not only because they had specific issues to address but also because they were unwilling to suppress an important component of who they were in the name of feminism. In assuming that their experience and culture were normative, middle-class, white Christian women denied voices to those whose experience and culture differed from theirs, and particularly to those who had loyalties to a group that transcended their gender. Black women had written of this problem with eloquence. In 1980 the poet and activist Audre Lorde proclaimed in a speech at Amherst College, "Refusing to recognize difference makes it impossible to see the different problems and pitfalls facing us as women."[18] Yet, black as well as white feminists did not recognize Jewishness as a legitimate source of identity and seemed oblivious to its erasure.

By 1980 Jewish feminists identified trends within the American women's movement that in the best light revealed anti-Jewish biases and at worst were themselves expressions of anti-Semitism. In the pages of *Lilith* Judith Plaskow and Annette Daum, coordinator of the Reform movement's Department of Interreligious Affairs, attacked the tendency of Christian feminists to blame Judaism for the birth and survival of patriarchy, the cultural system that oppressed women. The traditional Christian claim of Judaism as inferior to Christianity and as the source of evil in the world was now clad in new feminist garb.

Plaskow pointed to the creation of a "new myth" in Christian feminist circles—that before the ancient Hebrews came onto the historical scene, "the goddess reigned in matriarchal glory, and that after them Jesus tried to restore egalitarianism but was foiled by the persistence of Jewish attitudes within the Christian tradition."[19] One Catholic theologian, Leonard Swidler, published an article in 1971 with the title "Jesus Was a Feminist" and proclaimed in a later book that "feminism [was] . . . a constitutive part of the gospel, the good news of Jesus," while the rabbis were the central disseminators of misogyny within Western religious traditions.[20] As Plaskow pointed out, Christian feminists read the Jewish tradition selectively, highlighting only the negative passages about women. Most importantly, she noted, "Feminist research projects onto Judaism the failure of the Christian tradition unambiguously to renounce sexism. It projects onto Judaism the 'backsliding' of a tradition which was to develop sexism in a new and virulent direction. It thus allows the Christian feminist to avoid confronting the failures of her/his own tradition."[21] Similarly, Annette Daum saw the feminist attack on Judaism, by both Christians and pagan worshipers of the goddess, as a feminist reformulation of the traditional charge against the Jews of deicide in the crucifixion of Jesus.[22] Susannah Heschel, like Plaskow, a scholar of religion, has continued to press the issue, asserting that Christian feminists have created a new theodicy "that blames the Jews for the suffering of women and the existence of violence." The Jews thus replace women in bringing about the Fall.[23] Heschel challenges Christian feminists to refrain from distorting Judaism in their attempts to deal with the problems of misogyny in their own tradition, problems that are, she notes, "ultimately . . . so similar to our own. Their problems will not be resolved through a manipulative ideology that projects Christian problems (or human problems) onto Jews."[24] By addressing the position of Jews and Judaism in feminist theology and in feminist reflections on patriarchy, Jewish feminists have focused attention on the (perhaps) unconscious continuation of anti-Jewish stereotypes that have a long history in Christian and secular Western thought. Because Jewish feminists are raising these issues from within feminist ranks, they have access to an audience that is unlikely to read rabbis' sermons or Anti-Defamation League press releases.

Jewish feminists also pointed out that much of the general American women's movement displayed discomfort with the issues of Jewish identity and anti-Semitism. Here Jewish lesbian feminists took the lead in expressing their dismay at the denial of difference that they found in the American women's movement. Although the women's movement seemed ready to respond to charges of racial and class bias, there was little discussion of the dismissal of Jewishness as a legitimate category of difference and of anti-Semitism as a form of oppression. Alienated from Jewish religious tradition because of its sexism and homophobia, Jewish lesbian feminists, in the words of activist Melanie Kaye/Kantrowitz, were "pulled back to the theme of danger as the shared Jewish identity."[25] They were also sensitive to issues of difference because of their sexual orientation; within the lesbian feminist movement they expected to find respect for the full complexity of their identities. Yet they felt triply marginalized: as feminists within the Jewish community, as lesbians within the Jewish feminist movement, and as Jews within the lesbian community. The poet and lesbian activist Irena Klepfisz first articulated her sense of unease with the silence surrounding the subject of anti-Semitism in a letter she sent in 1981 to *Womanews,* a New York City feminist paper, a letter that resulted in an entire issue devoted to the topic. Klepfisz's contribution to that issue described the feelings of many Jewish feminists. Although few shared her sense that anti-Semitism was a serious phenomenon in American society, they did recognize with pain her encounter in the lesbian feminist community of "an antisemitism either of omission or one which trivializes the Jewish experience and Jewish oppression."[26] Similarly, in an article published in 1985 in a general book of feminist thought, Judith Plaskow brought to American feminists an analysis of anti-Semitism as "the unacknowledged racism" of the women's movement. Jewish feminists, she recounted, heard anti-Semitic jokes and references to anti-Semitic stereotypes such as the "JAP" at women's meetings and yet were accused of paranoia when they complained of anti-Semitism.[27] By raising these issues Jewish activists within feminist circles and Jewish feminist scholars who participate within women's studies programs have challenged the position that only persons of color have their own political goals that merit support or distinctive cultures worthy of study.

Most painful of all was the acceptance by some in the international feminist community of an anti-Zionist stance that descended into anti-Semitism. At the International Women's Conference in Mexico City and at the 1980 International Women's Conference in Copenhagen, both sponsored by the United Nations, Jewish feminists encountered not only opposition to Israeli policy but denial of Israel's right to exist. In Copenhagen a Program of Action was adopted that called for the elimination of Zionism (i.e., the State of Israel) and delegates heard such statements as, 'The only way to rid the world of Zionism is to kill all the Jews.'" Although Jewish women formed a caucus to respond to the attacks and Bella Abzug spoke with her customary power and Jewish pride, the experience for Jews who were present was one of fear and vulnerability.[28]

Letty Cottin Pogrebin, who, like Abzug, bridged the general American women's movement and Jewish feminism, publicly brought the issue of anti-Semitism to the American feminist community in 1982 in the pages of *Ms.* magazine. Her article spoke eloquently about anti-Semitism on the right and the left, about feminists' failure to see the parallels between anti-Semitism and sexism, and about black-Jewish relations. Most importantly, she identified what she called the "three i's" that Jewish women experienced as anti-Semitism: "invisibility (the omission of Jewish reality from feminist consciousness)," "insult," and "internalized oppression (Jewish self-hatred)." Perhaps her most poignant question was this: "why [could] the Movement's healing embrace encompass the black woman, the Chicana, the white ethnic woman, the disabled woman, and every other female whose struggle is complicated by an extra element of 'outness,' but the Jewish woman [was] not honored in her specificity?"[29] Pogrebin's piece drew what the magazine called "one of the largest reader responses of any article published in *Ms.*" The editors added that "the overwhelming majority of the letters expressed support of Letty Pogrebin for taking on a topic of such complexity, gratitude for an analysis that challenged their own assumption, and relief that someone had named for them a problem that had brought pain to their own lives." Nonetheless, the magazine's editors, despite Pogrebin's objection—she was then an editor at *Ms.*—decided to publish only three long letters, all critical of her position.[30] Because of the prominence of *Ms.* magazine, however, Pogrebin's article lent legitimacy to Jewish women in the American feminist movement to name their discomfort with hiding their Jewishness and to reconcile their identification as both feminists and Jews. As Pogrebin reflected a decade later, the article and its responses also "exposed some feminists' anti-Semitic feelings and inspired movement activists to analyze this behavior constructively in workshops and conferences."[31]

Pogrebin was also a founder of a group called Feminists Against Antisemitism, which included, among others, the writers E. M. Broner and Aviva Cantor, the psychologist Phyllis Chesler, Judith Plaskow, Susan Weidman Schneider, editor of *Lilith*, and me. The group organized a panel, entitled "Antisemitism: The Unacknowledged Racism," at the 1981 meeting of the National Women's Studies Association. About three hundred women attended the session. The panel's five participants—Andrea Dworkin,

Broner, Chesler, Plaskow, and I—discussed contemporary manifestations of anti-Semitism in anti-Zionism and the links between anti-Semitism and antifeminism.[32] A plenary session on racism and anti-Semitism, held at the 1983 conference and organized by lesbian activist and scholar Evelyn Torton Beck, drew an audience of some fifteen hundred persons and resulted in the formation of a Task Force on Jewish Issues that established a Jewish Women's Caucus within the association the following year. The Caucus asserted that "Jews were a cultural/religious minority within American society," a minority that was still "mocked, despised, feared and scapegoated." It called for integrating the experience of Jewish women "as Jews" in feminist organizations. Already at the 1983 Women's Studies Association conference there were six additional sessions on Jewish women's history and literature.[33] The experience of anti-Semitism—an issue of what we might now label identity politics—thus brought together Jewish feminists who worked primarily in the Jewish community and Jewish feminists who worked primarily in the American feminist movement. Members of this alliance called attention to, and delegitimated, anti-Semitism within the women's movement, and explained how it could be cloaked in the guise of anti-Zionism. In doing so, Jewish feminists sensitized a portion of the American Left, where the Jewish Establishment is disdained, to take seriously the legitimacy of Jewish particularity and Jewish concern for Israel. They also spurred the American Jewish Congress to found a National Commission on Women's Equality in 1984, with Betty Friedan as one of its cochairs.

Jewish feminists rarely criticized the American women's movement except where anti-Semitism and anti-Zionism were concerned, but they often avoided themes that became prominent in general American feminism. They differed with American feminism in their attitudes to the family and with regard to essentialism, the assertion that women's biological and cultural differences should be celebrated and should become the basis of a separate women's culture. To be sure, some Jewish feminists have incorporated symbols and forms of women's spirituality from other, often pagan, religious traditions into their rituals in a form of syncretism, but they have had little impact on institutionalized Jewish religious life, with the exception of the Reconstructionist movement, which, however, has formally repudiated any reference to pagan gods.[34] As of now, these syncretistic rituals, which often focus on issues related to domestic life or with women's life-cycle events, remain an aspect of what has been called "New Age" Judaism.

American feminists were widely perceived as elevating professional accomplishment and public activity over women's traditional domestic roles. Although feminists spoke about empowering women and giving them choices, in the early years of the women's movement they seemed to portray housewives and mothers simply as drudges. Many feminists depicted the nuclear family only as a source of women's oppression, failing to acknowledge the satisfactions it also offered to women (as well as to men). They made light of the stress experienced by women who sought to combine careers and family life. As Betty Friedan asserted in her 1981 book, *The Second Stage,* because of their perceived hostility to the family, feminist ideologues were failing to reach the majority of American women, who were rooted in family life and connected their sense of self to their domestic roles. "The women's movement," she noted, was "being blamed . . . for the destruction of the family."[35]

Jewish feminists disseminated a different vision of the family. To be sure, they expressed concern about calls from communal leaders for Jewish women to have more children to compensate for the Holocaust or for the growing rate of intermarriage in America. They recognized that promoters of traditional Jewish family life often romanticized the past and blamed mothers for the perceived decline in Jewish identification among American Jews. Their concern was driven by the fact that the promotion of higher fertility in Jewish families was too often accompanied by attacks on feminism and was rarely followed by communal efforts to alleviate the high costs, particularly for large families, of raising Jewish children.[36] But Jewish feminists refrained from statements of radical individualism. They did not denigrate the family as such, for they were aware of its role as the central unit in Jewish communal life. As the writer Anne Roiphe later put it in an article offering a feminist perspective on the Jewish family, "A truly feminist position does not mock the family and a Jewish feminist position must by definition cherish the home and value the work that is done there."[37]

Jewish feminists, both male and female, did suggest, however, that Jews had embraced many family patterns throughout history, depending on socioeconomic conditions, and should expand their concept of family to respond to the actual Jewish families that comprised the American Jewish population.[38] They noted that, like American families over the course of the past two generations, Jewish families have changed. There are now far more singles, single parents, and gay couples and parents among American Jews than ever before.[39] Serving the needs of all American Jewish families, including those who depart from the stereotype, Jewish feminists have argued, strengthens the Jewish community. Not only does an inclusive, wel-

coming policy draw otherwise alienated Jews into contact with Jewish institutions, but, as Martha Ackelsberg suggests with regard to gay and lesbian Jewish families, it provides opportunities for communal discussions of
sexuality and of the ways in which nonparents can promote intergenera-
tional Jewish continuity. Feminists conclude that serving the needs of families broadly defined is also rooted in Jewish concepts of communal responsibility.[40] This relative family friendliness on the part of Jewish
feminism predated the reconsideration by mainstream American feminism
of its attitude toward family life.

The emphasis of American feminism in the 1960s and 1970s was the
identification of women's oppression and exclusion from power and the
definition of strategies to secure self-empowerment and political change.
Perhaps because most leaders of American feminism were white and middle class, their primary goal was for women to attain a fair share of the material wealth and status available to white men in American society. Jewish
feminism mirrored this goal in its early articulation of an "equal access"
platform, seeking equity for women in Jewish communal life and in the
synagogue. In the late 1970s American feminism began to highlight some
of women's differences from men as positive attributes. To cite the historian Hester Eisenstein once more, "the woman-centered perspective located specific virtues in the historical and psychological experience of
women. Instead of seeking to minimize the polarization between mascu-
line and feminine, it sought to isolate and define those aspects of female
experience that were potential sources of strength and power for women,
and more broadly, of a new blueprint for social change."[41] Just as American
feminists began to celebrate women's culture, as expressed in particular art
forms or in styles of storytelling, so Jewish feminists began in the early
1980s to articulate the need for women's interpretation of classical Jewish
texts and creation of liturgy that reflected the ways in which women
named, and experienced, God. They struggled with the tension between
the need to innovate, so that liturgy might reflect deeply felt spiritual beliefs, and the desire to remain attached to a liturgy whose authenticity was
rooted in its age and communal usage.[42] As Judith Plaskow has noted of
feminist reinterpretation of rituals and reworking of—or creating new—
liturgy, "women are seeking to transform Jewish ritual so that it acknowledges our existence and experience. In the ritual moment, women's history
is made present."[43]

This project of feminist-inspired change suggested that Jewish culture
as a whole would benefit from the infusion of women's perspectives, that

these could become a blueprint for change. And, in fact, feminists have stimulated much liturgical creativity, leading to the production of new prayer books by the Reform and Reconstructionist movements, feminist Haggadoth for use at family Passover seders or at special third feminist seders, and the publication in 1996, for example, of the poet and Hebraist Marcia Falk's innovative *The Book of Blessings*. Falk has pioneered in the creation of a Hebrew liturgy that incorporates feminist understandings of God.[44]

The validation of female culture within American feminism led some radical feminists to develop an ideology often called "essentialism," or "cultural feminism." As opposed to "liberal feminists," who see men and women as basically the same and seek therefore to rectify inequities in the treatment of women, essentialists argue that women and men are basically different. Women have a different way of speaking, of constructing reality, and of learning. Differences between men and women are not simply the product of their social conditioning, as liberal feminists would have it, but are inherent in their femaleness, in physiological distinctiveness. As opposed to adherents of Western cultural paradigms who see females as different and inferior, essentialists sees females as different and superior. To give just one example, according to essentialists, women must be free to design and administer their own schools, giving full recognition to women's nonlinear and nonrational styles of learning. Essentialists have inverted antifeminist presumptions, celebrating women's modes of being in the world as morally superior to men's.

Essentialism is virtually absent from Jewish feminism; Jewish feminists by-and-large still fall into the liberal camp. Although they believe that women may have a distinctive perspective to offer in the interpretation of Jewish texts and may display a different leadership style, they share Jewish cultural treasures with men and they seek to be partners with men in exploring the culture of the past and creating the culture of the future. They make no claim to female superiority. True, some Jewish feminists have rejected tallith and tefillin as male paraphernalia inappropriate to women and have suggested that women find more congenial garb for prayer. Some have reclaimed women's rituals linked to women's biological cycle, ranging from marking Rosh Hodesh, the beginning of the month, as a special day for women, to immersion in the *mikveh* (ritual bath) at the conclusion of their menstrual periods.[45] In both these cases Jewish feminists have reappropriated these rites as a way to link their own spiritual expressions to Jewish women of the past as well as to their own physiology. They have, however, adapted these practices to their own contemporary needs. They have created new ceremonies, often with a learning component, to mark Rosh Hodesh, which was acknowledged in the past as a half-holiday for women on which they might refrain from some of their household tasks but was not celebrated as such. And they have eliminated the negative elements that traditionally surrounded observance of the rules of family purity.[46]

Ironically, Jewish essentialists can be found more readily among ultra-Orthodox women than among feminists.[47] As Debra Kaufman found in her study of *ba'alot teshuva,* women who became Orthodox, those who affiliated with ultra-Orthodox sects saw themselves as sharing special qualities as women, such as a capacity for nurturing and a higher degree of spirituality. In their view these natural, indeed divinely bestowed qualities, fit them for their roles as wives and mothers, responsible for their families, and justified the sex segregation and women's exemption from mitzvoth (commandments) that characterizes ultra-Orthodox life. As Kaufman notes, "both newly Orthodox Jewish women and radical feminists see women's culture as the source for transformation of values for humankind."[48] However, unlike essentialist feminists who seek women's autonomy and power, Orthodox women accept the rules determined by men in a patriarchal system.

Despite its lack of a central address, Jewish feminism remains a vibrant voice, primarily within the various denominations of American Judaism. Like much of the American Jewish community, it seems to have turned inward. Jewish feminists participate in general feminist organizations, but they do so as individuals. Jewish feminist scholarship appears in general collections of articles in history, anthropology, and literature and is published by respectable university and trade presses. Yet most Jewish feminist scholars are more concerned with having an impact on the field of Judaic than on women's studies. Ideally, of course, they seek both. The inclusion of topics on Jewish women's history and literature at women's studies conferences and the explosion of work on women and gender in the annual conference of the Association for Jewish Studies has muted Jewish feminists' sense of isolation within the scholarly world. Although general feminist theory continues to proliferate, it has become so arcane and jargon-filled that it plays little role in the lives of most American women, whether secular or religious, Christian or Jewish.

In turning inward, the Jewish community and Jewish feminism as well reflect the fragmentation of society and culture in contemporary America. Jewish feminists are less concerned with making their voices heard as Jews in the institutions of the American women's movement than they were in the past. Their experience of anti-Semitism in American and international meetings has declined. They have chosen to direct their attention to the institutions of the Jewish community to realize feminist visions of equality, not only in terms of equal access but also in terms of cultural revitalization.

Many Jewish feminist activists have declared in one way or another, "Feminism enables me to be a Jew" or "Feminism has brought me back to my Jewishness." Because Jewish feminism has been successful in its efforts to end the exclusion of women from spiritual and communal leadership and to restore the experience of women to Jewish history, it has enabled many secular feminists of Jewish birth to find a place for themselves within the community of Jews. Letty Cottin Pogrebin recounts in *Deborah, Golda, and Me* how Jewish feminism provided her with an opportunity to overcome her alienation from Judaism, an alienation that dated back to her being excluded from reciting kaddish, the memorial prayer for the dead, after her mother's death when she was fifteen.[49] Only after she encountered anti-Semitism within the women's movement did Betty Friedan begin to reflect on the Jewish component of her identity. She traveled to Israel, joined a Jewish study group in America, and became involved with the organized Jewish community through the American Jewish Congress's Commission on the Status of Women. After the writer Anne Roiphe began a serious study of Jewish history and Talmud in the aftermath of the passionate negative responses to her *New York Times* article on celebrating Christmas as a secular Jew, she realized that she could join the Jewish community only if she found a synagogue to which she could take her daughters "without subjecting them to insults."[50] By the 1980s, when she was incorporating Judaism into her family's life, thanks to Jewish feminism, many egalitarian synagogues existed. The poet Adrienne Rich also turned to Judaism through her feminism. Born into a mixed Jewish-Christian household with its Jewish roots in the South, Rich was raised to deny her Jewishness. Her marriage to a Brooklyn-born Jew, of East European origin, in a ceremony at Harvard Hillel was in part a rejection of her parents' values. They recognized it as such and refused to attend the wedding. In a long poem written in 1960, she described herself as "Split at the Root, Neither Gentile nor Jew, Yankee nor Rebel."[51] When she came to the recognition of her lesbianism, she also affirmed her identity as a Jew and turned to Jewish feminist writings as resources. She has written poems on Jewish sources and was a founding editor of the Jewish feminist journal *Bridges*.[52]

In addition to prominent feminists whose encounter with anti-Semitism in the women's movement or with Jewish feminism led to an engagement with the meaning of Jewishness in their own lives, many women whose names are not known to us also use feminist ritual to connect with Jewish tradition. For example, the feminist seder organized by Ma'ayan, the Jewish Women's Project, in New York in 1996 attracted more than nine hundred women. Although this was a feminist celebration, it placed women's experience within a Jewish structure and within a Jewish time-frame. Adult women have also organized programs of study and have celebrated adult bat mitzvahs, marking their sense of full recognition as Jews.[53]

Although Jewish feminism developed under the impact of the American women's movement and diverged from it largely because that movement did not see Jewish women's specific concerns as of interest, Jewish feminism has developed a momentum of its own. Its adherents are aware of general feminist issues that transcend ethnic and religious lines, but their feminism is informed by Jewish communal concerns. With no central organizations, Jewish feminism depends on the energy of religious professionals and laypeople to bring its issues to local institutions, both mainstream and what a generation ago would have been called countercultural. The fragmented nature of American Jewry and of American society suggests that Jewish feminism in America will continue to be diversified; the history of the movement demonstrates that a relatively small number of persons, attuned to the currents of social and cultural change, can have an influence beyond their numbers.

Notes

1. Hebrew Union College ordained 417 female rabbis between 1972 and 2004, the Reconstructionist Rabbinical College 118 from 1974 to 2004, and the Jewish Theological Seminary 138 between 1972 and 2004. The sources of the data are the Hebrew Union College website, www.huc.edu, accessed February 2004; conversations with representatives of the Rabbinical Assembly, the Rabbinical School of the Jewish Theological Seminary; Barbara Hirsh, Dean of Administrators, Reconstructionist Rabbinical College, February 19–26, 2004.

2. Jack Wertheimer, *A People Divided: Judaism in Contemporary America* (New York: Basic Books, 1993), 21–22, 72–75.

3. Arthur Hertzberg, *The Zionist Idea* (New York: Atheneum, 1970); David Vital, *The Origins of Zionism* (New York: Oxford University Press, 1975).

4. Betty Friedan, *The Feminist Mystique* (New York: Norton, 1963).

5. On the countercultural background to radical feminism, see Alice Echols, *Daring to Be Bad: Radical Feminism in America, 1967–75* (Minneapolis: University of Minnesota Press, 1989).

6. Derived from figures provided in Moshe Hartman and Harriet Hartman, *Gender Equality and American Jews* (Albany: SUNY Press, 1996), 31–43. The data for their conclusions are drawn from the 1990 National Jewish Population Survey.

7. Kate Millett, *Sexual Politics* (Garden City, NY: Doubleday, 1969); Shulamith Firestone, *The Dialectic of Sex* (New York: William Morrow, 1970); Robin Morgan, ed., *Sisterhood Is Powerful* (New York: Random House, 1970). All three appeared in paperback editions by 1971.

8. Hester Eisenstein, *Contemporary Feminist Thought* (Boston: G. K. Hall, 1983), xi.

9. "Friedan at 55," *Lilith* 1, no. 1 (1976): 11.

10. On the beginnings of Jewish feminism, see Sylvia Barack Fishman, *A Breath of Life: Feminism in the American Jewish Community* (New York: Free Press, 1993), 1–9; and Paula E. Hyman, "Ezrat Nashim and the Emergence of a New Jewish Feminism," in *The Americanization of the Jews,* ed. Robert M. Seltzer and Norman Cohen (New York: New York University Press, 1995), 284–95. For the most comprehensive study, with an emphasis on individual biographies, see Joyce Antler, *The Journey Home: Jewish Women and the American Century* (New York: Free Press, 1997), 259–308.

11. See Trude Weiss-Rosmarin, "The Unfreedom of Jewish Women," *Jewish Spectator,* October 1970, 2–6; Rachel Adler, "The Jew Who Wasn't There," *Davka,* summer 1971, 6–11; Paula E. Hyman, "The Other Half: Women in the Jewish Tradition," *Conservative Judaism* 26, no. 4 (1972): 14–21; Judith Hauptman, "Women's Liberation in the Talmudic Period: An Assessment," *Conservative Judaism* 26, no. 4 (1972): 22–28; Ezrat Nashim's "Jewish Women Call for Change," my personal archive; program of the second Jewish Feminist Organization Conference, April 1974, my personal archive.

12. The Jewish Feminist Organization, Statement of Purpose, April 28, 1974, my personal archive.

13. For example, prominent Wiccan Starhawk (Miriam Simos), author of *The Spiral Dance: A Rebirth of the Ancient Religion of the Great Goddess* (San Francisco: Harper and Row, 1979), *Dreaming the Dark: Magic, Sex, and Politics* (Boston: Beacon Press, 1982), and *Truth or Dare: Encounters with Power, Authority, and Mystery* (San Francisco: Harper and Row, 1987), was born and raised a Jew.

14. Mary Daly, *Beyond God the Father: Toward a Philosophy of Women's Liberation* (Boston: Beacon Press, 1973), 55–59, 157–58. The first three citations are from pp. 56, 55, and 59 respectively, the fourth from p. 158, and the fifth from p. 74.

15. Judith Plaskow, *Standing Again at Sinai: Judaism from a Feminist Perspective* (San Francisco: Harper and Row, 1990), xi.

16. Elizabeth Koltun, ed., *The Jewish Woman: New Perspectives* (New York: Schocken, 1976), 217–40.

17. "From the Editors," *Lilith* 1, no. 1 (1976): 3.

18. Audre Lorde, "Age, Race, Class, and Sex: Women Redefining Difference," in her *Sister Outsider* (Trumansburg, NY: Crossing Press, 1984), 118.

19. Judith Plaskow, "Blaming the Jews for the Birth of Patriarchy," *Lilith* 7, no. 1 (1980): 11–12. The citation is from p. 11. Reprinted in *Nice Jewish Girls,* ed. Evelyn Torton Beck (Watertown, MA: Persephone Press, 1982), 250–54.

20. Leonard Swidler, "Jesus Was a Feminist," *Catholic World,* January 1971, 177–83. The citation is from *Biblical Affirmations of Woman* (Philadelphia: Westminster Press,

1979), 164. Swidler's *Women in Judaism: The Status of Women in Formative Judaism* (Metuchen, NJ: Scarecrow Press, 1976) asserted the rabbinic source of the disparagement of women in Western culture.

21. Plaskow, "Blaming the Jews." The citation is from p. 12.

22. Annette Daum, "Blaming Jews for the Death of the Goddess," *Lilith* 7, no. 1 (1980): 12–13. Reprinted in Beck, *Nice Jewish Girls,* 255–61.

23. See, for example, Susannah Heschel, "Anti-Judaism in Christian Feminist Theology," *Tikkun* 5, no. 3 (1990): 25–28, 95–97. The citation is from p. 27.

24. Heschel, "Anti-Judaism," 97.

25. Melanie Kaye, "Some Notes on Jewish Lesbian Identity," in Beck, *Nice Jewish Girls,* 38.

26. Irena Klepfisz, "Anti-Semitism in the Lesbian/Feminist Movement," in Beck, *Nice Jewish Girls,* 45–51. The citation is from p. 46.

27. Judith Plaskow, "Antisemitism: The Unacknowledged Racism," in *Women's Consciousness, Women's Conscience,* ed. B. H. Andolson, C. E. Gudorf, and M. D. Pollaner (Minneapolis: Winston Press, 1985), 47–65.

28. As cited in Letty Cottin Pogrebin, "Anti-Semitism in the Women's Movement," *Ms.,* June 1982, 48–49. The quotation was reported by a non-Jewish American activist. For a discussion of this issue, see Fishman, *A Breath of Life,* 9–12.

29. Pogrebin, "Anti-Semitism in the Women's Movement," 45, 46, 48–49, 62, 65–66, 69–70, 73–74. The "three i's" are discussed on pp. 65–66, 69–70. The essay is reprinted in abbreviated form in Pogrebin's *Deborah, Golda, and Me* (New York: Crown, 1991), 205–28.

30. *Ms.,* February 1983, 12. The three long letters that the magazine published criticized anti-Semitism but dissented from Pogrebin's understanding of Zionism and of the significance of anti-Semitism.

31. Pogrebin, *Deborah, Golda, and Me,* 204.

32. Minutes, Feminists Against Antisemitism, January 22, 1981, February 22, 1981, my personal archive; Pogrebin, "Anti-Semitism in the Women's Movement," 46; Vivian Scheinmann, "Jewish Feminists Demand Equal Treatment," *New Directions for Women,* July–August 1981, 5, 16.

33. *Lilith* 11 (fall–winter 1983): 5; and Antler, *The Journey Home,* 294. The quotation of the caucus's statement is from Antler.

34. Nurit Zaidman, "Variations of Jewish Feminism: The Traditional, Modern, and Postmodern Approaches," *Modern Judaism* 16 (1996): 54. Zaidman considers Jewish feminism that has sought equality for women within the various denominations of American Judaism as "modern," while "postmodern" feminism includes self-conscious attempts to bring together eclectic symbols and rituals from a variety of traditions in order to remake Judaism. She provides an analysis of a postmodern feminist ritual, the burying of a baby boy's umbilical cord, placenta, and dried foreskin, 54–57.

35. See Betty Friedan, *The Second Stage* (New York: Summit Books, 1981). The citation is from p. 22.

36. See my "Looking for a Usable Past," *Congress Monthly,* October 1975, reprinted in *On Being a Jewish Feminist: A Reader,* ed. Susannah Heschel (New York: Schocken, 1983), 19–26.

37. Anne Roiphe, "The Jewish Family: A Feminist Perspective," *Tikkun* 1, no. 2 (1985): 71.

38. Steven M. Cohen, "The American Jewish Family Today," *American Jewish Yearbook* (1982), 136–54.

39. On the demographic changes among American Jewish families, see Cohen, "American Jewish Family Today," and Steven M. Cohen, *American Modernity and Jewish Identity* (New York: Tavistock, 1983), 113–31.

40. Martha Ackelsberg, "Redefining Families: Models for the Jewish Future," in *Twice Blessed: On Being Lesbian or Gay and Jewish,* ed. Christie Balka and Andy Rose (Boston: Beacon Press, 1989), 107–17.

41. Eisenstein, *Contemporary Feminist Thought,* xii.

42. Rita Gross, "Female God Language in a Jewish Context," in *Woman Spirit Rising: A Feminist Reader in Religion,* ed. Carol Christ and Judith Plaskow (San Francisco: Harper and Row, 1979), 167–73; Ellen Umansky, "(Re)Imaging the Divine," *Response* 41–42 (1982): 110–19, and "Creating a Jewish Feminist Theology," in *Weaving the Visions: New Patterns in Feminist Spirituality,* ed. Judith Plaskow and Carol Christ (San Francisco: Harper and Row, 1989), 187–98; Susannah Heschel, introduction to *Being a Jewish Feminist,* xii–xxxili; Judith Plaskow, "The Right Question Is Theological," in Heschel, *Being a Jewish Feminist,* 223–33; Martha Ackelsberg, "Spirituality, Community, and Politics: B'not Esh and the Feminist Reconstruction of Judaism," *Journal of Feminist Studies in Religion* 2 (1986): 109–20. The Women's Institute of Continuing Jewish Education, located in San Diego and directed by its founder, Irene Fine, has published a number of volumes of women's midrashim (interpretations), including Jane Zones, ed., *Taking the Fruit: Modern Women's Tales of the Bible* (San Diego: Woman's Institute for Continuing Jewish Education, 1981, 2d ed. 1989); Jacquelyn Tolley, ed., *On Our Spiritual Journey: A Creative Shabbat Service* (San Diego: Woman's Institute for Continuing Jewish Education, 1984); Jane Zones, ed., *San Diego Women's Haggadah,* 2d ed. (San Diego: Woman's Institute for Continuing Jewish Education, 1986); Irene Fine, *Midlife: A Rite of Passage / The Wise Woman: A Celebration* (San Diego: Women's Institute for Continuing Jewish Education, 1988); Elizabeth Levine, ed., *A Ceremonies Sampler: New Rites, Celebrations, and Observances of Jewish Women* (San Diego: Women's Institute for Continuing Jewish Education, 1991).

43. Judith Plaskow, "Standing Again at Sinai: Jewish Memory from a Feminist Perspective," *Tikkun* 1, no. 2 (1985): 33.

44. See the Reconstructionist siddur *Kol Haneshamah,* ed. David Teutsch (Wyncote, PA: Reconstructionist Press, 1993); the Reform *Gates of Prayer for Shabbat* and *Gates of Prayer for Weekdays and at a House of Mourning,* both edited by Chaim Stern (New York: Central Conference of American Rabbis, 1992); Marcia Falk, *The Book of Blessings: New Jewish Prayers for Daily Life, the Sabbath, and the New Moon Festival* (San Francisco: HarperCollins, 1996).

45. See Peninah Adelman, *Mirriam's Well: Rituals for Jewish Women around the Year* (Fresh Meadows, NY: Biblio Press, 1986).

46. Many women no longer wait seven days after the end of their menstrual periods, and unmarried women, whose sexuality belongs only to themselves, are also using the *mikveh* (ritual bath).

47. Debra R. Kaufman first noted this parallel in her book *Rachel's Daughters: Newly Orthodox Jewish Women* (New Brunswick, NJ: Rutgers University Press, 1991), 149–54.

48. Kaufman, *Rachel's Daughters*, 153.

49. Pogrebin, *Deborah, Golda, and Me*, 42, 48–52, 54–80, 236–56.

50. Anne Roiphe, *Generation without Memory: A Jewish Journey in Christian America* (New York: Simon and Schuster, 1981), 203–4.

51. Adrienne Rich, "Split at the Root," in Beck, *Nice Jewish Girls,* 67–84. The citation is from p. 67.

52. Antler, *The Journey Home*, 301.

53. Ma'ayan brochure. On adult bat mitzvah rituals, see Stuart Schoenfeld, "Integration in the Group and Sacred Uniqueness: An Analysis of Adult Bat Mitzvah," in *Persistence and Flexibility: Anthropological Perspectives on the American Jewish Experience,* ed. Walter Zenner (Albany: SUNY Press, 1989), 117–33 and his "Ritual and Role Transition: Adult Bat Mitzvah as a Successful Rite of Passage," in *The Uses of Tradition: Jewish Community in the Modern Era,* ed. Jack Wertheimer (New York: Jewish Theological Seminary, 1992), 349–76.

Giora Feidman, Temescal Canyon Beach, Pacific Palisades, 2000.
Courtesy of Bill Aron.

The Paradoxes of American Jewish Culture

Stephen J. Whitfield

A Culture of Recoil

Perhaps no fin de siècle intellectual was more rancid in his estrangement from his own country than Henry Adams, grandson and great-grandson of presidents, whose autobiography begins with a sneer. Had his surname been Cohen, "born in Jerusalem . . . and circumcised in the Synagogue by his uncle the high priest . . . , he would scarcely have been more distinctly branded, and not much more heavily handicapped in the races of the coming century, in running for such stakes as the century was to offer." Adams contrasted himself with Jews recently arrived from Warsaw or Krácow, "still reeking of the Ghetto, snarling a weird Yiddish to the officers of the customs—but [who] had a keener instinct, an intenser energy, and a freer hand than he—American of Americans, with Heaven knew how many Puritans and Patriots behind him."[1] How curious that the grandson of an actual immigrant named Cohen, born on the Fourth of July two years before these ruminations, would personify that facility of adaptation to modernity that the bitterly anti-Semitic Adams could not accomplish. Cohen's grandson, Lionel Trilling, would become the first tenured Jewish professor in the Department of English at Columbia University. While teaching the Anglo-American literary canon, he would also doubt the viability of a Jewish-American culture and make its very possibility problematic.

"My existence as a Jew is one of the shaping conditions of my temperament," Lionel Trilling conceded, "and therefore I suppose it must have its effect on my intellect. Yet I cannot discover anything in my professional in-

This essay was originally presented on April 6, 1992, at the Jean and Samuel Frankel Center for Judaic Studies, University of Michigan, Ann Arbor.

tellectual life which I can specifically trace back to my Jewish birth and rearing. I do not think of myself as a Jewish writer. I do not have it in mind to serve by my writing any Jewish purpose. I should resent it if a critic of my work were to discover in it either faults or virtues which he called Jewish." In 1944, Trilling accepted that designation primarily "as a point of honor," and admitted finding "no pride in seeing a long tradition, often great and heroic, reduced to this small status in me," especially when so many Jews were suffering so greatly for sharing that condition of ancestry. Otherwise the assistant professor of English could see only sterility and complacency, complaining that modern Judaism had not produced "a single voice with the note of authority—of philosophical, or poetic, or even of rhetorical, let alone of religious, authority." Having helped edit the *Menorah Journal*, he knew something of Jewish cultural movements firsthand and concluded that neither then nor earlier had "the Jewish community . . . give[n] sustenance to the American artist or intellectual who is born a Jew. . . . Writers . . . have used their Jewish experience as the subject of excellent work; [but] . . . no writer in English . . . has added a micromillimetre to his stature by 'realizing his Jewishness,' although . . . some . . . have curtailed their promise by trying to heighten their Jewish consciousness."[2]

Such recoil was not quite typical even of the prominent critics of Trilling's own generation. Far more affirmative, indulgent, and even sentimental responses were to arrive in succeeding decades—from Alfred Kazin, the *Walker in the City* (1951) who defiantly labeled himself a *New York Jew* (1978); from Irving Howe, the cicerone of Yiddish literature as well as the elegist of the *World of Our Fathers* (1976); from Leslie Fiedler, the explainer *To the Gentiles* (1972) and the entertaining *Fiedler on the Roof* (1991); and even from the managing editor of that issue of the *Contemporary Jewish Record* in which Trilling's just-quoted remarks appeared, Philip Rahv (whose estate went to the State of Israel in 1973). Their postwar burst of influence has seemed in retrospect a vigorous—and therefore almost inevitable—displacement of the genteel custodianship of Anglo-American letters once associated with such august figures as Harvard's Barrett Wendell, who once told a young immigrant: "Your Jewish race is less lost than we, of old America. For all [its] sufferings . . . it has never lost its identity, its tradition, its existence." "As for us," he added, "we are submerged beneath a conquest so complete that . . . I feel as I should think an Indian might feel."[3] How fitting that Wendell's correspondent, Horace M. Kallen, soon became the prophet of a "cultural pluralism" that would sanction the opportunity for Jewish life to flourish. With that heterogeneous ideal of democracy, Jewry was cleared for takeoff and would vindicate the case for diversity in the New World.

Jewish Culture on Native Grounds

The challenge that Trilling posed over half a century ago nevertheless remains a problem for those who wish to realize their Jewishness on native grounds, for those who would synthesize their American birthright with their Jewish sensibility. It has become increasingly apparent that the persistence of Jewish identity depends upon the vitality of culture. A Jewish community in the United States will not sustain itself merely upon memory, or sentiment, or vague feelings of obligation; nor will it endure if fueled by xenophobia or paranoia. It will have to cohere around shared and salient values, merging the components of tradition, adaptation, and creativity. Contemporaneity as well as history will have to be addressed. Jewish culture will need something to affirm, and not merely something to remember. "I don't want to live in the past," J. J. Gittes (Jack Nicholson) remarks in the film *The Two Jakes* (1990). "I just don't want to lose it." In a society that, in effect, makes even so cohesive a minority "Jews by choice," Gittes offers the perspective on which their subculture might pivot.

Yet it is paradoxical how glancingly the scholarly literature treats this topic. Standard anthologies ignore it (like Marshall Sklare's *Understanding American Jewry* [1982] and his *American Jews: A Reader* [1983], or like Marc Lee Raphael's *Jews and Judaism of the United States: A Documentary Reader* [1983]), or give it fairly cursory notice (like Gladys Rosen's *Jewish Life in America* [1978]). An erstwhile vehicle for the voices of the next generation, like James A. Sleeper and Alan Mintz's 1971 volume, *The New Jews*, omits the topic. Peter Rose's *The Ghetto and Beyond* (1969) should be partially exempted from this complaint, but its separate chapters on religion, literature, politics, and identity force the reader to make the necessary links and to wonder whether these facets add up to something distinctive.

The shelves bulge with studies of American Judaism that are only infrequently integrated into an analysis of the larger pattern of values to which its adherents might also have subscribed. Monographs in American Jewish literature have also forced acquisitions librarians to work overtime, and the postwar development of a body of serious fiction has become central to any understanding of the community, if not the faith, that nurtured such talent. But the connections have been so ambiguous that Philip Roth could echo Trilling's complaint two decades later: "If there are Jews who have begun to find the stories the novelists tell more provocative and pertinent than the sermons of some of the rabbis, perhaps it is because there are regions of feeling and consciousness in them which cannot be reached by the oratory of self-congratulation and self-pity."[4] The players in whatever makes up American Jewish culture have rarely seen themselves as engaged in the same enterprise, as members of the same team.

No wonder then that, in writing the history of the Jewish Publication Society, Jonathan D. Sarna discovered that "not a single book length survey of American Jewish culture existed, much less one that placed Jewish literature and scholarship within an historical context." While he found himself more impressed with that culture than other observers have been, he conceded that "the problem . . . lies not with the production of Jewish culture in America, of which there is a great deal, but rather with its distribution and consumption. Too much of what *is* produced lies unsold, unread, and unappreciated."[5] Sarna's case study is invaluable for its close scrutiny of a nonreligious institution that has shaped Jewish literacy. But the theme promised in the subtitle is subdued, and the index does not include "American Jewish culture" (nor any of its variants), perpetuating the impression that scholars have exercised their Miranda right to remain silent.

I know of only three recent essays devoted to this topic, two by the same author—Harold Bloom—who has doubted the viability of a phenomenon that "is not American, not Jewish, not culture." He is disheartened, not disdainful, because no American Jew has reached the stature of Freud, Kafka, and Scholem, writers who worked the night shift with such originality that the meaning of Jewish identity has been enlarged. With "text-centeredness" in decline among the young, Professor Bloom fears for an emergent Jewish culture: "A Jewry can survive without a Jewish language . . . but not *without language;* not without an intense, obsessive concern that far transcends what ordinarily we call literacy." This version of culture is limited, however, not only by its remorseless and forbidding elitism but also by Bloom's almost exclusively literary scope; though here at least, Robert Alter has shared his gloomy estimate of the caliber of American Jewish fiction. For Alter, it is "an expression of Jews in transition . . . , and by virtue of that problematic fact, it cannot really meet our test of authentic Jewishness or powerful high culture." Therefore "the exploration of an ambivalent identity . . . does not uncover firm enough or deep enough ground for the creation of what we would like to think of as a culture."[6] Professor Alter instead looked for promising directions in the academy—in the emergence of Jewish studies—for the outlines, however tentative, of an American Jewish culture that would not be oxymoronic.

Three thoughtful essays do not amount to a foundation upon which further reflections on the topic can steadily build, and anyone daring to do so must elide the disjunction between communal exigency and scholarly lacuna, the paradoxical gap between the importance of a phenomenon and the interest shown in it. Perhaps the definition of an American Jewish culture has remained elusive, if not insoluble, because "culture" is so polysemous. It is saddled with so many definitions, around which so many elaborations and clarifications have been constructed, that the threat of additional lexicographical forays can drive audiences to the exits as quickly as hurling a tear gas canister. The obligatory distinction should nevertheless be noted between the anthropological and the prescriptive (between Herder's version and Arnold's). Both definitions are enmeshed in the study of American Jewish life and require some explanation.

The first sort of "cultural system" Clifford Geertz has described in terms of shared "conceptions embodied in symbolic forms," according to which "men communicate, perpetuate, and develop their knowledge about and attitudes toward life."[7] Such "structures of meaning," for instance, account for our responses to suffering. In 1990, the United Jewish Appeal (UJA) received more dollars than any other American charity, except local United Way groups (to which Jews of course also contribute). The UJA received triple the total of private contributions to Catholic Charities and the Catholic Relief Services, even though Roman Catholics, the largest single sect in the United States, outnumber Jews by a ratio of ten to one. In a nation that is off the charts in its record of private generosity and its faith in a thousand points of light, the UJA attracts double the donations of the American Red Cross, almost four times what the American Heart Association receives, and almost ten times what Yale University receives, though all of these institutions count on gifts from Jews as well.[8] "Structures of meaning" can also affect our very nature; our bodies are not synonymous with ourselves, which vary according to the ideals that we have inherited. Anthropologists who have studied the tolerance for torment have discovered that for Irish Americans "pain becomes an endless road of lonely suffering, at the end of which is only death." Their thresholds of pain are "well above" those of American Jews, who are, in comparative terms, kvetches, quick to seek medical relief. One subculture places a certain premium upon martyrdom; the other does not inhibit those who want a second opinion.[9]

Though explanations for such variations are necessarily cultural, the second major definition of the term is quite different. It is normative, honoring the finest aesthetic and intellectual achievements of European civilization. Confined to the best that the Western imagination has achieved, its approach is mandarin, its purview the masterpiece. *Sulamith,* founded in 1806 as the first German-language Jewish periodical, proclaimed its aim in its subtitle: "A Journal for the Promotion of Culture and Humanity Among the Jewish Nation." Its editors and readers, as well as their descendants, considered *Kultur* to be "high culture." Along with *Bildung* or "education—the cultivation of reason and aesthetic sensibility," Paul Mendes-Flohr has observed, " 'culture' would make it possible for the Jews to 'embrace Europe.' " Their worship of art and learning would presumably entitle them to full emancipation. This ideal of "high culture" affected Eastern European immigrants, who transposed their sense of its richness to the United States within the next century.[10]

That set of ideals and those forms of expression are generally what Jews in the West have meant by "culture"; and, because of the cosmopolitan claims attached to *Bildung,* it has obscured the problem of defining a Jewish culture in particular national settings. The norms of the educated elite among the majority became the standards of Jews eager to participate in the cultural and intellectual life of the society surrounding them. Even when the theoretical illuminations of mandarin culture were disproportionately the work of Jews, these creative figures were usually quite deracinated. Those giants whom George Steiner dubbed "meta-rabbis"—Marx, Freud, Einstein, Wittgenstein, Lévi-Strauss, Roman Jakobson—became surrogates for actual rabbis, extracting from their Judaic heritage "an intense, perhaps pathological concentration on the life of the word, a profound historicity and bias to historical diagnosis, a commitment to analytic totality, to the ordering of all phenomena under laws and principles of prediction—these three traits accompanied the Jewish intelligentsia as it entered gentile culture."[11] They generally invigorated modern culture more powerfully than they sustained the particularities of Jewish experience. This is a point that need not be elaborated. But in an era when a Harvard professor of English proclaims that "there can be no culture without the transvestite,"[12] it may seem a bit quaint and overcautious to consider how little modern culture there might have been without the Jew.

But so much was given that often too little remained of Jewish identity itself, which accounts for another sort of duality that stalks the very definition of Jewish culture in the United States. A minimalist categorization would include any intellectual or artistic activity done by Jews in the United States, whether or not such work bears the traces of Jewish content or specificity. Allon Schoener's handsome volume *The American Jewish Album* (1983), for instance, includes portraits of Bob Dylan, Bette Midler, and Stephen Sondheim, none of whose careers can be said to serve an explicitly

The Paradoxes of American Jewish Culture 249

Jewish purpose. Schoener's hospitable principle of selection also governs a new encyclopedia which is designed to show how "the Jewish-American presence has made significant contributions to American history and culture."[13] A promotional flyer for the volume, whose entries were written largely by academicians, spotlights Lenny Bruce·more than anyone else. This is reminiscent of an advertisement for the movie *Uncle Buck* (1989), "He's crude. He's crass. He's family." But does Bruce also personify Jewish history and culture in the United States?

In the wake of such lax criteria, allowing editors to move freely about the cabin, attempts have sometimes been made to find a distinctive perspective in artifacts that are stripped of Jewish content. Since few American Jewish works have been done "under strict rabbinic supervision," perhaps they are at least "kosher style." Sometimes claims have been advanced for the very likely or even necessary provenance of such works as Jewish, claims excavated from broader generalizations that would cause positivistic social scientists to shudder. Arguing that "the characteristic genius of the Jew has been especially a moral genius," Edmund Wilson conjectured that "it was probably the Jew in the half-Jewish Proust that saved him from being the Anatole France of an even more deliquescent phase of the French belletristic tradition." Or take the example of Joseph Heller's *Catch-22* (1961), in which there are no Jewish characters. One critic, nevertheless, found "hard to imagine anyone but a Jew writing that book—so visibly Jewish is the curious combination of self-pity and self-irony that lies behind Heller's humor, so little whole-hearted is the nihilism to which he aspires."[14] The illustrations of this critical tendency could easily be multiplied. The trouble is that so could the range of Jewish expression, which is far too various to be covered by any assumption of what only a Jew or a half-Jew could have voiced.

The maximalist definition of American Jewish culture requires that such works be conceived and created not only by Jews but bear directly on their beliefs and experiences as a people. This definition finds space for Heller's *Good as Gold* (1979) but not *Catch-22;* for Leonard Bernstein's *Jeremiah Symphony* (1942) and *Kaddish Symphony* (1963) but not his *West Side Story* (1957), much less his *Mass* (1971); for Neil Simon's dramatic trilogy *Brighton Beach Memoirs* (1983), *Biloxi Blues* (1985), and *Broadway Bound* (1986) but not his other autobiographical forays *Come Blow Your Horn* (1961) and *Chapter Two* (1977); for films like Woody Allen's *Zelig* (1983) and *Crimes and Misdemeanors* (1989) but not, presumably, his *Play It Again Sam* (1972) or *Sleeper* (1973).

The maximalist definition therefore establishes a consensus of what is

Jewish, but at the cost of sabotaging a full critical appreciation of particular artists, whose identity may be as fluid as that of other Jews. Ethnicity and religion are hardly the only influences that are likely to shape such artists. Professor Alter's praise of Jewish studies programs, for example, finds their status in the American academy intriguing and promising not because their object of scrutiny is Jewish, which is a given, but primarily because they are American. His curiosity is piqued by the national habits and features that its scholarly practitioners have acquired. The maximalist definition therefore shifts the angle, inviting questions of how Americans have contributed to Jewish scholarship or to Jewish artistic expression. The maximalist definition encourages the tracing of, say, the poetic imagination from King David through Judah Halevi and Heinrich Heine down to Allen Ginsberg, a self-described "Buddhist Jewish pantheist"[15]—Walt Whitman's kid brother. The son of a Communist mother and a poet father, Ginsberg has been the quondam bard of a lyrical Jewish leftism who opened himself to the charge of selling his birthright for a message about pot and homosexuality. But such an angle might obscure the greater impact that Ginsberg exerted on American culture, in accelerating its latitudinarian and libertarian tendencies. To highlight his Jewish identity may be to fudge and misjudge his significance as a poet and a presence.

More broadly, as Harold Rosenberg once noted, "though art may be characterized by its subject matter, subject matter does not characterize it as art." This third duality is a conundrum out of which even the *New Yorker* art critic could not wriggle, for Rosenberg invalidated the notion of a "Jewish art in the sense of a Jewish style in painting and sculpture. . . . Still . . . while Jewish artists have not been creating as Jews, they have not been working as non-Jews either. Their art has been the closest expression of themselves as they are, including the fact that they are Jews, each in his individual degree."[16] It was a loss to Jewish art, for instance, that George Gershwin never fulfilled his contract with the Metropolitan Opera to adapt S. Ansky's *The Dybbuk,* but it is hardly a loss to art that he composed *Porgy and Bess* (1935) instead. The critical pursuit of how that folk opera was not the work of a non-Jew should, however, be called on account of darkness. The maximalist definition sanctions the exploration of so little American expression that too many dry holes are hit. The minimalist definition encourages the examination of so much, however, that contributions of Jews seem to dissolve into a melting pot that allows little that is peculiar to this people to be savored.

Through the Lens of Assimilation

Thus another paradox can now be formulated. In the light of American culture, the impact of Jews has been striking; from the perspective of Jewish culture, however, the contribution of Americans is so thin it is virtually anorexic. To Barrett Wendell the Jews looked tenacious preserving their identity; to Harold Bloom, who has been teaching Wendell's field at Yale, an American Jewish culture may be stillborn, in large part because his own Jewish students show no special flair for the reading of texts. To those who study America, the role of one particular group looks impressive; within that group, however, the fissures can loom large.

Two decades ago, for example, Philip Taylor's standard history of immigration, *The Distant Magnet,* concluded with a plea for books that needed to be written. On "community life and leadership among ethnic groups," the University of Hull historian claimed that "only rural Norwegians and the Jews have been at all adequately treated; and I sometimes feel that the greatest service to the subject would be rendered if Jewish scholars would cease from studying their own people and turn their brilliant talents to *any* other group." The most gifted of those historians of the uprooted was undoubtedly Oscar Handlin, the successor to Marcus Lee Hansen (whose mother had been born in Norway). Yet Handlin's study of the Irish is better known and developed than his work on the Jews, and among the six dozen dissertations that he supervised at Harvard, only one was devoted to Jewish history—Moses Rischin's 1957 thesis on the immigrant Jews of New York. When *World of Our Fathers* was published, Father Andrew Greeley committed the deadly sin of envy by conceding: "By us Irish, we should be so lucky to have an Irving Howe," who could "so adroitly describe" immigration and adaptation with a synthetic power that would serve as the model for a "future . . . history of the Irish Americans—or the Italian or Polish or Croatian or Armenian Americans." Yet shortly before, Seymour Martin Lipset had noted that "with relatively few exceptions, Jewish social scientists with a general reputation in their discipline have . . . abstained from writing about American Jews." (He admittedly excluded "men employed by Jewish institutions, and . . . those with specific appointments to posts on Jewish topics.")[17] The first paradox of so little scrutiny of so pressing a subject may therefore be related to the second one, because an American Jewish subculture looks drab in the light of an American culture that Jews have helped to energize, a mass culture that has dazzled the world.

Of course, an appreciation of the general culture is not easy either, and its hospitality and robustness marked America off from the mother country. Over the last three centuries, "the toleration that made possible the successful integration of English Jews was hostile to the notion of cultural diversity," historian Todd M. Endelman has argued. "Circles and institutions quite willing to tolerate Jews as intimate associates were not willing to endorse the perpetuation of a separate Jewish culture or to see any value in the customs or beliefs of the Jewish religion. Their unshakable faith in the superiority of their own way of life seduced those Jews eager to join them into believing that this was really so. The stigma of Jewishness, however slight, however muted, persisted, continuing to work its corrosive effect on Jews whose faith and ethnicity were already receding." Though Endelman added that "no Western society has ever developed the kind of cultural pluralism that might have discouraged . . . radical assimilation," an exception, especially in the late twentieth century, might be made for the United States, where its culture is up for grabs, where English influence itself could be contested. American society was such a novelty that Alexis de Tocqueville had asked a friend to imagine "a society formed of all the nations of the world . . . people having different languages, beliefs, opinions: in a word, a society without roots, without memories, without prejudices . . . without common ideas, without a national character. . . . What serves as the link among such diverse elements? What makes all of this into one people?"[18] To this polyphony, the voices of Jews could be added as well.

They could also help form the mass culture around which a disparate people could cohere. As middlemen, packagers, and showmen, they could merchandise their cultural wares with such acumen that a dispersed people might be unified into an audience—for Leonard and Phil Chess's black musicians (on Chess Records), for Abe Saperstein's Harlem Globetrotters, for the Feld family's Ringling Brothers and Barnum & Bailey Circus, for Michael Eisner's rejuvenated Disneyland and Disney World. As motion picture moguls, they could invent and promote the nation's icons (and sometimes marry them). As successors to Joseph in Egypt and Freud in Vienna, they could serve as interpreters of dreams, as well as advisors on everything from ethics ("Ann Landers" and "Dear Abby") to etiquette ("Miss Manners"), from dance (Arthur Murray) to language (Edwin Newman, William Safire) to sex (Dr. David Reuben, Dr. Ruth Westheimer). They could compose the unofficial national anthem, Irving Berlin's "God Bless America" (1938) or other unabashedly patriotic pieces like Aaron Copland's *A Lincoln Portrait* (1942), which has most recently been recorded by the Saint Louis

Symphony, with Leonard Slatkin as conductor and General H. Norman Schwarzkopf as narrator. They could assume virtually any identity they wished. Amid the flux that Tocqueville had emphasized, the option of consent could displace the category of descent, giving even erstwhile pariahs so many chances to hit the jackpot that the cherries, grapes, and lemons all seemed to come up at once.

The promise of free choice has seemed so glorious that we need an outsider's perspective to underscore its implications. Franz Kafka's only comic novel (unfinished, of course) is eerily set in *Amerika*, a land that he never had a chance to visit. In the eighth and last chapter, the protagonist is hurtled into the "Nature Theatre of Oklahoma," where careers are open to talent, upward mobility is sanctioned, and all seem to be welcome for employment. In this huge and "almost limitless" forum, the author intended Karl Rossman to find freedom and fulfillment.[19] The Nature Theatre of Oklahoma is surprisingly fussy with identity papers, however, and therefore the tone of the novel is a bit edgier than the sunny-side-up optimism of a work of musical theater like *Oklahoma!* (1943), in which the urbane New York Jews who wrote it—Richard Rodgers and Oscar Hammerstein II—celebrated cowboys who "know we belong to the land! And the land we belong to is grand." But *Amerika* is still too light to be Kafkaesque; it is picaresque. Put a Kafka hero in Central Europe, and authorities are sinister and unresponsive, guilt is imposed for crimes that are ambiguous or uncommitted, verdicts are inflicted by distant but demanding fathers. But put the Kafka hero in America, even when his first name begins with the fatally enigmatic *K*, and mass culture invites fantasies of emancipation. Then put a Kafka admirer in America, and Philip Roth will invent an "Assistant Commissioner of Human Opportunity" desperate to free himself from the memories of a Newark family dominated by Sophie Portnoy. It is also amusing that Roth's comic exposé became the first foreign novel to be translated into Czech under a post-Communist government in Prague. Testifying to the allure and vitality of American culture, an in-joke had surmounted national as well as ethnic frontiers.[20]

The Politics of Jewish American Culture

The Judaism to which neither novelist could subscribe has itself been transformed in the United States, changing from a true-false test into multiple choice. But Judaism has also been enfeebled because its historic manifestations could not be squared with the dominant ideals of American society.

The prevalence of freedom and happiness had led Jefferson, rather exuberantly, to boast that America had passed the test of civilization, thus upending Freud's theory that freedom and happiness had to be curtailed as the *price* of civilization. His tragic view is closer, however, to traditional Judaism, which is so exacting in its authority, so interdictory in its texture, Louis Finkelstein once remarked, that "it demands of its people what other religions demand of those in religious orders. Because Judaism demands so much, it never gets 100%." The conflict between religious imperatives and American freedom is hardly confined to Judaism; a flick of the dial, when televangelists are on the air, can disclose how Christianity has been historically altered as well. But belief in the Savior has nevertheless flourished in the United States, which by some indices harbors the most pious Christians in the Western world (other than the Irish and the Maltese). Because in any given week more Americans (about 40 percent) attend church than sports events, the nation's real religion seems to be neither football nor even baseball; it is religion. Nine in ten Americans claim never to have doubted the existence of God and profess to pray at least once a week. Half believe in angels, a third in a personal devil.[21] Despite the phoniness of much of the nation's piety, Americans are far more faithful than any other advanced industrialized people.

Yet among such citizens the Jews are eccentric. To be sure, about two-thirds claim to fast on Yom Kippur, about four-fifths to light Hanukkah candles, and almost nine-tenths to participate in a seder. But then the signs of religious commitment and renunciation falter—though in exculpation Finkelstein was amazed that the austere requirements of Judaism elicited even a 1 percent response. Asked what their religion is, 1.2 million Jews (or one in five) answered "none," making the category of Jews as a "religious group" a bit of a misnomer. (It's the denominational equivalent of fresh-frozen food and hard-top convertibles.) This "religious group" is riddled with intellectual free agents who are reluctant to penetrate the mysteries of existence through faith and observance or to incorporate God as a referent in their discourse. Gallup polls reveal that Jews "lag well behind the general population in congregation membership, worship attendance, and the importance they place on religion in their lives." A clear majority is not affiliated with any synagogue.[22] Eleanor Roosevelt once privately reminisced: "We were Victorians. I knew my obligations as a wife and did my duty," or, as her biographer delicately paraphrased it, "sex was an ordeal to be borne."[23] Judaism for huge numbers of its American adherents has been as sex was for at least some eminent Victorians—an experience not to be enjoyed but to be endured. The secularism even of those who *are* affiliated has meant that sanctity has resembled certain parking spaces—reserved for clergy. Or, in the words of one joke that has made the rounds: "How big is your synagogue?" one rabbi asks another. Answer: It sleeps six hundred.

The pathos that such humor reveals has been registered by Leonard Fein, the wisest contemporary guide to the perplexed, who explained to a disaffected correspondent that the typical rabbi finds

> no great joy to enter a calling that has teaching as its central aspect, and then . . . discover[s] that your students cut almost all their classes. . . . Come the high holidays, they look out at a sea of people—most of them as much in search as you—who sit there and say, "Show me." There is less an air of expectancy than a brooding skepticism. Strangers have come together, for a wide variety of reasons, from a wide variety of back-grounds, and the poor rabbi, who knows better than you this is his own annual opportunity to work a piece of magic—and who also, if he's like most, has his own personal agenda with God that day—must charm, educate, inspire, convert. "Be charismatic," the audience (for it is not a congregation) says; "you've got two hours, or three, to defeat the massed forces of secularization, of modernism, of alienation and assimilation. Make it happen."

Fein adds: "And that's the best of the assembly; the rest just want out as quickly as possible." Call it sleep. He conceded that "it is unfortunate . . . that the tradition has somewhere been ruptured, that one cannot simply enter the house of Judaism and find there an ongoing congregation, into which one fits most naturally."[24]

The ricketiness of that house cannot be ascribed to the general pressures of secularism but rather to the particularities of contemporary Jewry, which is largely tone-deaf to the sort of sacred music that so many other Americans hear. In their practicality and respect for common sense, in their reliance on science and rationalism, in their distaste for obscurantism, and indeed even in their pursuit of business and commercial opportunities, American Jews unwittingly remain among the most loyal disciples of Benjamin Franklin, whose career in desacralization Max Weber had made into the epitome of modernization, and whose scientific vocation helped diminish the "fear of natural phenomena" like lightning, which were once "divinely inspired" bolts of anger, according to Harvard's eminent historian of science Bernard Cohen (and, incidentally, Lionel Trilling's cousin).[25] American Jews are also heirs of the commitment of Franklin's Enlighten-

ment contemporaries to a very high wall separating religion and government, which is why no one should be surprised by *Lee* v. *Weisman*. In a possibly landmark case in its significance for church-state relations, victorious
young Deborah Weisman joined her parents in complaining about a prayer
delivered at her middle school graduation in Rhode Island because the
clergyman had offered thanks to God for "the legacy of America, where diversity is celebrated and the rights of minorities are protected"—even though
the clergyman who uttered these innocuous sentiments was a rabbi.[26]

As the most ancient as well as the most modern of peoples, Jews thus
exhibit a curious duality. Their ethical monotheism can be traced to the
most distant origins, and yet their dedication to education has also armed
them more than others with an antidote to what can be impugned as su-
perstition. The result is that the people responsible for imagining the deity
that their neighbors worship has been losing the capacity of doing so itself.
Asked if they believe in God, 99 percent of Protestants answer in the
affirmative, 100 of Catholics, compared to 75 percent of Jews, with the proportion declining. Over two-thirds of Christendom believes in heaven. But
only 6 percent of American Jewry can acknowledge such faith, which even
Job, whose ordeal was far worse, could manage when he questioned the
benevolence of God but never His existence.[27] Because religion circum-
scribes conduct, its effectiveness is bound to be partial at best, and the relationship between preaching and practice is of course imponderable. Still,
Judaism is probably less successful than Christianity in propounding veri-
ties that are not only eternal but believed. For example, though Jews were
once famous for family cohesiveness and loyalty, and though the Seventh
Commandment would appear binding, a fourth of Jewish women "could
envision situations when sex with someone other than one's spouse is not
wrong." This proportion can be contrasted with only a tenth of other
American women,[28] who may be less affected by modernity.

An admittedly tiny sample of literary evidence may also be suggestive.
In his later years Edmund Wilson was consistently attracted to only three
younger American writers of fiction: James Baldwin, Edwin O'Connor, and
J. D. Salinger—one Afro-American, one Irish American, and one half-Jew,
as it happened. Within this rainbow coalition, it may be merely coinci-
dental that Baldwin made the black church the locale of his first novel, *Go
Tell It on the Mountain* (1953), that O'Connor used a priest to narrate his
Pulitzer Prize winner, *The Edge of Sadness* (1961), but that Salinger failed to
treat Jewish religious experience at all. Indeed, if his favorite characters,
the Glasses, are even Jewish, it is hard to detect any identifying features. In-

deed, *Franny and Zooey* (1961) features a prayer to Jesus and reveals "the Fat Lady" to be "Christ Himself, buddy."[29] Had Wilson's taste included the canonized American Jewish novelists who were contemporaries of these three writers, he still would have found none who treated the challenges of faith or depicted fully persons engaged in a specifically Judaic quest. However, Wilson did promote Isaac Bashevis Singer, whose only novel set in America, *Enemies, a Love Story* (1972), features a Holocaust survivor who serves as a ghost writer for a Rabbi Milton Lampert, a womanizing, real estate–rich philistine.

Or take the evidence of best sellers, which moves us far beyond Wilson's own perhaps eccentric syllabus. There have been blockbusters about valiant, gun-toting Israelis; anecdotal sagas of the upward ascent of the *all-rightniks;* brooding portraits of estranged intellectuals; even a law professor's recent plea for greater ethnic pride and civic assertiveness in an indifferent gentile world. But although Boston rabbis like Joshua Loth Liebman and Harold Kushner published therapeutic works aimed at general audiences, only one best seller can be classified as articulating an explicitly Judaic vision—Herman Wouk's *This Is My God* (1959). The freakish popularity of this introduction to Orthodox Judaism may testify to the religious revival that characterized the 1950s in the United States and also to the widespread assumption that, even when explaining the hermeneutics of rabbinic interpretation, *anything* Wouk wrote must be compellingly readable.

This Is My God was predictably less successful, of course, than *The Caine Mutiny* (1951) or even than a novel published little more than a decade earlier, Laura Zametkin Hobson's *Gentleman's Agreement* (1947). Sales of over 1.6 million copies made her assault on snobbery the most famous literary blow ever struck at American anti-Semitism. Yet the author herself was an agnostic, and her autobiography, *Laura Z* (1983), revealed no interest in Judaic religion or values. The success of *Gentleman's Agreement* is symptomatic of the primary impulses of her fellow Jews, who have been far better at defending the freedom to worship than in practicing it, in asserting their rights than in actually exercising them, in expressing bemusement with the contingency of Jewish identity than in cultivating its mysteries—which was, incidentally, the challenge that Jean-Paul Sartre had issued from an existentialist perspective a year before Hobson's novel was published. *Anti-Semite and Jew* had urged Jews to make an accident meaningful, defining their own freedom in a way that erased the images of their enemies. And yet, by the time he had written his tract, the erudite French philosopher had not bothered to read a single book on the Jewish experience.[30] What

Jews might have been defending themselves *for*, what sort of heritage they might transmit to their descendants—these issues were unexplored in these otherwise very different artifacts from European high culture and American mass culture.

In the admittedly arcane field of theology, American Jewry has always suffered from manpower shortages. The thinkers who are most commonly seen as influencing the study of God have been almost invariably foreign-born or educated, like Abraham Joshua Heschel, Emil Fackenheim, Joseph Soloveitchik, or (in his own way) Elie Wiesel. Exceptions should be granted for Mordecai M. Kaplan, who immigrated from Lithuania at the age of nine, and Will Herberg, who arrived from Russia at the age of three. With *Judaism as a Civilization* (1934) and *Judaism and Modern Man* (1951), each made his reputation in this field with only one book, though Kaplan wrote prolifically and his thought engendered an entire movement. Herberg was an even more special case. In the wake of a close brush with Christianity, from which the Rev. Reinhold Niebuhr had deflected him, he taught at Drew University, a Methodist institution. Even their impact on leading Judaic thinkers cannot be said to be prepossessing, however. One major symposium revealed that the thinker who exercised the greatest effect on Judaism in the immediate postwar era was probably Franz Rosenzweig, who was not even a rabbi, much less an American.[31] Scholarly specialists in religion, like Harry A. Wolfson of Harvard (or, for that matter, Gershom Scholem of the Hebrew University), may not have given credence to Judaism, the object of their study; the evidence is uncertain. Those intellectuals who have defended the value of religion on social or moral or political grounds, like Irving Kristol, have not formulated an extensive case for Judaism itself. Daniel Bell, who had predicted the return of the sacred in the 1980s, could muster only a sense of its transcendent sanction and appeal, without explaining how Judaism might fit within such a scheme in civil society.

Religion on the Margins

Such immunity to faith has been stressed because of its implications for an already small community, threatening the adherence of those born into Jewish and part-Jewish families in the future. The Judaism that is central to Kaplan's conception of Jewish civilization has been marginal to the values by which much of American Jewry seems to live. Its culture cannot be said to oppose religion explicitly, nor have tumbleweeds been blowing through the portals of the synagogues. But American Jewish culture has become increasingly dependent upon its least dependable feature—the final paradox entangled in this topic, which can no longer be imagined as lasting beyond religion.

For ethnicity itself is fading, receding over the horizon of immigrant experience and memories. Hebraicists, socialist Yiddishists, and Zionist secularists once represented possibilities of Jewish culture without religion; by now they mostly belong to the actuarial tables. Their flip side is now the *baal teshuvah* or even more strikingly the convert, who hints at the possibility of religion without Jewish culture. The prospect of "a Quaker-like future for American Judaism" did not thrill one leading scholar of traditionalist sympathies,[32] for a ruptured sense of historic peoplehood would mark a community in which some of our best Jews are Friends. The spirit of *klal yisrael* has nevertheless been slipping through the fingers of succeeding generations in America, and yet, despite the battering it has received, the religious sensibility might be just recalcitrant enough to survive in a modern or postmodern era.

"If someone wants to convert," Edmond Jabès once pointed out, "never will a real rabbi ask him at the start if he believes in God. You don't see that. He'll say to him, 'Why do *you* want to be Jewish? What madness has come over you that you want to be Jewish?'" The writer, who had been born in Cairo in 1912 and died in Paris in 1991 and was therefore attuned to the mysterious sense of peoplehood in the diaspora, explained that Judaism is "an ethic . . . of questioning, of being open, of solidarity, of memory."[33] But what happens when questioning starts and ends outside the traditional framework, when being open means disaffiliation, when solidarity and memory are too fragile to bind Jews together or to make the slogan "We are one" truly adhesive? The question has become more insistent: what links Jews to their ancestors if not religion, if not uttering the same prayers to a historic deity?

The link cannot be the language in which those prayers are uttered, the language that was jump-started in Palestine by Eliezer Ben-Yehuda, whose daughter managed to marry a long-standing Jerusalemite who nevertheless could not speak the holy tongue. When asked whether he felt ashamed of his ignorance, he agreed but added: "Believe me, it is much easier to be ashamed than to learn Hebrew."[34] American Jews seem determined to emulate Ben-Yehuda's son-in-law. Nor, even more obviously, can the link be forged in Yiddish, which was once so pervasive that, when Herberg happened to have mentioned to an elderly audience that Maimonides had spoken Arabic rather than Yiddish, one immigrant listener burst out: "Eikh mir a Yid?" (You call him a Jew?).[35] No one would have called Abraham Cahan anything other than a Jew, and yet the editor of the most widely circulated of all Yiddish newspapers, the *Forward,* introduced so many English words that, according to a rival from the *Freiheit,* Cahan's readers eventually "didn't know English *or* Yiddish."[36] But nowadays, the popular Judaica lecturer Moshe Waldoks complains, young Jews think that *nachas* means corn chips.

That language once flowed through a powerful set of folkways that Weber called a lifestyle and that others have seen exemplified in *Yiddishkeit.* In 1939, just more than half a century ago, over four out of every five of the world's Jews had either resided "in the old Polish lands, or descended from Jews who lived there. Of the six million Jews murdered during the following years, half were citizens of the Polish state, [and] most of the remainder were descended from Polish Jews." Those fortunate enough to reach the Holy Land have now become a minority of the Israeli population, and though the overwhelming majority of American Jewry traces its ancestry to those who had lived in the lands associated with the Polish Commonwealth for nearly a millennium,[37] their histories are strikingly discontinuous. This is clearly seen in I. B. Singer's haunting tale "The Son from America," the story of a Jew who returns to visit his parents in the Polish village of Lentshin. He is so tall and so finely dressed that they do not recognize him; his Yiddish is so mixed with English that they barely understand him—and so he departs with the realization that his wealth means nothing in a place where needs are simple, where the riptides of modern history have not yet come to sweep away the old traditions.[38] Totalitarianism would intervene soon enough to devastate the centers of *Yiddishkeit* in Eastern Europe and ensure that they cannot be replenished. For a tectonic shift has occurred, making the postwar Jewish world largely bipolar.

Can religious life pulse in the part located in the United States, where more Jews have resided than in any place since Abraham left Ur of the Chaldees? Can an American Jewish culture be grounded in faith and observance? Or, because secularism is so commonplace, would such investment in religion mean a death warrant for American Jewry? These are the questions that linger. Much will depend on the resilient powers of Judaism, which obligates its adherents to differ from their neighbors—and yet has also sanctioned its believers in America to diverge even more from their ancestors. The problem of preserving Judaic tradition within the groove of modernity happened to strike me with magnum force shortly before Rosh Ha-Shanah in 1990, on the Brandeis University campus. While waiting in line at the post office, I overheard an undergraduate tell another young woman: "This will be the first time I've been home since last Passover. I know I've got to go to services. It'll be a big deal because since my last time at home my mother has become a rabbi. She wants me to attend, and yet she warned me that my boyfriend and I might not feel comfortable there. His father is a Congregationalist minister, you know, but that's not the reason. She said we'd stick out because the *shul* is really for gays and lesbians."

A supple proclivity for adapting to the environment has long characterized American Judaism, which has often pushed past the breaking point the motto that every Jew has his own *Shulkhan Arukh* (code of laws). My aunt, for example, has acknowledged only one dietary restriction, refusing at Passover to put ham on *matsah*. Others have tried harder to maintain consistency with tradition, and their rituals have been creative and even ingenious. The Bohemian-born, Cincinnati-based Reform rabbi Isaac Mayer Wise found himself in the midst of citizens who seemed to devour oysters that, because they are embedded in the ocean floor, he attempted to have reclassified from a shellfish to a vegetable.[39] He failed, but the gesture is significant. Called to Atlanta, an Orthodox rabbi named Tobias Geffen ensured that Coca-Cola would pass muster as kosher; in 1935 he was able to have the celebrated, presumably top-secret syrup formula slightly altered. Rabbi Geffen seemed to agree that things go better with Coke: "Because it has become an insurmountable problem to induce the great majority of Jews to refrain from partaking of this drink, I have tried earnestly to find a method of permitting its usage. With the help of God, I have been able to uncover a pragmatic solution."[40] Such agile efforts to put Judaism on fast-forward may not be sufficient, and later generations might not care what the laws once dictated; but confidence in the possibility of such synthesis is an inescapable aspect of American Jewish ideology.

According to the historian of political theory J. G. A. Pocock, a republican tradition of civic humanism managed to sustain itself over four centuries in Europe and even to stretch itself to the New World (all the way down to the embattled conservative revolutionary who was the great-grandfather of Henry Adams). This was a tradition that tried to sustain communal ideals of *virtù*, an irrepressible legacy Pocock dubbed "the Machiavellian Moment." For their part, Jewish historians might speak of the Mendelssohnian Moment, which began quite precisely in 1743, when, according to a probably apocryphal account, the guards at one of Berlin's gates recorded the passing of "six oxen, seven pigs, [and] one Jew,"[41] a Jew who inaugurated the struggle to synthesize the culture of the Enlightenment and the Judaic legacy. "Still reeking of the Ghetto," the philosopher helped to translate the Hebrew Bible into German and became the eponymous model for Lessing's *Nathan the Wise* (1779), though all of his descendants became Christians within two generations. Ever since then the bulk of Ashkenazim has been breathing the Mendelssohnian Moment. The reconciliation of religious sentiment and knowledge with the imperatives of modernity has been the destiny of most American Jews, as they have grafted at least the vestiges of Judaism upon contemporary culture and dared to hope that the tension might be creative.

Among those who collaborated in the final Jewish translation of the Bible into German was Martin Buber, who repudiated early in his career the temptation "to shed the culture of the world about *us*, a culture that, in the final analysis, has . . . become an integral part of ourselves." For "we need to be conscious of the fact that we are a cultural admixture, in a more poignant sense than any other people." But then Buber posed the challenge that still bedevils his coreligionists: "We do not . . . want to be the slaves of this admixture, but its masters."[42]

Notes

1. Henry Adams, *The Education of Henry Adams,* ed. Ernest Samuels (1918; Boston: Houghton Mifflin, 1973), 3, 238.

2. Lionel Trilling, "Under Forty: A Symposium of American Literature and the Younger Generation of American Jews," *Contemporary Jewish Record* 7 (February 1944): 15–17, reprinted in Trilling, *Speaking of Literature and Society,* ed. Diana Trilling (New York: Harcourt Brace Jovanovich, 1980), 198–201.

3. Barrett Wendell to Horace M. Kallen, December 6 and December 30, 1914, quoted in Moses Rischin, "The Jews and Pluralism: Toward an American Freedom Symphony," in *Jewish Life in America: Historical Perspectives,* ed. Gladys Rosen (New York: Institute of Human Relations Press/Ktav, 1978), 77.

4. Philip Roth, "Writing about Jews" (1963), in *Reading Myself and Others* (New York: Farrar, Straus and Giroux, 1975), 168–69.

5. Jonathan D. Sarna, *JPS: The Americanization of American Jewish Culture* (Philadelphia: Jewish Publication Society, 1989), ixx; Lloyd P. Gartner, "Jewish Historiography in the United States and Britain," in *Jewish History: Essays in Honour of Chimen Abramsky,* ed. Ada Rapoport-Albert and Steven J. Zipperstein (London: Peter Halban, 1988), 218.

6. Harold Bloom, "Free and Broken Tablets: The Cultural Prospects of American Jewry," in *Agon: Towards a Theory of Revisionism* (New York: Oxford University Press, 1982), 321; Bloom, "The Pragmatics of Contemporary Jewish Culture," in *Post-Analytic Philosophy,* ed. John Rajchman and Cornel West (New York: Columbia University Press, 1985), 114, 116; Robert Alter, "The Jew Who Didn't Get Away: On the Pos-

sibility of an American Jewish Culture" (1982), in *The American Jewish Experience*, ed. Jonathan D. Sarna (New York: Holmes and Meier, 1986), 272–73.

7. Clifford Geertz, *The Interpretation of Cultures: Selected Essays* (New York: Basic Books, 1973), 89–90.

8. Felicity Barringer, "In the Worst of Times, America Keeps Giving," *New York Times*, March 15, 1992, sec. 4, p. 6.

9. Mark Zborowski, *People in Pain* (San Francisco: Jossey-Bass, 1969), 235, quoted in John Duffy Ibson, *Will the World Break Your Heart? Dimensions and Consequences of Irish-American Assimilation* (New York: Garland, 1990), 135–36.

10. Paul Mendes-Flohr, "Culture," in *Contemporary Jewish Religious Thought: Original Essays on Critical Concepts, Movements, and Beliefs*, ed. Paul Mendes-Flohr and Arthur A. Cohen (New York: Charles Scribner's Sons, 1987), 120, 121, reprinted in Paul Mendes-Flohr, *Divided Passions: Jewish Intellectuals and the Experience of Modernity* (Detroit: Wayne State University Press, 1991), 414, 415; Irving Howe, "The Eastern European Jews and American Culture," in Rosen, *Jewish Life in America*, 97–108.

11. George Steiner, "Some 'Meta-Rabbis,'" in *Next Year in Jerusalem: Portraits of the Jew in the Twentieth Century*, ed. Douglas Villiers (New York: Viking, 1976), 66–67, 75–76.

12. Quoted in Bruce Barcott, "Coming of Age," *Boston Phoenix*, March 6, 1992, sec. 1, p. 18; Marjorie Garber, *Vested Interests: Cross-Dressing and Cultural Anxiety* (New York: Routledge, 1992), 389–90.

13. Jack Fischel and Sanford Pinsker, introduction to *Jewish-American History and Culture*, ed. Fischel and Pinsker (New York: Garland, 1992), xiii.

14. Edmund Wilson, *To the Finland Station: A Study in the Writing and Acting of History* (1940; New York: Farrar, Straus and Giroux, 1972), 358–59; Norman Podhoretz, "The Rise and Fall of the American Jewish Novelist," in Rosen, *Jewish Life in America*, 143.

15. Jane Kramer, *Allen Ginsberg in America* (New York: Vintage, 1970), 23.

16. Harold Rosenberg, "Is There a Jewish Art?" (1966), in *Discovering the Present: Three Decades in Art, Culture, and Politics* (Chicago: University of Chicago Press, 1973), 227, 230.

17. Philip Taylor, *The Distant Magnet: European Emigration to the U.S.A.* (New York: Harper and Row, 1971), 309; Andrew M. Greeley, review of Irving Howe, *World of Our Fathers, Moment*, March 1976, 74; Seymour Martin Lipset, "The American Jewish Community in a Comparative Perspective," in *Revolution and Counterrevolution: Change and Persistence in Social Structures*, rev. ed. (Garden City, NY: Doubleday Anchor, 1970), 149.

18. Todd M. Endelman, *Radical Assimilation in English Jewish History, 1656–1945* (Bloomington: Indiana University Press, 1990), 209; Alexis de Tocqueville to Ernest de Chabrol, June 9, 1831, in Tocqueville, *Selected Letters on Politics and Society*, ed. Roger Boesche, trans. James Toupin and Roger Boesche (Berkeley and Los Angeles: University of California Press, 1985), 38.

19. Franz Kafka, *Amerika*, trans. Edwin Muir (New York: New Directions, 1946), 272–99.

20. *New York Review of Books*, April 12, 1990, 2.

21. Quoted in Ari L. Goldman, "At 90, Judaic Scholarship Is Still Finkelstein's Pas-

sion," *New York Times*, September 1, 1985, sec. 1, p. 57; Garry Wills, *Under God: Religion and American Politics* (New York: Simon and Schuster, 1990), 16.

22. Charles S. Liebman and Steven M. Cohen, *Two Worlds of Judaism: The Israeli and American Experiences* (New Haven: Yale University Press, 1990), 123; Goldman, "Judaic Scholarship," 57; Harold Schulweis, "Are We Losing the Faith?" *Reform Judaism* 20 (spring 1992): 5; Jeffrey K. Salkin, "The Jews We Don't See," *Reform Judaism* 20 (winter 1991): 5.

23. Quoted in Joseph P. Lash, *Eleanor and Franklin* (New York: Norton, 1971), 146.

24. Leonard Fein, "Searching for the Self: An Exchange of Letters," September 1979, reprinted in *Jewish Possibilities: The Best of Moment Magazine* (Northvale, NJ: Jason Aronson, 1987), 21–22.

25. I. Bernard Cohen, *Benjamin Franklin's Science* (Cambridge: Harvard University Press, 1990), 30.

26. Nancy Gibbs, "America's Holy War," *Time*, December 9, 1991, 62.

27. Andrew M. Greeley, *The Denominational Society: A Sociological Approach to Religion in America* (Glenview, IL: Scott, Foresman, 1972), 137; Nahum N. Glatzer, "Introduction: A Study of Job," in *The Dimensions of Job: A Study and Selected Readings*, ed. Glatzer (New York: Schocken, 1969), 5.

28. Sylvia Barack Fishman, "The Impact of Feminism on American Jewish Life," *American Jewish Year Book* (1989), ed. David Singer (Philadelphia: Jewish Publication Society, 1989), 16; Wills, *Under God*, 17.

29. Edmund Wilson, "An Interview with Edmund Wilson" (1962), in *The Bit between My Teeth: A Literary Chronicle of 1950–1965* (New York: Farrar, Straus and Giroux, 1965), 546–47; J. D. Salinger, *Franny and Zooey* (New York: Bantam, 1964), 36–37, 196, 198, 202.

30. Judith Friedlander, *Vilna on the Seine: Jewish Intellectuals in France since 1968* (New Haven: Yale University Press, 1990), 143.

31. Milton Himmelfarb, introduction to *The Condition of Jewish Belief: A Symposium Compiled by the Editors of Commentary Magazine* (New York: Macmillan, 1966), 2.

32. Charles S. Liebman, *The Ambivalent American Jew: Politics, Religion, and Family in American Jewish Life* (Philadelphia: Jewish Publication Society, 1973), viii.

33. Interview with Edmond Jabès, in *Writing at Risk: Interviews in Paris with Uncommon Writers*, ed. Jason Weiss (Iowa City: University of Iowa Press, 1991), 193.

34. Israel Shenker, *Coat of Many Colors: Pages from Jewish Life* (Garden City, NY: Doubleday, 1985), 234.

35. Will Herberg, *Protestant-Catholic-Jew: An Essay in American Religious Sociology* (Garden City, NY: Doubleday Anchor, 1960), 202 n. 22.

36. Sid Resnick, quoted in Shenker, *Coat of Many Colors*, 245.

37. Michael C. Steinlauf, *Beyond the Evil Empire: Freedom to Remember or Freedom to Forget?* (Melrose Park, PA: Gratz College, 1991), 9.

38. Isaac Bashevis Singer, *A Crown of Feathers and Other Stories* (New York: Farrar, Straus and Giroux, 1973), 102–9.

39. L. Finkelstein, introduction to Shimon Finkelstein, *Seder tefilah im biur siah Yitshak* (Jerusalem, 1968), 10. I am very grateful to Jonathan D. Sarna for the citation and translation.

40. Personal communication from Jonathan D. Sarna; Tobias Geffen, "A *Teshuvah* Concerning Coca-Cola" (1935), trans. Louis Geffen and M. David Geffen, in *Lev Tuvia: On the Life and Work of Rabbi Tobias Geffen,* ed. Joel Ziff (Newton, MA: Rabbi Tobias Geffen Memorial Fund, 1988), 120.

41. Quoted in J. P. Stern, *The Fuhrer and the People* (Berkeley and Los Angeles: University of California Press, 1975), 206.

42. Martin Buber, "Judaism and the Jews" (1909), in *On Judaism,* ed. Nahum N. Glatzer (New York: Schocken, 1967), 19.

Couple, Bronx, New York, 1976. Courtesy of Bill Aron.

A Demographic Revolution in American Jewry

Egon Mayer

In his erudite and entertaining profile of Jewish elites in England from the mid-seventeenth century to the prewar decades of the twentieth, Todd Endelman illustrates an apparently inexorable process in the Jewish encounter with tolerant Christian societies:

> The gradual, multigenerational character of the process of Jewish disaffiliation has worked to mask the extent of the phenomenon everywhere. For subtle and undramatic transformations, however great their cumulative impact, arouse less interest, both at the time and in historical retrospect, than dramatic and decisive ruptures.[1]

Over the course of successive generations some of the most prominent families "pass out" of the Jewish community through the portals of exogamous matrimony into status-appropriate ranks in the wider society.

> Harts, Frankses, Goldsmids, Gompertzes, Montefiores, Cohens, Jessels, Franklins, Beddingtons, and Sassoons . . . disappeared from the ranks of the communal nobility. . . . The departure of these families, once the pillars of the Jewish establishment, indicates that radical assimilation is not an extraordinary event, a phenomenon on the periphery of Jewish life, but rather a common occurrence, eating away at the maintenance of group solidarity.[2]

After examining the relentless tide of "radical assimilation" among English Jewry, Endelman leaves off with what continues to be one of the pro-

This essay was originally presented on April 16, 1991, at the Jean and Samuel Frankel Center for Judaic Studies, University of Michigan, Ann Arbor.

found challenges of modernity for Jews the world over. "The question remains," he writes, "why so many Jews with feet in both worlds were unable to transmit their sense of Jewishness, however they defined it, to succeeding generations."[3] This essay attempts to answer that question on the basis of an analysis of what one might call, following Endelman, the "radical assimilation" of American Jews in the late twentieth century. As such, the essay explores some cold facts, some hard truths, some soft speculations, and concludes with some warm hopes.

The Basic Thesis

To help focus the reader's attention on what will amount to a rather detailed analysis of demographic trends and attitude patterns, it is only fair to state plainly the contention of this presentation: that modern America is different! Its culture and social structure have presented Jews with a novel setting in which to explore the relationship between Jewish particularity and the implied invitation extended to Jews by modern society "to become like everyone else."

In virtually all previous Diaspora communities, no matter how benign and receptive they might have been, Jews (along with other religious and ethnic minorities) have had only one of two ways to adapt: isolation or assimilation. Whether imposed from without or voluntarily chosen from within, isolation provided Jews with a cocoon around their culture and social order that protected them from erosion and hindered them from creative change. It enforced, too, a high degree of demographic homogeneity that, willy-nilly, tended to further foster group solidarity as well as a monolithic image of the community. Innovation and creativity, not to mention social deviance of any kind, were unwelcome in such a community.

Not surprisingly, the opportunities provided by modernity for economic and cultural creativity burst that cocoon asunder in England, France, Italy, Austro-Hungary, and Germany. From the dawn of the Industrial Revolution, energized by the liberalizing currents of the Enlightenment and the French Revolution, a multitude of opportunity-starved Jews came spilling out of the cocoon. They looked to their increasingly welcoming host societies not only for ways to improve their economic and political circumstances, but also for novelty, creativity, aesthetic experience, pleasure, and new bases of social ranking through financial accumulation and professional expertise. Those Jews who were most successful in taking advantage of the new opportunities soon found that the psychological and material benefits conferred by their host societies exceeded the comparable benefits conferred by life in the cocoon. They learned, moreover, that if they wished to continue reaping the benefits of the latter, they might risk losing the benefits of the former.

European modernity and, indeed, American modernity in its early stages were not nearly so pluralistic as to countenance a Jew simultaneously attaining the rewards of universalism and hanging on to the pleasures of particularism as well. Hence there existed a great deal of pressure, psychological as well as social, for assimilation, the end point of which was reached through intermarriage and the loss of Jewish identity. For many Jews bent on assimilation intermarriage became the vehicle of entry into the respectable echelons of the host society. By the same token, for those committed to "tradition," intermarriage became the ultimate symbol of Jewish withdrawal, and rejection of it served as the ultimate symbol of survivalism.

The terms of American modernity since the turn of the twentieth century, the terms that have governed the influx of massive waves of immigrants, of Jews and many others as well, are quite different from those of previous societies. American pluralism, the steady decline of the proportional majority as well as the cultural hegemony of white Anglo-Saxon Protestants, the growing assertiveness of all sorts of minorities throughout the twentieth century, the total separation of state and religion, and the nearly total separation between the public domain of economic life and the private domain of family and neighborhood—these factors have combined to produce a society in which universalism and particularism have grown less and less antipodal.

Indeed, the mid-1960s ushered in an era of ethnic reassertiveness, followed in the 1970s by a revival of religious sectarianism and fundamentalism, which made particularisms of all sorts not merely acceptable but even chic. The cultural open-endedness of late-twentieth-century America has not only allowed for the reemergence of all sorts of traditionalism; it has also permitted the emergence of innovations within them (e.g., neo-Hassidism on the one hand and women rabbis and gay synagogues on the other). In short, American pluralism has come to encompass not only a respect for the diversity of traditional cultures and religious groups, but also a growing respect for diversity within them. Moreover, it has fostered that diversity by allowing, perhaps even encouraging, members of minorities to combine their participation in the wider culture with their participation in their respective subgroups, to blend the universalistic components of

American identity with the multitude of particularisms. It is in this evolv- ing context of American pluralism that I will examine the demographic transformation of American Jewry by intermarriage between 1970 and 1990.

Unlike the craft of the historian, which proceeds from personal docu- ments, organizational records, legal documents, and even works of fiction, the craft of the sociologist-demographer (at least in the present instance) proceeds from a carefully constructed survey of population. The "facts" about the population under study are generated out of responses to a stan- dardized questionnaire, its items designed to reflect personal, ideational, religious, and other facets of individuals' lives. These facts are held to be reflective of the entire population under study due to the representative manner in which individuals are selected from the whole population to be part of the sample surveyed.

National Jewish Population Survey: 1970

Since the U.S. Census does not ask questions regarding religion, American Jews have had to depend on their own, communally sponsored surveys both for purposes of general enumeration and also for gaining any sense of proportion about the makeup of the Jewish population. Because American Jewry has virtually no central organizing structure, much less authority, it has been able to carry out surveys of itself only on a highly localized basis. Between 1960 and 1990 more than fifty different Jewish community stud- ies were conducted under the sponsorship of local Jewish federations.[4]

Due to their varied sponsorship and purposes, the differences in the time period during which each was conducted, and the differences in sur- vey methodology, these studies have proven to be but an imprecise source of information about the size and composition of the American Jewish population as a whole. They have also proven to be a weak source of infor- mation about important trends in the American Jewish experience.

To correct for these deficiencies, the Council of Jewish Federations un- dertook sponsorship, for the first time in 1970, of a National Jewish Popu- lation Survey (NJPS). That survey made use of membership lists of major Jewish organizations throughout the country as well as of names selected at random from local phone directories with the aid of a list of distinctive Jewish surnames (DJNs) to construct a national sample of about seven thousand households in which at least one adult respondent identified himself or herself as Jewish.[5]

The NJPS of 1970 found that American Jewry consists of approximately

5.4 million Jews living in about two million households, households that also include about 430,000 "non-Jews."[6]

Successive revaluations of the 1970 NJPS have determined that the American Jewish population in 1990 was somewhere between 5.5 and 6 million persons. It was a population whose overall growth was slightly diminished by low fertility, probably even less than what is required for "zero population growth" (ZPG), but enriched by immigration.

One of the most dramatic findings of the 1970 study pertained to the changing composition of the Jewish family due to intermarriage (viz., a marriage between a person of Jewish parentage and upbringing and a person of non-Jewish parentage and upbringing). The change in Jewish marital selection patterns that started in the early 1960s was abrupt (table 1). While the percentage of Jews who married persons of non-Jewish origins had remained relatively constant from the early 1940s to the end of the 1950s, it nearly *doubled*, quite suddenly, from the end of the fifties to the midsixties, and nearly *tripled* from the midsixties to the early seventies, when the first NJPS was concluded.

The percentage of non-Jewish spouses who converted to Judaism had fluctuated from a low of around 3 percent in the 1940s to a high of 26 percent in the midfifties and around 23 percent in the early seventies. This last statistic is of particular significance because it lends numerical support to the common observation of the early 1970s that the American Jewish community was experiencing an influx of "new Jews," that is, converts or "Jews by choice," as many came to prefer to be called.

TABLE 1. Jews Married to Non-Jews by Year of Marriage (in percentages)

Year	Percent	Non-Jewish Spouse	Converted? Yes	No
Pre–1924	1.7	0.3		1.4
1925–29	2.6	0.5		2.1
1930–34	3.4	0.4		3.0
1935–39	3.9	0.5		3.4
1940–44	5.9	0.2		5.7
1945–49	6.5	0.3		6.2
1950–54	5.1	0.6		4.5
1955–59	6.6	1.7		4.9
1960–64	11.6	1.7		9.8
1965–71	29.2	6.7		22.5
Average	8.1	1.3		6.8

Source: NJPS 1970; Schmelz & DellaPergola, "The Demographic Consequences of U.S. Jewish Population Trends," *American Jewish Yearbook* 83 (1983): 162 (table 10).

New Facts and Their Consequences

The relatively high proportion of conversions in intermarriages was occurring precisely at the time that the incidence of intermarriage had reached an unprecedented extent on the American Jewish scene, fueling a growing recognition that the impact of intermarriage might be more complex than previously thought. Intermarriage had been historically associated not only with religious and cultural disloyalty but also with Jewish demographic erosion. The trends of the early 1970s raised for the first time the realistic possibility that, at least in the American cultural context, intermarriage could produce a large population of converts; this possibility had profound implications not only for Jewish demography but for Jewish religious life and culture as well. Those trends and prospects led the Union of American Hebrew Congregations (UAHC), the congregational institution of the Reform branch of Judaism, whose members comprise about a third of American Jewry, to establish a Task Force on Reform Jewish Outreach at the end of the 1970s (with David W. Belin as its chairman).[7]

While Jewry throughout the world had long abandoned any programmatic effort to "missionize" to the gentiles, it never broke entirely with the creed of the prophet Isaiah, who believed that Israel shall be "a light unto the nations, that My salvation may reach the ends of the earth." David W. Belin, who has played a major role in transforming American Jewish attitudes toward "outreach to the Gentiles," founded the Jewish Outreach Institute at the end of the 1980s, citing Isaiah's vision of the day when the house of the One God would be called "a house of prayer for all peoples."

Jews as a group have never believed that the faith of Israel is a prerequisite for spiritual salvation (as Christians believe in the necessity of accepting Jesus as savior). But most Jews have believed—and most probably continue to believe—in the world-perfecting efficacy of a life lived according to the social ethics of the Torah and the Talmud. The formal break with sixteen hundred years of Jewish diffidence about welcoming converts actually occurred less than three decades ago. Its consequences, however, are just beginning to crystallize in lives of hundreds of thousands of families and in the multitude of Jewish institutions that comprise the organized Jewish community in modern America.

On December 2, 1978, Rabbi Alexander Schindler, president of the Union of American Hebrew Congregations, proposed that Jews, or at least Reform Jews, begin to "reach out" to the religiously unaffiliated, particularly those who have married Jews. "I believe," he said in his address to the

Board of Trustees of the UAHC, "that the time has come for the Reform movement . . . to launch a carefully conceived outreach program aimed at all Americans who are unchurched and who are seeking religious meaning. . . . Have we not, we Jews, water to slake the thirst and bread to sate the great hunger? And having it, are we not obliged—for our own sake as well as for those who seek that which we have—to offer it freely and proudly?"[8]

These were remarkable words for the religious leader of a community that has *not* sought converts since the fall of the Roman Empire. Schindler's words and the approach behind them were not welcome in all Jewish quarters. Traditional Jews, particularly in the Orthodox camp, were outraged at the chutzpah of a Reform rabbi proposing to "make Jews" by standards that are contrary to traditional Jewish law, known as halacha. Apart from its general hesitancy to welcome converts, halacha requires that converts "accept the yoke of the Torah," that is, obey the complex Jewish ritual system, undergo ritual immersion in a *mikvah* (a ceremony that is historically the forerunner of Christian baptism), and, in case of males, have themselves circumcised. Even as it pioneered "outreach," the Reform movement relaxed most of the traditional standards for conversion. The Conservative and Reconstructionist movements (about 40 percent of American Jewry), which soon followed the Reform lead on "outreach," also take a more lax attitude toward the bases on which they will accept converts to Judaism.

Indeed, the battles during the 1980s in the Israeli Knesset over the "Law of Return," battles over who is a Jew, were largely stimulated by Schindler's 1978 manifesto and the programs of outreach that flowed from it. In the United States one group of militant Orthodox rabbis, calling itself the Shofar Association, took out full-page advertisements in the *New York Times* and other newspapers, warning readers to beware of "Counterfeit Conversions" to Judaism. The Association of Sephardic Rabbis, another traditionalist group, placed a complete ban on any and all conversions to Judaism.[9]

Liberal and secular American Jews were frightened that Schindler's call for "outreach" would upset the entente in Jewish-Christian relations that had been in effect at least since Vatican II, an understanding that Christians would not actively seek to convert Jews. Some feared that a "Jewish outreach" program would rekindle theological anti-Semitism and possibly undermine American support for Israel.

More importantly, the masses of American Jews who were the target audience for Schindler's message did not (and do not) possess the religious zeal it takes to fuel a missionary movement. Few could see themselves as being "a light unto the nations" in any but the most secularized sense.

More personally, Jews who had married gentiles were most reluctant to up-set the emotional balance of trade that seems to regulate the handling of re-ligious and cultural differences in interfaith families.

The reaction from Protestant and Catholic quarters, Jewish fears to the contrary notwithstanding, has remained a resounding silence. As the renowned sociologist of religion Peter Berger observed in a May 1979 article in *Commentary* magazine, "The mainline Christian churches are in a state of theological exhaustion and are most unlikely to be roused from it by a little Jewish proselytizing. . . . It seems unlikely that the conversion to Ju-daism of a few lapsed Presbyterians would produce anti-Semitic reactions—except among those already so disposed. It is equally hard to imagine that irate Presbyterians [or anyone else] would launch a missionary counterof-fensive."[10]

If the Christian denominations were not roused to "defend the faith" against the call for "Jewish outreach," neither were the various branches of Judaism moved to *actively* seek out America's "unchurched" and bring them to temple. Although Schindler's own covenant created a Commission on Reform Jewish Outreach in 1983, its principal task from the very begin-ning was to *facilitate* rather than to *instigate* conversion.

Though professing philosophical support for the idea of outreach, nei-ther the Conservative nor the Reconstructionist branches of American Ju-daism made the least effort to seek out the religiously unaffiliated or even to aid those seeking entry into Judaism of their own volition.

The major secular Jewish organizations, which each year collect hun-dreds of millions of dollars for Jewish philanthropies in Israel and in the United States, and which provide such services as local community centers for education, culture and recreation, and social services for troubled fami-lies, have remained aloof from the issue. Even long-established community relations agencies, like the Anti-Defamation League of B'nai B'rith, the American Jewish Congress, and the American Jewish Committee, agencies that have many decades of experience in interfaith dialogue and coopera-tion, took a position of "benign neglect" when it came to promoting out-reach. They studied it, earnestly discussed it at conferences, maybe even hoped for it. But, in fact, they did nothing to advance it.

How, then, did it happen that by the end of the 1980s there were ap-proximately two hundred thousand adult converts to Judaism—up from only about a third as many twenty-five years earlier? How, then, did Amer-ica's Jews arrive at a change of heart on the issue of conversion, as was shown by a survey completed in 1990, and to be described below? That survey, tapping the attitudes of more than two thousand American Jewish leaders, including rabbis, synagogue presidents, Jewish community service professionals and other lay leaders, found that between 80 and 90 percent favored the conversion of the gentile partner to Judaism in cases of intermarriage. The answers to these questions are less likely to be found in the policy postures of any denomination or Jewish organization, or in programs of "Jewish outreach," than in what might be called the continuing demographic revolution in American Jewry.

National Jewish Population Survey: 1990

Twenty years after the first NJPS, the Council of Jewish Federations initiated a second national survey of American Jewry to coincide with the 1990 U.S. Census. The purpose of the new NJPS was to see how American Jewry had changed in the past two decades. The new study was also designed to correct some of the deficiencies of the previous one, arising from the reliance on lists and on distinctive Jewish surnames and from the restrictive selection criterion of choosing only respondents who report themselves to be Jewish.

The 1990 NJPS utilized a national probability sample of more than 110,000 U.S. households selected by means of random-digit telephone dialing. This method completely avoids any selection biases inherent in organizational or surname lists. Respondents thus contacted were asked to indicate their religion, whatever it might be.[11] In addition, they were asked a series of questions about their own religious background as well as about the background of other members of the household. As a result of its more sophisticated methodology, the study found that about 4 percent of those contacted had at least one Jewish parent. Of these respondents 2,441 agreed to participate in the study.

On the basis of this method the 1990 NJPS found that in the United States there were then 3.2 million households that had residing in them at least one person who was of at least some Jewish parentage. There were thus about a third as many more households in the 1990 survey with at least one person of Jewish parentage than there were in the 1970 survey.

Because of its more precise sampling methodology and its more encompassing selection criteria, the 1990 NJPS was able to identify not only more households with a Jewish connection, but also a much richer variety of ways in which people can be counted as part of the American Jewish population. Barry A. Kosmin, the research director of the 1990 NJPS, identified the key components of the American Jewish population; they are given in table 2. Kosmin further found that in terms of their distribution by type of household, of the 5.5 million persons identifying in 1990 as Jewish, 72 percent (3,980,000) were living in households that were entirely Jewish, while 26 percent (1,430,000) were living in households that also included one or more non-Jewish adults. The remaining 2 percent were to be found in institutions (hospitals, nursing homes, prisons, college dormitories, and other institutionalized living arrangements).

This broad demographic description of the American Jewish population bears clear testimony to the impact of intermarriage. As in the 1970 NJPS, intermarriage continued to be the critical variable in the transformation of the population. Indeed, probably no other trend in the population continued to change as rapidly and with such potentially profound consequences as the incidence of intermarriage.

A closer look at that trend is provided by figures 1 and 2. In 1990 only about 68 percent of all married Jewish persons were married to someone who was born or raised Jewish also (figure 1). About another 4 percent were married to a convert or "Jew by choice," and approximately 28 percent

TABLE 2. Components of U.S. Jewish Population, 1990

Population Segment	Estimated Size
Persons who were born / raised as Jews and now consider their religion Jewish	4,200,000
Persons who were born / raised as Jews, consider themselves Jewish but say they "have no religion"	1,100,000
Persons who were *not* born / raised as Jews, but now consider their religion Jewish	200,000
Total Currently Jewish	5,500,000
Persons who were born / raised as Jews, but now identify with another religion	200,000
Persons who report having at least one Jewish parent, but were raised in another religion	400,000
Total with Jewish Lineage	6,100,000
Persons who are not Jewish, but are living in a household containing one of the above	2,100,000
Total in households including one or more of the above	8,200,000

Source: Barry A. Kosmin.

were married to non-Jews. As we saw in table 1, in 1970 the NJPS found that only about 8 percent of the Jewish married population was married to someone who was not born or raised Jewish.

Figure 2 provides a graphic illustration of the quickening pace of inter-marriage over the two decades following the 1970 NJPS and helps to explain why the overall proportion of intermarriage rose from 8 percent to 31 percent. The figure indicates that the proportion of born or raised Jews marrying a spouse who was similarly born or raised Jewish slid from 89 percent among the segment of the population that married prior to 1965 to 69 percent for 1965–74 marriages, to 49 percent for 1975–84 marriages, and further still to 43 percent for post-1985 marriages.

Incidentally, it might be noted that while the 1970 NJPS found the intermarriage rates of marriage cohorts prior to 1965 to be well under 10 percent, the 1990 NJPS found that about 11 percent of that population segment had intermarried. The reason for this discrepancy is probably explained, at least in part, by simple random variation from one sample to another; but it is probably also due to the more accurate sampling and screening methodology of the later study.

Mixed Truths behind Clear Facts

If intermarriage reflects as well as portends the "radical assimilation" of Jewry, as Todd Endelman has shown for the English, and as many now fear for the Americans, then the data in figures 1 and 2 give ample cause to lament the coming decline of American Jewry. But a more detailed analysis of the social origins of the intermarriers among America's Jews and of the Jewish content of their lives subsequent to intermarriage suggests more equivocal conclusions. It suggests, too, that the long course of Jewish history will be shaped less by inexorable demographic trends than by voluntary responses that individuals, families, and the community as a whole make to those trends.

Intermarriage and Denominational Origins

The broad trend in intermarriage among America's Jews between 1970 and 1990, as shown in figure 1, masks considerable variation among the branches of Judaism. There appears to be a direct relationship between denominational origins and the likelihood of intermarriage (figure 3). Among those raised in Orthodox families, 87 percent were married to a spouse who

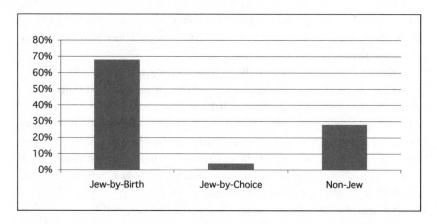

Fig. 1. Currently married Jews-by-birth, by religion of spouse

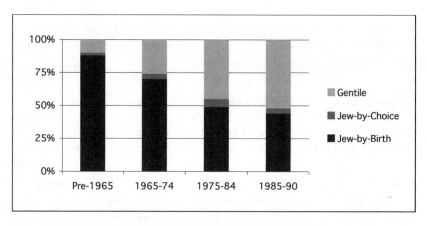

Fig. 2. Year of marriage and religion of spouse for persons born Jewish

was also born or raised Jewish; among those raised in Conservative families, 73 percent were married to such a spouse; and among those raised in
Reform families, 58 percent were married to such a spouse. When one looks
at these denominational differences in even finer detail by year of marriage, as shown in table 3, even more interesting insights emerge.

This table highlights a number of important features of the relationship
between intermarriage and denominational background. First, it reveals
that the intermarriage differences between those of different denominational background were relatively small until the mid-1970s. Indeed,
among those marrying prior to 1965, differences by denominational back-

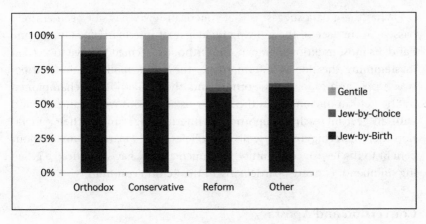

Fig. 3. Denominational background by religion of spouse

TABLE 3. Religion of Spouse by Denominational Background and by Year of Marriage (in percentages)

| | Denominational Background and Spouse's Religion | | | | | | | | |
| | Orthodox | | | Conservative | | | Reform | | |
Year	JBR	NJ	JBC	JBR	NJ	JBC	JBR	NJ	JBC
Pre–1965	96	3	1	87	12	1	91	6	
1965–74	85	12	3	74	22	4	68	31	1
1975–84	70	28	2	55	42	3	51	45	4
1985–90	73	23	4	49	48	3	36	58	6

Note: JBR = Jew born and/or raised; NJ = non-Jew; JBC = Jew by choice.

ground are under 10 percent, which might almost be explained away due to random sampling variation.

After the mid-1970s there appears to be a sharp break between those of Orthodox background and those of Conservative and Reform backgrounds. The intermarriage rate of the former increases much less than do the intermarriage rates of the latter. Among the Orthodox the rate of intermarriage actually seems to diminish from the early 1980s to 1990, while the rates of the other two groups have continued to mount. Those of Reform background, who happen to have had the highest incidence of intermarriage as well as the greatest growth in the proportion of intermarriage from the pre-1965 period to 1990, also seem to have had the highest proportion of spouses who are Jews by choice.

What these data suggest is that American Jewry has not been entirely passive in the face of the growing incidence of intermarriage. On the one hand, its most traditional branch, the Orthodox, seemed to have succeeded in stemming the tide of intermarriage; the rate actually diminished between 1985 and 1990. On the other hand, the liberal policies championed by the Reform movement in the late 1970s and 1980s went hand in hand with an ever increasing proportion of intermarriage among their generation then marrying; but these liberal policies were apparently not without benefit to the Jewish community, inasmuch as they have produced a growing number of converts, particularly in the Reform community.

Conversion and Apostasy

The issue of conversion and apostasy is far more complex than can be treated in this essay, but it is important to note several related phenomena that could fairly be attributed to the liberal "outreach" movement in Judaism that was pioneered by the Reform movement.

There were in the American Jewish population of 1990 about 200,000 "Jews by choice" and about an equal number of apostates, that is, persons who were born or raised as Jews but now profess another religion (table 2). Table 4 reveals the trend that produced those outcomes; it shows that, in fact, conversion out of Judaism among the intermarried was on the decline in the decades prior to the 1990 survey. Indeed, conversion in general was on the decline both into and out of Judaism. However, among the Reform it seemed to have increased somewhat (table 3). Moreover, the simple numerical increase of the intermarried, coupled with the more ready availability of conversion programs due to the popularity of outreach, resulted in a growing *number* of conversions into Judaism, as shown in figure 4, even as the overall *proportion* of intermarriages that involve conversions diminished.

While these numbers hardly suggest a major population infusion re-

TABLE 4. Intermarriages and Conversions (in percentages)

Year	N	No Conversion	Into Judaism	Out of Judaism
Pre–1965	94,320	44	20	36
1965–74	100,210	61	18	21
1975–84	265,380	72	13	15
1985–90	211,180	82	9	9

sulting from the phenomenon of conversion, they do suggest a modest off-setting of the common fear about intermarriage resulting in a Jewish population erosion. More importantly, these figures suggest that at least some of the danger posed by intermarriage is resolved in the favor of Jewish continuity through the choosing of Judaism by the non-Jewish partner.

The Jewishness of Jews-by-Choice

Apart from the demographic impact of conversionary intermarriages on the Jewish population, one of the more critical questions concerns their effect on the quality of Jewish life. Practically speaking, do such families produce Jewish children? Do such families participate in the life of the community? The unequivocal answer to both questions is a resounding yes. Children raised in families where the formerly non-Jewish spouse is a "Jew by choice" are overwhelmingly raised as Jews and identify as Jews. Moreover, the religious affiliations and practices of such families are consistently more identifiably Jewish than is typical for American Jews in general.

Jewish Outreach Institute Survey

In the over ten years after Rabbi Alexander Schindler boldly invigorated Jewish public discussion by calling for outreach "to Americans who are unchurched" (December 1978), many more tens of thousands of young American Jews married gentiles.[12] The relentless rise in the rate of Jewish intermarriage, from the early 1970s on through the 1980s, gave American Jewry in general and the Reform movement in particular ample opportunity to take Rabbi Schindler's revolutionary call for outreach to heart.

While a full assessment of the Reform movement's philosophy and programs of outreach is yet to be done, a survey by this writer holds important clues to some of its triumphs as well as to its remaining challenges. In the spring of 1990 a national Jewish leadership survey on attitudes pertaining to intermarriage was conducted under the auspices of the Jewish Outreach Institute. Founded by David W. Belin, former chairman of the UAHC Task Force, and later, Commission on Reform Jewish Outreach, JOI is an independent think tank and public information organization that devotes its efforts solely to issues of Jewish intermarriage. Responding to the revolutionary demographic challenges posed by intermarriage, JOI has devoted itself to serving as a forum for debate and discussion about all issues pertaining to Jewish intermarriage and as a resource for community organiza-

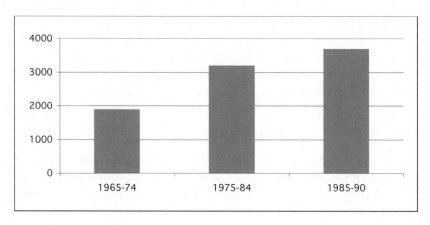

Fig. 4. Number of Jews-by-choice per year

tions, laypeople, and professionals, who might seek to help intermarried families meet their own needs within the Jewish community.

On a scale never before attempted, the survey sought out a large cross section of the major rabbinic and lay leadership groups in the organized Jewish community. The focus on leadership was chosen in the belief that the attitudes of this group will be critical in the years ahead in dealing effectively with the demographic revolution resulting from large-scale intermarriage.

The current demographic revolution, like the political and economic revolutions of the previous century, has generated intense debate within the Jewish family as well as within the organized Jewish community on issues of self-definition and relations with gentile neighbors, of standards of membership and participation in the life of the community, and of the religious status of marriages that have historically been anathema. This demographic revolution could effect a dramatic decline in size of the American Jewish population and an erosion of its cultural, religious, and even political vitality in a matter of just a few decades. Alternatively, this same social tide could also be the harbinger of creative change within the community, resulting in numerical growth as well as cultural enrichment. Which way it will turn out depends only in part on the private choices of the multitude of American Jews and their families. In large measure it will also depend on communal policies, program initiatives, and funding priorities decided on by leaders of the organized Jewish community.

Much has been made of the great conflicts that exist between the major branches or denominational movements in the Jewish community over some of the issues surrounding intermarriage. Notably, the issues of patrilineal descent and standards for conversion have been seen as key points of division between the Orthodox, Conservative, and Reform groups. The findings of this study demonstrate that tensions *within* the Conservative and Reform movements may be as great as their differences *between* each other and the Orthodox. The study hints as well at some surprising changes in Orthodox thinking that have not been generally noticed in the din of the contemporary debate. Finally, the study points to broad areas of consensus across the denominational movements and across the various groupings of leadership and laity that may well serve as the basis for cooperative activity among all segments of the Jewish community.

Of all the movements in American Judaism, the Reform movement has taken the most liberalizing steps to deal with intermarriage since the end of the 1970s. In 1979 it instituted an outreach program whose mission was to attract the gentile spouses of Jews to identify and affiliate with the Jewish community. In 1983 the movement formally reaffirmed its long-standing policy to recognize the children of gentile mothers and Jewish fathers as Jews, even if the children themselves were not converted, as long as they were raised as Jews. Though the Reform rabbinate has steadfastly discouraged intermarriage, it has left the decision whether to officiate at a wedding involving intermarriage to each individual rabbi. A large number of Reform rabbis do, in fact, officiate at intermarriages, most conditioning their officiation on a commitment by the couple to raise their children as Jews.

The positions associated with the different denominational bodies express themselves in both the attitudes of individuals and in the programs of institutions. However, the attitudes of individuals, be they laypeople or leaders, are not only shaped by or associated with the ideological stances of denominations; they are also shaped by or associated with the different institutional sectors that are the person's primary linkages to the Jewish community. One would expect that the attitudes of rabbis and synagogue lay leaders (viz., presidents and board members) are more reflective of the "official" positions of their respective denominations than the attitudes of their laity.

In addition to the synagogue the organized Jewish community also includes a complex of "secular" institutions, such as Jewish community centers, catering largely to the social, cultural, and recreational needs of American Jews, social service agencies under the umbrella of local federations. Because of the essentially nonreligious nature of these institutions, they are able to cater to a much broader cross section of the Jewish population than synagogues. Their professional staff and lay leadership are drawn from the broad spectrum of the Jewish community rather than from any particular denomination. Consequently, one would expect that the attitudes expressed by the professionals and lay leaders of Jewish communal agencies would reflect more liberalism on the aforementioned issues.

The purpose of the survey was to provide a solid base of information about the prevailing attitudes concerning the issues outlined above. It was undertaken to help all who are concerned about how the American Jewish community is to respond to the complex challenges posed by the rising rate of intermarriage.

The Method and Sample

The survey entailed a questionnaire mailed to the rabbinic and lay leaders of the American Jewish community, people whose decisions affect the quality of Jewish life, as well as to a representative sample of typical American Jews, herein referred to as "the laity." The target populations included the following:

a. pulpit rabbis in the United States in each of the major denominations;
b. synagogue presidents and board members in each of the major denominations;
c. executive directors of federations and federation agencies as well as
d. their lay chairpersons and board members;
e. executive directors of Jewish community centers and Jewish family service agencies and
f. their respective lay chairpersons and board members;
g. a selected group of "young leaders" in the Jewish community (members of the Wexner Heritage Foundation);
h. the national executive and regional board members of B'nai B'rith Women; and
i. a sample of American Jews with distinctive Jewish surnames, drawn from the local telephone directories of five major cities.

In all, a total of nine thousand questionnaires were mailed to prospective respondents between April and July 1990 in a single rolling wave. By the end of August a total of 2,179 had been returned completed, for a response rate of 24 percent.

Table 5 presents the general profile of the sample in terms of respondents' denominational identification, role in the community, gender, and age. There are several points to be emphasized. First, the sample was not designed to replicate the general demographic distribution of the American Jewish population. Rather, it was designed to yield large numbers of respondents in the designated Jewish leadership categories so as to facilitate some meaningful comparisons between various groups. Consequently, the sample overrepresents the Orthodox.

Second, because the survey was self-administered, the final sample shows a certain unevenness in response rates. For example, the thousand questionnaires sent to Reform rabbis resulted in 416 completed responses, a response rate of about 42 percent, while the thousand questionnaires sent to Conservative rabbis resulted in only 97 completed responses, a rate of just barely 10 percent. By contrast, nearly as many lay leaders of Reform synagogues (115) returned completed questionnaires as did Conservative lay leaders (141). Thus, the final sample significantly overrepresents Reform rabbis and underrepresents Conservative ones.

For the purposes of this brief report it is important to stress that the sample included 920 Reform respondents, of whom 45 percent were rabbis, 13 percent were temple presidents, 37 percent were other communal professionals or lay leaders, and the balance of 5 percent were lay men and women. As such, the sample provides a significant opportunity to examine the attitudes of various categories of Reform leadership and laity on some of the critical issues surrounding intermarriage and outreach.

TABLE 5. Profile of JOI Survey (Number of Cases)

| | Denomination | | | | |
Role in Community	Orthodox	Conservative	Reform	Other[a]	N
Rabbis	52	97	416	31	596
Synagogue lay leaders	29	141	115	15	300
Communal professionals	72	110	89	53	324
Communal board members	24	148	96	39	307
Laity	107	76	55	80	318
Combination	46	106	149	33	334
Total	330	678	920	251	2,179
	15%	31%	42%	12%	100%
Men	163	348	630	116	1,257
Women	167	330	290	135	922
Median Age	47	49	40	47	

[a]Other indicates Reconstructionists.

The Questionnaire

The survey questionnaire focused on the following key issues:

1. the acceptability of intermarriage,
2. rabbinic officiation at intermarriage,
3. the Jewishness of children from an intermarriage where the mother is not Jewish, and
4. the acceptability of one's gentile sons- or daughters-in-law in the family, and in communal institutions,
5. the willingness to encourage conversion, and
6. the willingness to expend resources of the Jewish community on programs of outreach.

At the heart of the survey was a highly "personal" story concerning a Jew, either a woman named Ruth or a man named Michael, who is about to marry a gentile spouse. Half the sample received the "Ruth" version of the questionnaire and half received the "Michael" version to see if respondents' attitudes differed significantly on the key issues depending on whether the intermarriage in question was that of a Jewish man or a Jewish woman. The objective of this approach was to get respondents to focus on the issues in direct human terms rather than in terms of abstract ideology. Terminology used in this report assumed "intermarriage" to mean marriage between Jew and gentile *without conversion.*

The "female" version of the questionnaire read as follows.

Ruth is a 35-year-old Jewish college professor. She has never been married, though she would very much like to be. Although she works in a large department with about a dozen Jewish men, nearly all are married (about half to Gentile women). The others are too old for her. The reality of her daily life is that she meets very few "eligible" Jewish bachelors. In fact, she has not had a date with a Jewish man in about three years.

At age 35 Ruth also realizes that if she is to have any children, which she wishes for very much, her "biological clock" is ticking away with alarming speed.

In the past six months Ruth met Henry, a non-Jewish colleague from another department, who is 38 years old, an agnostic of Methodist origins. The two have fallen in love, much against Ruth's early resistance, and Henry has asked Ruth to marry him.

While Ruth is eager to marry and loves Henry, who is socially, intellectually, and in virtually all other ways an ideal match, she also has very strong feelings about wanting to have a "Jewish family." "I want to have Jewish children," she says.

She was brought up in a rather traditional Conservative Jewish home. She went to Hebrew school three days a week until a year past her Bat Mitzvah. She attended a Jewish summer camp for several years during her early adolescence, spent two summers in Israel, all positive experiences that have remained wellsprings for her continuing Jewish self-identification.

She asked Henry if he would ever consider converting to Judaism. But he is resistant to the idea. He says he has not given religion much thought as an adult and has felt little need for it. On the other hand, he has a close relationship to his widowed mother, who has belonged to the same church virtually all of her adult life. He is very concerned that she would feel "crushed" by his conversion.

On the other hand, Henry is very understanding of Ruth's feelings (precisely because of his mother's attachment to her church) and has made it clear that he will be fully supportive of Ruth's raising their future children as Jews. Indeed, since the two have become "serious" about each other, Henry has gone with Ruth to her parents' home on many Friday evenings for Shabbat dinners as well as to several Friday-night and Shabbat-morning services at Ruth's synagogue. As a political scientist he has also taken an interest in some of the publications that he finds lying about in Ruth's apartment, publications she receives from some of the Jewish organizations of which she is a member. If he agreed to convert, Ruth would marry Henry in a minute. But she is also afraid that if she pushes the conversion issue too hard she will either lose him or get him to do something for which he might later resent her.

Apart from the deep emotional reasons, Ruth is also afraid that if she loses Henry she may not get a chance to marry for a long time, if at all. She may have to relinquish her hopes of ever having a child.

How would you advise your own daughter or granddaughter if she was like Ruth? What, if anything, should the Jewish community do about her marriage plans?

The "male" version was identical in all respects except that "Ruth" was replaced by "Michael" and "Henry" by "Cynthia" as the dramatis personae of the story, and all other pronouns were changed accordingly.

Findings

The questions that followed the presentation of the case focused on the six issues outlined above.

Acceptability of Intermarriage

The first of these questions involved the acceptability of intermarriage for a Jewish woman or man as described in the case. The overwhelming majority of respondents wanted to see Ruth or Michael get married, even though it means that they would be marrying a gentile spouse (figure 5). This was particularly true since there was reasonable assurance that the children would be raised as Jews. Rabbis and temple presidents were somewhat more inclined to want to see "preconditions" set for the marriage. Among the laity a substantial proportion wanted to see Ruth married even if there were no explicit prior agreement that the children born to the marriage would be raised as Jews.

In short, the preference for marriage seemed to take precedence over the resistance to intermarriage for the majority. And that preference is marked when the marriage in question involved an unmarried Jewish woman who is "thirty-something."

Interestingly, on this issue the study found a high degree of similarity between the attitudes of the Conservative and Reform laity. The overwhelming majority of both were willing to see Ruth or Michael marry even if their respective spouses did not convert to Judaism, as long as there was a commitment to raise the children as Jews. The majority of Reform laity would have Ruth marry even if there was no prior agreement to raise the children as Jews.

The similarity in attitude of Conservative and Reform laity was most noteworthy with respect to the marriage of Michael because, even if there were an agreement to raise the children as Jews, according to Conservative ideology the children of a gentile mother are not considered Jewish. The fact that so many Conservative respondents were prepared to endorse a marriage in which the couple would consider their children Jewish without the blessings of their denomination represents a telling indication of possible boundary shifts in ideology.

Rabbis are likely to be the first, and often the only, Jewish professionals to be consulted by a young couple contemplating marriage. Orthodox rabbis, like Orthodox laity, stood in sharp contrast with their non-Orthodox colleagues. A much higher percentage of them than their non-Orthodox colleagues were prepared to advise Ruth or Michael simply not to marry. Very few Conservative or Reform rabbis were prepared to advise Ruth or Michael not to marry. The majority of Conservative rabbis (53 percent and 52 percent respectively) would advise Ruth or Michael to marry if their gentile spouse was willing to convert.

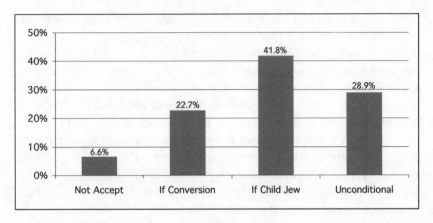

Fig. 5. Willingness to accept intermarriage

Among Reform rabbis more than half (61 percent) would advise Ruth to intermarry and nearly half (48 percent) would advise Michael to do so as well if there was agreement "to raise the children as Jews." Another surprising finding was that a little more than a quarter of Conservative rabbis (26 percent) would also advise Michael to intermarry as long as there was agreement to "raise the children as Jews." Finally, the survey found that between a quarter and a third of Reform rabbis would accept the intermarriage of Ruth or Michael without any precondition regarding children or the possible conversion of the gentile spouse.

Rabbis of all three of the major Jewish denominations were less accepting of intermarriage than the laity of their respective movements. However, there appeared to be a greater similarity on this issue at least, between laity and rabbinate among the Orthodox than among the Conservative or the Reform.

If one were to use respondents' advice to Ruth or Michael not to marry as an indicator of the most restrictive attitude toward intermarriage, one would have to say that Orthodox synagogue presidents and board members were, on the whole, less restrictive than Orthodox rabbis or even than Orthodox laity. The overwhelming majority (71 percent for presidents and 79 percent for board members) were willing to see Ruth or Michael intermarry if the gentile spouse converted.

A high degree of similarity was again found between Conservative and Reform respondents among synagogue leaders on the issue at hand. However, Conservative synagogue presidents, like Conservative rabbis, were far less likely than Conservative laity to accept the intermarriage of a Jewish male without prior agreement to raise the children as Jews. For Reform temple presidents no such difference obtained.

The professionals and lay leaders who run a variety of Jewish communal service organizations are rarely called on to advise couples contemplating intermarriage, except within their own families. However, because of their positions within the Jewish community, their attitudes are of great importance on all issues surrounding intermarriage. Except for those who are Orthodox, Jewish communal professionals on the whole seemed to be somewhat more accepting of intermarriage than rabbis, synagogue presidents, or the laity. Jewish communal professionals who identified as Conservative seemed to be more willing to accept Michael's intermarriage without any preconditions than to accept Ruth's. This, too, differentiated them sharply from Conservative rabbis or synagogue presidents, but brought them closer to the thinking of Conservative laity. A close similarity was also found in the attitudes of Conservative and Reform Jewish professionals.

Similar also were the attitudes of the board members of Jewish communal agencies. The Conservative and Reform respondents who were members of the boards of Jewish communal agencies were not only highly similar to one another, but they also seemed to be much more liberal on the issue of tolerance for the marriage of a Ruth or a Michael than rabbis or synagogue presidents in the same denominations.

The survey found that among the twelve leadership groups, Jewish communal professionals who personally identified as Reform Jews were the *most* accepting of intermarriage. The attitudes of the Reform laity were closely mirrored by those of other categories of leadership who identified as Reform—except for Reform rabbis, who tended to prefer some preconditions before they accept an intermarriage.

Rabbinic Officiation

The second issue dealt with in the survey was the highly divisive one of rabbinic officiation. First, the survey asked respondents in what type of marriage ceremony they would prefer to see a couple marry: should it be a civil ceremony only or one in which a rabbi officiates? If they prefer to see a rabbi officiate, should it entail the condition that the children be raised as Jews or should there be no conditions? If they prefer a civil ceremony, would they help to give it some Jewish content or not? Putting the question in a more personal way, respondents were then asked what they themselves would do or would like their own rabbi to do if they were approached by a couple like Ruth and her gentile fiancé or Michael and his gentile fiancée to officiate at their marriage.

Among the Conservative laity, 70 percent expressed a preference for rabbi-officiated marriage, regardless of whether the intermarrying Jew was female or male. A quarter to a third of these set no preconditions as far as the children from the marriage are concerned.

Among the Reform laity the percentage expressing a preference for rabbi-officiated marriage is even higher (88 percent and 89 percent respectively for Ruth and Michael). Between a half and two-thirds of these preferred such a marriage ceremony even without any preconditions regarding children.

These figures revealed, again, the great similarity between Conservative and Reform laity on these issues. They also indicated that as far as this issue is concerned the gender of the intermarrying Jew was of small relevance.

Asked if they would wish to see their own rabbi officiate at an interfaith marriage, about 80 percent of Reform laity said "yes," as did about 57 percent of Conservative. About 90 percent of Orthodox were unequivocally opposed (figure 6).

As one might expect, rabbis were much more likely to express a preference for marriage ceremonies that were consistent with the official positions of their denominations. Nonetheless, Conservative and Reform rabbis were far more divided among themselves about what type of marriage ceremony is *most* desirable for the intermarrying couple. Their divergences of opinion were different both from the Orthodox and from each other.

While the majority of Conservative rabbis preferred to see only a civil ceremony for the couple, regardless of whether the Jewish partner was a woman or a man, a few more were willing to help add a Jewish component to the ceremony if the intermarriage in question involved a Jewish woman rather than a man. It is also interesting to note that more rabbis indicated a preference for rabbi-officiated marriage if the intermarriage in question involves a Jewish man (10 percent) than a Jewish woman (6 percent).

If the principal division of opinion for Conservative rabbis was whether or not they should add a Jewish component to a civil ceremony, the key division of opinion in the Reform rabbinate was whether or not the marriage should be officiated by a rabbi, and, if so, conditionally or unconditionally. More than half (55 percent) of Reform rabbis indicated a preference for rabbi-officiated marriage if the intermarrying Jewish person is a woman, including 14 percent who would not insist on the condition that the children be raised Jewish. Just under half (46 percent) expressed such a preference if the intermarriage in question involved a Jewish man,

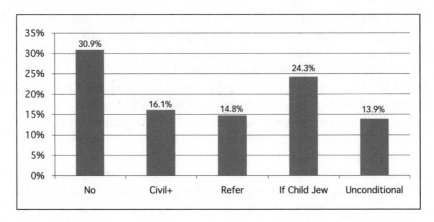

Fig. 6. Willingness to officiate

including 16 percent who would not set any preconditions about the children being raised Jewish.

How would they themselves respond to a couple seeking their officiation? About 42 percent said they would officiate at the ceremony of Ruth if there was a commitment made to raise the children Jewish, while 34 percent said they would officiate at Michael's if there was a commitment made to raise the children Jewish. The difference might indicate a residue of "matrilineal" sentiment among Reform Jews.

On the issue of rabbinic officiation, as on most of the other issues treated in the study, presidents of synagogues and members of synagogue boards proved to be quite similar to rabbis of their respective denominations. Presidents of secular Jewish organizations and members of their boards, on the other hand, proved to be far more liberal, regardless of their personal denominational identification.

Jewish communal professionals are involved primarily with the cultural, educational, political, and social service needs of the community. Indeed, there is almost something of a church-and-state separation in the attitude of Jewish communal professionals toward matters of religion. Yet Jewish communal professionals, who function in settings like community centers, family service agencies, schools, and homes for the aged, encounter vast numbers of ordinary American Jews precisely in situations where the laypeople feel most at liberty to express feelings about the Jewish tradition without regard to religious authority. Jewish communal professionals are thus often seen as a kind of "secular clergy" and are looked to for some of the pastoral and leadership functions of rabbis—but without the aura or ceremony of religion. Consequently, their opinions can be a source of considerable influence even in such matters as rabbinic officiation.

Eighty-two percent of professionals who are Reform Jews would opt for rabbinic officiation for Ruth and 63 percent for Michael if there was a commitment to raise the children as Jews. Would they want their own rabbi to officiate? Sixty-eight percent and 62 percent respectively said yes for Ruth and Michael, where there is a commitment to raise the children as Jews.

The lay leaders of Jewish communal agencies are, along with the lay leaders of synagogues, the closest to what might be called democratically elected representatives of the Jewish public. By virtue of their positions in decision-making roles, they also have the ability to affect the life of the organized Jewish community—at the very least, through their ability to determine how the agencies of the Jewish community spend and deploy their resources. Thus their opinions regarding rabbinic officiation are of paramount significance, as are their opinions on all other matters pertaining to intermarriage. The study found that they, too, were overwhelmingly in favor of rabbinic officiation.

The Jewish Identity of Children

Perhaps the central Jewish communal question concerning the children of the intermarried is whether or not they will be Jewish. To the extent that such a question refers to the person's subjective identity, it matters not what anyone else thinks. However, within the organized Jewish community the status of people does depend on whether they are regarded as Jewish by other members of the community.

Traditional Jewish law maintains that the children of Jewish mothers are automatically Jewish by birth, whether or not the father is Jewish; children who are born to a gentile mother and a Jewish father are not considered Jewish unless they are converted. The Reform and Reconstructionist movements have modified the traditional stance on this issue by regarding the child of either a Jewish mother or a Jewish father as Jewish, even if the other parent is not Jewish, as long as such a child is raised as a Jew.

How do various segments of the Jewish laity and leadership regard children of gentile mothers and Jewish fathers; that is, what is their position on the issue of "patrilineal" Jewishness? To address this issue in highly personal terms, respondents were asked, "If your Jewish son and his gentile wife were raising their children as Jews, would you consider your grandchildren Jewish?"

Between 94 and 99 percent of all Reform Jews—rabbis, leaders, and laity alike—answered this question in the affirmative. Among Conservative Jews the affirmative responses ranged from 41 percent among rabbis to 78 percent among lay men and women.

These numbers underscored the overwhelming sentiment in the organized Jewish community in the United States, except among the Orthodox, to consider children Jewish if one parent is Jewish by birth and the children are raised as Jews (figure 7).

Outreach for What: Conversion or Inclusion?

To what extent do respondents wish to see the *community* extend its boundaries to be more inclusive? Specifically, should the community attempt to attract the gentile marriage partners of Jews to convert to Judaism? Or should the gentile marriage partners of Jews be accepted as bona fide members of the Jewish community even without religious conversion?

The Reform movement, as indicated earlier, has taken the most public position on the issue of conversion by establishing the Task Force on Reform Jewish Outreach in 1979, succeeded by a permanent commission in 1983. The goal was, and remains, to attract the gentile partners of intermarrying Jews to convert. Responses to the Reform initiative have been diverse. It is in the context of such discussion that respondents were asked two questions pertaining to a situation after an intermarriage had taken place:

a. Would you want your Gentile son- or daughter-in-law to become Jewish?
b. Would you make any effort to help your Gentile son- or daughter-in-law become Jewish?

These two questions were meant to tap both the attitude of respondents toward conversion as well as their willingness to facilitate it. The response alternatives included three possibilities:

1. No to both of the questions,
2. Yes to (a), and no to (b), or
3. Yes to both (a) and (b).

These alternatives produced the following results. First and foremost, the great majority of *all* categories of respondents, across *all* denominations, were in favor of the conversion of the gentile partners of Jewish in-

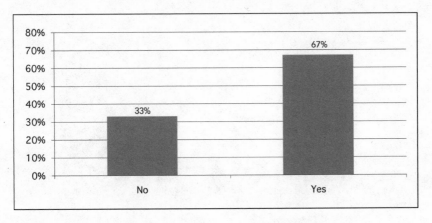

Fig. 7. Consider grandchildren Jewish

termarriers (figure 8). Respondents in *most* categories and across *all* denominations favored the conversion of the gentile regardless of the gender of the Jewish partner. This finding is particularly surprising in light of the well-established fact that conversions to Judaism are far more likely in cases where the gentile spouse is a female than where the gentile spouse is a male.

Another important surprise is that Reform laity were *less* likely to favor the conversion of their gentile sons-in-law than either Conservative or Orthodox. Reform laypeople were also *less* likely than their Conservative counterparts to favor the conversion of a gentile daughter-in-law.

In general, the laity appeared to be *less* favorably disposed to encouraging the conversion of their gentile sons- or daughters-in-law than most categories of the leadership. It was found that communal professionals who identified as Reform Jews were the *least* likely to want a gentile daughter-in-law to convert. At the other end of the spectrum, a Reform Jew who was a board member of a Jewish communal organization was the *most* likely to desire and facilitate the conversion of a gentile son- or daughter-in-law.

Generally speaking, synagogue leaders, in the persons of the rabbi or synagogue president and members of the board, were more favorably disposed to encouraging conversion than the laity. Rabbis as a group were the most favorably disposed toward conversion, regardless of denominational differences or the gender of the prospective convert. Orthodox rabbis appeared to be as far from Orthodox laity on this issue as were Reform rabbis from their laity.

Conservative respondents across all groups manifested the greatest de-

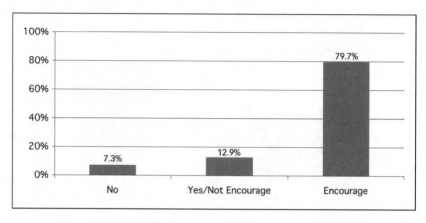

Fig. 8. Preference for conversion

gree of consensus, with the great majority in all groups expressing both the
desire for and the willingness to facilitate the conversion of a gentile son-
or daughter-in-law.

If Jews have had little experience with conversion over the last sixteen
hundred years, they have had even less experience with the inclusion of
gentiles in their communal structure. While Jews rightly take pride in being a hospitable and liberal folk, in fact, Jewish communal institutions
have not had to deal much with the question of whether to permit the inclusion of gentiles among their members, much less within their leadership
cadres. However, the high rate of intermarriage between 1970 and 1990
brought increasing numbers of families with gentile members into the orbit of synagogues, Jewish community centers, and the like. The presence of
such families within the community has raised the question of whether
and in what capacity gentiles could be members of key Jewish communal
institutions. The degree to which respondents were prepared to allow for
the inclusion of gentiles within the Jewish community was measured by
four questions:

Would you welcome your Gentile son- or daughter-in-law to:
a. membership in your synagogue,
b. membership in a Jewish organization that you support,
c. serve on board committees of your synagogue,
d. serve on board committees of a Jewish organization you support?

For purposes of a baseline comparison, respondents were also asked:

e. Would you welcome your Gentile son- or daughter-in-law to participate in Jewish holiday celebrations in your home?

Acceptance of a gentile son- or daughter-in-law in one's home was virtually universal, at least among Reform and Conservative respondents. Between 90 and 99 percent of all Reform Jews were also ready to welcome
their gentile in-laws to membership in either the synagogue or in secular
Jewish organizations. The more surprising finding was that, with the exception of Reform rabbis, the overwhelming majority of Reform Jews—
leaders, professionals, and laity alike—were quite ready to accept their gentile in-laws in positions of board leadership as well, without prior
conversion to Judaism.

Resource Allocation for Outreach to the Intermarried

The final issue addressed by the study was whether the Jewish community
ought to expend resources for programs of outreach to intermarried families. The issue was addressed by two questions:

a. Do you want to see any special programs in which the Gentile partner in an intermarriage might become better acquainted with and attracted to Judaism?
b. Do you want to see more resources devoted by the organized Jewish
   community to programs designed to help intermarried families be a
   part of the community?

Taken together, the answers to these two questions may be regarded as
an indication of how much importance respondents assigned to the issue
of formalized outreach to the intermarried by the Jewish community.

Out of the entire sample *less* than 10 percent responded in the negative
to both questions; 11 percent responded in the affirmative to only one of
the questions; and 80 percent responded affirmatively to both questions. In
other words, the idea that the organized Jewish community should sponsor
programs of outreach to the intermarried was endorsed by at least 80 percent of its leadership as well as the laity.

These figures provide robust confirmation of the fact that the great majority of American Jewish leaders at the time of the study, along with

laypeople, favored devoting at least some of the resources of the community to the development of programs of outreach to help bring the intermarried into the Jewish fold.

Conclusions

The conclusion that emerges from this analysis of the demographic revolution visited on American Jewry by intermarriage is that American Jewish leaders were not afraid of the supposed link between intermarriage and assimilation. They were further not likely to allow such a link to be forged. To the extent that the Reform call for outreach has been a message for the entire Jewish community, the findings of the JOI survey suggest that the message was widely heard and internalized.

On the controversial issue of "patrilineal descent" the overwhelming majority of Jewry—with the notable exceptions of the Orthodox and of the Conservative rabbinate and synagogue presidents—took the affirmative position: the child of a Jewish man, if raised as a Jew, is a Jew.

On the controversial issue of rabbinic officiation both the Reform and Conservative laity seemed to be at odds with their respective rabbis. In addition, the Reform rabbinate itself seemed to be deeply split on the issue.

Perhaps the greatest puzzle that emerged from the JOI study was that while the great majority of the Jewish community seemed to have heard and accepted the message of outreach, the Reform laity appeared to be the least interested in encouraging the conversion of their gentile sons- or daughters-in-law. This same group was also ready to accept their gentile in-laws into membership as well as leadership positions in synagogues and other Jewish organizations. One cannot help but wonder whether such apparently boundless tolerance is a healthy reflection of outreach or a sign of the perilous erosion of any distinguishing boundaries that define "Jewishness" within the Jewish community.

However one answers that question, by 1990 it appeared that American Jewry had taken a radically new attitude toward intermarriage and toward those non-Jews coming into the orbit of the Jewish family. The welcoming attitude toward converts in the Jewish community reflected a sense of realism about what it takes for a religious minority to survive in a free, open, and pluralistic society. The realization that intermarriage cannot be stopped led American Jews in most cases to a fundamental philosophical change, which might be summed up, albeit somewhat glibly, in a twist on an old cliché: If we can't beat 'em, let them join us.

Notes

1. Todd M. Endelman, *Radical Assimilation in English Jewish History, 1656–1945* (Bloomington: Indiana University Press, 1990), 6.

2. Endelman, *Radical Assimilation,* 6.

3. Endelman, *Radical Assimilation,* 206.

4. A full list of these studies and the data sets on which they are based has been compiled at the North American Jewish Data/Graduate Center of the City University of New York, with the support of the Council of Jewish Federations.

5. Fred Massarik, "National Jewish Population Study," *American Jewish Yearbook* 75 (1975): 296–302; Bernard Lazerwitz, "An Estimate of a Rare Population Group— the U.S. Jewish Population," *Demography,* August 1978, 389–94.

6. U. O. Schmelz and Sergio DellaPergola, "The Demographic Consequences of U.S. Jewish Population Trends," *American Jewish Yearbook* 83 (1983): 142–43.

7. David W. Belin, "A Summary of the Report of the Joint UAHC/CCAR Task Force on Reform Jewish Outreach," New York, Union of American Hebrew Congregations, 1981. In 2003, the UAHC changed its name to the Union for Reform Judaism.

8. "Outreach: The Case for a Missionary Judaism," address by Rabbi Alexander M. Schindler to the Union of American Hebrew Congregations Board of Trustees, December 2, 1978, Alexander M. Schindler Papers, Box 24, File 2, American Jewish Archives, Cincinnati.

9. "Will Counterfeit Conversions Destroy the Jewish People?" *New York Times,* October 24, 1985, advertisement taken out by Shofar Association.

10. Peter Berger, "Converting the Gentiles?" *Commentary,* May 1979, 35–36.

11. Barry A. Kosmin, "The National Survey of Religious Identification, 1989–90," copy from the Graduate School of the City University of New York, March 1991; also Ari L. Goldman, "Portrait of Religion in U.S. Holds Dozens of Surprises," *New York Times,* April 10, 1991, 1.

12. Schindler, "Outreach."

Chuppah and microphone, Los Angeles, 2006. Courtesy of Bill Aron.

Relatively Speaking: Constructing Identity in Jewish and Mixed-Married Families

Sylvia Barack Fishman

New Perceptions of Peoplehood

Concepts such as ethnicity and religious difference, which once seemed determining and solidly significant factors in people's lives, are today "a matter not of essence but of choices," a voluntary and perhaps even an "artificial" construct.[1] It is the individual, rather than the group, who decides what his or her affiliation—or lack of affiliation—with a particular group may mean. Individuals also differ in their interpretations of the character and significance of the social groups themselves. This individualism or personalism in understanding the meanings of social groups has been ratified by many social scientists. During the past century, cultural historians have transformed the way communal stories are interpreted. Rather than depicting the evolution of a particular national, ethnic, or religious group as "a grand narrative in which the many individuals are submerged," some currently influential methods focus on the "micro" picture, a multiplicity of small stories, "a multifaceted flow with many individual centers."[2]

A preference for analyzing social change through myriad small details, called "thick description" and advocated by cultural anthropologist Clifford Geertz, fits felicitously in some ways into contemporary social scientific analysis of the American Jewish community.[3] This essay explores my research on the internal dynamics in American Jewish and mixed-married families, based on 254 in-depth interviews with husbands and wives in four

This essay was originally presented on October 17, 2001, at the Jean and Samuel Frankel Center for Judaic Studies, University of Michigan, Ann Arbor.

American locations (New England, New Jersey, Atlanta, and Denver) augmented by four focus group discussions with teenagers growing up in mixed-married households. I analyze the texts provided by these many and diverse individual stories, as each of the informants has interpreted his or her own life, behaviors, and goals.[4]

I am especially interested in the ways in which husbands and wives negotiate the ethnic and religious character of their households, the ways in which these negotiations change over time, and the impact of extended family members and friends on these continuing negotiations. I asked my informants to recall both the quotidian and the life-transforming, to describe their daily, weekly, and yearly routines. I asked them many questions about the ways in which they interpret the events and decisions in their own lives.

But sometimes my interpretations of informants' lives differ from the ways in which they understand themselves. When ethnoreligious societies seemed relatively defined and stable, social scientists measured characteristics through formally defined yardsticks, often derived from the behaviors and attitudes that characterized these particular societies in the past. However, today, in our times of enormous societal flux and change, it is much less clear what particular behaviors may mean—what their significance is to the individuals, societies and families who do or do not perform them. Today, it is not a given that the social scientist is "objective," and has authority beyond that of his informants to interpret and analyze observations. The task of the social scientist becomes especially complicated under these conditions.

In the current intellectual climate the semiotics or meaning of behaviors—rather than the behaviors themselves—have become the primary focus of exploration for some of my colleagues. Society, and the "social structures and processes that were seen as the determinants of a society . . . are now increasingly viewed rather as products of culture."[5] Cultures are themselves defined by networks of meanings, in some ways not appreciably different from those in a literary text. In Geertz's words:

> Man is an animal suspended in webs of significance he himself has spun. I take culture to be those webs, and the analysis of it to be therefore not an experimental science in search of law but an interpretive one in search of meaning.[6]

Like literary texts, the significance of social behaviors is viewed as depending on individual interpretation. In some cases, this reluctance to assign meaning or value to particular behaviors veers into relativism: what a behavior means, whether it is appropriate or good, depends on the way it is seen, understood, and interpreted. Later in this essay, I suggest that tendencies toward relativism pervading some academic circles are also prevalent in liberal Western society at large, and have played a significant role in the decline of certain traditional Jewish family and communal values once regarded as self-evident. I argue that these tendencies have contributed to the erosion of "tribal" feelings of loyalty among Jews, both on a personal and on a communal level. Finally, I show that an environment of relativism has also had an impact on the exclusively Jewish ethnoreligious commitments in some Jewish and especially mixed-married households.

Constructing American Hybrid Identities

Most American Jews share the liberal and tolerant worldview characteristic of the highly educated Americans in their socioeconomic cohort. Many liberal Americans believe that all conflicts can be solved through compromise and negotiation, that every situation can be seen in another way, and that tribal appeals are almost always suspect. Chester Finn reports that educators are made profoundly uncomfortable even by the word *patriotism,* and that they do not educate children and teenagers to understand the need for it:

> In the case of September 11 . . . assumptions forged during the Vietnam conflict and then tempered by the postmodern doctrines of multiculturalism and diversity, have overwhelmingly shaped the pedagogical and curricular guidelines for elementary and secondary school teachers that has poured forth from educational organizations, state and federal agencies, and a plethora of commercial groups.[7]

If highly educated liberal Americans have trouble articulating an absolute loyalty to their own country, it should not be surprising that within this liberal ethos the attempt of a particular ethnoreligious group to promote endogamy and to advocate against exogamy—marriage across ethnoreligious boundaries—can appear to be a racist enterprise. American Jews have been influenced by the notion that advocating for Jews to marry Jews may be somehow un-American.

In an October 14, 2001, *New York Times* column, for example, "The Ethicist" Randy Cohen was asked the following question:

Some friends and I use a Jewish Internet dating service. When I mentioned an ad placed by a Hispanic woman who likes to date Jewish men,
a female friend of mine remarked that "they should stay away from our
stuff." I argued that the Hispanic woman was upfront about her ancestry and so did nothing wrong. Please shed some light.[8]

This question and Cohen's multilayered response reward close attention and deep description. Cohen transmits a very interesting gender difference in responses to this question. The male questioner assumes that
any honest American has the right to use the Jewish Internet dating service. However, the female friend is upset with the idea that those eligible
Jewish men who use the dating service looking for Jewish women—a category of persons reputedly in short supply—may be captured by an enter-
prising non-Jewish woman.

Cohen's answer to the questioner is instructive. The first paragraph of
Cohen's answer reflects the current assumptions of the great majority of
American Jews that intermarriage is inevitable, and not necessarily prob-
lematic, in an open society.

You can, of course, be Hispanic and Jewish—Jews in Barcelona do it
every day—and if that's the case here, problem solved. But even if the
controversial Hispanic woman is a gentile, I still see no problem. She
has been open about her background and her desires. (Although she
may want to examine the feelings that draw her to a group rather than
a particular individual.) If another participant in the dating service finds
her appealing, then the two of them can rendezvous. It's not for some
third party to veto that decision. The Jewish dating service should be a
way for people who wish to date Jews—perhaps primarily but not exclusively other Jews—to do so; it ought not be a segregated Semite preserve.[9]

Recent research shows that fewer than half of American Jews today actively oppose mixed marriage. According to a study recently published by
the American Jewish Committee, when asked whether "it would pain me if
my child married a gentile," only 39 percent agreed with this statement, including 84 percent of Orthodox, 57 percent of Conservative, 27 percent of
Reform, and 19 percent of "Just Jewish" respondents. Of Jews who said that
Jewishness was "very important" to their lives, only 54 percent said it
would pain them to have a child marry a gentile.[10]

However, the second paragraph of Randy Cohen's answer effectively articulates the reasons why many American Jews are concerned about the impact of mixed marriage on Jewish families and communities:

> Needless to say, a whites-only dating service would be repugnant, trading on racism, on superficial characteristics over which people have no control. By contrast, a Jewish dating service defines people by their behavior and beliefs, by something volitional. In theory, anyone can choose to embrace Jewish customs and to search for a like-minded spouse with whom to establish a Jewish household and live according to Jewish precepts. That is, members of a minority culture, eager to preserve and practice a way of life, may honorably seek each other out online or in person. That isn't to say, however, that you may impose this belief on other people. So let the Hispanic woman and her Jewish suitors dance the night away.[11]

Note that Cohen begins this paragraph by distancing Jewish concern about endogamy from racism. The concept of Jewish peoplehood is fraught with discomfort for most American Jews today, especially outside the Orthodox world. The traditional Jewish construct of the "chosen people," repeatedly articulated in biblical texts and foundational to Jewish thinking for much of Jewish history, has been rejected or explained out of recognition by many American Jewish thinkers, as well as ordinary American Jews. Thus, although many would agree with a definition of ethnic groups as "a collectivity within a larger society having real or putative common ancestry, memories of a shared historical past, and a cultural focus on one or more symbolic elements defined as the epitome of their peoplehood,"[12] Cohen's formulation skirts ethnicity by *descent*—that is, an ethnicity that comes to a person by virtue of their forebears, and emphasizes ethnicity by *consent*—an ethnic group identification entered into voluntarily.

Conceptions of ethnicity in general (not just Jewish ethnicity) have undergone profound change during the second half of the twentieth century. Scholars utilize constructionist theories of ethnicity, which view ethnic identity as fluid, continually being negotiated and renegotiated.[13] They propose that race and ethnicity are social constructs, perceptions of difference created by persons both internal and external to the perceived group. Some social scientists emphasize the importance of boundaries in creating discrete ethnic groups.[14] To use a homely metaphor, ethnographers who emphasize boundaries see ethnicity as a kind of shopping cart being pushed across time and space; the contents of the shopping cart keep changing, although the cart retains the same name, and thus its distinctiveness.[15] In contrast, another group of social scientists emphasizes "the nuclei, the centers of ethnic culture," rather than the boundaries, which may be porous and changing. According to this theory, it is exactly the "cultural stuff" at the heart of ethnic group life that maintains dynamic group distinctiveness and cohesiveness.[16] Thinking about these two theories of ethnic distinctiveness and referring back to the dilemma posed to ethics columnist Randy Cohen, we see that Cohen emphasizes the cultural nucleus of Jewishness, and accepts the boundaries of peoplehood mostly as a way of protecting "a minority culture, eager to protect and preserve a way of life."

Herbert J. Gans noted decades ago that for Jews, as for other white ethnic Americans, ethnicity is largely voluntary and symbolic, rather than externally enforced. The voluntary, symbolic nature of ethnicity has become more pronounced as the years pass and educational, occupational, and social boundaries within American society have become increasingly permeable.[17]

The resilience of ethnic appeal over the decades came as a surprise to some assimilationists, who expected ethnic differences to disappear. However, as Nathan Glazer and Daniel Patrick Moynihan and later Michael Novak noted, ethnicity, instead of disappearing, seemed to be "unmeltable."[18] Richard Alba demonstrated that interest in ethnicity is actually greater and more persistent among highly educated and socioeconomically successful white ethnic Americans; the more educated and successful the white ethnic American, the more interested she is in passing ethnic identity along to the next generation of children.[19]

However, as Mary Waters has illustrated in her study of diverse American ethnic Roman Catholics, American ethnic identification and behavior is more and more selective, multisourced, and idiosyncratic to individual family units. In other words, any one family may well combine elements of Italian, Irish, German and Polish customs and behaviors, for example. As Waters demonstrates, children within that household will often think of their idiosyncratic, hybrid family traditions as classically derived from one ethnic tradition, "typically Irish," or "typically Italian." Moreover, children will pick out the ethnicity they think of as being more socially desirable in their peer group to describe their own family tradition.[20]

Romeo, Juliet, and Mixed Marriage in America

It is most appropriate to view Jewish behaviors within the context of other hyphenated American ethnoreligious groups. The Jewish experience in

America has been and continues to be strikingly, distinctively American, as American Jews coalesce Jewish and American values and behaviors to produce hybrid American Judaisms. American Jewish life's multicultural ethos and permeable boundaries—while they have emerged gradually—represent a new and challenging chapter in Jewish history, and one for which the past offers few clear precedents. In the United States today Judaism as a faith tradition has been strikingly Americanized, creating commonalities and bridges between Jews and non-Jews who occupy the same socioeconomic, educational, geographical, and political milieus. Contemporary American Jews routinely merge American and Jewish ideas, incorporating American liberal values such as free choice, universalism, individualism, and pluralism into their understanding of *both* Jewish *and* American identity. Indeed, not only have American Jews created a coalesced American Judaism, they have also created a distinctly Jewish notion of what defines the "true" America, in their own image.[21] My research on mixed-married families, families whose ethnic and religious heritage makes them "Jewish and something else," focuses on the specific ways these couples construct the ethnic and religious identities of their households, taking coalescence several important steps further.

Mixed marriage is both a symbol and a result of the voluntary nature of ethnoreligious identification in America. To many, America's promises are dramatically symbolized and fulfilled by marriage across religious and ethnic lines. Americans following their own hearts, unfettered by familial and communal preferences, illustrate the triumph of Romantic values such as the sanctity of the individual and the sacredness of personal passions—the very incarnation of life, liberty, and the pursuit of happiness. Religious bigotries and ethnic hatreds seem conquered when Americans whose grandparents were Irish or Italian Catholics, Orthodox Greeks, English Episcopalians, Chinese Buddhists, or Lithuanian Jews walk down the aisle, gazing at each other with love. The proliferation of mixed marriages, moreover, helps to diminish cultural mistrust and hatred, as family members from diverse backgrounds get to know and care about each other. In what seems to many observers a beneficent cycle, Americans marry across ethnic and religious lines because boundaries have become so permeable—and boundaries become ever more permeable as more Americans create interethnic and interfaith homes.

Opposing mixed marriages, as a result, carries the odor of demanding that Romeo and Juliet choose between the Montagues and the Capulets. Compared to prior social expectations, relatively few Americans today believe that ethnic and religious choices are necessary, because contemporary American culture encourages individuals and families to combine multiple heritages. Americans share in the festive events and symbols of many cultures: on St. Patrick's Day we can all be a "little bit Irish" through "the wearin' of the green." Eastern religious strategies are incorporated into Western lives through yoga and meditation tapes. Protestant churches sponsor seder programs for their congregants. Unlike societies in previous times, and in less tolerant countries today, marriage across ethnic and religious lines is not automatically viewed as apostasy or cultural betrayal. Jews can marry Christians without the baptism of one, or the circumcision of the other. Intermarriages are viewed by some as doubling, rather than diminishing, the family's cultural capital.

American Jewish resistance to intermarriage has in recent years been replaced by the view that intermarriage is normative, as we have noted earlier. Despite the pluralism and multicultural openness of American society, however, many observers worry about the impact of mixed marriage on American Jews and Judaism. The 1990 National Jewish Population Survey showed that the proportion of Jews in America is static or falling. This stagnation of the Jewish population arises from a combination of factors including a relatively small number of Jewish immigrants; and the pronounced tendency of American Jews to postpone marriage and childbirth, and to have fewer than two children per family, a fertility rate demographers consider well below replacement level. The 1990 NJPS also revealed a recent Jewish mixed-marriage rate (marriages in the five years prior to the survey) of about 50 percent. Of these mixed-married families, fewer than one-third said they were raising their children as Jews.[22] Looking at the shrinking proportion of Jews in America, the rising rate of recent mixed marriages, and the dramatic preference in mixed-married households for not raising Jewish children, some Jewish communal and religious leaders warned that the blessings of multiculturalism and pluralism might well cause a distinctive, coherent ethnoreligious Jewish culture to be virtually loved out of existence in twenty-first-century America.

Within America's open society, with ethnoreligious distinctiveness waning, large numbers of Jews have for decades been defined as much by what they were *not* as by what they were. Thus, Robert Bellah wrote in 1987, "It is part of Jewish identity and the maintenance of the boundaries of the Jewish community to deny that Jesus is the Christ, the Messiah."[23] Peter Medding further suggested that "paradoxically, as the religious aspects of

Judaism have become relatively less central to the core of Jewish identity, and shared feelings have become more important, being *not* Christian has taken on greater salience as a defining element of Jewishness."[24]

Negotiating Two-Heritage Households

Is "not being Christian" still a defining characteristic of the religious identity of children growing up in mixed-married households? This is just one of many questions we face in our attempt to understand American Jewish families today. One important piece of the answer lies in the perhaps surprising fact that despite popular messages that blur religious differences, only a tiny minority of in-married American Jewish families celebrate non-Jewish holidays. The incidence of Christmas celebrations in in-married Jewish households has actually declined over the past few decades, probably as a result of the increased acceptability of Jews and Judaism in mainstream American settings.

However, in mixed-married households, in dramatic contrast, the intermingling of holidays from the faith traditions of both parents is one of the most prevalent characteristics. Most mixed-married families report some connection to both Christmas and Hanukkah, to both Passover and Easter. How these dual connections are handled depends on the way the household has designed its religious identity.

The great majority of mixed-marrieds incorporate substantial Christian celebrations into their family life. In our sample of predominantly Jewish-identified mixed-married households, nearly nine out of ten families talked about participating in Christian activities of some sort during the year. Christmas celebrations were the most frequently reported Christian activity in mixed-married families, with Easter celebrations second. In contrast, among conversionary households, fewer than 10 percent celebrated Christmas at home. No conversionary families in our sample went to church, and about half celebrated in the homes of extended family members. Among in-married households in our study, only 4 percent had Christmas celebrations at home.

In holiday celebrations, as in other aspects of family religious life, the gender of the Jewish parent made a difference. In households with a Christian mother, Christmas was celebrated at home in three-quarters of the households, and in church as well as home in 22 percent of the households. In mixed-married households with a Jewish mother, the percentage celebrating Christmas at home was 72 percent, but fewer than 1 percent went to church. In mixed-married households with a Jewish mother, 20 percent had no Christmas celebration in their home; but with a Jewish father, only 1 percent had no Christmas celebration in their home.

Husbands and wives in mixed-married families often feel they are involved in an ongoing process of negotiating and juggling "yours, mine, and ours" religious identities. Concerns about these issues become especially focal in the yearly cycle of religious holiday observances, during the time period when formal religious schooling may be initiated, when the family makes decisions about institutional affiliations, and when individuals encounter joyous or sad life cycle events.

Yiddishkeit versus Menshlichkeit?

One of the most striking aspects of our interview data was the empathy of spouses whose religion held the primary position in the household toward those whose religion was relegated to secondary status, especially when Judaism was the official family religion. Jewish spouses often said they felt as though their Jewish concerns wrestled with their love and compassion for their Christian husbands and their in-law families—as though there was a battle between *yiddishkeit* and *menshlichkeit*. Spouses who had insisted before marriage that their children must be brought up as Jews often became more and more concerned as the years passed that they were not being "fair" and had "taken too much away" from their fellow-traveler spouses. This guilty anxiety often became a vehicle for introducing or reintroducing Christian symbols into the household.

Thus, in households where both spouses had initially agreed that they would celebrate only Jewish holidays in their own house, and would celebrate Christian holidays in the homes of their Christian extended family, these resolutions often broke down gradually over the years. One of the most common reasons for the reintroduction of Christian festivities was the aging of the non-Jewish grandparents. As one Jewish wife put it:

> I really love my mother-in-law. Every year we went to her house for Christmas and Easter dinners, and it was a special time for the whole family. But now she's older and it's too hard for her to do it. So I said I would do Christmas and Easter dinner in my house for the family. So every year now I make the Easter ham. Except one year when Easter came out on Passover. That year I still had Easter dinner in my house, but I didn't make the ham.

Strikingly, in many cases mixed-married spouses felt like their Jewish loyalties were at war with their empathetic family feelings. If they "deprived" their Christian spouse of Christian symbols, they felt guilty. On the other hand, if they reincorporated Christian symbols they had been determined not to incorporate, they also felt guilty.

Just as the ethnically hybrid Roman Catholic families in Mary Waters's study often functioned in the absence of "context with a wider ethnic community beyond the family," and communal standards for behavior, therefore developing very idiosyncratic familial patterns of behavior,[25] mixed-married families in my study also constructed idiosyncratic family traditions that blended diverse religious elements. In both cases, fewer families than might be expected want to have no ethnoreligious celebrations in their household. It is important to them as Americans to include ethnic and religious symbols and ceremonies, even if the symbols and ceremonies they choose blend two or more religious cultures.

Speaking Up for Jewish Families

Observers of the American Jewish community often attribute the rise in mixed marriage to the overwhelming pattern of Jewish youth attending colleges, and graduate and professional schools away from home. The assumption underlying this perception is that teenaged Jews do not date non-Jews when they are under parental supervision, and it is only when they leave home that they initiate romantic relationships with Christian partners. However, most Jews married to non-Jews who participated in our study said they had mixed friendship groups and dating partners while they lived at home, under their parents' supervision.

We can recall the diffidence with which Randy Cohen answered his questioners in his *New York Times* column when we note that among mixed-married participants in my study, 62 percent said their parents had made no comments to them discouraging them from marrying outside the faith. This absence of parental communication vis-à-vis dating and marriage was more pronounced among Jewish men married to non-Jewish women than among Jewish women married to non-Jewish men. Even when informants had contemplated college choices, few of their parents made it clear that they wanted their children to attend schools where they could meet and marry Jews, or that marrying Jews was an important family priority.

Where parents did attempt to guide their children, however, there was a positive relationship between parental guidance and the type of marriage entered into. One-third of both in-married and conversionary participants said their parents had strongly discouraged them from marrying out of the faith, and another 29 percent of in-married and 17 percent of conversionary households said their parents had mildly discouraged them. Only 38 percent of in-married participants said their parents had not commented on dating, marriage, and religion. Interestingly, although American parents often say they are nervous about advising their children on dating practices because they fear a backlash, negative reactions to discouragement of mixed marriage was reported in fewer than 5 percent of cases.

Socioeconomic issues were unpleasantly linked to ethnoreligious considerations according to some informants, who said that their parents' standard "speech" about dating Jewish girls was heavily tied into a kind of bourgeois package that included the Jewish girl, her parents' money, professional career direction, and so on. According to these respondents, this Jewish-girl-as-a-middle-class-norm undercut the significance of a Jewish marriage as a value in and of itself. As one respondent put it, by marrying a Jewish princess he could become himself a "crown" prince:

> You know, the standard parental thing. How did they express it? My mother was sort of a social climber, so she was always—she always had this fantasy of finding some, you know, wealthy Jewish princess or something, I think. That would sort of—what's the word—serendipitously elevate her status somehow. Marry a crown.

Another described his parents' directives as a Jewish version of the all-American dream:

> I knew what they wanted. They wanted me to be a doctor and they wanted me to marry a Jewish girl and they wanted me to have two-and-a-half kids and have a picket fence and probably live in another two-family house right next door to their house.

In comparison, in-married respondents recalled their parents speaking to them about Jewish homes and Jewish values in very direct ways that were not linked to economic and social mobility issues:

> They were visibly pleased for me to have a Jewish girlfriend, bring her to dinner, bring her to Friday nights. And as it was, it had become pretty clear pretty quickly to anybody I dated that I couldn't go out Fridays, couldn't do much of anything until Saturday night. And that always

means because I'm Jewish and my dad wouldn't let me out on those days and so on and so forth. Those things never lasted too long.

In contrast to these families in which resistance to interdating was part of a multifaceted, Jewishly active environment, according to many respondents, parental laissez-faire attitudes that were commonplace about their dating patterns extended to the prospect of mixed marriage as well. Indeed, even when parents were unhappy or agitated about an upcoming mixed marriage, they did not openly encourage as yet unattached siblings to date Jews exclusively.

American Judeo-Christian Households

Just as children growing up in other mixed ethnoreligious American households come to accept as normative the blended traditions of their families, the American construct "Judeo-Christian tradition" is not an abstraction for many children of mixed marriage. While some of these children will eventually choose to become exclusively Jewish, the great majority of the children of mixed marriage bring their Judeo-Christian outlooks with them into their new homes and as they participate in American Jewish communal life. Moreover, individuals and families go through ethnoreligious evolutions, responding to internal and external changes in their own lives, and in the families and various communities around them.

Our study has shown that many, perhaps most, potential marital partners in interfaith relationships explore questions of household religion as soon as they perceive their relationship to be "serious" and heading toward marriage. Whether these first negotiations take place before marriage, or when the couple contemplates or embarks on childbearing, many sensitive issues are involved. Some couples decide to raise children with two faiths, some with no faith, some with both, and some with one faith only. Later, the birth of a child, the death of a parent, a shake-up in the workplace, the divorce of a friend—any of these events can and do precipitate spiritual responses and reevaluations of decisions on the religious character of the home. In some cases, these lead to a deepening attachment to Judaism and to the Jewish community. In other cases, the resoluteness of early decisions about the Jewish character of the household gives way to a variety of new negotiations. For mixed-married couples who have decided to raise children as Jews only, it is difficult to maintain an exclusively Jewish household environment.

These nearly inevitable Christian aspects of mixed-married family life stand in contrast to families in which the born-Christian partner has become a Jew by choice. In conversionary households, Jews by choice usually feel that they and their households are unambivalently Jewish. Jews by choice often announce to their own Christian parents and siblings: "We are a family. Please don't send our children Christmas presents or Easter baskets." In mixed-married households that have pledged to raise their children as Jews, however, it is much more difficult for parents to maintain an unambivalently Jewish profile. As long as one spouse does not consider him- or herself to be a Jew, it is hard to exclude Christian rituals, ceremonies, and culture from family life.

Many non-Jewish spouses cheerfully participate in their Jewish children's holiday celebrations. However, a substantial proportion find themselves feeling increasingly resentful about the fact that their children are growing up in a different faith tradition than theirs. Even when they say they have been warmly received by family members and Jewish synagogue communities, non-Jewish spouses often find themselves longing for their own traditions in their own households. Some report that they are disturbed by their children's use of Hebrew in household and holiday prayers—and yet they have decided that they do not wish to learn Hebrew themselves. Some say they harbor deep distaste for organized religion, and look forward to the day their children are old enough to share these feelings.

Adolescent children grow close to extended-family members on the basis of many factors, including their own personality and intellectual and extracurricular interests. Non-Jewish grandparents, aunts, uncles and cousins become admired role models for many raised-Jewish children in mixed-married households.

Again, the comparison with conversionary households is useful. Although conversionary families also have a full set of Christian extended-family members, their relationship to them is different. They face their beloved Christian family with unambiguously Jewish eyes. As one Jew by choice commented:

> We tell our children that grandma and grandpa's holidays belong to them only, just like a person's birthday belongs to them only. So we'll go there to visit before or after Christmas, not on Christmas, that's not our holiday. And if grandma gives them a goody bag to take home, well that's like taking a goody bag home from someone else's party. We can have the goodies, but the party doesn't belong to us.

Religious Integrity and Inclusiveness

One important coalesced American Jewish value is inclusiveness. American Jews pride themselves on their empathy for, and feelings of solidarity with, all people of goodwill, perhaps because Jews historically have frequently been vilified as "exclusive" or "clannish," and because Jews have suffered historically by being excluded, not only in Europe, but in the United States until relatively recently as well. As a result, as we noted earlier, the tribal passages in the Hebrew Bible or Jewish liturgy, and the historical Jewish concept of a "chosen people," make many American Jews uneasy. Although some still retain a feeling that there is an essential core of Jewishness that makes Jews more comfortable with each other than with non-Jews, this attitude is far more prevalent among older American Jews than among their children and grandchildren.

This American Jewish predilection for inclusiveness is important in analyzing personal and communal responses to rising rates of mixed marriage, since it makes inclusiveness feel more "comfortable" to most American Jews than exclusiveness. When unprecedentedly high rates of mixed marriage are placed in the context of the delight and pride American Jews feel about their perceptions that Jewish tradition harmonizes with American ideals, the stage is set for the powerful appeal of the "inclusivity and outreach" message.

Another very important American Jewish value is egalitarianism. Although historical Jewish societies were stratified into numerous hierarchies, including gender hierarchies, many American Jews believe that religiously based social inequality is unacceptable, even repugnant. In part because of this coalesced American Jewish preference for religious egalitarianism, and in part because of the demographic fact that large numbers of Jewish men had married non-Jewish women, the American Reform movement rejected the principle of matrilineal descent, declaring that either patrilineal or matrilineal descent could make a child Jewish. This decision was hailed by many as more fair and just, since it did not discriminate against Jewish men in favor of Jewish women.

Both statistical studies and my interviews, however, strongly indicate that the cultural and religious impact of a Jewish mother in a home is greater than that of the father. The likelihood that children will be raised completely as Jews, rather than partly as Jews and partly as non-Jews, and the type and extent of Jewish education received by children, as well as terms of holiday observances and social networks, depend greatly on the gender of the Jewish parent.

It should also be noted that the principle of matrilineal descent favored and privileged Jewish women as wives, giving them somewhat of an advantage in the marriage "market." This was an important factor, because Jewish women in the United States today are delegitimated and disadvantaged by the negative stereotypes prevalent in contemporary American media, film, literature, and popular culture.[26] These stereotypes are deeply "nonegalitarian" in that they target Jewish women far more than Jewish men. The fact that Jewish women have lost the protection afforded by matrilineal descent, and yet are still subject to American cultural negative stereotypes, contributes to rising rates of mixed marriage.

A paradoxical trend in American culture today is the celebration of ethnoreligious differences as testimony to the sameness of all Americans. Americans share the experience of deriving from diverse, particularistic heritages, and the contemporary liberal ethos simultaneously accentuates and transcends differences. Valorizing the differences that unite, liberal Americans are fond of emphasizing commonalities that seem to span ethnic and religious boundaries.

Striking evidence of this ethos of unification through difference is found in department store decorations, magazine illustrations, and in a new species of greeting cards now proliferating in stationary shops, exemplified most directly in the "Mixed Blessings Greeting Card Company." One card, for example, shows children who have respectively lit the solstice-based lights of Christmas, Hanukkah, and Kwanzaa holding hands in front of their tribal candelabras. The message inside this card prays that the season of lights will "unite us all." These pictures, illustrations, decorations, and cards convey the impression that the messages of all religions are the same, only the packaging differs.

However, research on American Jewish life shows that distinctiveness is a necessary attribute for the ethnoreligious survival of minorities in an open society. The very NJPS data sometimes cited to claim that mixed marriage is inevitable clearly show that mixed marriage does not occur on a random basis. In-marriage and mixed marriage occur according to clear patterns. In-marriage is closely correlated to three factors: (1) Jewish education, both formal and informal, which is intensive and continues through the teen years; (2) a Jewishly connected home, which provides multifaceted Jewish experiences in family settings; and 3) Jewish friendship circles. Each of these alone, and exponentially all three of these together, dramatically predispose an individual to marry a Jew and to establish a new Jewish family. In other words, the more Jewishly connected the parental family and the more Jewish education an individual receives, the more likely that individual is to establish a Jewishly connected home of his or her own.

We can usefully look to the ethnographic theories we spoke of earlier in analyzing Jewish communal approaches. Some policy planners take the approach that the most effective strategy is to reinforce the nucleus of Jewish life. Others take the approach that the community must reinforce its boundaries. The "nucleus" people believe that if they make Jewish experience and education compelling enough, they can keep the boundaries around Jewish identification low. Those who favor more well-maintained boundaries feel that the permeability of boundaries is in itself problematic, and in many ways a betrayal of historical Jewish behaviors.

Ultimately, American Jewish communities will create their own list of priorities, either through a process of thoughtful deliberation or through default and indecision. The inclusive model is currently attractive because of its "political correctness," since it avoids boundary maintenance and judgmentalism—except against those who themselves seem to be passing judgment.[27] The alternate communal strategy for dealing with the challenges of rising rates of mixed marriage calls for focusing communal will into the intensification of a broad spectrum of identifiably Jewish cognitive and experiential opportunities for Jews of all ages. This strategy is opposed by some because it calls for painful reallocation of communal resources and difficult assessments as to what comprises authentic Jewish activities and attitudes. Moreover, such an emphasis would almost inevitably be accompanied by some shrinkage in terms of computable Jewish population size. Serious economic and political ramifications accompany a reduction in the number of persons who can be counted as Jews, and some observers are frightened at the prospect of a smaller Jewish community.

There is no doubt that the dramatic increase in the proportion of mixed-married households has already had a profound effect on communal psychology among both Jews and non-Jews. On a very positive note, the acceptance of Jews and Jewishness in American culture is surely due, at least in part, to the fact that numerous Christian families include Jewish members. Conversely, most American Jewish families include some mixed-married members.

Jewish communal laypeople and leaders alike are concerned about the occurrence and ramifications of mixed marriage in their own families. Their concern is not based on "racism," as is sometimes alleged, but on familial and communal issues of continuity, popularly articulated in the question, "Will my grandchildren be Jewish?" As we have seen, by seeking to transmit what *New York Times* ethicist Randy Cohen calls their "minority culture" and their Jewish "way of life" to the next generation, American Jews today are responding not only to the models of Jewish history, but also to the models provided by their non-Jewish ethnic neighbors. The contemporary American Jewish quest for cultural continuity is, to an extent not often realized, an articulation not only of traditional, historical Jewish values but of prevalent American values as well.

Notes

1. Tamar Jacoby, "An End to Counting by Race?" in *Commentary,* June 2001, 39.

2. Georg G. Iggers, *Historiography in the Twentieth Century: From Scientific Objectivity to the Postmodern Challenge* (Hanover, NH: Wesleyan University Press, 1997), 103.

3. Clifford Geertz, "Thick Description: Toward an Interpretive Theory of Culture," in *The Interpretation of Cultures* (New York: Basic Books, 1983).

4. See Sylvia Barack Fishman, *Jewish and Something Else: A Study of Mixed Married Families* (New York: American Jewish Committee, 2001). A more complete exploration of these data is in *Double or Nothing? Jewish Families and Mixed Marriages* (Waltham, MA: Brandeis University Press; Hanover, NH: University Press of New England, 2004).

5. Iggers, *Historiography,* 123.

6. Geertz, "Thick Description," 5.

7. Chester E. Finn, Jr., "Teachers, Terrorists, and Tolerance," *Commentary,* December 2001, 54.

8. Randy Cohen, "The Ethicist: Group Dating," *New York Times Magazine,* October 14, 2001, 40.

9. Cohen, "The Ethicist," 40.

10. *2000 Annual Survey of American Jewish Opinion* (New York: American Jewish Committee, conducted by Market Facts, 2000).

11. *2000 Annual Survey.*

12. R. A. Schermerhorn, *Comparative Ethnic Relations: A Framework for Theory and Research* (Chicago: University of Chicago Press, 1978), as cited by Werner Sollors, *Theories of Ethnicity: A Classical Reader* (New York: New York University Press, 1996), xii.

13. Developed by such thinkers as Peter Berger and Thomas Luckman, *The Construction of Reality: A Treatise on the Sociology of Knowledge* (Garden City, NJ: Anchor, 1967); and Malcom Spector and John Kitsuse, *Constructing Social Problems* (New York: Aldine, 1977). The constructionist theory of ethnicity has been evaluated by James A. Holstein and Gale Miller, eds., *Reconsidering Social Constructionism: Debates in Social Problems Theory* (New York: Aldine, 1993).

14. Anthropologist Fredrik Barth is among the more prominent advocates of the view that it is the "ethnic boundary that defines the group, not the cultural stuff that

it encloses." *Ethnic Groups and Boundaries: The Social Organization of Cultural Difference* (Boston: Little, Brown, 1969), 15, 17.

15. Joane Nagel, "Constructing Ethnicity: Creating and Recreating Ethnic Identity and Culture," *Social Problems* 41, no. 1 (1994): 153.

16. One example of those who favor the nuclei as the definers of ethnic distinctiveness is John Higham, *Send These to Me: Jews and Other Immigrants in Urban America* (New York: Atheneum, 1975).

17. Herbert J. Gans, "Symbolic Ethnicity: The Future of Ethnic Groups and Culture in America," *Ethnic and Racial Studies* 2 (January 1979): 1–20.

18. Nathan Glazer and Daniel Patrick Moynihan, eds., *Ethnicity: Theory and Experience* (Cambridge: Harvard University Press, 1975), "Ethnicity and Social Change," 157–69; and Michael Novak, *The Rise of the Unmeltable Ethnics: Politics and Culture in the Seventies* (New York: Macmillan, 1973).

19. Richard D. Alba, *Ethnic Identity: The Transformation of White America* (New Haven: Yale University Press, 1990), 199.

20. Mary C. Waters, *Ethnic Options: Choosing Identities in America* (Berkeley and Los Angeles: University of California Press, 1990), 61–62, 121.

21. See Sylvia Barack Fishman, *Jewish Life and American Culture* (Albany: SUNY Press, 2000), 13.

22. Ariella Keysar, Barry A. Kosmin, and Jeffrey Scheckner, *The Next Generation: Jewish Children and Adolescents* (Albany: SUNY Press, 2000), 48–58.

23. The term *ethnoreligious identity* is drawn from John A. Armstrong, *Nations before Nationalism* (Chapel Hill: University of North Carolina Press, 1982). The changing role of religious belief in ethnoreligious identity is discussed in Robert N. Bellah, "Competing Visions of the Role of Religion in American Society," in *Uncivil Religion: Interreligious Hostility in America,* ed. Robert N. Bellah and Frederick E. Greenspahn (New York: Crossroad, 1987), 228.

24. Peter Y. Medding, Gary A. Tobin, Sylvia Barack Fishman, and Mordechai Rimor, "Jewish Identity in Conversionary and Mixed Marriages," in *American Jewish Year Book 1992* (New York: American Jewish Committee, 1992), 15.

25. Waters, *Ethnic Options,* 130–31.

26. Sylvia Barack Fishman, "I of the Beholder: Jews and Gender in Film," Hadassah International Research Institute on Jewish Women Working Papers Series, 1999; and Riv-Ellen Prell, *Fighting to Become Americans: Jews, Gender, and the Anxiety of Assimilation* (Boston: Beacon Press, 1999).

27. See Bernard Susser and Charles Liebman, *Choosing Survival: Strategies for a Jewish Future* (New York: Oxford University Press, 1999), for a full development of this idea.

Contributors

Hasia R. Diner is Paul S. and Sylvia Steinberg Professor of American Jewish History at New York University. She is the author most recently of *The Jews of the United States.*

Arnold M. Eisen is Chancellor of the Jewish Theological Seminary of America. He is the author of *Rethinking Modern Judaism: Ritual, Commandment, Community,* among other works.

Sylvia Barack Fishman is Professor of Contemporary American Jewish Life at Brandeis University. She is the author of *Double or Nothing? Jewish Families and Mixed Marriages.*

Arthur Green is Dean of the Rabbinical School of Hebrew College. He is the author of *Seek My Face: A Jewish Mystical Theology,* among other works.

Jeffrey S. Gurock is Libby Klaperman Professor of Jewish History at Yeshiva University. He is the author most recently of *Judaism's Encounter with American Sports.*

Paula E. Hyman is Lucy Moses Professor of Modern Jewish History at Yale University. She is the author of *Gender and Assimilation in Modern Jewish History,* among other works.

Egon Mayer is the author of *Love and Tradition: Marriage between Jews and Christians.* A pioneering Jewish social scientist, Mayer was the founder of the Jewish Outreach Institute.

Deborah Dash Moore is Frederick G. L. Huetwell Professor of History at the University of Michigan. She is the author most recently of *GI Jews: How World War II Changed a Generation.*

Alvin H. Rosenfeld is Professor of English at Indiana University. He is the author of *A Double Dying: Reflections on Holocaust Literature, The Americanization of the Holocaust,* and other works.

Jonathan D. Sarna is Joseph H. and Belle R. Braun Professor of American Jewish History at Brandeis University. He is the author of *American Judaism: A History,* among other works.

Stephen J. Whitfield is Professor of American Studies at Brandeis University. He is the author of *In Search of American Jewish Culture; American Space, Jewish Time: Essays in Modern Culture and Politics;* and other works.

Index

Brownsville (Brooklyn, NY), and World
War II war effort, 33
Bruce, Lenny, 249
Buber, Martin, 133, 210, 262
Buchenwald, 32, 35
Buddhism and feminist spirituality, 224
Buffalo, NY, Jewish life in, 179
Burstein, David Reuven, 177
Burt, Robert, 36

Cahan, Abraham, 260
Camp Kvutzah (NY), 110
Cantor, Aviva, 229
Cargas, Henry James, 53, 54
Carter, Jimmy, 49, 50
Catholic Church and sexism, 225
Catholicism: and feminism, 224–25; and
Jewish perceptions of the U.S., 29; and
Judaism, 6; and Protestant polemics,
122; and Catholic Charities, 247
Catholic Relief Services, 247
Célan, Paul, 215
census, U.S., 148, 149, 170, 175
Central European Jews, 143, 149
chaplains, 28; and Jewish, 31–32
Charleston, SC: Jewish life in, 184; and
Jewish revival, 141, 142
Chesler, Phyllis, 229, 230
Chess, Leonard and Phil, 252
Chicago, IL, 5, 24, 27, 37
Chicago, Judy, 58–62, 63, 76
Christian Broadcasting Network, 63
Christian evangelicals, 62–63
Christian holidays/symbols and mixed
married households, 309–11
Christianity: and American ideals, 35; and
inter-religious relationships, 309–18;
and religious liberty, 144–47; 226
Christian Science Monitor, 53
church-state separation, 139, 148
Cincinnati, OH, 149; denominational
conflict in, 187
citizenship, 4, 121
civil liberties, 7
civil rights, 6, 7; and American wartime
ideals, 30; and feminism, 103; and
Holocaust, 12, 57
civil rights movement, 1, 3, 4; and Civil
War, 149; and feminism, 223; and Holocaust, 91, 103
class, 25, 223, 228

Cleveland Jewish Center (Cleveland, OH),
174
Cleveland, OH, 5; Jewish life in, 174
Clinton, William, 68
Coca-Cola, 261
Cohen, Arthur, 207
Cohen, Bernard, 255
Cohen, Gerson, 25
Cohen, Herman, 210
Cohen, Randy, 303–6, 311, 318
Cohen, Steven, 127
Cold War: and American anticommu-
nism, 86; and Holocaust politics, 100,
108
Cole, Tim, 100–102
Commentary, 274
Commission on Reform Jewish Outreach,
274, 281
communism: and Holocaust politics, 86,
101; and immigrant Jews, 4
concentration camps, 32, 34, 45; and
Holocaust memorialization, 86, 96, 110.
See also death camps
Conference on Science, Philosophy and
Religion and Their Relation to the
Democratic Way of Life, 35
Conference on New Politics, 1
Conservative Jews, 15; acceptability of intermarriage among, 288–90, 304; likelihood of intermarriage among, 277–80;
opinions of, on conversion, 297–98;
opinions of, on rabbinic officiation of
intermarriage, 290–93; and Orthodox
Jews, 159–71; and Orthodox Jews
(1900–1960), 171–85; and Orthodox
Jews (1960–2000), 185–90; and outreach to intermarried families, 298
Conservative Judaism, 15; and egalitarianism; 143; and Orthodoxy, 159–63;
163–71; and Orthodoxy (1900–1960),
171–185; and Orthodoxy (1960–2000),
185–90. *See also* Judaism; religion
Conservative Judaism (magazine), 109
Conservative movement, 160, 224, 273,
283, 293; development of 1960–2000,
185–90; and Orthodoxy (1900–1960),
171–85; post-World War II growth of, 37;
and Union for Traditional Judaism, 163
Conservative Rabbis, 162, 285; acceptability of intermarriage among, 288–89;
circa 2000, 160–63; officiation of inter-